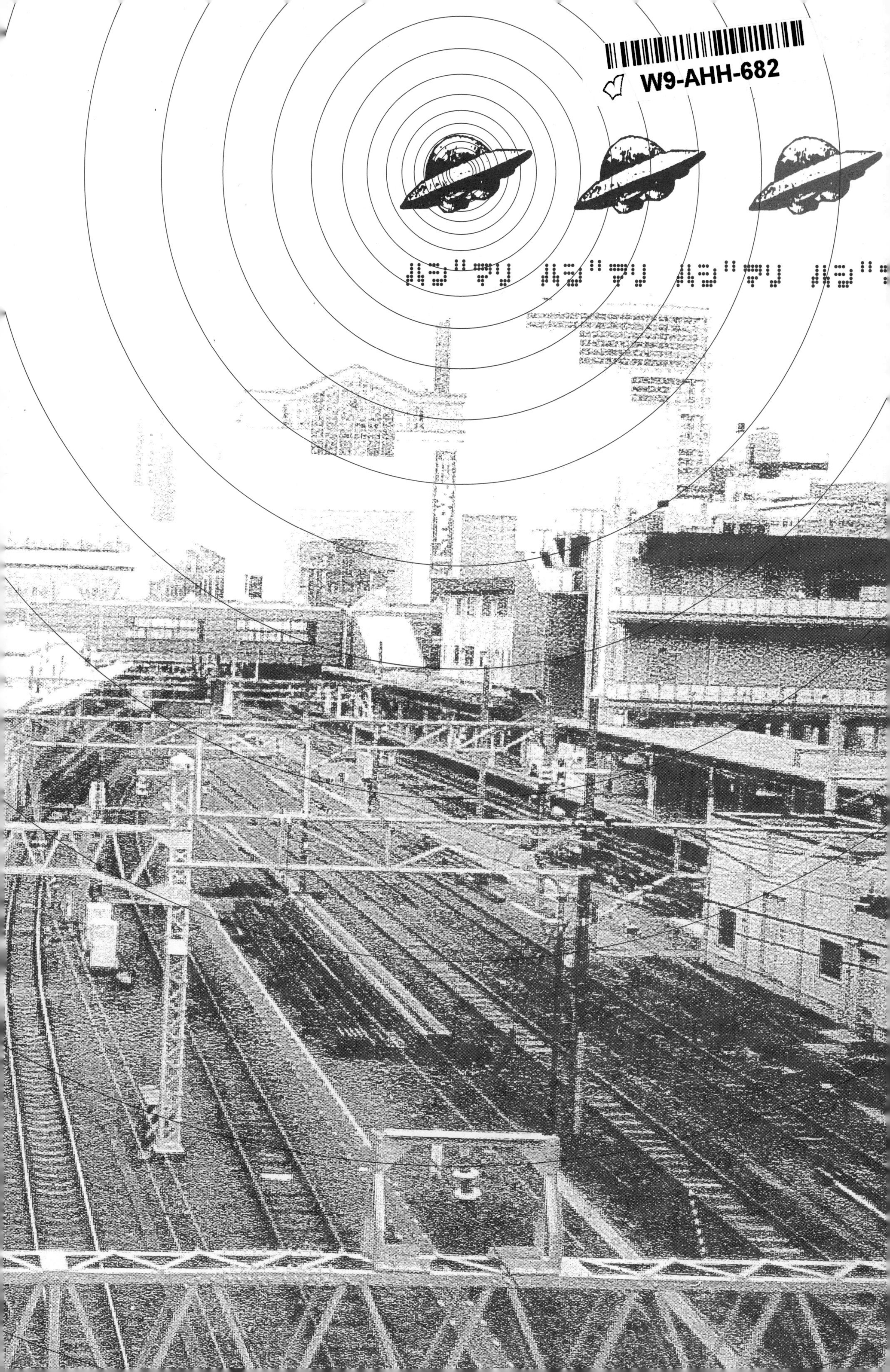

japan edge

The Insider's Guide to Japanese Pop Subculture

hokkaido

osaka

kobe

tokyo

okinawa

kanagawa

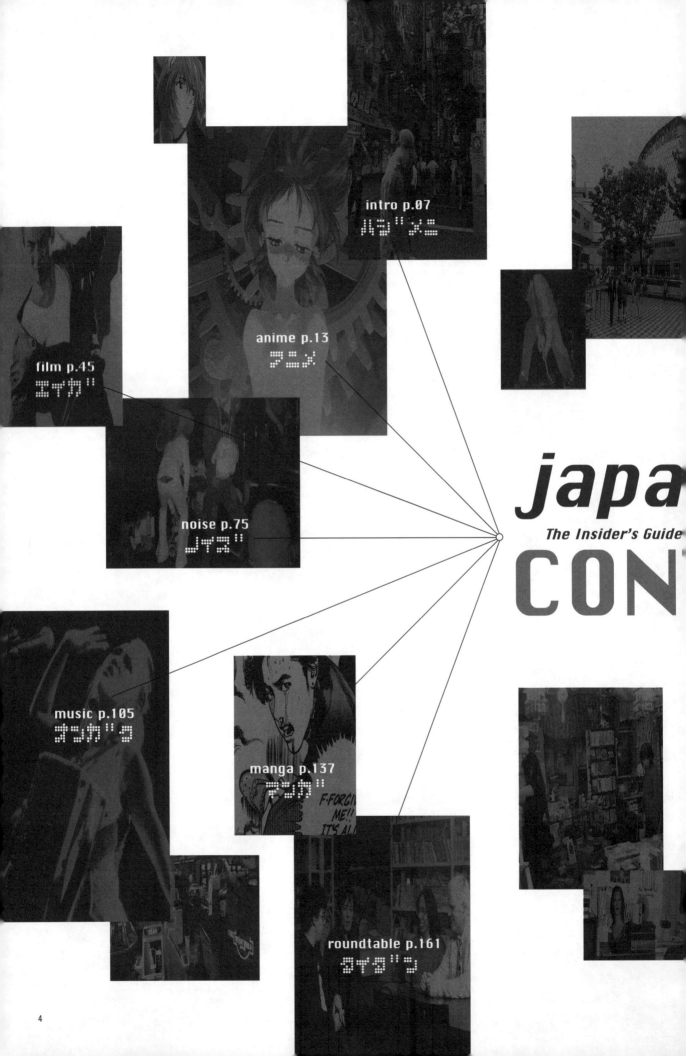

japa
The Insider's Guide
CON

edge

se Pop Subculture

NTS

japan edge

Contributing Writers
Carl Gustav Horn
Mason Jones
Patrick Macias
Yuji Oniki
Matt Thorn

Editor
Annette Roman

Book Design
Izumi Evers

Editorial Consultant
Alvin Lu

Director of Sales & Marketing
Oliver Chin

Managing Editor
Hyoe Narita

Editor in Chief
Satoru Fujii

Publisher
Seiji Horibuchi

Printed in Canada

ISBN 156931-345-8

First Printing, May 1999

Cadence Books

A division of Viz Communications, Inc.

A subsidiary of Shogakukan, Inc.

P.O. Box 77010

San Francisco, CA 94107

intro

East Meets West (You Know the Rest)

Patrick Macias

In 1959, at the age of fifty-one, English writer **Ian Fleming** traveled to Japan at the behest of his employers at the *Sunday Times*, who were publishing his essays on travels to the "thrilling cities of the world."

Before arriving in Tokyo, Fleming was highly suspicious of the country and its people. "After all," he wrote, "during the war [England and Japan] had been bad enemies, and many friends had suffered at their hands." He began to grudgingly prepare for "a great deal of hissing and bowing."

But Fleming was soon won over. After a bathhouse scrubdown from a girl named Kissy and the purchase of an old atrocity print of a man being beheaded, he fell in love with a country which, like himself, had "an unquenchable thirst for the bizarre, the cruel, and the terrible."

This was more or less the same Japan that **James Bond**, that ultimate Westerner, visited in Fleming's eleventh Bond novel, *You Only Live Twice*. A departure from the typical 007 formula, two-thirds of the book were devoted to a

leisurely travelogue of Japan, one that comes within inches of reinforcing the idea that beneath the exterior of every average Japanese male is a samurai warrior, while Japanese women are all willing geishas. But a careful reading shows that Fleming ultimately rejected such conclusions (although his books were marketed and sold thanks to them), especially in his handling of Bond girl **Kissy Suzuki** who, in the end, emerges as far more substantial than a submissive "Oriental doll."

Fleming's original novel is quite unlike the now better-known 1967 film adaptation of *You Only Live Twice*. (There's no space to discuss it, even though its production history is another telling East-meets-West parable, beginning with **Sean Connery** unwisely proclaiming to the international press upon his arrival in Japan that "Japanese women are just not sexy.") The book ends with an amnesiac James Bond, believing he is a simple Japanese fisherman, setting sail for Russia and leaving Kissy Suzuki behind, never to know that she is pregnant with his child.

Whatever the plans were for 007 and

Kissy's progeny, they died, along with Ian Fleming, in 1964, soon after the publication of *You Only Live Twice*. The child, **James Suzuki**, briefly appears and plays a key role in the 1997 short story *A Blast From the Past*, but its author is **Raymond Benson**. Without the existence of the original storyteller's grand design, we too are left to wonder, to speculate, just as far and wide, about how the mysterious child might have grown up.

I'm going to wager, as did Benson, that the child would be a he. I doubt that James Bond's superbly masculine DNA would produce anything else. Perhaps the child would have grown up in that remote fishing village—not remote for very much longer as radio waves and television signals soon ruined its isolation. Kissy Suzuki would have held on to the secret as long as she could. Her affair with Bond was, after all, the offshoot of a top secret mission.

Besides, the boy was, for now, happy enough and certainly distracted by toys, movies, manga, television, and the transistor radio. Having dodged the standard pre–May '68 diet of "Marx and Coca-Cola," the child would grow up with Japanese pop culture as a guide and surrogate father. After all, from a three-year-old's perspective, 1968 wasn't the year that the Left failed to turn the tide but the year that the last episode of *Mach Go! Go! Go!* (a.k.a. Speed Racer) was televised and *Kaiju Soshingeki* (a.k.a. Destroy All Monsters!) was released to local movie theaters.

Still, the child is destined to come of age in the '70s, becoming as adept at *Space Invaders* as he is at handling a yo-yo, worshipping **Bruce Lee**, and collecting bromide cards of idol singer **Momoe Yamaguchi** and **Star Wars** edition Coca-Cola bottle caps.

By his late teens, more possibilities emerge. Perhaps the fantasy-addled boy becomes an in-betweener at an animation studio, or a biker with an outrageous mohawk and a well-maintained speed habit, or simply goes to college, an adored *Beatle*-esque pop singer only in his daydreams.

Now it's the late '90s, and in his thirties, the boy is a well-paid computer analyst living in California's Silicon Valley, a bachelor (and something less ferocious than a closet samurai) who watches Japanese TV on the **International Channel** and buys clothing off the Internet. He eats at Taco Bell weekly, consumes ramen and gyoza just as often, but is troubled by a growing craving for "grilled soles, *les oeufs des cocotes*, and cold roast beef with potato salad."

A craving that eventually leads him to confront his mother, Kissy Suzuki, once and for all.

"Who was my father?" he asks.

"A British Cold War spy," she eventually answers.

"Oh God, how clichéd."

Hey, it could happen. Like the man said, nothing is real. And if you're out there, bastard child Bond Jr./James Suzuki, you really ought to drop us a line. Your thoughts as the pop cultural product of two cultures would be most welcome in these pages.

The collective authors of this book must also be considered as the figurative children of 007 and Kissy Suzuki—East meets West and all that—American or Japanese by birth, once receivers, now transmitters in a great international simulcast.

For the sake of brevity, let's call the Japanese side of the broadcast "J-pop" and let it invoke the whole of Japanese pop culture without having to refer to the stuffy sounding phrase "Japanese pop culture" again and again. As part of the deal, you'll get "pop" as in popular, "pop" as in pop art, "pop" as in pop music, "pop" as in anything-but pop music, "pop" as in a prelude to an eruption.

At the moment, J-pop is better known as a uniquely Japanese style of brazenly commercial music performed by beautiful and disposable idols. But for our purposes, that's only part of the story. The J-pop that *Japan Edge* promotes is all-inclusive. Inclusive to a fault. This is, in fact, a very greedy book, claiming affiliation with everything under the Japanese pop culture banner: television shows, fads, fashion trends, girls' comics, boys' comics, and most certainly anime, manga, movies, and music. You know...J-pop!

And since we've already admitted to the vice of greed, J-pop is going to have to bear the weight of Japanese subculture as well. Dirty movies, noise music, student movements, self-published zines, weird comic books, strange people and their alternative histories.

The time is ripe. Already many of Japan's pop signifiers have firmly twisted their way into the Western world. The odds are that you already have some examples deeply embedded in your consciousness—maybe it's just the opening theme of *Ultraman*, the climactic mutations of *Akira*, or a **Nissin Cup Noodle** having its way with your stomach. And we'll presume you already know what manga and anime are without needing a glossary.

The spores of J-pop have fallen far and wide beyond our star-spangled backyard as well. In Mexico, children grow up with **Fujio-Fujiko**'s atomic-powered cat *Doraemon*, just as Japanese kids do, and joyfully bash unlicensed papier-mâché **Power Rangers** piñatas. In the U.K., musician **Gota Yashiki** works behind the scenes as drummer–rhythm programmer for VH-1–ers such as **Simply Red** and **Soul 2 Soul**, while his solo projects do respectable business on the charts. In Italy, manga artist **Go Nagai** has opened an Italian branch of his **Dynamic Productions** company to translate and publish his own and **Osamu Tezuka**'s works all across Europe.

Yet it is in America that the J-pop craze takes on a particular cultural significance. To examine how it has touched and influenced the fabric of the red, white, and blue is to add yet another layer to the extraordinarily complex relationship between Japan and the U.S. (I now refer you to author **Frederik Schodt**'s excellent book *America and the Four Japans: Friend, Foe, Model, Mirror*, which examines this relationship from a number of highly readable interpretations and angles); it's a saga that stretches all the way back to **Commodore Perry** to the postwar occupation to **George Bush** losing his lunch in **Prime Minister Takeshita**'s lap.

Either way, after a long period of cult worship and the occasional inconclusive affair with the mainstream, now J-pop is just another minimall on the American landscape. Only a handful of J-pop artifacts will go on to do blockbuster business (which is, let's face it, the only real measure of success in capitalist-minded countries, Japan and the U.S. alike). But merely raking in the megabucks is not what makes the growing presence of J-pop in the U.S. such a unique

phenomenon.

And it *is* unique, although a cold, clinical dissection won't turn up much insight. Our only hope lies in a shotgun approach: a scattering of different observations, perspectives, and personal testimonials, some hitting the bull's-eye dead on, some sneaking up on key cultural issues from behind, but all pointing towards the same goal: to show how J-pop is unique to Japan...even as its audience has gone global.

But first, we've got to slow down a bit and look beyond nations and borders. And it's here, in the tricky realm of cultural theory, that the first clues to thematic unity appear.

Admittedly, it's tempting to throw around terms like pop culture and subculture without ever stopping to supply a working definition. After all, nowadays pop culture is a Pepsi Cola ad campaign and the '80s anime *Voltron* is selling Sprite (just as "subculture" is certain to one day sell oversized sandwiches). But if we are to proceed on course as a book about J-pop and the further adventures of East meets West, then we've got to get our definitions straight.

If only it were so simple.

Cultural theorists have been busily occupied for decades now with a never-ending attempt to put the finger on exactly what manner of beast pop culture—and even "real" culture—truly is. Once again, we are in the realm of no easy answers, only

speculation.

In our *own* mad little quest to define what makes J-pop unique and why our contributors have devoted such a significant portion of their lives to it, we must now look to that most elementary of geometric shapes, the triangle.

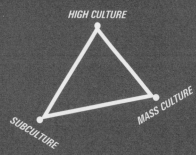

At the top of the pyramid rests high culture, far and away removed from the coarse, crowded din of mass culture. This is the art gallery of the establishment, the home of the classics: ballet, opera, literature, kabuki, and Gray Poupon Dijon mustard. In short, the best that "civilization" believes it has to offer. Its eternal mission to appreciate and reinforce the confines of reality is the polar opposite of pop culture's offering of unlimited fantasy. If it's difficult for the layperson to take up an interest and get involved in "culture," then so much the better. They'd only get dirt all over the rug. Trouble is, the high priests of high culture continually risk wasting away from isolation and irrelevance.

Clockwise to the right lies the great shopping mall of mass culture, a.k.a. media culture, a.k.a. pop culture (if you like the word pop): in other words, the mainstream. Here rest the box-office receipts of *Titanic* and the Star Wars saga, back issues of *Teen People* magazine and supermarket tabloids, whatever passes for programming this week on **MTV**, and, yes, Ian Fleming's James Bond novels. Call it mass-produced culture if you want.

Of the multiple definitions of mass culture, some of the most influential have depicted it as a ruthless economic phenomenon, the commodity-minded by-product of capitalism (the culture industry, as the Frankfurt school puts it). Others say it's an unrelenting brainwashing machine designed to keep regular folks in a clueless and distracted state while the people on top tug away at the reins of real power while relishing real culture. More optimistically, others say it's a complex linguistic-based playground of symbols, a way to decode meaning from our lives and environment.

In many ways, the basic characteristics of Japanese pop culture aren't so different from the American equivalent. That's one reason we seem to get along so well. Both varieties, at worst, promote, as **Christopher Frayling** says in his absolutely brilliant book *Spaghetti Westerns*, "a gimmick culture of nonsense, a commodity culture for captive consumers." At best, it gives us prisoners of planet Earth pastimes, entertainment, and social history. Angel or

devil, either way, you might as well get used to it. We're stuck with pop culture from cradle to grave.

Down to the lower left dwells subculture, an alternative space in opposition to—and yet closely allied with—both mass and high culture. It's here that attitudes, fashions, and styles are invented and pioneered. Through discovery, action, and participation (as opposed to the one-way receivers that pop culture and high culture would turn us into), individuals and small tribes create and feed their own culture. What's great is that this sidesteps a number of economic straitjackets. Whereas the success of pop culture depends on how well it sells, and the supposed "value" of high culture is priceless, in subculture, all that's really important is the participant's individual satisfaction. While consumers of mass and high culture receive media from on high, subculture can transmit and make creators out of audiences. Inevitably enough, the innovations are sure to trickle upwards to shape the tastes of mass culture and, one day, high culture. Do the weirdest thing you can imagine. The odds are, if someone else thinks it's cool, it'll be devoured by the hungry culture industry one way or another. And two hundred years from now, its origins will be debated in elliptic academic circles.

Is it any wonder that people want alternatives? Especially now that the mentality that **Fredric Jameson** described in

1977 as "that suburban Los Angeles–type decentralization, dominated by multinational corporations and transcontinental networks of various kinds in which only professional castes and individual networks of acquaintances are able to feel any kind of group identity" is threatening to spread out from West L.A. to dominate the entire developed world. Clearly, there is a staggering need for ways to get out and survival guides.

And despite the many points of similarity and the promise of mass acceptance, that's just what J-pop is. An alternative. It's founded on all three groups—high culture, mass culture, and subculture—but the end product is far greater than the sum of its parts.

Just as Occidentals in the grip of New Age philosophies experiment with exotic deities and chants because they believe the East offers spiritual and intellectual wisdom, students of J-pop also experience the world through a different psychological perspective. Its informal name is Asian chaos.

Asian chaos is Tokyo. Kansai. Hong Kong. San Francisco's Chinatown. A playground of media and populace. Crowded, noisy for sure. Lights, language, pictures everywhere. Faces. Advertisements. Foreigners. Buildings and shops crammed together with little regard for architectural harmony. Sick as we all are now of that 1980's buzzword "postmodern," here it is in flesh and blood. Glass and plastic. A place where the boundaries between high culture, pop culture, and subculture no longer matter or exist. There's a lightness here, a lack of tensions and divisions that cause cultural anxiety elsewhere. To a Westerner, it can be a terrifying state of disorder. But to the natives, it's home, and it has an underlying unity—one that's open to anyone, even outsiders, who can learn to read the signs and signifiers. Once again, it's "a commodity culture for captive consumers." But it's also *alive*, teeming with vitality and possibilities. Asian chaos gives life back to the cities and its citizens. Best of all, it's a human and cultural game preserve, a sanctuary from the encroaching impersonal Orwellian order of West Los Angeles. And it leaves plenty of room for subcultures and hybrid creatures to breed in the cracks.

That's why J-pop is unique. And that's why J-pop is going universal.

We are all potential importers and exporters, despite however bad the international economy may be. Fans are beginning to meet and have dialogues with Japanese musicians, artists, and filmmakers face to face, through the Internet, in myriad situations. What are the odds that a great hybrid culture will arise, one in which imitations and the products of cultural imperialism (sorry about that, Mr. Fleming) won't be bought and sold as they used to be?

Western J-pop devotees are on the cusp of something old, new, and authentic. The American show *Star Blazers* used to be the Japanese anime *Space Cruiser Yamato*. The 1960's group sounds band **The Gold Cups** once recorded **James Brown**'s **"I Got You (I Feel Good)"**. The recent foreign film *Shall We Dance?* was shorn of several minutes of its Japanese running time by its American distributor. The truth is found somewhere between both sides of the flow. Between the signs and signifiers.

On the beat are: **Carl Horn**, with his uncompromising belief in the power of anime and manga. There's **Mason Jones**, creating "international incidents" through 'zines and noise. **Yuji Oniki** and his kaleidoscopic history of Japanese pop music and insightful **"Tokyo Diary"**. My own hyperbolic gaze backwards into a cult cinema darkly. All of us are citizens of California, a state that, we are only too happy to point out, is roughly analogous in size to the entire nation of Japan. Draw any conclusion you choose from that. Do whatever you wish with our observations and information. We're not going to judge you, readers and critics.

But know this. Anything is better than **Herbert Marcuse**'s grim bottom-line statement that culture, any kind, makes an unbearable condition bearable by dulling the pain of existence. We hope that in writing with enthusiasm, and some degree of knowledge, we can create something more worthwhile than a painkiller or a time waster.

The J-pop dialogue must grow and evolve. We risk a fool's errand, drawing conclusions from popular culture and casual observation. Stereotypes can get reinforced. Definitive answers seldom arrive. "Reality" is forever stranger and more elusive.

As in **Sidney Pollack**'s 1975 film *The Yakuza*, in which **Richard Jordan** tells a nonplused **Robert Mitchum** (both men buck naked in a bathhouse), "When an American cracks up he opens up the window and shoots up a bunch of strangers. When a Japanese cracks up he closes the window and kills himself. Everything's in reverse, isn't it?"

Well, no, not really. And anyway, you'd better look out. A tattooed hitman is about to crack up and attempt to kill the *both* of you. And how does that oxymoron fit into your amateur philosophy?

Like an American Godzilla movie.
Like Disney and anime.
Like teriyaki bowl donut shops.
Like Japanese noise music.
Like Japanese pop music.
Like J-pop.
Like James Bond and Kissy Suzuki.

Like East meets West.

Patrick Macias, 1999

California, ヴァーチャル日本

た睡眠薬を大量にのみ

ンターネット上に開設

カリを送付していた。

この東京都内の主婦は

て調べている。調べによると、塾講師は青酸カリを購入した際、運転免許証

　抑える劇物のスコポラミン一グラムを三千五百円で買っていた。塾講師に

だけが所在不明。六人のうち杉並区の女性は宅配便で届いた青酸カリ入りの

　もらった睡眠薬を大量にのみ、逃亡し○生存○○○この○○

師がインターネット上に開設したホームページで、電子メールを交換。白

で、青酸カリを送付していた。練馬区の女性に薬物を譲渡していた東京都内

ていた。この東京都内の主婦は薬物の任意提出を拒否しているという。塾講

　フィルムケースのような容器（長さ約七センチ、直径約二・五センチ）に

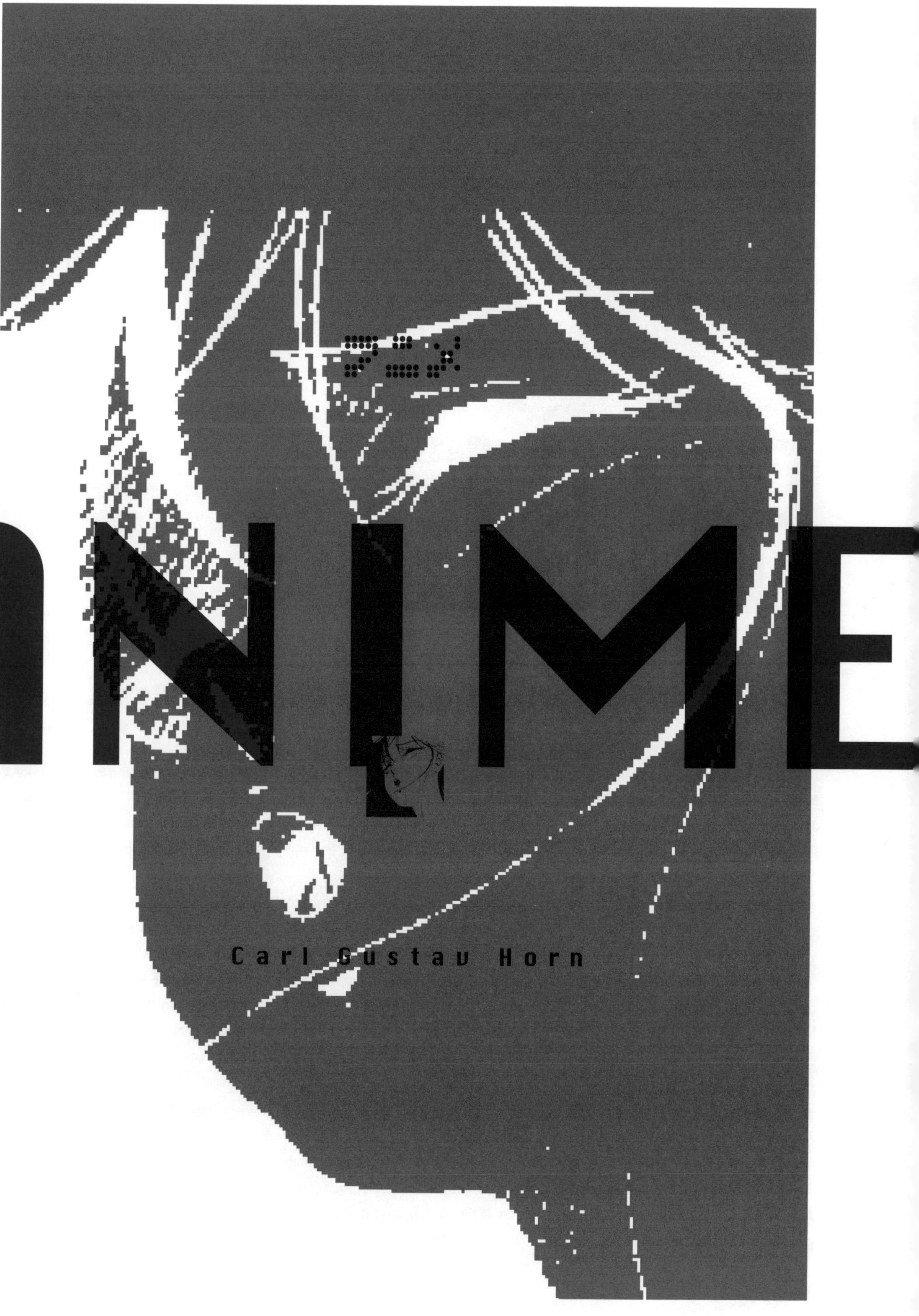

アニメ

ANIME

Carl Gustav Horn

overview

They All Look Like Speed Racer...
Anime From America to Japan and Back Again

Let's start with an anime quiz. I've heard all three of these statements about Japanese animation lately. Which of them is incorrect? (a) Japanese animation, or "anime," is *the hot new thing*, (b) Japanese animation is *not for kids*, or (c) Japanese animation is *twisted...bizarre...uniquely imaginative*.

Strangely enough, only a and b are complete bullshit; there is a lot of truth to c. Not too long ago, when you heard about all of those Japanese children suffering seizures from watching a particular episode of the anime program *Pokémon*, *USA Today* sought to reassure its readers that American viewers were safe because, as they put it, "While the **Cartoon Network** does air Japan's *Speed Racer*, made thirty years ago, and *Voltron*, about ten years old...neither show is in the style of anime." (Estimates of the extent of the *Pokémon*

incident, by the way, were based in part on what happened the next day when Japanese schools announced to their students that "anyone who doesn't feel well can go home"....)

If *USA Today* had written instead, say, "While your cable system airs the United States' program *Bewitched*, made thirty years ago, and *Miami Vice*, about ten years old...neither show is in the style of American television," wouldn't you have spotted the logical fallacy? Sure, and you'll get an easy five points on this quiz if you realized that saying that *Speed Racer* is not "in the style of anime" is just as ridiculous.

To show why I've got more confidence in you than in *USA Today*, let's return to their article. It went on to explain that anime (Remember? That stuff you *don't* have to worry about seeing on the Cartoon Network) is "that fast-paced style

of animation...rarely seen on TV in the USA.... ABC, NBC [and] UPN...don't air the graphic Japanese cartoons known as 'anime.' Nor do the major cable outlets for cartoons: Nickelodeon, the Cartoon Network.... Where you will find anime is in video stores, where anime sections are stocked with imports of Japanese cartoons." *USA Today* then quoted Mike Lazzo, vice president of programming for the Cartoon Network: "[Anime] is so different from what airs here. It's far edgier...and violent...driven by intense moments. The story is hard to follow."

Again, the little alarm bell goes off in your head. *Edgy...violent...driven by intense moments...hard to follow...* Wait a minute...isn't that a pretty good description of *Speed Racer?* Five more points. And—depending on how long you've been around—you may have grabbed some more bonus questions off *USA Today* by remembering that you *did* in fact once see "that fast-paced style of animation" on NBC (**Astro Boy**, **Kimba The White Lion**), and on ABC (**8th Man**), and on UPN (**Teknoman**), and on Nickelodeon (**The Mysterious Cities Of Gold**), and even on the Cartoon Network. *Of course* **Voltron** and **Speed Racer** are anime. They were made in Japan years ago, by the studios **Toei** and **Tatsunoko** respectively, and by some of the same Japanese animators still working in the field today. And being anime, **Voltron** and **Speed Racer** are, as Mike Lazzo put it, very different from what airs here. They stood out; that's why you remember them. I mean you, American, whomever you are.

Second question on the anime quiz: Who discovered anime in America? (a) cultish secret conclaves of obsessed U.S. fans who first appeared in the '70s (their Japanese equivalent are sometimes called *otaku,* meaning literally, in an affected way, "thou"); (b) today's youth, wearing knock-off Plastik and Hook-Up shirts on Melrose Avenue and hungry for a new disease; or (c) ordinary Americans who grew up watching it on TV over the last thirty years.

Answer from the back of the book: *(a)*

It is true that the cult gave rise to the anime sections you see in your Blockbuster and Tower video stores today, that many of the U.S. companies releasing these anime videos in English are staffed by otaku, and that otaku formed the original market for these companies when they first sprang up in the early '90s. (b) It is also true that the teenagers now making anime a fad are greatly expanding the market for these same videos. Now, I'm part of a, and I'm glad to see b happening. But by now you've figured out how this test works: the correct answer is c.

Anime isn't just an imported cult or a foreign fad; in the brave year of 1999, anime is as American as apple pie, pizza, and sushi. Neither the core cult of a few thousand fans in scattered clubs nor the new "anime look" on the street explains fully why American ad agencies—not just now, but over the past five years—have spent millions of dollars selling Americans products bearing images from **Speed Racer** and **Voltron**, whether the targeted consumer demographic be traditionally pale (NASCAR, Volkswagen) or what they like to call "urban" (Sprite). That kind of push reflects the affection many *mainstream*

Americans under thirty-five have for anime, anime as it truly is: colorful, exciting, strange, and Japanese.

It may come as a surprise to many Americans to hear that much of the anime they consider "adult" is not regarded as such in the country of its origin. To go back to the first question—wrong answer b—lots of anime *is* for kids. Actually, not very much anime is intended for people old enough not to get carded. The confusion is understandable. Since graphic violence, crude humor, and explicit eroticism are not considered "appropriate" entertainment for young people in America (although, of course, most young Americans like seeing it), many Americans assume that anime with such content is intended for adults. But this is not true, and doesn't recognize that anime is the product of a very different culture. While there is a recognized class of outright pornographic anime in Japan directed at adults only (released in this country under such labels as **Kitty**, **SoftCel** and **Anime 18**), eroticism or violence in anime, as such, is not an infallible indication of the target audience.

Many foreign observers have been so

shocked by such casual "transgressions" in material meant for children as well as adults that they have drawn some strong conclusions about the Japanese character. **Ian Buruma**, in his valuable study of Japanese pop culture heroes, *Behind the Mask*, concludes that the Japanese are, rather, more honest about the common desire (of all ages and societies) to transgress, and allow this to be expressed in a much freer *fantasy* life than Americans, with their Puritanism and legal concept of "obscenity."

Another "Ian"—and a giant of Western pop culture—**Ian Fleming**, wrote in his James Bond novel *You Only Live Twice* of the "unquenchable thirst of the Japanese for the cruel, the bizarre, and the terrible," a taste that he himself, of course, shared. In his travelogue *Thrilling Cities*, Fleming praised the Japanese for lacking certain hypocrisies treasured in the West. The *real* Japan is, of course, one of the most conformist, materially comfortable, and law-abiding—one is tempted to say *bourgeois*—societies on Earth, while the *real* America tolerates unconscionable violence and

poverty among its youth while vowing to protect them at all costs from pornography on the Internet.

In fact, far fewer adults in Japan watch anime on a regular basis, than read comic books—*manga*. Manga are a much, much bigger business in Japan than anime, and whereas it has long been viewed as "normal," if not always admirable, for Japanese adults to devour manga (much the way watching TV is regarded in America), the same, until very recently, has not been true of anime. It's an odd situation for Americans to understand; it's as if it were okay in the U.S. for a grown man to read the *Batman* comic book but a little suspect to be into *Batman: The Animated Series*.

But the analogy is inexact. It's not a prejudice towards animation *per se*, so much as the fact that anime has traditionally offered so much less to Japanese adults than manga. In part, this is because of the application of Sturgeon's Law that ninety percent of everything is crap; it must be reiterated that manga is so much *bigger* than anime. There are currently fifty anime TV series episodes broadcasting new episodes week-

ly in Japan; perhaps fifteen original anime videos (OAVs) come out there every month, and a few anime films every year. But there are well over 200 manga magazines printed in Japan, most with at least eight and some with as many as forty-five serialized stories, and many other non-manga magazines carry a manga story as a regular feature. At any given moment, then, the average Japanese has literally *thousands* of different, ongoing manga stories to choose from, and there is simply going to be more of that good ten percent in all those comics than those few dozen anime.

Anime is less prevalent because of the production demands. A complete manga story, ready to print and sell, can be completed by one person (and often *is*, though just as many creators have a small staff of assistants) for the price of some pens and paper. Various deals may follow, but the *creative* work is finished. And while manga magazines carry some advertising, it is remarkably little; the 320-page *Big Comic* carries eleven pages of non-house ads, as many as the average thirty-two-page American comic book. Manga, by and large, stands or falls on the strength of its stories alone, not through the sales of other products.

To produce an anime, however, the deals must come first to secure the financing—ranging from as little as $50,000 for a cheap OAV to as much as $20 million for a cutting-edge movie—to pay for the dozens, hundreds, or even thousands of production staff members one must have to make an anime. Whereas manga are largely unsupported by ads, anime must lean heavily on merchandising, cross promotion, and soundtracks. With other people's money—and quite a bit of it—at stake, anime faces a situation like many deal-driven Hollywood movies: it risks being precompromised, conservative, and formulaic, especially when it is an "original" story. Ironically, when it is an adaptation, it can lean on the creativity found in the freer medium of manga.

This entails considerably more than the common Hollywood practice of adapting movies from books, for a manga provides the anime not only with a basic plot and dialogue, but many of its visuals as well. (A case in which the same creator made the manga and anime version of a story simultaneously, as with **Hayao Miyazaki**'s *Nausicaä of the Valley of Wind* or **Yoshiyuki Sadamoto**'s *Neon Genesis Evangelion*, is another matter.) **Frederik L. Schodt**, author of *Manga! Manga!* and *Dreamland Japan*, has described the anime-manga relationship as "parasitic." **Toshio Okada**, former president of anime studio **Gainax** and now a lecturer at Tokyo University, believes anime should use original scripts because a good manga cannot be improved upon by making an anime version of it. To Okada, for animators to use their skills to merely adapt manga is "a waste of time, opportunity, and money."

A typical thirty-five-year-old, non-otaku Japanese will have no problem finding a manga that appeals to their age group, but he or she will have considerable trouble finding a suitable anime. **Sadao Otomo**, editor of *Big Gold*, a middle-aged manga magazine, is quoted by Schodt as saying

that most of his readers have read manga all their lives, and intend to keep doing so. Clearly, some within the manga industry planned for manga to grow up with the population who began reading it in the '50s and '60s. TV and feature-length anime began in that same period. And, for a time, it too catered to an evolving demographic; the fairy tales and short-pants romance of anime such as *Alakazam the Great* and *Gigantor* gave way in the late '60s and early '70s to the freak-out adolescence of **Go Nagai**'s *Cutey Honey* and *Devilman*, the young, outlaw, radical chic of *Lupin III*, and even spicy film adaptations of *The Thousand and One Nights* and the story of *Cleopatra* made by *Astro Boy* and *Kimba* creator **Osamu Tezuka** himself.

But, generally speaking, the wave crested and broke on the college-age audience. While manga for older readers (such as *Galaxy Express 999*, published here in *Animerica* magazine, but in Japan in *Big Gold*) is by no means devoid of young characters, and many Japanese have long enjoyed in secret anime meant for younger viewers, an older audience tends to relate to older characters and a plot that reflects a more considered outlook on life. It's a perspective hard to find in anime, where major characters are rarely older than teenagers, protagonists stamped out like coins fed through slot-machine scripts that rarely pay off. Compromises are necessary in the production of anime, whether it is based on a manga or an original screenplay written by the animators themselves. An otaku has a love for anime on its own terms: as it was, as it is. Yet through that same passion, one can see anime for what it may yet be.

The passionate otaku finds fault with much of Japanese animation for its lack of vision, its reluctance to take chances with its stories, and its unwillingness to appeal to a wider demographic. The current anime boom in Japan and its unprecedented financial success (such success is, after all, the very goal of production deals), is the result of two hit anime, *Neon Genesis Evangelion* and *The Princess Mononoke*, which *did*

take chances and *did* appeal to a wide demographic. They were produced by **Ghibli** and **Gainax**, two studios of very different generations that nevertheless recognize each other as part of the same artistic tradition in anime and equally part of its future. If it is true that the Japanese (and American) mainstream is only now beginning to fully appreciate this exciting form of world cinema and television, they will find that that 10 percent of quality indeed exists, and that there are many more veteran directors besides, both young and old, for them yet to discover: **Noboru Ishiguro, Yoshiyuki Tomino, Taro Rin, Gisaburo Sugii, Tomoharu Katsumata, Osamu Dezaki, Shoji Kawamori, Mamoru Oshii, Katsuhiro Otomo, Satoshi Kon**. Each certainly deserve their own chapter. Nor is the first part of the essay which follows this overview, "To The Revolution Now," any more than one perspective on the long and varied works of Ghibli and Gainax.

Part two of the essay, "Pictures From The Drowning World," is "a memoir of sorts" (to borrow from the autobiography of World War II cartoonist **Bill Mauldin**) of some of my own encounters with Japanese animation as a—if you will pardon the expression—Gen-X American. It may be of interest, it may be entertaining, but it certainly is not anything more than a self-analysis—it is not intended as a statement about "anime fans" in general. I don't feel entirely comfortable making such statements, and you probably wouldn't feel entirely satisfied reading them. That's because, just as every anime is the singular creation of each artist in the industry, each anime is viewed in a unique way by each member of its audience. There is *History* with a capital H and then there is the secret history we all write for ourselves—just as true, and often more meaningful. No matter how co-opted, commercialized, or played out your strange love may become, remember that, at its heart, it's never about a clique or trading conformity with the masses for conformity with the underground. The ultimate, most sincere subculture will always be the individual.

"As you are, as you were,

PART ONE
TO THE REVOLUTION NOW:
STUDIO GHIBLI AND STUDIO GAINAX
At the End of the Century, Two Generations of Radicals Rule Japanese Animation (and Japan) Together...as Father and Son

History Without End

In September 1959, the leader of the Communist world, Soviet Premier **Nikita Khrushchev**, was unhappy. It was his first visit to the United States and they wouldn't let him into Disneyland; he was told they couldn't guarantee his safety. But he got his revenge. Nine months later, the leader of the free world, President **Dwight Eisenhower**, wasn't let into Japan; the government couldn't guarantee *his* safety. Mobs of Japanese leftists, taking their cue from Khrushchev, were rioting against the U.S. in the worst disorders in Japan since the end of World War II. Little did two young radicals with dreams of making great anime suspect that there would someday be a Tokyo Disneyland a stone's throw from the demonstrations, or that Disney would—after the two became the greatest of Japan's animators—buy the English language rights to their life's work.

The two were **Hayao Miyazaki** (b. 1941) and **Isao Takahata** (b. 1935), the founders of Japan's most critically acclaimed and financially successful anime production house, **Studio Ghibli**—named for the hot desert wind of the Sahara. No two men have played a more important role in establishing animation in the eyes of mainstream Japan as a respectable and popular form of cinema for all ages; the honors and rewards heaped upon the partners are unequaled. Studio Ghibli was formally established in 1985, but the partnership between the two director-producers was

already twenty years old when Miyazaki's *Nausicaä of the Valley of Wind* became the first anime ever to make the yearly top ten poll in Japan's premier journal of film, *Kinema Jumpo*, in 1984. One decade later, in 1994, Takahata's *Heisei Tanuki Gassen Ponpoko* (Modern-Day Tanuki War [goes] 'Tum-Tum') was considered worthy to represent Japanese film to the world, becoming the first anime to be offered by Japan to the Academy of Motion Picture Arts and Sciences in consideration for the Oscar for Best Foreign Film.

And in 1996 came the deal through which Disney associated its famous name with Ghibli's achievements by purchasing the rights to eight of their films—a move that attracted international media attention and which has begun to come to fruition with the successful video release last year of an English version of Miyazaki's 1989 film, *Kiki's Delivery Service*. Phil Hartman played his final role in it, a sarcastic interpretation of Kiki's black cat, Jiji. Disney has lined up equally notable talent for this summer's Miramax/Dimension release to American theaters of the Miyazaki masterpiece *The Princess Mononoke*: Claire Danes, giving an English voice to its heroine, will front a cast that includes Billy Bob Thornton and Gillian Anderson.

How did the strange journey from Japanese student radical to imported Disney icon begin? Takahata was a graduate of Japan's top university, Tokyo University, and Miyazaki attended Gakushuin, a prestigious private university

with close ties to Japan's imperial family. But, as **Mark Schilling** observes in his *Encyclopedia of Japanese Pop Culture*, the elite educational status of the pair made a Marxist influence almost inevitable. After the disaster of World War II, Communists gained new moral clout in Japan for having resisted their country's aggression overseas, while the liberal reform policies of the American occupation made left-wing economic ideals seem natural and desirable. Only five years later, though, in 1950, the Korean War began, and Japan entered its long role as "America's unsinkable aircraft carrier," with Asian Communism the target. When, at U.S. urging, Japan began to build up its military again, idealistic college youth such as Miyazaki and Takahata felt the postwar dream had been betrayed. It was their mutual love of world animated cinema, however, including experimental Euro-Soviet productions, that led the pair to the rather unusual decision to take their degrees to the then-flowering animation division of Japan's hallowed movie studio, Toei.

They left none of their politics behind; one of the first things Miyazaki did when he arrived was to march in a union demonstration in front of the studio building. He became friends with Takahata through the animator's union; in 1964 Miyazaki became its chairman and the older Takahata his deputy. The pair became comrades in art during the three-year effort at Toei to make their first collaboration: *Horus, Prince of the Sun*, directed by Takahata. The making

as I want you to be"

of *Horus* was like a scene from *The Princess Mononoke* thirty years later: a band of outcasts working their iron forge, making weapons in a compound under siege. It wasn't the army who dogged the animators, but the dubious Toei higher-ups who questioned whether an anime film could, or even needed to be what Takahata and Miyazaki envisioned—a complex, layered story with realistic emotions. Moreover, *Horus* was a protest both as art and as commerce: the pair intended to smash preconceived barriers as to what anime was visually capable of, while suggesting that it was worthier for animators to aspire to this rather than dissipate their talent in the cheaply-done (and poorly-paid) world of TV anime that had arisen since the 1963 debut of *Tetsuwan Atom* (*Astro Boy*).

What Takahata wanted to accomplish in animation had already occurred in Japanese comics. The idea that manga—even a historical fantasy—could reflect a radical social consciousness, had been accepted. **Frederik Schodt** notes that the ninja stories—full of peasant rebellion—by **Sanpei Shirato**, published in the mid-'60s by the avant-garde manga magazine *Garo*, had become "a substitute for Marx" for many students. Former *Garo* editor **Chikao Shiratori**, in his column for the American manga magazine *Pulp*, has remarked on how well Shirato's comics were synchronized with "the movement." But as Takahata recalled for *Kinema Jumpo* in 1995, "There was no anime like that"—until *Horus*. Its theme of medieval villagers rising up together against an evil king resonated not only with audiences in 1968—the time of its release and the most radical year of the '60s—but also with the solidarity among the animators during the making of the film itself. Takahata recalls, "In an unsatisfying situation with low pay, heavy workloads, frustrations, and such

things, we had comrades with whom we could talk not only about the work we were doing but also about other things, and anime was created out of those interactions. It was that kind of era."[1]

"Comrades" would continue to be the byword as Takahata and Miyazaki shuttled around together from one studio and project to another for the next fifteen years. But it was to bring to fruition a concept that Miyazaki had been forming in his head since childhood that Studio Ghibli—the alliance that would bring them both undreamed-of success—was founded. The concept was, in many ways, Miyazaki's lifelong vision: a story about the human race in conflict with itself and nature, in which an empathic princess embarks on an adventure to negotiate peace between nations and monstrous creatures of the wild. In 1982, Miyazaki began drawing this epic as a manga, named *Nausicaä of the Valley of Wind*, a comic that, when it reached America in the 1990s, would be called "the best graphic novel ever" by **Stepan Chapman** of *Comics Journal*. When he was approached two years later to transform the unfinished *Nausicaä* into an anime movie, his only condition was that Takahata be the producer.

The anime was a success, but Miyazaki was unsatisfied, and grappled with the theme again and again over the next twelve years as he attempted to finish—in his spare time between anime films—the thousand-page manga version. During the same period, Ghibli gained fame with each successive film. Yet while Miyazaki, with his love of flight, made the literal children's flights of fancy *The Castle in the Sky* (1986), *My Neighbor Totoro* (1988), and *Kiki's Delivery Service* (1989), Takahata took a more adult-oriented approach, bringing anime, with his humanistic realism, to a level of mastery and discipline never before seen—whether

1. Takahata's *Horus* was in fact well received in the U.S.S.R.; it won a recommendation from the Ministry of Education. Films with child heroes were quite popular in the Soviet Union of the '60s, a notable example being **Andrei** (*Solaris*) **Tarkovsky**'s debut feature, *Ivan's Childhood*. Later, Miyazaki would say admiringly of Tarkovsky, "This S.O.B. does just as he pleases!" Americans have already been introduced to the work of fellow Tarkovsky admirer and anime director **Mamoru Oshii**—his 1995 film *Ghost In The Shell* received an enthusiastic endorsement from no less than James Cameron. Lesser known is Oshii's own association with the Japanese Left during his '70s youth (his best work, the 1993 anime techno-thriller *Patlabor 2*, targets the contradictions of the postwar Japan—U.S. military relationship) leaving him in a suitable position to observe Ghibli from both an artistic and political perspective. In Oshii's judgment, the art and politics were, at Ghibli, much the same thing: "I think that for them, making a movie is still a kind of extension of the union movement."

That was the very reason why, despite his continuing admiration for Ghibli's work, Oshii withdrew from what might have been a fascinating collaboration—the never-made mid-eighties film concept *Anchor*. In a 1995 *Kinema Jumpo* interview, Oshii compared Ghibli to the Kremlin: "The real one is long gone, but they're still sitting in the middle of the field in Higashi Koganei (Ghibli's address)." Oshii thought of the expert animators of Ghibli as the "steel-like athletes" from Communist nations viewed in the Olympics. "You can value [that system] because it cultured such talent, but if you ask me if it's totally right, I'd say, I don't think so."

2. "Various questions inside me became overwhelming," Miyazaki told the June 1994 issue of *Yom* magazine—a special issue marking the end of his *Nausicaä* manga, in which its princess rejects an offer of a scientific means to perfect humanity and society. "During the time I was trying to conclude *Nausicaä*, I did what some might think is a turnabout. I totally forsook Marxism. I had no choice but to forsake it. I decided that it is wrong, that historical materialism is also wrong, and that I shouldn't see things through it.... At first, I even hesitated to make Nausicaä a princess. I thought some might say [she's] in a sort of elite class, so I thought of ways [to justify it]. But these things became meaningless to me.... When I first saw Mao receiving cheers from the big crowd in Tiananmen Square...I felt his face was really inauspicious and ill-favored. But since I was told that he had a big warm personality or such

in the elegiac *Grave of the Fireflies* (1988) or the life-affirming *Only Yesterday* (1991).

Miyazaki was making "worry-free adventure stories" in animation while putting his deeper, troubled thoughts into the long *Nausicaä* manga, which had already diverged widely from the 1984 anime movie. And the world he had always believed in changing *was*, in a way that began to burn holes in what he drew: in *Nausicaä* he created fantasy empires that fell in fantasy wars, while in the real world he watched the Soviet Union collapse and Yugoslavia revert to barbaric strife and genocide as if nothing had been learned or gained in the entire century. For Miyazaki the animator, the fall of the old Communist order signified a liberating, but not comforting change.[2] The turn began with his film *Porco Rosso*; based on a light-hearted comic he had drawn of a (literally) pig-headed aviator who hunts pirates over the Depression-era Adriatic, Miyazaki shaded the 1992 anime version with glimpses of rising Fascism and ironic postcard views of the same Balkan coastline towns that history slated for destruction in our own time. Miyazaki told *Yom* magazine, "If I think about going back there again, I feel really dark, but I think I have to accept that. I think I have to see things on my own.... It's painful to go back to the world of *Nausicaä*, and I don't want to go back."

He did, though. 1997's *The Princess Mononoke* was his return journey to the themes of *Nausicaä*, the journey of a man no longer at ease, but with his eyes fully opened to a lifetime's experience. Miyazaki abandoned neither his abiding love of nature nor his observations on social justice—indeed, Miyazaki chose to set *Mononoke* in fifteenth-century Japan because class and sex roles had not yet rigidified. The film centers around an armed commune of outcasts who build primitive muskets in their own factory. What changed

was the resolution of the story, or rather, Miyazaki's realization that there can never be any. It is indeed his darkest film, presenting the struggle between man and nature with a shadow of primitive terror, an ancestral memory of man's first art: *Mononoke* conjures the violence and sympathetic magic, the fear and hunger and awe, that thrust spears into painted boars on cave walls.

But as one watches *Mononoke*, it is tremendously exciting to see how Miyazaki's craft has leapt forward—despite the phantasmagorical imagery, his disciplined staging and shots make the narrative seem real and immediate in a way *Nausicaä* never was. *Mononoke* became Miyazaki's first truly adult film—and his signal achievement in a lifetime of films that have charmed all ages. An astounding experience reminiscent of the finest human passion of the late **Akira Kurosawa**, *Mononoke* was one of the best motion pictures to have been made anywhere in the world during the 1990s. Earning $133 million, it broke *E.T.*'s fifteen-year boxoffice record in Japan, and briefly became the top-grossing film in Japan of all time. It was deposed only by the international sensation *Titanic*—a film, it should be noted, that had ten times *Mononoke*'s budget behind it.

Thirty years after *Horus*, Ghibli achieved a different kind of revolution. *Mononoke* is a vast banner unfurled on the screen, one side green in the sun—the other moonlit, full of vicious colors and shadowy folds. Yet in the end, it all rolls to fit into a human hand. Clarity, Miyazaki explained to *Yom*, will be found in the appropriate scale. "There is a huge gap between generalities and particulars. But a human can often be satisfied with particulars. If we see...from the top of a mountain or from a plane, we feel it's hopeless, but if we go down, and there's fifty meters of nice

road, and the weather is fine and shining, we feel we can go on.

"I drive a car and cause pollution. If everyone has to stop, I'll stop, but even so, I'll continue to drive to the last. Go ahead and raise the price of gas to 300 yen per liter..." Miyazaki laughs. "Gee, I'm shooting my mouth off just as I please, aren't I?" Of course, as he pleases: the car Miyazaki drives is no Lexus or Acura, but a funny-looking little red rocket, a three-wheeled thing with a miniature rollbar to cradle his grey head at the highest speeds. Like his movies, he made that car himself, with his own two hands.

The Children of Miyazaki and Coca-Cola

Jean-Luc Goddard's minimalist science-fiction classic, *Alphaville*, became both the name of an '80s band and a sideways influence on *Neon Genesis Evangelion*, the anime that stormed the barricades of TV in Japan as *The Princess Mononoke* did the theaters. But when it comes to describing the company that made *Evangelion*, Studio Gainax—named after a slang term for something really big—it's Godard's *Masculine-Feminine* that comes to mind, with its priceless opening line: "This film could be called *The Children of Marx and Coca-Cola*." The people who make up Gainax are just like that—except that they are the children of Coca-Cola and Miyazaki.

The Gainax animators are from the first generation to grow up with anime as a pop-culture given; they were born in the years when Toei was first putting it on the screen and Tezuka was first putting it on TV—in short, Gainax is of the otaku generation, as they put it in their wincingly honest, and sometimes truthful, 1991 *Spinal Tap*-like "autobiography," ***Otaku no Video***. "Otaku" was a dirty word then in Japan. Gainax, however, suspected there was an otaku inside everyone just waiting to emerge—and *Otaku no Video* predicted (in a manner not unlike ***Ed Wood***'s Amazing Criswell) the otakuization of all Japan by 1999.

Gainax's ***Neon Genesis Evangelion*** would eventually become the national phenomenon to make the prediction come true. Gainax (their name even sounds like Gen-X) understood the culture of international postmodernism that draws everyday lessons from ***Bewitched*** and reserves the big, abstract issues for ***Star Wars***. But what made Gainax special was their insistence that this was all, on some level, true and authentic. The '60s generation claimed that a ninja comic was a Cliff Notes for Marx. Gainax had no need to plead a higher authority; they saw nothing wrong with finding guidance just in the ninja comic itself. They had a special kind of self-knowledge sometimes accessible to those who grow up playing not with the world but with other people's models of the world, to those who contemplate not creation but artifice.[3]

Like Miyazaki and Takahata's political fables, Gainax's know-thyself anime ran on a partnership of two directors. The critical detail for Gainax is that the "moment of clarity"—as American otaku **Quentin Tarantino** would have it—for **Hiroyuki Yamaga** (b. 1962) and **Hideaki Anno** (b. 1960), came at decidedly different speeds. For Yamaga, the perception came first, as a burst from deep space: illuminating with a brilliant, light-speed flash. Long years later, the shockwave arrived for Anno, cracking his private world apart.

Yamaga presented as a fairly respectable, athletic young man with an inner passion for creative and financial success in the film world, when he arrived at college in 1980—just like Kubo, the freshman protagonist of ***Otaku no Video***, which Yamaga wrote under a pseudonym. The college he attended was no Todai or Gakushuin, but the arts university of Japan's heavy industrial center, Osaka. Walking through the quad one day early on in his student career, he found himself suddenly in the midst of a live-action battle between wild costumed students, one side dressed as ninja, the other in SWAT gear. "When that becomes a daily occurrence, what am I supposed to say?" Yamaga exclaimed to American fans in 1997 upon a visit to Silicon Valley's massive annual anime gathering, Fanime Con. Then, a tall, gangling, and mysterious upperclassman named Hideaki Anno introduced himself not with the customary hello but by confiding that he knew practically every line in ***Space Battleship Yamato*** (***Star Blazers***) by heart. "I think I forgot what was normal at that point," recalled Yamaga.

Soon he found himself making 8 mm ***Power Rangers***-type superhero films with Anno and his friends, and, of course, anime—cutting up industrial plastic sheeting into cels to save money. The anime shorts were not so much narratives as collections of pop-culture rhyming-and-stealing, as frantic as a **Beastie Boys** track. In an Anno-Yamaga student production, cities got A-bombed just for effect while Playboy bunnies crossed light sabers with Darth Vader. Yamaga, who, when he arrived at college, had no intention of becoming an otaku, much less an anime-maker, became both by the time his group incorporated in 1984 as Studio Gainax.

It was the year of ***Nausicaä***, and only three years later, Gainax would make an anime epic of their own—***Royal Space Force: The Wings of Honneamise***.[4] The concept for the film, said Yamaga, came to

things, I thought maybe he happened to be ill and wasn't photogenic on that day." Miyazaki laughed, but said it was the truth. "I should've trusted my first instinct. I did such things many times. I always tried to overpower my feelings with my ideals. I stopped doing so. And this is a bit hard. Even now, I sometimes think that things would be easier if I had not changed..."

Anno

3. **Pauline Kael**'s comments on *Masculine-Feminine* in *The New Yorker* fit Gainax's conception of the otaku perfectly: "This community of unbelievers has a style of life by which they recognize each other; it is made up of everything adults attack as the worst and shoddiest forms of...dehumanization. It is the variety of forms of 'Coca-Cola'—the synthetic life they were born to and which they love, and which they barely make human and more beautiful and more 'real' than the old just-barely-hanging-on adult culture. Membership is automatic and natural for the creatures from inner space...they have the beauty of youth which can endow pop with poetry, and they have their feeling for each other and all those shared products and responses by which they know each other."

Gainax's passion is, then, a French kiss-in-cheek, a tongue stuck out, but saying some lovely things. Hideaki Anno and Hiroyuki Yamaga, both born when the Beatles were still a Chuck Berry cover band, are the Lennon and McCartney of Gainax. At least, Yamaga maintains that Anno *looks* like "the smart one," while personally disclaiming any resemblance to "the cute one." (But neither of the two are fans, particularly; Anno loves the sound of retro-SF themes and classical music, while Yamaga has shown a penchant for the '80s electronica of **Ryuichi Sakamoto** and '90s trance-Goa pioneer **DJ Tsuyoshi**, both of whom Yamaga picked to score his movies.) "If anybody's going to get shot, though, I would want it to be Anno," he says, laughing as he speaks of his comrade of many years. "Supposedly he made *Evangelion* for a target age of fourteen, but I think he really made it for people his own age—about thirty-five."

Yamaga

4. At Fanime Con, Yamaga described how they raised the money for the film. One might say that Gainax decided to walk into Jabba the Hutt's palace with a thermal detonator. Freshly dropped-out of college, they entered the corporate headquarters of Bandai, the multibillion-dollar Japanese toy giant that produces half the anime in Japan, including titles familiar to Americans, such as *Sailor Moon*. Gainax presented Bandai with a ten-year business plan they had drawn up—not for *Gainax* to follow, him in that most Gen-X of cathedrals, the coffeehouse. It was a product of otaku consciousness. "I thought how [anime] should reflect society and what it should represent, and to me it seemed it should be like a mirror in a coffeehouse—a double space, an illusion. We have a limited time here in our lives, but we feel that through television and film, we can understand a great deal more... In school, you may be taught that the world is round, but with your *own* eyes, you'll only be able to confirm, to directly experience, a very small part of that world, a very small part of what we're capable of *imagining*... We wanted to *create* a world, and we wanted to look at it from space."

Gainax made good on their ambition; under Yamaga's direction, an explosion of twenty-something creative energy gave **The Wings of Honneamise** the most sophisticated and cosmopolitan art direction of any anime film made before or since. In an achievement beyond even that seen in the movies of **Terry Gilliam** or **Ridley Scott**, the team crafted an imaginary alternate world in every fascinating detail, from the bongs to the jet planes. It was a kaleidoscopic mirror, for the setting of **Honneamise** contained every element of our modern lives: class, faith, science, war, and of course, television—but all with the jumbled look of no particular country, or many countries, in an international visual language.

Yamaga imagined an ordinary young man in his early twenties, named Shiro, for the protagonist of **Honneamise**. However, in a brilliant plot conceit, the director turned the clock of Shiro's parallel world back to a time when space travel was a dream few believed possible. Shiro always says he wants a simple life, but a childhood vision of flight flickers within him. Without the grades to get into aviator school, he falls in with a tiny, no-budget government program, whose mumbling commandant styles his bored young students the Royal Space Force, and

talks of one day sending the first man into orbit. For no better conscious reason than to impress a girl who seems to believe in him, Shiro astounds everyone by volunteering. The story begins from there, as Shiro begins his long journey to the rocket.

His ill-considered decision changes him from a man content to stare, into someone who, for the first time in his life, must take a good look around. Before he will ever get to leave the ground, the would-be astronaut has to explore his own fallen world and the inner space inside him. What begins for him as a sci-fi joke becomes shadowed by assassination, terrorism, social unrest, and war, as both he and his mission become public sacrifice pawns in the global power game. Yet the question of whether the first man *will* go into space is to be decided privately, as Shiro confronts his own capacity for violence and delusion in moments without a witness. Few motion pictures of any kind have so well used the make-believe of movies in such a powerful and sustained metaphor as **Honneamise**. As an anime, it remains in many ways unsurpassed.

Anno had been the special-effects genius on **Honneamise**, and unlike Yamaga, Hideaki Anno never had any doubts that he was either an otaku or an animator. On the cusp of adolescence, he withdrew from the realm of the senses into a world of watching anime and making 8 mm movies. Girls avoided him like the plague, and he avoided them—an *entente cordiale* of the kind portrayed in 1991's *Otaku no Video*. It was oddly appropriate that after *Otaku no Video* strobelit Anno and his friends like a string of firecrackers, Gainax fell silent in the smoke for the next four years as they struggled fruitlessly with an abortive plan to make a second motion picture.

The reason lay in large part with Anno himself, who never had any doubts because he never asked himself any questions. When he at last asked, with an anime called **Neon**

Genesis Evangelion, he was to change the face of anime once again, as Yamaga's **Honneamise** had years before—only this time, the public would respond to the seeds Gainax had sown. And when Anno had the answer, it was a high school girl who got it from him. One day in August of 1998, while visiting students to research his next show, she came up to him, full of admiration, to say that she loved **Evangelion**, believed in pursuing one's dreams, and intended to grow up and one day make anime herself. He warned her: "You've got it all wrong. This is the only thing I can do.... I've managed to get this far because I gave up everything else."

By the time he was twenty-four, while still a student filmmaker, Anno was being mentored by Hayao Miyazaki, who gave him key work on **Nausicaä**—and hailed as a rising star. After **Honneamise**, he directed and cowrote for Gainax both the 1988 romantic space-war epic video series **Gunbuster** and the 1990 TV anime **Nadia**, a Jules Verne–like adventure set in a fantastic nineteenth century (and a concept originally developed for Miyazaki). Then it was all over, not from a lack of success—Anno's two directorial efforts had proven popular—but because he had broken quietly one day. For four long years he was unable to make anime anymore. It was when he realized that, in a world full of life, not making anime was for him the same as not living, that the shockwave hit. On October 4, 1995, he began at last to speak about it, with the premiere of a TV series four years in the waiting, **Neon Genesis Evangelion**— ancient Greek for New Beginning Gospel.

Evangelion takes place in 2015— fifteen years after the second-to-Last Judgment. On September 13 in the year 2000, a massive explosion in Antarctica triggers a global catastrophe that leaves half the world dead. The official story is that the blast is caused by a giant meteor. The truth though, as they say, "is out there," and there may be time to discover it as humanity makes its last stand in Tokyo-3, a super-tech fortress city under assault from the hideous, uncommunicative entities code-named the Angels.

Evangelion follows the course of this war and, most especially, the personal conflict between the three different generations at NERV: the fourteen-year-old "Children" who pilot the equally-monstrous biomechanical Evangelion Units against the Angels, their twenty-something commanding officers, and the Children's parents, scientists who know far too much and tell far too little. The 1995–96 *Eva* TV show was a phenomenon in Japan; ten million people tuned in for its final episode. The 1997 *Evangelion* movies, which presented a different version of the TV show's controversial ending, made about $28 million, the merchandising well over $200 million.[5]

Anno claims no spiritual beliefs but the animism of Shinto. In fact, many of *Evangelion*'s religious elements—most particularly his use of the Kabbalah—come not through religion per se but the psychological theories of **C. G. Jung**, who considered the Kabbalah a valuable set of symbols with which to understand the human psyche. Thus, in *Eva*, the Angels' and Man's battle for their place in the scheme of creation becomes a dramatic and meticulously considered device that allowed Anno to stage spectacular fights and showcase fantastic technology, all in the service of his own personal lake of fire, a public burning every Wednesday at 7:30 p.m. nationwide.[6]

Today Japanese animation, in its search for the next *Eva*, populates its new series with the *Eva* look—the exotic technology called *mecha* in anime and a cast of sad tomatoes—without perhaps ever realizing what kind of commitment another *Evangelion* would require from its creators. Pretty faces and cool

devices drew *Evangelion*'s initial audiences, but it was the unraveling of the strands of the life of a real human being that captured older Japanese audiences who would have never admitted to watching anime before—that brought in the outsiders. In a savage irony, many hardcore otaku—despite the anime's requisite portion of cute girls and hi-tech action—felt robbed by *Eva*, and wanted to know what kind of a show was ultimately about nothing more than a person's unresolved soul.

Postscript: Somewhere/ Anywhere

There isn't likely to be "another *Evangelion*." Nor is that particularly desirable. What *Eva* has led to is much better—its success has spawned an explosion of new anime shows in Japan on a level unseen since the early '80s; it's just like the exciting college days that encouraged Gainax to enter the industry in the first place. Some shows are taking chances and trying to move anime along. Others are simply providing anime with the diversity of demographics and themes that the medium so desperately needs to catch up with the success and respect manga already enjoys in Japan.

Gainax is not the **Beatles**; first of all, that was Ghibli's generation. In a 1998 interview with the author, Yamaga invoked the Fab Four not as history, but as myth, for he is well aware that to the Japanese—as well as to their American fans—he and Anno have themselves become myth as much as history. Yamaga accepts their fame with a cautionary wink: "The press is saying good things about us.... If they were insulting us or saying nasty things—yeah, then I would

but Bandai! In the stunned silence that followed, Gainax president Toshio Okada (who went to college just to join the science fiction club and today teaches at Takahata's alma mater) managed to fashion a movie budget with the help of a creative-minded young executive at Bandai, Shigeru Watanabe, who quickly became a fervent disciple of Gainax's vision. Watanabe remains the patron behind some of Japan's most progressive anime films—films that he and *Honneamise* took the blows to make possible. The thermal detonator bit proved no joke: the movie bombed. *Honneamise* was a classic example of the film too far ahead of its time that today everyone acknowledges as the work of genius. At least someone understood, though: Yamaga may have taken some paternal comfort from Miyazaki's praise of his film in an interview in *Kinema Jumpo* in 1995 (the year after *Honneamise* finally began to turn a profit). Miyazaki saw kindred spirits in the makers of Gainax's breakthrough film; their approach reminded him of his work with Takahata on the making of *Horus*. "*Honneamise* is the proof [that] it's still possible.... Those who made it were amateurs in terms of experience. In their mid-twenties, they made it by themselves, living and eating together, with no distinction between the work and their private lives."

5. Although *Evangelion* has remained strictly on video for now in the United States, it has been a considerable success, which has made the persistent rumor that it might be picked up by MTV seem credible. When Houston's A.D.V. Films released the final episode here, their print ads, trading on *Eva*'s renown in the American market, were mysterious and text-only, showing no anime images at all—the first U.S. anime ad to dare such an approach. Some elements of *Eva*'s success needed no English translation, such as the visual design which Emmy-award winning CG programmer **Allen Hastings** (*Babylon 5*) has described as the most sophisticated of any anime TV series ever, or the attractive characters drawn by **Yoshiyuki Sadamoto**—most notably, the Zen beauty of Rei Ayanami, whose appeal as The Face in Japan during '96 to '97 proved portable when she appeared on a popular bootleg T-shirt worn by a character on NBC's *Veronica's Closet*.

Like the majority of anime, *Evangelion* was made with no audience in mind but the one in Japan. Nevertheless, to the Westerners who see it, it has a special resonance. *Eva*'s use of Judeo-Christian symbolism, eschatology, and esoterica are exotic and fascinating decorations for the Japanese, but they are part of the actual cul-

"It's good to be young.
You can bet all of yourself
on the smallest of hopes."

—from *Adieu Galaxy Express 999*

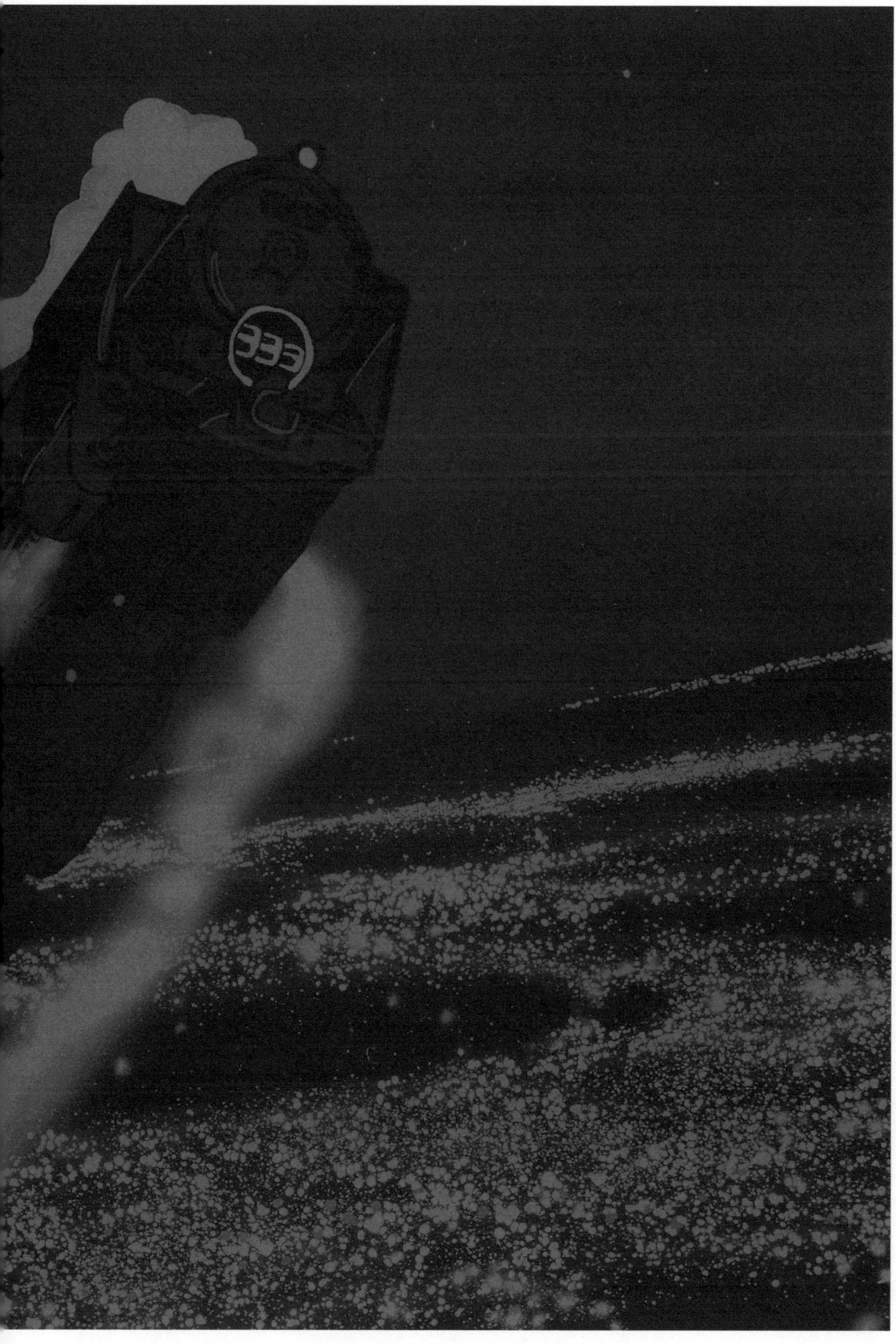
333

be motivated to go out and correct them. As I make my own living writing stories that aren't true.... Look at all the things they said about the Beatles. If you do, you'll probably find a lot of stuff that was made up as well.... Well, it would be great if we could be as successful as *them*... The main thing the industry has learned from *Evangelion* and *Mononoke*", says Yamaga drily, "is that there's a lot of money to be made in anime."

Currently, Yamaga is at work on his very long-awaited second film, *Blue Uru*, while *Honneamise* has been rediscovered by astounded audiences in Japan. So far, Gainax is famous only in their own country, while Ghibli is being hoisted up before America in the four-fingered, white-gloved, massive mouse hands of one of the largest, most famous, most successful, and most revered institutions in the world, America's giant robot: the Walt Disney Company.

Those same hands, even gloved, are not likely to touch Gainax. Perhaps it says something about them that it was **Manga Entertainment**—whose parent company **Islandlife**'s **Chris Blackwell** brought ska and reggae to the world—which released *Honneamise* here, while *Evangelion* has

come to the U.S. through Houston's **A.D.V. Films**, whose producer once ran the local anime club—the club the guys from NASA, literally right across the street, attended. However long Gainax manages to fly low and fast under the American radar, they may also resist simple definitions like "fine family entertainment" and "an ecological message" that Ghibli now risks from the media here (as if *Mononoke* were *FernGully*). Not, in the most important sense, that it matters. Whether in a thousand theaters or direct-to-video, Ghibli and Gainax are both here now, and part of the machine. But as creators, they will always be a world away.

They say, "To live is to change," as Anno wrote in a letter introducing *Eva* to the public in the months before its television premiere. Miyazaki had used that phrase at the very ending of the *Nausicaä* manga, when his heroine rejects the very concept of a cleansed and at-peace soul that can still be called human. There is a hard wisdom to walk by there. "If I trust his words, I can live," Shinji says of his father, just this side of the apocalypse. The director of *The Princess Mononoke* had tasted ashes in his own mouth. "This is the end of everything. The

forest is dying," *Mononoke*'s heroine says. "This is not the end. We are still alive," proclaims the voice of its hero.

Recently, Miyazaki and Anno took an extraordinary journey together, an air safari across the Sahara in a vintage plane, which retraced the path of aviation pioneer and author of *The Little Prince*, **Antoine de Saint-Exupéry**. Landing in the middle of that desert from whose winds Ghibli takes its name, the two posed for a picture on a dune, striking the statuary poses of bearded, bespectacled leaders of the revolution. Miyazaki, with the dignity of a grey suit, the shade of a sensible hat, points straight ahead. Anno, in a black pullover, his bare head covered with scraggly curls, raises his arm high in the air; after a moment you realize he's doing an *Ultraman* pose. Sorry—it's not "look upon my works, ye mighty, and despair," because anime is just in the hands and the imagination; there's nothing ever there to see but the man. And it's not like they're going to stick around waiting to be covered by the sand—father or son, they've got places to go still. Whatever place you want to put them, they'll leave that somewhere behind. They prefer anywhere.

PART TWO
PICTURES FROM THE DROWNING WORLD: SCREAMING LIFE, AMERICAN OTAKU

Thou shalt call, and I will answer thee: thou wilt have a desire to the work of thine hands. For now thou numberest my steps: dost thou not watch over my sin? (Job 14: 15-16)

welcome to the land of real guns in real faces (June 4, 1996 and Before)

I suppose the closest I ever came to being shot to death was in an anime store.

When I was a student, I was once warned not to take a course with a certain professor

because he was too "intense." He wrote a poem that began, *Don't be afraid of dying,* and ended with, *Lie down here, next to Empedocles. Be joined to the small grains of the brotherhood.* I have brothers in Houston: Jean and Hip of **Planet Anime**, the first all-anime shop in the United States, which opened in early 1994. There had been places before, across the country, where you could get your goods, but these were all comic shops, bookstores, and Japanese boutiques. Planet Anime was the first to be founded on anime alone.

Location: no dismal strip mall or shit-pile brick block—of which Houston has plenty, believe me. Planet Anime is flanked by tobacconists, antiquaries, even a store selling that shiny revived Swedish Modern, the scratched knockoffs of which you sat on in the third grade. Right near the sprawling Texas Medical Center, PA's racks of *La Blue Girl* and *Night on the Galactic Railroad* are pawed by both trauma surgeons in green and gangbangers in various, all part of an interlocking economy. Naturally, I was most pleased to have such a shop in my town of residence, so I went to the flower stalls on Main and brought a pot of yellow chrysanthemums with me as I first stepped through Planet Anime's doors. That's how I made friends with Jean and Hip.

Those were good times for the city. The **Rockets** won the NBA championship two years in a row; it was the first time Houston had ever won *anything*. We all watched the playoffs in the store, drinking Shiner Bock. We were even watching when the game was interrupted by the coverage of O. J.'s skedaddle *en el Bronco*. I remember how pissed we were, wanting them to get back to the game, to trade reality for spectacle. But reality, if you'll recall, was poorly lit and hunkered down in that Brentwood driveway. We popped another bottle, sighed, and, I believe, may have actually put a tape off the shelves into the VCR. All in all, I couldn't have asked for a better anime club.

It was those after-hours habits that got me into trouble, though. It was June 4, 1996, two days after A-Kon. I had gone back to Cali, but had flown out for the convention and a visit afterward to H-Town. (An omen of the drama to come: I thought I saw **Bushwick Bill** out of **Geto Boys** at Hobby Airport; it may have been him—there can't have been too many other black, one-eyed dwarfs at the baggage claim). That night, I hung out at Planet Anime until nine, then went to Japon's across the street and had some eel. An assistant was closing the store; Jean walked by and joined me at the table. Looking over at the store, he saw a red pickup parked outside. He said something was going on, and told me to wait there. I didn't; I followed him. It was later established that the time was 9:20 p.m.

As soon as I stepped through the door, I saw the case where **Skuld** dolls raised their mallets in euphoric command. I saw the rows of *El-Hazard* tapes, the models of the Zaku and the Yamato. I saw the assistant with two other guys; a third was out of my line of vision; they were covering the store. One of them pulled a gun on Jean and myself. It was held casually at bent arm: if Kenichi Sonoda were to ask, it might have been a Ruger, or maybe a Beretta. They all had guns. They told me to go in back, under the **Urushihara** poster with the maid outfit and clamps, and get face down on the floor.

When I was a child, I was scared by a book we had about the **Tutankhamen** exhibition. It was a thick British volume, full of photos from the opening of the tomb; in 1920s black-and-white, it looked deader than dead. But how childish indeed were those fears. The young king still lies there, his desiccated corpse now in a plain glass box; they removed all the important parts to a museum. He is remembered; he lives today. Not for his pemmican skin but for his immortal portion, the goods of a famous character. About his body were heaped the shiny figurines of those he worshiped; on the walls they were painted flat and bright.

ture of the West, most especially America, where fallen presidents have prayer breakfasts, citizens claim in polls to still believe in the God of Abraham, and many fear a millennial Armageddon—or seek to help it along with a little fertilizer and gasoline.

 6. It is as much a metaphor for the real violence within the intricate depths of Anno, who speaks with a different aspect of his persona through every character—from his cowardly, desolate "son," Shinji, who motivated him to create *Eva* in the first place to the cryptic, dictatorial "father," Gendo, who the driven director was said to resemble as the series neared the wracking end of its production. "Your God is dead/And no one cares/If there is a Hell/I'll see you there," is the scream from **Nine Inch Nails'** song **"Heresy"** off *The Downward Spiral*, an album that Japanese social critic Kenji Sato, late of M.I.T. and *The New York Times Magazine*, compares to the feeling of *Eva* as the series approaches the whirlpool of its end.

Eva isn't really about the end of the world, but the personal apocalypse. Some American fans had already made this association independently, or saw in Anno's intimations of suicide not **John Lennon** but **Kurt Cobain**. Certainly neither **Nirvana** or **NIN** had any direct connection with *Evangelion* or the show's musical style, but it's natural that young fans tied into the U.S. music scene should associate the show that, for once, really meant it, with the songs that in the four years before *Eva*'s 1995 premiere made pop music mean something again. Anno also made *Eva* as a comment on the desolation of youth and culture in Japan, but American teens don't have giant robots to command in their rage. They have semiautomatic rifles. It is the emotion, too, of *Evangelion*, that needs no translation.

 7. Lots of people say they never knew which of the animated shows they watched as kids were from Japan. But I was clued in from the very beginning that *Speed Racer* was Japanese, because my parents remarked upon names like K. Fujita in the credits. I never saw any real Japanese in Iran. There *were* Chinese though, looking, with their Mao jackets and red-star caps, just like they do in *Ranma 1/2*. My sister and I had blond hair then, and this seemed *ling-ling* to them; in the supermarket aisles they would pinch our cheeks as if pulling taffy. Actually, my parents thought the people doing the English voices in *Speed Racer* were themselves Japanese, an impression brought on by the show's notoriously bizarre syntax ("A secret

Having all he needed for eternity, he was sealed within. I looked peaceful, lying there in my suit, hands composed behind my head. If the bullet came, it would be through those hands: a surprise, as I suppose death always seems. I thought about none of those things then; I thought of nothing at all. But it was an interesting discovery that I felt no fear. Looking down at the nap of a cheap synthetic carpet with strong tiny loops of nylon, I was looking up at a shroud. As God is my witness, I felt what I felt whenever I look out a window seat into clear blue sky, where there is no end to vision and no point to fix your eyes upon.

Nativity scene (Racer-X in Iran)

My first memories are of *Speed Racer* and soap operas dubbed in Farsi: *Days of Our Lives* and *Another World*, in which Rachel sounds about as stupid as she does in English. In 1967, when *Speed* premiered in Japan under the shag-a-delic name of *Mach Go Go Go* (*go* means five, baby), my father was building moon rockets on acid: white shirt, tie, and security clearance. James Bond was having the hair plucked from his chest to look Japanese in *You Only Live Twice* and kids both here and there in the '60s knew the U.S. would lead the way to a future sky spangled with fifty times fifty stars, filled with Pan-American scramjets, flying to a Ho-Jos high above the Earth.

My daddy would drop before a showing of *2001* and then drive back to Hermosa Beach in his Corvette more on than ever. Everyone knows LSD came in stronger

doses in those days; I used to ask him how he could steer. He replied, "You just push everything out into a tunnel so there's a path of clarity." He was twenty-seven, the same age I am now. At raves nowadays you taste vinegar, a weak acid: things have gone sour. We burn in place with a roof over our heads and the plug-in stars shine in seizure. In 1973, when I was three years old, the future was all over and done with. The last American had walked on the moon the year before; the odd-and-even days at the gas station had begun. Japan began its switch from the petro-dependent heavy industry that had been SPECTRE's cover in the Bond movie to the electronics and fuel-efficient vehicles that would fulfill their dream of world domination.

As for my family—we moved to our only Mideast friend with any oil: the Iran of **Shah Reza Pahlavi**. I liked Iran, and I always tell people so, because, admit it, you haven't gotten the best impression in recent decades. It's not some no-account pile of sand, but one of the world's oldest civilizations, a land of prophets and poets: **Mani**, **Zoroaster**, **Omar Khayyám**. The Magi, who journeyed from the East to attend Jesus's birth? Yep, Iranian. And the food is great; any country whose major exports include pistachios and caviar can't be all that bad. I grew up eating caviar; an odd thing I remember is that it was peanut butter that was exotic in Iran. The gift of Jif was appreciated.

Speed Racer was on the Armed Forces Radio-Television Service, which had the predictably-pronounced acronym AFRTS. I sat on godawful German blood-red felt furniture and watched it on black-and-white TV; I didn't know TV could *be* in color until we returned to the United States. AFRTS featured things like the Rose Bowl on time delay, public service announcements on how to use a fire extinguisher, a remarkably optimistic version of Watergate

and Vietnam, and, of course, the muezzin's call to prayer. There was a children's show hosted by a probably not very high-ranking soldier called Uncle Peewee. But *Speed Racer* wasn't on Uncle Peewee—*Speed Racer* was *prime time.* Even then, it had mass expatriate appeal for my countrymen, and the whole family was glued to the set, drawn into its timeless whirlpool of rubber, asphalt, chimps, candy, and **Jackie O** bouffants.[7]

I walked by the American Embassy every day on the way to school and never saw the future. I didn't know Mehrabad International Airport, which we were there to build, was lining pockets full of graft, or that inflation would run out of control, or that the Shah would be Audi in just a few years. I don't know whether the current dictatorship is better than the one it replaced. I don't know if they still show *Speed Racer* in Iran. I like to think that they've used computer graphics to give him a fringe of beard and Trixie a head scarf, and that Rex now works for the *Komité-yé Enghelab-é Eslami* (the religious secret police), and that Flash Marker became **Salman Rushdie**, and that Speed stands over his flaming wreck at the end saying "Burn in hell."

fast train/slow train (The National Anime Man-Boy Love Association)

I didn't see any more anime until I came back to the U.S. It was the death of an ancestor that brought me home. My mother's father was a patriarch worthy of **Coppola**, except that he just made concrete; he didn't put anyone into it. He came, a Serb, from Bosnia-Herzegovina; you've heard of the people and the place. They say I get my sturdy peasant features from him, but I wish I had received more of his character. The company he started with his partners poured stone over and under the waters of the west, coalescing dams and aqueducts, highways and bridges. He cut life to his size. It was death he was larger than; I watched them lower him into the common estate, six feet down, but he was six foot seven.

The slow cars of the Bay Area Rapid Transit ran through the San Francisco environs, where we settled after the funeral. BART seemed futuristic to an eleven-year-old, but it was, again, a '70s kind of future, one going nowhere at fifty-five miles an hour. I was into role-playing then, and San Francisco was certainly a good place for it. That the Bay Area became the sacred, flaming heart of Japanese animation in America should be no surprise to anyone.

February 13, 1982—the night before St. Valentine's, when love gets written down in secret. I am at a gaming convention held at the castle-shaped Dunfey Hotel in San Mateo, its Rankin-Bass ambiance just perfect for a boy whose voice is yet to break. *On the second floor is a small, narrow chamber. You see humanoid figures seated in rows before a dimly-glowing altar, from which a strange tongue emanates. A spark leaps from its clear face; you fail your saving throw.* On the TV set in the room, there it is: an episode of *Space Pirate Captain Harlock*.

You can see him in English in *Galaxy Express 999* and *Adieu Galaxy Express 999* and many other movies and shows. He was never famous here, like Speed, but Harlock is *the* great heroic figure of anime, walking with his shadow flag, fighting both alien invaders and the government of a decadent future Earth that has turned its back on space. Uncle Joyce compared him to Ragnar Danneskjöld, the freebooter of *Atlas Shrugged*. "Uncle Joyce" was *the red-bearded ogre you see before the altar, beckoning you forward.*

He and his wife were fixtures at gaming and SF conventions all over the Bay Area, where they would bring a stack of Betas and put on an anime medicine show. Heap big medicine. That night he was showing Harlock in the original Japanese: episodes once subtitled for broadcast in Hawaii, that hapa-paradise for otaku where you could grow up watching all the *Ultraman* you wanted. Joyce was a genteel Hell's Angel, a good-natured creature who invited me up to his castle, perched high on a hill in South San Francisco. I entered freely and of my own will a rickety and rotting Victorian, a redolent sepulcher inside, piled high with hoarded anime tapes and anime books and anime LPs. Like the leader of Iran's medieval cult of assassins, I had been drugged by the Old Man of the Mountain and given a vision of paradise in need of Mop 'n' Glo.

Such was the way for a lad: this was the graffiti of otaku generation 1982, an age of culture clubs doing the *kaiju* thing on MTV and bands named for *Barbarella* bad guys featuring men proudly wearing lip gloss and mousse. There was no Japanese animation section in Blockbuster; there was no Blockbuster. Uncle Joyce directed me to a scattered underground group, the first formal American anime fan club in existence; perhaps four hundred people belonged to it in all. Local meetings were held in the back of public libraries and, curiously, banks, and always seemed to be run by middle-aged men with my-side-lost-the-war mustaches and pocket protectors bearing the names of pre-consolidation aerospace firms. A strange double exposure would hit me as I beheld them, remembering my father's two childhood warnings: be wary in public bathrooms and never become an engineer.

Fortunately, I met two teens there, named Bruce Bailey and Brian Fountain, who ran a little refuge for their fellow run-

meeting is about to take place, secretly!") and frequent exclamations of "Ohhhhhhh." But, no, they were Americans, led by **Peter Fernandez**, the voice of Speed and the English scriptwriter. Fernandez is on record expressing pride that *Speed Racer* was a show in which no one ever got killed. Perhaps he was thinking of a different program; that fellow whose car jumps the railing and explodes into a million pieces even before the opening credits end certainly doesn't look well.

8. In those '80s days of manga such as *Banana Fish* and *Pineapple Army*, young Japanese wanted to spend time in New York City, for then it was the high tide of the city's reputation as an exciting land of violent death. For them, to escape from NYC alive meant you had truly *lived*. A little strange, then, that *we* were running around Miramonte High School with Japanese play guns, called airsoft guns. These weren't like those pink and green paintball guns; airsofts fired 6 mm plastic pellets but looked *exactly* like the real brand name—be it Uzi, HK, or Smith & Wesson. Strangely, no one ever fussed; today, a school would call the cops faster than you can say "CNN Special Report."

Sure, even then, some suburban kid (city school violence, then as now, wore a collective face, and of a color poor for ratings) might pull a Jeremy out of their Jansport. You especially wanted to watch out for those who wore double straps, and of course they'd always find a copy of *The Bachman Books* in his locker. But while we did in fact have a murder in my class, it was by knife. Now that I think about it, that's very Japanese. It was a fairly famous murder, one written up in *Rolling Stone* and made into a TV movie starring **Tori Spelling**. A girl stabbed another for reasons of popularity, just like in *Heathers*. Our junior prom theme, by the way, was **"In The Air Tonight"**, a slow dance number about death and deceit. Anyway, don't bother looking for airsoft guns here today; they were outlawed for safety reasons. Fortunately, it is still legal to buy the real ones.

9. From an industry standpoint, *Robotech* can be viewed as simply a failed scheme to market its accompanying Matchbox robot toys. The commercials, often coming after some particularly dramatic moment, showed a crude animation of the characters blasting their way towards you with the musical slogan "Robotech to the Rescue;" it made anyone over ten feel like a fucking fool for watching. *Robotech* was *written* for a teen audience, but its major marketing was towards children, and in most American cities it literally aired at preschool

"Did you sleep well?
How do you like your new body?"

—from *Key the Metal Idol*

aways from that scene. They would show me copies of Japan's *Animage* magazine and play **Agnostic Front**'s *Victim in Pain*. Through them I began to understand that this was a vital, golden age for anime, that things were *happening* over in Japan. It was they who introduced me to shows like *Lupin III*, *Dirty Pair* and *Fist of the North Star*, which we watched with many a "huh-huh-huh." They showed me that anime wasn't just an all-male world; there was heterosexuality and lesbianism as well in an anime called *Pop Chaser*. Years later, I would find out that *Evangelion*'s Hideaki Anno worked on it, although he has written that he only did the explosions. Which explosions, he didn't specify.

It all made quite an impression at fourteen; *epiphany* would be the right dirty word. Imagination got the best of me once again. Even as I rode BART, delays from station to station and the days of my youth unwound at six-hour speed; I was a starchild, looking through glass at strange colors in a blur. The future was bright and garish: anime was my bullet train.

hat am i dreaming of?
(Ron and Yas's Amerasian Blues)

For Japan had become both my today and tomorrow. I had discovered the purest rock form of anime in the intersection of the immortal god-king of my generation, **Ronald Reagan**, and the one Japanese prime minister people tend to remember, **Yasuhiro Nakasone** (imagine a country where *every* president is **Gerald Ford**). In

the '80s, it was assumed that the future belonged to Japan, that the Japanese would buy everything worth owning and make everything worth having. Perhaps someone should have remembered the '70s, when it was the Arabs with their oil who were going to rule the world. But then, those who fail to learn history are doomed to be employed.

In America, despite the fear that our cars were never going to start again, times were good.[8] Eschewing the ruinous tax-and-spend policies of the Democrats, Reagan borrowed and spent, taking out a $2 trillion student loan for us all. As with most loans of that type, we had a lot of fun with the money but didn't learn very much from the experience. The national debt was a worry for future generations. You might call it a tax on the unborn—fitting for a president who believed that they are people, too. Flush with cash, we coveted exotic imports like **Nastassja Kinski**—my first video girl ai—and the Porsche 928. A friend of mine's dad had one, and yes, we ganked it whenever we could, just like Tom Cruise in *Risky Business* (the first film I ever recorded off that open-admission sex-ed class of my generation, cable). President Reagan's own son, Ron Jr., satirized the movie when he hosted *Saturday Night Live*. We all understood who our father *really* was; as **George Lucas** wrote in *The Empire Strikes Back* in the year Reagan took forty-four states: search your feelings, you know it to be true.

And we asked him for war toys. This was the age of *Voltron* and *Transformers*, and in an act of voodoo origami, the

hours; San Francisco, where it showed in the afternoon, was a notable exception.

Robotech also remains controversial from a creative standpoint, for far greater liberties were taken with its original material than would be considered acceptable today. The show's chief developer, **Carl Macek**, edited together eighty-five episodes from three separate series with plots that were unconnected in the original Japanese. Further, *Robotech*'s voice-acting, narration, and music often left something to be desired. Yet on balance, I believe **David Chute** of the *Los Angeles Herald-Examiner* was correct when he called it in 1985 "the best new entertainment series on TV." Incidentally, a large part of the reason for *Robotech*'s failure was Reagan's Treasury Secretary **James Baker**'s idea that our trade deficit with Japan could be wiped out simply by making the dollar weaker against the yen. It didn't work, but the sudden currency plunge wrecked the international deals holding the *Robotech* production together. Although I am almost certain this is mere coincidence, James Baker later became secretary of state under Bush during the Gulf War.

10. I also bought a copy of **Giyûgun**'s *Itsumi Sensation* (very mid-'80s in style, with its instant lovers still edged with that **Toshihiro Hirano** baby fat) at **Animate** in Ikebukuro, and chucked it over the wall of the Canadian Embassy in a brown paper bag. Looking back, I'm not exactly sure why I did that. In Tehran, my mother always told me that if I was ever in trouble abroad, it was best to go to the Canadians for help. You may remember how they later smuggled some of our people out of Iran when things got bad. Their embassy in Tokyo was near my hotel, so it gave me a good feeling; perhaps I wanted it to be mutual. It might have been some kind of political gesture; all the Canadians I know love porno manga, but their government gives them a hard time over it. Commodity fetishism flies like a red rocket, as someone would say in an *Appleseed* postscript. Perhaps socialism *can* work as **Masamune Shirow** envisioned it in *Appleseed*: people first, biotech lingerie, and the best life for all. Those who complain that ex-radical **Mamoru Oshii** somehow added fan service when he directed Shirow's *Ghost in the Shell* have apparently never read the original manga. In fact the old pol made Shirow's Kusanagi as sexy as denatured alcohol—see my comments regarding the Planet Anime robbery below. The way I figure it, my action *had* to have been some kind of political gesture; as Oshii himself pointed out in his *Patlabor* OAV, *The Seven Days of Fire*, the problem with the Left is that it's always fighting with itself.

Defense Department folded two thousand thousand thousand thousand dollar bills into toilet seats and Trident submarines. Yet there was indeed more than meets the eye in *Robotech*, the epic tomorrow that Japan gave American TV in 1985. Its saga of soldier teens—who sometimes flew *Top Gun* pseudo-F-14s that transformed into big robots in a war against authoritarian aliens—would have seemed a product of its times, if the script hadn't been so subversive. Its characters constantly questioned the necessity of the war, which was often portrayed as driven more by ignorance and politics than the actual security interests of Earth. And, in the age in which the TV special *The Day After* challenged the official position that nuclear war was "winnable," *Robotech* portrayed the situation Richard Rhodes would later describe in *Dark Sun: The Making of the Hydrogen Bomb*: how honorable military virtues—duty and bravery—are mocked by the hideous machinery of technocratic, push-button mass destruction.

A haunting scene in *Robotech* has a soldier throwing his arms around a little girl, trying ineffectually to protect her as a fireball swallows them and their city. Compare to *G.I. Joe*, a contemporaneous American *cartoon d'combat* in which characters always ejected safely from their burning planes. *G.I. Joe* was known for tacking on a little safety lesson at the end of each episode, to qualify as an "educational show." The lesson's refrain was "Knowing is half the battle." *Robotech* let you spell out the lesson for yourself; its portrayal of battle was knowing. Some of the friends with whom I watched the show joined up after high school. One who was in the Marines during the Gulf War asked me if I thought it wasn't a "bullshit war, like in *Robotech*."[9] Indeed, hardcore as *Robotech* was in its depiction of megadeaths, its focus was on the life of the common soldier; it

insisted that living was more interesting than killing. The cast often seemed too busy drinking, miscegenating, and cross-dressing to fight; *Robotech* had strong elements of soap opera.

And as Shirley Conran said in that other great romantic saga of the times, *Lace II*, "Which one of you bitches is my mother?" Who indeed? For me, at least, that hot milk had to taste of Prime Minister Nakasone. Whatever the wishes of Ron Reagan Sr., G.I., I was no son raised to battle but a love child, Baby, a wandering half-caste. Love? Tokyo seemed the most romantic city in the world to me, *the* place to be young and alive in the '80s, as Paris might have been to Americans in the '20s. How did I know? From anime—the today Japan gave me in **Noboru Ishiguro**'s *Megazone 23*. It had much of the same staff and much of the same look as *Robotech*, but was set against a backdrop of Tokyo, 1985. Its locations were all based on real life, its cast the free-living teenagers—bikers, dancers, musicians, filmmakers—who had opted out of the cram-school-towards-corporation stereotype. And yes, in the story, a shadow of war hung above them. *Megazone* reflected images and dreams enough to serve as a mirror. But compared to my American suburbia, their reality—speeding down Meiji-Dori Avenue, riding double down Omotesando, cruising the circle of Yoyogi Park—seemed more like looking into a stream and seeing a stone, while the water rushed right over me.

Tokyo was the city; and when I ventured to the underage paradise of San Francisco's Hard Rock on Van Ness or even the Get-laid-ium on Kearny, it was images of Shibuya and Harajuku that flashed in my mind. When I went to Japan at last after high school, I visited every place I had seen in the anime.[10] But until then I mapped it onto my own days. Sure, slacker brother, I too followed **Molly Ringwald** and **Andrew**

McCarthy through *Pretty in Pink*, but in truth Yui Takanaka and Shogo Yahagi from *Megazone* meant as much, or more. The night of the junior prom, you see, she and I played **O.M.D.**'s **"If You Leave"** in the car; we listened to *Megazone*'s Kumi Miyasato sing about pretending you're not sentimental. I didn't fully understand the words, but it was in that time, after all, when we were in the confusion of tongues. And at the dance, I remember that the only song that got anyone moving was **James Brown**'s **"Living In America"** from *Rocky IV*, a movie all about a showdown between the U.S.S.R. and the U.S.A. But if you have a mouth for war, I believe you have a mouth for love. She drove me there, although I was old enough to learn.

The pillar of cloud by day and the pillar of fire by night (Even in His Youth)

Pomona College loved anime—and why not? The year I entered, it was *Rolling Stone*'s Hot Liberal Arts School. But I preferred to think of it then as the best school you could go to and still maintain a tan. Just look at my student I.D. and you'll use a big word: *Duuuuuuuuuude*. My head had gone south; my feet, they pointed north, under the sun. On the lawn to my west was a garage-kit apartheid-protest shantytown. In the desert to my east, the student contractors searched in vain for that stand of Joshua trees on the **U2** album cover. I'd lay out, body on the bare white concrete, the quartz baking every side a strictly temporary brown. When I arose, there was a sweat angel. No matter how dark I got, I always felt too pale. I cut a tragic figure: tanorexic. It was 1988—again, in the year of election, like the band said in "Desire."

If it was supposed to be the time for going somewhere new, then Hiroyuki Yamaga's *The Wings of Honneamise* and Katsuhiro Otomo's *Akira* were the vehicles for it.[11] They seemed the youthful moment in the history of Japanese animated film. I never started an anime club at Pomona, as I never did in high school. In part because I still walked funny from those early club experiences, but mainly because I truly believed anime was for everyone. Viewed one way, it's just TV shows, video, and movies; so why should you need a secret handshake to see them, any more than you do to watch *The Blues Brothers* or *Northern Exposure*? I would simply have showings of the anime on campus, as if it was unextraordinary film and television.

Honneamise was a declaration of independence, a statement of industry and purpose; *Akira* a revolutionary manifesto with a terrifying unmatched visual power. They were the pillar of cloud by day and the pillar of fire by night, a visible hand guiding anime to the future of possibility. Their strength was my resolve, and I felt supremely confident that these two films would reach out and bring a student audience together. I was right about them; how little did I know I was wrong about me.

The shadow couldn't be seen from the outside, the way I saw that *Honneamise* was haunted by the ghost contrail of the *Challenger* or that *Akira* was a bloody prescience of Tiananmen Square or that Japan's 1980s bubble economy was iridescent and acetate-thin. I saw those things, because that's the kind of thing I see. But this shadow was personal, not political: something had happened that I didn't understand and couldn't escape from.[12] The anime showings were always

a triumph, and I would repeat them again and again. But as those days went on, I began to feel strange, as if the full house was empty, and I would remain after it was, and I didn't know why.

As with DVDs, I would start to view scenes from a private angle. The crowd would cheer *Honneamise*'s space shot as it curved into the sky, but I would see it as the view through the eyes of a supine man, perhaps one of those dying on the field. From this vantage, the earth is not flat but a bowl, and you lie at its bottom. For you, the world is curved, but the wrong way, and the sun at the peak of the column is rising, a white memorial, leaving you behind. And so my classmates would breathe the dark in and out in rhythm with the excitement of *Akira*, but I fixed upon a moment in which a street rally preached not a new world, but an imminent end to it. The chanting priests burned television sets. One was still plugged in, showing a commercial seen in close-up for half a second before it cracked and boomed on the pyre. Before the screen went black, matching the color of the column of smoke, the color that fell upon me. Like **Art Alexakis** out of **Everclear** says, it can come from out of nowhere; as he knows perfectly well, it never, ever does.

In class, I painted the scene as a triptych with the rally itself on the screen: panel one, burn; panel two, burn; panel three, explode. I finished it late one night, stumbled out of the studio and back to the dorm, arms wide and not steadying, my face west, north, east, south. I couldn't see where I was going; think about it—when you can find someplace blind, you know you really aren't going to go anywhere new. I couldn't hear what was coming; only my Walkman, spattered with fresh acrylic crimson. It was playing a song from 1967, an odd number that didn't fit in at all with my view of that year, but I

11. The screening room for *Honneamise* was the Goldfish Bowl, a chamber of Walker Hall so named for its glass walls on all sides. They slid open, and as you might expect, every once in a while someone would turn it into an impromptu auto showroom. I believe I remember **No Doubt** playing on the lawn outside one time; ska was never out at the Claremont Colleges. I hate to drop the cliché—but I liked them better before they got big. The screening room for *Akira* was the basement of Oldenborg Hall, the language students' dorm: the idea was that by sleeping and eating together in one place, the experience would simulate the "total immersion" said to be so useful in learning a foreign tongue. "Maximum security" might have been a better term; Oldenborg is a square, blocky, *Führerbunker* of a structure. If the outside is fortresslike, the interior seems just as likely to foil invaders, for the 'Borg (yes, they say our Paramount alumni named *them* for *it*) is full of mysterious half-floors that seem to drop you off at right angles to known space: imagine a building composed entirely of mezzanines. And no one has ever explained why Oldenborg has separate men's and women's *laundry rooms*. I think it actually has something to do with anti-fetish reformers from the Japanese section—while Americans invented the panty raid, Japan made it work as a mail-order business.

12. November 8, as the East Coast returns began to come in over AM, I was in an upstairs room with a friend's Amiga 2000 laying down subtitles on *The Wings of Honneamise*. We went down to get monster cables and there was Dukakis conceding. He was larger than life, thanks to the forty-inch Mitsubishi. The friend wishes to remain anonymous to this day; I will say that he was the guy who introduced me at a very underage to drinking Laphroaig ("the Frog") with an apple slice and water chaser, to **Steve Albini**'s old group, **Big Black** ("**Power When You Need It**"), and to Canada's great hardcore band, **Dayglo Abortions**. It was another friend, **Mike Ebert**, who introduced me to *Honneamise*.

A tall and good-looking artist, he was one of the principal founders of *Animag*, America's first stab at a slick anime magazine, of which, between 1987 and 1992, fifteen intermittent issues were produced. Both *Animerica*'s **Trish Ledoux** and **Julie Davis** were *Animag* editors for much of its run; my own involvement in the magazine was very small, and limited to its first issues, but it gave me the opportunity, when I went to Japan at sixteen, to go as Jimmy Olsen. Looking back, it seems fair for a number of rea-couldn't stop listening to it. My generation knows it from *Apocalypse Now*, and if you're truly dedicated to the concept, from the heart of darkness.

Back home in Houston for the summer, I ran my hand along the rocket, the Saturn V they have at the Johnson Space Center. It was much, much taller than me, but it fell in pieces long ago above red anthills: a lawn gnome for the front yard of all mankind. A nice little camp piece from the period; they say men once rode to the moon in them—but that is, of course, before my first memory. My daddy was going down to the grass, but passing by once in those last days, he had enough concern to ask me—hearing the sounds of **"The End,"** taped off a record handed down from father to son—if I was now, or had ever been, considering that last inverted option. And I realized then that anime could be my kind of love. It's the kind that moves on; it's the kind that leaves me alone.

How i saw my shadow (June 4, 1996 and Afterwards)

In life, as in business, you don't get what you deserve, you get what you negotiate. I'm just an editor. It was fortunate for us that Jean was a businessman. One gunman was a silent partner. The other two were doing good-crook, bad-crook in English and Vietnamese. The bad gunman kept saying, "I'm a' kill you, I'm a' shoot you now." The good gunman said, "*Nhieu nguoi qua,*

diet khong duoc"–now there's too many to kill. They had planned to shoot the assistant and leave with their take. Then Jean came into the store, and I followed Jean. I wasn't entirely without value, as I made up one of the *too many*–an asset, if an inactive one. I like to think I helped to make the deal attractive.

But Jean was the kind of person who makes things happen. He had escaped Vietnam. He had been in business since he was sixteen, and knew he had worked too hard to let it end here. He kept his head clear. He calmed the gunmen down, made it clear that the merchandise wasn't worth anyone's life, appealed to their common heritage. And it wasn't easy for him to stay clear. Because besides waiting for the bullet to issue at any moment from any one of three people not in consensus (or simply to be the victim of a very itchy trigger finger bungled heist, the Gen-X movie way to die) he had to listen to the robbers shouting about how they were actually foreign agents, secret police, come because Planet Anime had downloaded information from the Vietnamese embassy.

Just like *Ghost in the Shell*, I thought, and then I kind of remembered how, while they cut out the part with the *femmes frotteurs* from both the movie and the American version of the manga, they left in the part with the guy getting shot to pieces. I don't understand their rationale, because in the scene they kept, you can see the guy's large intestine falling out, while in the scene they cut, you can't see the woman's labia—another

woman's hand covers it. Well, anyway, that was the gunmen's story, and that was why they were taking the computer and all the paperwork as well as all the import disks (all except two or three boxes of CDs) and all the knickknacks and character goods. They left the money. And the three of us alive.[13]

That Coppola patriarch said, "You asked America for justice, but you should have come to me." Jean did the work of solving the robbery himself. If the cops tasted the crime, it might have been something like: *fruity bouquet, a hint of insurance fraud.* It seemed pretty suspicious to Jean, too, but in an entirely different way. He recalled the many strange phone requests for business information the store had received. The gunmen had been shadowing their target. They had been in Dallas, observing the Planet Anime table at A-Kon. He called all his distributors, and then one day that fall, they began to call back. That red truck had been sighted parked on the Southside. Outside a brand-new anime store. Its two proprietors were among the robbers; the third remained unidentified. One of the two fled; the other was captured and made a full confession: they had seen how well Jean's business was doing and decided on a hostile takeover.

Word of the resolution came back to me only later. Returning home, I drove above the Bay. I had **Utatane**'s *Countdown* open in one hand; in the other hand, you will be relieved to hear, was the wheel. Night and fog had drawn in, but it was fine; the bridge was alloy straight and firm, supported by piers my grandfather had laid. I have sisters in San Francisco. I suppose the closest I ever came to telling one I loved her was at a party there. Its theme was the Japanese TV show *Iron Chef*, in which top cooks compete to win the title. There are guest judges; whoever is hot this week in Japan. Thus you were encouraged to come either as a celebrity or an exotic food item. Amongst the bell peppers and **Ryoko Hirosue**s, I was dressed as Hideaki Anno: rectangle shades, flip-flop feet, crepe-curly beard, kung-fu suit, Ultraman hands.

You've heard—God, you've heard—what a success his *Neon Genesis Evangelion* was in Japan. But some there say that the millions who were drawn in by *Eva*, who made it such a phenomenon, are new fans. That all the old-time otaku who grew up with anime hate *Evangelion*, are disgusted by its compromises and its failures. It could have been the beginning of something new, they say, but instead went nowhere, offering up shame and weakness and confusion as a story.

Anno even admitted as much in writing before the project began. "I tried to include everything of myself, a broken man who could do nothing for four years. A man who ran away for four years, one who was simply not dead.... It is a production where my only thought is to burn my feelings into film....I don't know what will happen...because I don't know where life is taking the staff.... I feel that I am being irresponsible. But...it's only natural that we should synchronize ourselves with the world of the production.

"I've taken on a risk.... [*Evangelion*] may end up as nothing more than a fascimile. And for now, I can only write this explanation. But perhaps our 'original' lies somewhere within there." They say he talked of a mystery, too, but never explained what it meant.

A TV party was a funny thing, because our hosts' TV screen was covered with a simple converter made of toilet-paper tubes, their ends fronted with wax paper. It made whatever may have been on into a grid pattern of silver-dollar pixels, turned it back into a scrambled code of light and color. I can't see; I just stare. In the bedroom, on a nice hardback version of

Ishinomori, I laid out my own traces, through short breaths, of a silly, lighthearted drug. A fifteen-minute thing, if you and her are lucky.

Sonic Youth's *Evol* was on the turntable, spiraling all the way down to its last track, its last verse: *mystery train/three way plane/expressway/to your skull.* And I admit the unattractive truth: dying was never a problem for me, the laying down. I just wanted to lay myself down hard. I wanted to be steel and strike myself off stone; I wanted to crash in a shower of sparks.

Consider that anime, whatever it may be, is at first and last the man who created it. Anime, just like the man, is made out of dreams, and it flies its trajectory through space and is still when the beam fails. It is made in single frames, a series of moments strung together, to which you give the persistence of memory. It isn't a camera you can switch on and roll; you don't get to catch the light of the world in a glass. You have the man all backwards; anime is a lens that must be turned the other way. Whatever light you see has had to make its way into the world from within, however dark that is. I understood that much, even though I'm never going to be the least bit Japanese. For a born American, anime is the eyes of a stranger, letting you see in from outside.

I could perceive through the tunnel that it was all tabloid faith in wise men from the East, a karaoke litany, a mass-merchandised genuine-imitation true cross, cheap and flimsy. Catching the sun, as it turned by angels and angles, it shone right at me, and that was how I saw my shadow. I'm always trying to warn people that it has no meaning, except that which you give.

for Rogers Nelson Horn, 1940–1997
even in his youth

sons to call *Animag* the foundation of my eventual livelihood. It was another founder of *Animag*, **Matt Anacleto**, who introduced me to *Akira*. Not tall, but tough and tough-looking, he laughed when I once told him that I thought he was six feet. He just seemed that way to me. Like **Benicio Del Toro** in *Fear and Loathing in Las Vegas*, whom he somewhat resembled, he was also a man with a profession; having hands of grace on the Mac, he was the first person I knew personally who was really doing things with desktop layout.

 13. Don't misunderstand me too quickly. I am an American, and it wasn't as if I had never seen, held, or fired a handgun before. Real guns, unfortunately, are for only one real purpose, and that is to kill people. We may not all have them, but at six bullets per revolver and up to ten for an automatic, between us, we have our neighbors, our coworkers, our community, the whole world on our hands. We live like that; the truth, like Japanese animation, is strange. But even if our side had been packing—with three men getting the drop, it would have been bad. In the end, it was a good deal for all sides; even, if they will pardon my saying so, for the gunmen.

Consider the demographics involved. If they *had* murdered the assistant and/or us, they might have all been pursued until caught; such persistence is one of the platinum-plus perks of being the victim of a capital crime in a fashionable precinct like Rice Village. And the jurisdiction, Harris County, Texas, sends more murderers to death row than any other in the nation; you end up strapped down with a syringe in your arm like a character in a sketch by **Benkyo Tamaoki**. But thanks to Jean's negotiation, they only ended up committing aggravated robbery and assault with a deadly weapon with intent to kill, and only *one* of the three was caught, and he got five years, instead of a lethal injection. You understand the moral of the story, don't you? All of us still get to be young men with a future.

"You are a
fiasco waiting
for a venue."

—from *Maison Ikkoku*

future trend

Those Western admirers who viewed **Akira Kurosawa**, in the final years before his death, as the frail link to a lost era of genius in Japanese film would probably not have understood Kurosawa's appreciation of what a "lost" Japanese cinema was achieving in anime; he counted **Katsuhiro Otomo** as a friend and even hoped to work with him someday. Kurosawa had to find honor abroad before he received it at home; there was a different, happy ending in the last days of the director who long before made the world respect Japanese cinema. For it was, this time, neither Western critics nor Western audiences but the Japanese who took hold of and carried high this anime art of Japan to triumphal success. *The Princess Mononoke* demonstrated that anime could give Japanese film the power to outearn a Hollywood blockbuster. *Evangelion*'s cathartic, liberating narrative approach inspired a change in the attitudes of the Japanese towards anime in general; the *Eva* phenomenon opened up for all Japan the neglected heritage of the last four decades of the medium.

Ten years ago, anime had been in the sole care of outsiders, of *otaku*—then an epithet in Japan. Today—just as Gainax predicted for the year 1999 in their *Otaku no Video*—Japan has become *otaku-ized*, with pundits and media figures, salarymen and homemakers, admitting that they have, in fact, been secret fans for decades. Hip magazines run the make on each forgotten treasure as it tumbles out and on the fascinating stories of creators who were expected to make no more than this year's new line of toys but who instead created for Japan a

new art form, changing and charging the medium with their love and sometimes with their anger. As the Japanese begin to feel free to enjoy the innocent joys and repressed memories of childhood, there is also much talk now of so-called "edge anime" that continues to push, fold, spindle, and mutilate the envelope. Three examples are coming to America this summer.

The TV show to best make use of the freedom *Evangelion* pioneered is *serial experiments lain*, written by *Armitage III*'s **Chiaki Konaka**, directed by newcomer **Ryutaro Nakamura**, and released through **Pioneer**. The confidence in its opening sequence puts you bolt upright. *lain*'s theme, **"Duvet"**, is sung in English, and the swooping and bleeding edits buzz-clip you into the quiet desperation of Lain, an ordinary—for once, ordinary—Japanese schoolgirl whose schizoid consciousness dissolves to reform into something stronger in the Tokyo of today—so easily seen as a spider web, its people wrapped and bound in transmission lines whispering data and humming with menace.

A similar breaking apart and putting back together of reality is to be found in Otomo protégé **Satoshi Kon**'s *Perfect Blue*, which has already drawn comparisons both to **Roman Polanski**'s *Repulsion* and **Dario Argento**'s recent *The Stendhal Syndrome*. With a narrative shaped like a chambered nautilus, *Perfect Blue*, released through **Manga Entertainment**, paints the portrait of a singer who embarks on an acting career shadowed by terror and murder. Is she being stalked by an obsessed fan or something more subtle and horrible?

Shinichiro Watanabe's *Cowboy Bebop*, released through **animevillage.com**, is a TV show that brings back, with jazzy *élan*, the outlaw ethic to anime. *Bebop*'s definitely old-enough-to-drink cast of adventurers cruise "intergalactic *plan-e-tar-y*" around the twenty-first century to a cool/hot soundtrack; the opening credits' monochrome, montage, and splitscreen recall a '70s cop show only appropriate for *Bebop*, with its unusually ethnic hero, Spike Spiegel, who runs into everyone from a clone of **Kareem Abdul-Jabbar** to an ancient Betamax.

In this calendar year that ends with the clock reset, we experience time, as Patrick Macias would have it, both backwards and forwards. Japanese animation reverses and then hits the nitro; it runs you over twice. So this new/old year is at last a grown-up party for anime; specifically, Japan is like **Andy Warhol**'s Factory in 1967, full of people milling about the super-retro icons of **Marilyn** on the wall while listening to the future as the **Velvet Underground** plays in the corner. And there's a lot of fun and tripping and gaping and falling down flat going on. **"The Exploding Plastic Inevitable"**—a good way to describe Japanese animation—was what Warhol called his happening. May I suggest you mix **Jonas Mekas**'s *Village Voice* review with your anime cocktail? "The place where...needs and desperations are most dramatically split open. At the Plastic Inevitable it is all Here and Now and the Future."

And the future, like my man **Sören Kierkegaard** said, is unwritten. Anime is my happening, baby, and, yes, it freaks me out.

EASY TO FIND

1. ROYAL SPACE FORCE: THE WINGS OF HONNÉAMISE
Movie, Manga Entertainment, 1987

Often considered by American fans to be the best anime ever made for its breadth of vision, the unmatched complexity of its imaginary world, and its startling dramatic metaphor of the first man in space in an alternate society: a very human adventure of both past and future. Due to script changes made to this already challenging film in the dub, the subtitled version is strongly recommended.

2. PATLABOR 2
Movie, Manga Entertainment, 1993

The masterpiece of the brilliant Mamoru Oshii—a director praised by *Titanic*'s James Cameron—and the most openly political of all anime movies. In a Tom Clancy–like techno-thriller told with the languid, symbolic lyricism that is Oshii's trademark, a black-sheep police detective pursues an enigmatic terrorist whose plans may include mass murder, a *coup d'état*—or even war with the United States!

3. THE PRINCESS MONONOKE
Movie, Disney/Miramax Pictures, 1997

Every few years, the very small theatrical Japanese animation industry brings forth a motion picture the equal of anything in world cinema; this film is one of these. Hayao Miyazaki gives more here than just the perfection of his eye and hand; *The Princess Mononoke* is also a beautiful and terrible catharsis from Miyazaki's troubled genius and great heart.

4. AKIRA
Movie, Orion Home Video and The Criterion Collection, LD, 1988

Katsuhiro Otomo's film is still unsurpassed as a vehicle of sheer chaos and destructive power. Under the klieg-high glitter of 2019 Neo-Tokyo march the armies of the night: soldiers, cops, punks, salarymen with bloody shirts and red banners. Mad street preachers go down under police clubs–screaming of the apocalypse, and the return of their "messiah," the psychic child Akira.

5. LUPIN III: THE CASTLE OF CAGLIOSTRO
Movie, Manga Entertainment, 1979

Miyazaki's first film paints master thief Lupin III as a knight-errant out to rescue a reluctant bride and crack the secrets of a tiny European nation whose fairy-tale beauty conceals one of history's great conspiracies. The result is a nonstop action-adventure with an immortal cast of characters. Supremely entertaining, this is anime's *Raiders of the Lost Ark*.

6. ARCADIA OF MY YOUTH
Movie, AnimEigo, 1982

Tomoharu Katsumata directs Captain Harlock, the great heroic figure of manga artist Leiji Matsumoto, whose visions (see also *Adieu Galaxy Express* and *Yamato/Star Blazers*, below) dominated anime for nearly a decade. An existential opera set in space rather than a familiar space opera, *Arcadia* takes a hard road by suggesting that free will is "a truth from which you cannot abdicate."

7. FAREWELL TO SPACE BATTLESHIP YAMATO
Movie, Voyager Entertainment, 1978

The anime movie that moved Japan more than any other: bouquets were offered to the screen and combat veterans spoke of its noble spirit. Although certainly as influenced by *Star Wars* (itself inspired in part by Japanese film) as many other SF movies, *Farewell* at heart reflects the very Japanese aesthetic of the tragic beauty of youth dying for a cause.

8. ADIEU GALAXY EXPRESS 999
Movie, Viz Video, 1981

Tetsuro Hoshino has already come of age as a resistance fighter on a shattered Earth, but to claim his future he must travel across space to confront the terrible order of the city of machines, Grand Andromeda. Like *Arcadia*, *Adieu* is an epic myth of the future. It remains the astounding masterwork of one of anime's great directors, Taro Rin.

9. NIGHT ON THE GALACTIC RAILROAD
Movie, Central Park Media, 1985

Gisaburo Sugii renders in beauty the 1927 Kenji Miyazawa novel whose Christian-Buddhist synthesis provided imagery that has echoed in *Galaxy Express* and *The Angel's Egg* (below). A young boy living a life of small-town poverty takes an allegorical journey by train across the Milky Way through symbolic landscapes and intimations of death, salvation, and the migration of the spirit.

10. ASTRO BOY
TV series, The Right Stuf International, 1963–66

This, the first half-hour anime TV show, was created by Osamu Tezuka, the man who also pioneered manga—at once establishing both the controversial relationship between the two media, founding the recurrent anime motif of father-son/creator-robot, and providing a classic iconography that fired up both the generation of Tomino, who trained working on it, and Anno, who grew up watching it.

11. STAR BLAZERS
TV series, Voyager Entertainment, 1974–75

A crew of young astronaut-soldiers has one year to save Earth as they cross a galaxy in a World War II ship refitted as a spacecraft. This well-regarded English version of Japan's beloved *Space Battleship Yamato* has the ironic effect of effacing the original's revanchist overtones and emphasizing the universal, humanistic spirit of Noboru Ishiguro's enormously resonant classic.

12. MOBILE SUIT GUNDAM: THE MOVIES I–III
TV series collected together with additional footage, animevillage.com, 1979–80, 1981–82

Yoshiyuki Tomino is cited by Gainax as their most important single influence. One might call his *Gundam* the first post-Vietnam mecha show, as Tomino, a veteran of *Astro Boy*, portrays a twenty-first-century realpolitik war between Earth and its own orbital colonies, where robots are not our new, incorruptible bodies but vessels for the bitter old wine of the human condition.

13. ROBOTECH PERFECT COLLECTION
Three TV series, Streamline Pictures, 1982–83, 1984, 1983–84

A unique opportunity, the *Perfect Collection* lets viewers have it either way: each tape contains two episodes of the English dub *Robotech* (an original storyline created by editing together three series, *Macross*, *Southern Cross*, and *Mospeada*, whose stories were unrelated in Japan) followed by those same two episodes in the original Japanese, subtitled.

14. MAISON IKKOKU
TV, Viz Video, 1986–88

Anime's great romantic comedy, adapted from the manga by Rumiko Takahashi, the world's best-selling female comics artist. Young Godai is trying to get into a good college while rooming at the falling-apart boarding house Maison Ikkoku, which is infested with weirdos and one very sad and beautiful landlady. A love story with a beginning and end and lots of wonderful in-between.

15. NEON GENESIS EVANGELION
TV, A.D.V. Films, 1995–96

As a science fiction story, *Evangelion* is the SF of Harlan Ellison and Phillip K. Dick. It became the most important TV anime show of the 1990s, perhaps precisely because it alienated many traditional fans while becoming a topic of discussion far beyond the traditional fan community and returning the attention of the Japanese public to the possibilities of anime.

WHERE TO FIND THEM

The Right Stuf International at www.rightstuf.com

Planet Anime, Houston and Dallas, at www.planetanime.com

Nikaku Animart, San Jose, at www.nikaku.com

Kinokuniya, New York City; Edgewater, NJ; Seattle; San Francisco, San Jose, Los Angeles, and Costa Mesa, CA; and at www.kinokuniya.com

Mikado Laser Japan, San Francisco, at www.mikadosf.com

Japan Video & Media, Inc., San Francisco, at www.japanvideo.com

Mandarake, Los Angeles, CA, at www.mandarakeusa.com

collection

HARD TO GET

1. **ONLY YESTERDAY** Omohide Poro Poro
Movie, Tokuma Communications, 1991

Part of the Disney-Ghibli deal, but not to come here before 2000. Don't wait—it is one of the five best anime films ever made. Flashing back between 1982 and 1966, in *Only Yesterday*, Isao Takahata gives a rich and quiet voice to an ordinary Tokyo office worker traveling to the countryside to reconcile with the ghosts of her childhood.

2. **GOLGO 13**
Movie, Pony Canyon, 1983

This highly stylized portrait of Takao Saito's infallible manga assassin was perfectly suited for the distorted images of passion and venality conjured by anime's Mannerists: the longtime team of director Osamu Dezaki and animation director/character designer Akio Sugino. Only available uncut as an import. An early wake-up call for anime, *Golgo 13* still hasn't lost its power to shock.

3. **MEMORIES**
Movie, Bandai Visual/Emotion, 1995

The Katsuhiro Otomo–produced *Memories* returns to the short-story format through which he first influenced manga in the 1970s. Koji Morimoto, Tensai Okamoto, and Otomo in turn direct "**Magnetic Rose**", "**Stink Bomb**", and "**Cannon Fodder**"—three black science fiction comedies about man's clever inventions readily amplifying simple folly into disaster. Although (surprisingly) never released here, the Japanese LD is English-subtitled.

4. **HORUS, PRINCE OF THE SUN** Taiyo no Oji:
Horus no Dai-Boken, Movie, Bandai Visual/Emotion, 1968

The struggle by Takahata to direct his first film, with key animator Miyazaki, marked the start of their thirty-year partnership, but it did more: *Horus*, the best anime film of the 1960s, stands as an early example of directorial vision overcoming doubt. A dub, *The Little Norse Prince*, appeared on U.S. TV through the 1970s but had no commercial video release.

5. **SUPERDIMENSIONAL FORTRESS MACROSS: DO YOU REMEMBER LOVE?**
Macross: Ai Oboete Imasu Ka?, Movie, Bandai/Emotion CAV LD, VHS, DVD, Pioneer/Shogakukan, CLV LD, 1984

Kawamori codirects this "pop song '84" with Ishiguro; the movie is a strange and spectacular experience that rewrites the original *Macross* TV story into a film that is exciting and moving, yet claustrophobic. There are dogfights amidst Saturn's rings and the human fight-or-shop response within a battleship—ultrachic space mall. The pivot that turned anime's view of SF from Matsumoto to the era of *Megazone*.

6. **MAZINGER Z VS. THE GREAT GENERAL OF THE DARKNESS** Mazinger Z tai Ankoku
Dai-Shogun Movie, Toei Video, 1974

It's hard to imagine a better endorsement than the one given by the Italian Parliament to the electric transgressions of the man who corrupted Mangaburg, Go Nagai: his robot anime was denounced as an "orgy of annihilating violence, a cult of allegiance to great warriors, a worship of the electronic machine." That about describes it; and in Toeiscope, to boot.

7. **NEON GENESIS EVANGELION**
TV/Movies, Starchild; revised TV and *The End* on VHS/LD vols. 11–14, or DVD 6–7; *Death* in movie boxed set only, 1997-98

In Japan, considerable *Evangelion* material exists that was produced after the U.S. deal for the original TV series and hasn't been released here. This includes new scenes added to episodes 21–26 and two movies: *Death*, an elliptical "remix" of footage from the first twenty-four episodes; and *The End of Evangelion*, a new, brutal, and surrealistic "alternate take" on the final two episodes.

8. **FUTURE BOY CONAN**
Shonen Mirai Conan, TV series, Bandai Visual/Emotion, 1978

Spanish-language television sometimes airs *Conan, El Niño del Futuro*; yet, the only TV series directed nearly in its entirety by Hayao Miyazaki has never been shown in English. High adventure in the air, on the sea, and on the little land left of a post apocalyptic Earth: *Conan*'s "electromagnetic bombs" were so powerful they didn't raise the oceans–they lowered the continents!

9. **LUPIN III**
The First TV Series, TV, VAP, 1971–72

Revived for anime many times since, the first nine of this twenty-three-episode series were closest in feel to the original manga by Monkey Punch: Lupin as a cold-blooded young crook, Fujiko as a faster pussycat, and original gangsters pulling ripoffs with Sten guns. The remainder, featuring the increasing influence of Takahata and Miyazaki, are colorful and exciting in a more genial style.

10. **KENJI'S SPRING** Iihatove Genso: Kenji no Haru,
OAV, Bandai Visual/Emotion, 1996

Author Kenji Miyazawa would walk in the country and see the mountains in a roadside stone. He saw also the uselessness of nature's wonders to those around him living in rural poverty, and tried to live so as to link his beliefs in the brotherhood of man with that of the unity of creation. Director Shoji Kawamori astounds here with his versatility.

WISH LIST

1. **THE ANGEL'S EGG** Tenshi no Tamago,
Movie, Tokuma Communications, 1985, 128AH-8, ¥12800 VHS; 88LX-6, ¥8800 LD

A girl clutching a great egg and a man bearing a cruciform rifle explore a city of shadows in this bleak film with the beauty of fossils and tombs. In some ways the other side of Miyazawa's *Galactic Railroad*, with which it shares its symbols, *The Angel's Egg* suggests the death of director Mamoru Oshii's youthful faith in Christianity.

2. **MEGAZONE 23**
OAV, Victor, VTG-94, 1985, ¥13800 VHS; W78L-1003, ¥7800 LD

A phenomenal popular success upon its release, *Megazone* was followed by several sequels that included neither its spirit nor its principal staff. Find the Japanese original of Noboru Ishiguro's original video, that took an intriguing, action-filled SF con-spiracy story and suffused it with a real sense of what it felt like to be young, in a country that was once the future.

3. **CREAM LEMON**
OAV series, Pony Canyon, boxed set PCLS-00001~13, 1984–86, ¥46800

Although not to be oversold, the mid-'80s were the boogie nights for anime, a time when the new format of the OAV promised experimen-tation and liberty for the medium. In that atmosphere, pornography had not yet been firewalled, and the high-profile series *Cream Lemon*, whose premises ranged from lighthearted farce to gothic horror, could both approach semirespectability and involve important talent.

4. **TO-Y**
OAV, CBS/Sony/Shonen Sunday Video 00ZG-105, 1987, ¥12000 VHS; 96LG-105, ¥9600 LD

Mamoru Hamatsu's vibrant and stylized snapshot of the nightclubs, studios, and street scenes of mid-'80s J-pop gives a short but vivid portrait of a garage band amidst manufactured stardom. *To-Y* still looks ahead of its time, a fact demonstrated when San Diego fan group Seishun Shitemasu intriguingly transposed the setting of this obscure video to '90s Seattle in a parody/tribute dub!

5. **LUPIN III**
Movie, Japanese title Lupin III tai Fukusei Ningen [Lupin vs. The Clone People], released in U.S. by Toho in theaters only, 1978

There is a newer dub (*The Mystery Of Mamo*) that's easier to get, but you definitely want to find this *first* one, which screened on occasion at U.S. art houses during the 1980s. With a wild plot soaked in '70s spirit and featuring veterans of clas-sic chop-socky, this dub somehow conjured the verve of *Lupin*'s immortal characters like none ever since.

BIO

CARL GUSTAV HORN was born in Long Beach, California, on September 4, 1970, but his twin sister (future *kibbutznik*, nightclub owner, and pilot) had, predictably, beaten him by three minutes. His mother, a Beat-era Mills graduate who worked under Pierre Salinger at the *San Francisco Chronicle*, passed on to her son an affection for the East Bay. Together with his father, a surfer-scientist-scheduler who put on his résumé "sent three men to the moon and returned them safely to Earth," the family moved nineteen times throughout the United States, Europe, the Middle East, and Australasia during his first twenty years.

Mr. Horn studied history at Pomona College and law at Santa Clara University. He was a contributing editor to the second edition of **Trish Ledoux** and **Doug Ranney**'s *The Complete Anime Guide* and to *Anime Interviews*, Trish Ledoux, editor. He has written dozens of articles on anime and manga for magazines in the United States, Canada, and the United Kingdom, and has provided commentary on the field for *Wired*, *Newsweek*, *Newsweek Japan*, and *Aera*. He lives in Oakland, California, and is proud to have Jerry Brown as his mayor.

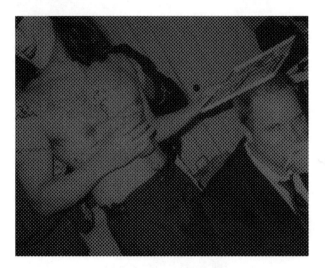

Q&A

What is the size of your collection?

This may sound a bit disappointing, but it's relatively small. I have about 120 VHS tapes of anime, the oldest a six-hour Scotch duped around the first Mondale-Reagan debate. There's one LD and two LD box sets; having no LD player has rescued me from having to buy any more. I have a fifteen-inch TV and mono Funai VCR; I'm really kind of a lo-fi otaku.

What's the most expensive item?

Again, it's a bit yen-y-ante: my *Daicon Film* LD, bought directly from the manufacturer, **Gainax**, for 14,800 (about $175 at the time). It's got laser rot, but in those days, they probably etched the grooves with a quill pen. The real punchline is that when Mr. Yamaga visited here in 1997, he pointed out the teeny-tiny kanji on the LD jacket that say "not for sale." It seems you were actually supposed to pay that 14,800 for the "making of" book—the accompanying LD was a free bonus.

Years later, I bought that book separately from an American dealer. How do you say, "This way to the egress" in Japanese?

Which item would you most boast about?

Perhaps my unbuilt garage kit of the space capsule from *Honneamise*, also made by Gainax. Mr. Yamaga offered the additional caveat that "no one ever managed to put one of *those* together." However, Rick Sternbach, the *Star Trek* SFX genius, says that he achieved this, once.

What is the total value of your collection?

You can't put a dollar price on pictures of Asuka without her clothes on. I have thought, though, of leaving it all to the Honnold Library of the Claremont Colleges, on the condition they get rid of those little lime-green vests.

What are your main interests other than watching anime?

Just as I write and think about anime and manga for a living rather than having it as a hobby apart from my livelihood, I'm not interested in anime as a form of escapism. I'm interested in anime for the way it

intersects with my life and with everything else in the happening world.

Anime, like live-action film and television, whether fiction or fact (which includes documentary footage) is never the same thing as the real world; it's an abstract or model derived from some aspects of the real world and real experience. But consider the physical definition of anime: it creates that model, or miniature, through a long series of two-dimensional windows and walls, which, unlike live-action film frames, have no origin in three-dimensional reality. The windows are the cels, and the walls are the backgrounds.

I use the term lens or mirror to describe anime because these "flat" glasses redirect and distort, as well as focus and clarify, our perception of our three-dimensional reality: the real world we move through. When the medieval writers discussed optics, their properties were often considered magical. Modern writers speak of these effects in psychological terms, but their hold on the imagination remains unchanged. We use the same terms when we speak of how we "project" our real feelings onto images or symbols that are, in and of themselves, abstract, mythical, or insubstantial. The very concept of three dimensions needs two-dimensional space to define it and give it form.

Although the viewpoints and evaluations expressed are the author's own responsibility, the following (in addition to works already mentioned in the text) were valuable and recommended references: Mark Schilling's superb *Encyclopedia of Japanese Pop Culture*; *The Oxford History of World Cinema*, Geoffrey Nowell-Smith, ed.; Pauline Kael's *For Keeps*; Toby Clark's *Art and Propaganda in the Twentieth Century*; Mikiso Hane's *Peasants, Rebels and Outcastes*; W. G. Beasley's *The Modern History of Japan*; William Manchester's *American Caesar* and *The Glory and the Dream*; Wolfgang Fuchs and Reinhold Reitberger's *Comics: Anatomy Of A Mass Medium*; and the three most valuable books in English for understanding Japanese comics and animation: Frederik L. Schodt's *Manga! Manga!* (Kodansha), *Dreamland Japan* (Stone Bridge Press), and *Anime Interviews* (Cadence Books), Trish Ledoux, ed..

Much of the political background discussed in "History Without End" was found in the absolutely wonderful archives of the **Hayao Miyazaki Web** (www.nausicaa.net); from there, I must thank Ryoko Toyama, Brian Stacy, Mark Hairston, and Tyler King. The first paragraph of **"Welcome to the Land..."** contains lines from **"Couplets: 20"** of *Evening Wind* by Robert Mezey (Wesleyan University Press, 1987), and is reprinted by permission of the author. At Pomona College, I am grateful to the late Professor Richard Harrison and to Professors Sam Yamashita and Richard Barnes; at Miramonte H.S., to Mr. Chuck Whyte and Ms. Martha Schimbor. I must express my particular gratitude to my friend, Mr. Hiroyuki Yamaga, for his great hospitality and humor in confronting my perceptions, as well as to longstanding comrade Michael House, staff translator of Gainax's remarkably forthcoming web site (www.gainax.co.jp). Scott Frazier, the first American to become an anime director, has always been a friendly source—there may be people who don't like and admire him, but I've never met any. I still owe a great deal to Toren Smith of Studio Proteus and to Mr. Ken Iyadomi of Bandai. "Special" juku-session master Kyle Johnson gave me the hook-up for parts of **"Future Trend."** Neil Nadelman contributed a number of valuable insights, as did Dave Fleming of the University of Illinois, Urbana-Champaign. For the manga section, I appreciate the help of Dan Kanemitsu, Kenichi Sonoda, Scott McCloud, Tomoko Saito, Robert deJesus, and Adam Warren. Thanks in Indianapolis to Magnum Opus Productions; in San Diego to Seishun ("Eddie Vedder") Shitemasu and in Atlanta to Corn Pone ("Ian MacKaye") Flicks...and in Oakland to *kanrinin-san* Anne Jones. Great portions of this were written using the house current and Sunrise Blend of Gaylord's on Piedmont Avenue—the best coffeehouse in the East Bay. Most especially I want to thank Andrew Lloyd and Don Thornburgh for their fraternity.

May 28

I've finally gotten over my jet lag enough to be able to jot down some coherent thoughts and observations here in Tokyo.

It's different.

It's been four years since I last lived here, three years since the Aum Shinrikyo religious cult poison gas incident, and exactly one year since my last visit. The police billboards depicting Aum fugitives that last year were pasted on every subway wall with the relentlessness of some insurance ad campaign only appear intermittently now. I see fewer cellular phones being flaunted in public spaces, fewer slouch socks worn by high school girls, and fewer drunks. Everything is slightly reduced, and this slightly is enough to make me realize something that's only been a hazy news statistic until now: there's a recession going on.

The aura of intensity is tapering off. Maybe it's no accident that there have been no Big Incidents this year. The bizarre tends towards the extreme in times of prosperity.

Everyone is griping about the economy. It's in the news, it's in soap operas, it's in the daily chatting of housewives on the street corner. In Japan, the number four is unlucky, because it's pronounced the same as the word for death (*shi*), and

right now, four percent is the red zone figure for unemployment. Riding the train, even catch the headline of a sports news paper that reads: "**Nomo** Unemployed! Which isn't technically true, but given the enthusiasm two years ago for this Japanese baseball player when he started pitching for the **Dodgers**, his being offered up for trade is further proof that, whether you're a professional star or an anonymous salaryman, as long as you're Japanese, you're all in the same boat on the sea of economic decline.

Tokyo doesn't look all that different but the urban psyche seems slightly traumatized, as if consumer culture in ruins isn't so much a state of things collapsing but things sitting still. The department store window displays are like paintings in a failed art exhibition, unconsumed Japan's population is still extremely fashion conscious, but I see more guys wearing scruffy jeans not so much because it's the hip thing but because they're cheap and comfortable. They remind me of the hippie college students when I was living here as a kid during the '70s. Instead of recession, retrogression might be a more apt description.

I pick up a cab near the **Imperial Palace**. The cab driver mentions something about the royal residence being empty right now while **Emperor Akihito** is on his controversial visit to London. British veterans are upset because the emperor has only vaguely acknowledged the atrocities of World War II and has neglected to apologize for his father's share of war crimes. Apparently, though, the time his father spent in London as prince before the war was his best time ever, his Roman Holiday.

Strange to be driving through the city instead of taking the subway. I know the city better from underground; like one of those connect-the-dots pictures, each subway station is represented by a point, and I have only a vague impression of how the districts aboveground connect. Most of the buildings and streets don't look all that familiar, especially at night. For all I know, the driver could be taking a long detour. I take note of all the other cabs whizzing by us with their "empty car" signs lit up. Last time I was here, salarymen were stumbling over each other to hail a cab.

"It's terrible," the cabbie gripes the moment I tell him I'm an American. "The country's finished." He begins to rant about Tokyo's economic Armageddon. When I ask him about the recession's effect on cabbies, he shrugs his shoulders, "Y'know, taxi drivers in Japan are the worst off in the world. Companies used to give allowances to their employees to go out and paint the town red, but now they've cut back completely. Everyone either just goes home or takes the train. No one is spending. You know how it is in Japan; everyone tilts to one extreme or another. That's why Americans are great, they keep on spending even when things take a turn for the worse. Hurray for America! Everyone's hoarding here in Japan, so the money's not moving. Pathetic, absolutely pathetic. A downward spiral!"

I ask him whether he has ever been to the States. "Oh yeah, when I was a student. I saved up my money and went to Texas." I repeat the word Texas as if there could be no stranger state for a Japanese to visit. I mean, New York, California, or even Florida, but *Texas*? Was he a JFK conspiracy nut?

"I love horses," he replies. He proceeds to recount the story of his trip, adding a nostalgic touch here and there with a flourish. "And she was so fine, with

bright blue eyes and blond hair.... I can't tell what he's talking about anymore—horses or women?

He lets me off at Shimo-kitazawa, which is where I end up meeting most of the musicians I'm interviewing for this book. First stop is **dohb discs**, the recording label for **Demi Semi Quaver**, **Super Car**, and **Tomovsky**. The office contains a studio where **Zak**, engineering whiz for **Buffalo Daughter**, is mixing down DSQ's upcoming release. **Masahiko Ogawa**, dohb discs' label manager, is on his cellular, even though he should be in bed since he has pulled a back muscle. **Yuji Katsui** and **Emi Eleonala** from DSQ are waiting around in the hall.

Zak emerges from the studio and the three of us go in to listen to the rough mix. It sounds spectacular. Katsui and Eleonala (who always goes by Emi) point out split-second spots to change, but otherwise they seem content. They turn to me and ask, "How about a drink?" By then it's midnight. For them the night is just beginning. Myself, I've got two jet lags to deal with, as I always do when I come here, the normal plus-seventeen-hour adjustment on top of this afterhours four-in-the-morning-I-hear-the-birds-chirping-mebbe-it's-time-to-get-some-shut-eye Tokyo time. I'm dead tired, but as usual I can't say no.

"I know a really great sushi bar. It's cheap and awful," Emi says, laughing. She's wearing the same kind of outfit she wears on stage with wild sparkling hair and makeup that puts **Maki Nomiya** of **Pizzicato Five** to shame. For Emi, the line between performance and everyday existence isn't blurred, it's obliterated. The gaudy outfit, hair wildly dyed different colors, and starry makeup, doesn't reveal some repressed side of her that only comes out during their live shows. In broad daylight you can spot her a mile away, walking in the middle of a crowd of pedestrians and talking to them. I finally get it, this is her job, playing the part of Emi Eleonala, night and day.

TAKASHI LEARNS VIOLENCE IS POWER BY KNOCKING MS. FATSO'S BLOCK OFF. BY: FURUYA USAMARU

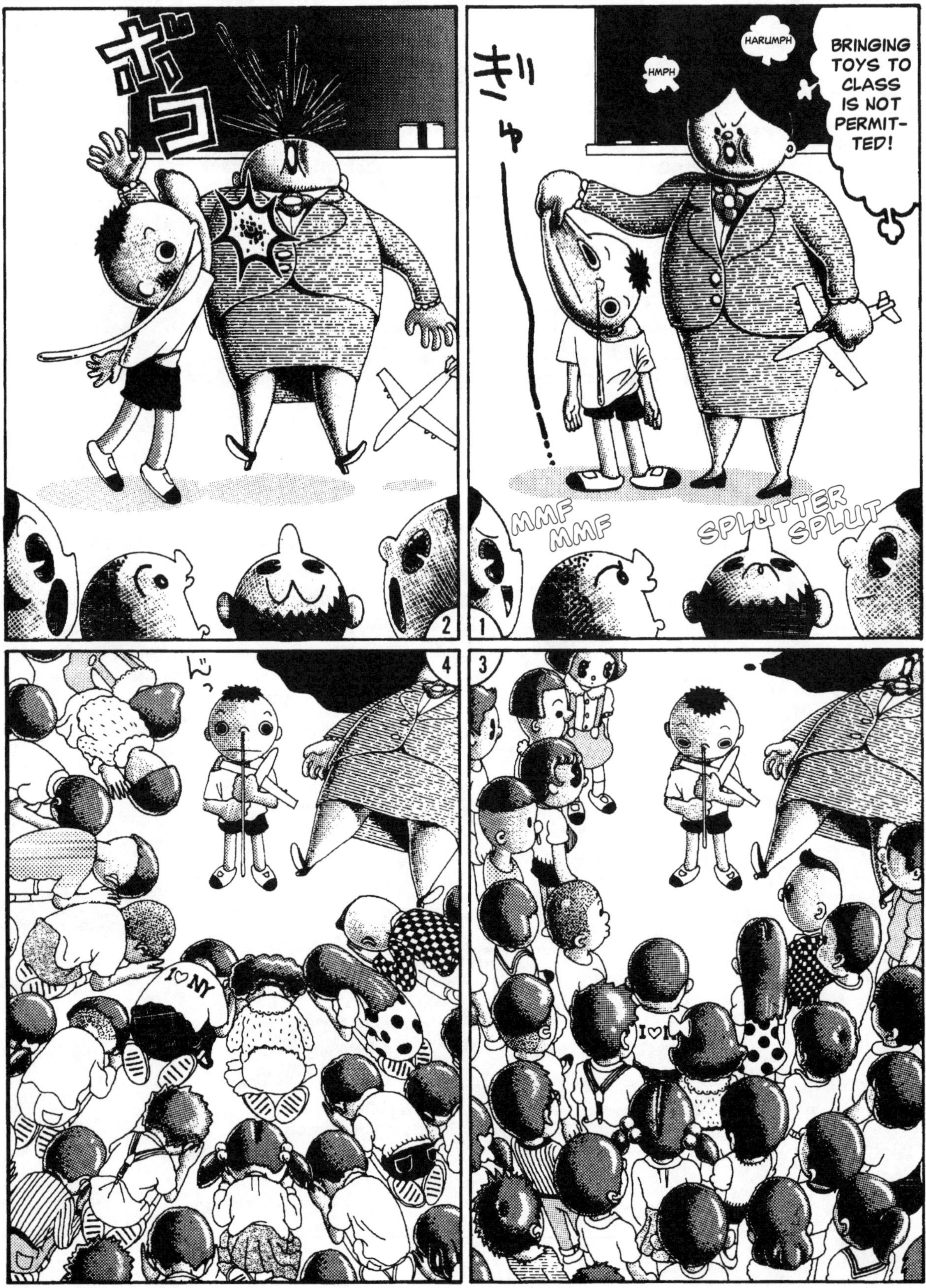
HARUMPH
HMPH
BRINGING TOYS TO CLASS IS NOT PERMIT-TED!
MMF MMF
SPLUTTER SPLUT

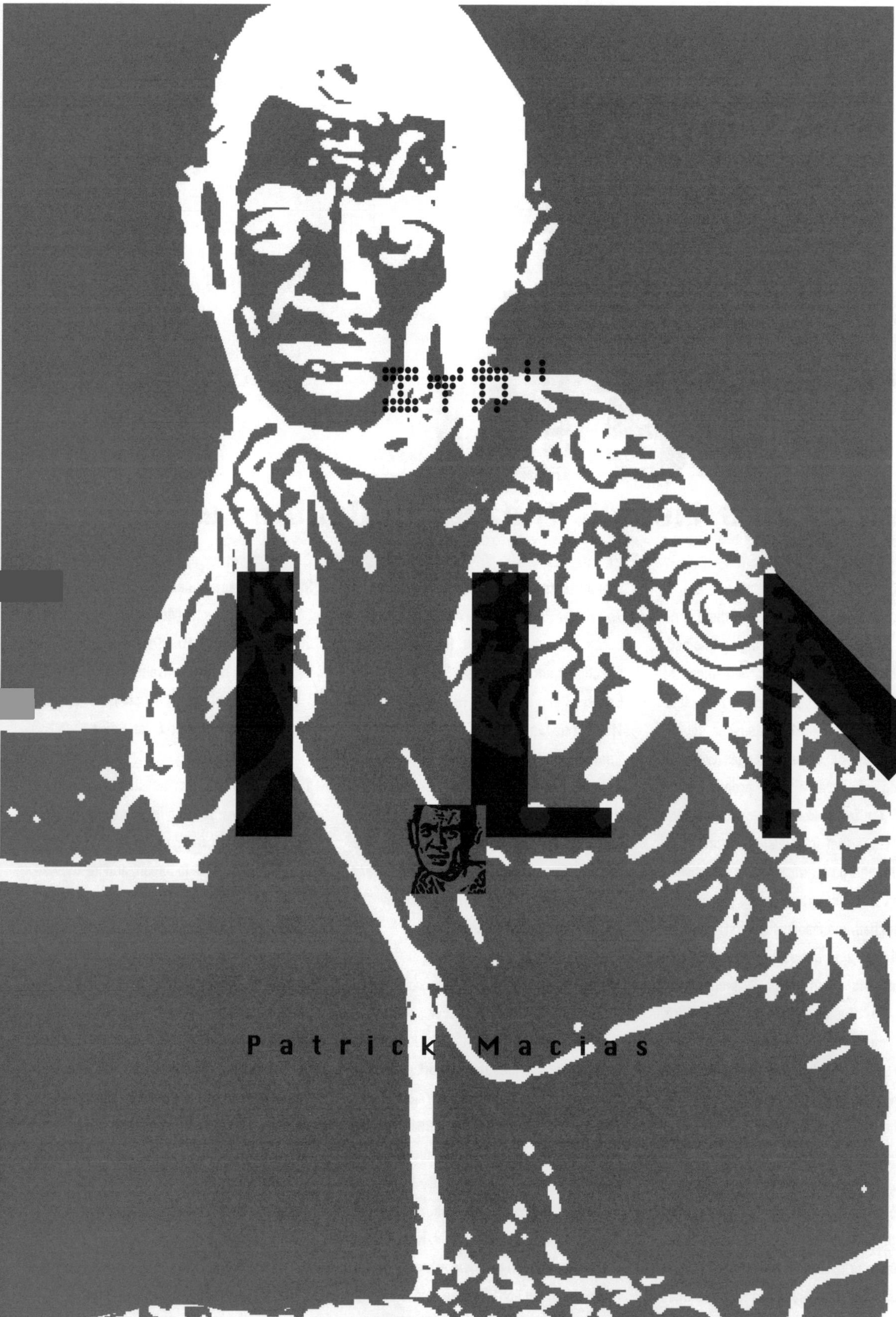

エイガ

FILM

Patrick Macias

overview

Denki-Kan & Electric Theater (A Double Feature)

Tokyo, 1903. Japanese film has been a reality since 1898 or so, and yet there is no venue entirely devoted to bringing this new medium to a paying public. Screenings of foreign and domestic productions take place infrequently, in kabuki theaters or department stores. All of this changes with the opening of Japan's first proper movie palace: the **Denki-kan**, or "electric theater." In the years that follow, studios form, consolidate, and go forward in the established Hollywood mold, with contract players and theater-chain monopolies. At first, musicals are all the rage, but as World War II hits, light entertainment turns to propaganda. Still, the studios—**Nikkatsu**, **Shochiku**, **Toho**, and, in 1953, the yakuza-derived upstart, **Toei**—prosper by rolling with the punches, giving the people what they want, and changing with the times.

1953, Hollywood, New York. Eugene Lourié, a former costume designer and art director, is working on his directorial debut, a B-movie to be called *The Monster From Beneath the Sea*. Given limited resources and a $10,000 special-effects budget, young stop-motion animator **Ray Harryhausen** creates the **Rhedosaurus**, a giant dinosaur who is awakened by atomic testing. When released in June as *The Beast From 20,000 Fathoms*, the film becomes a worldwide hit, less for Lourié's direction than its savage, startlingly *alive* Beast. Blueprinted in 1925's *The Lost World*, fine-tuned in 1933's *King Kong*, the "monster-on-the-loose" film is about to explode...like an H-bomb. But not for Lourié. His first taste of directorial success binds him tightly—too tightly, in fact—to the genre. His successive films—*The Giant Behemoth* and *Gorgo*—are cursed by the law of diminishing returns.

1953. Flying over the Pacific Ocean, forty-three-year-old film producer **Tomoyuki Tanaka** fears for his job. The Indonesian government has just denied work permits to the cast members of his new project, *In the Shadow of Glory*. On the sweat-inducing flight back to Japan, Tanaka quickly comes up with a backup plan to pacify his bosses at Toho Studios. Forget the *Shadow of Glory* and war films altogether. He will pitch a monster movie. A *giant* monster movie. Given the green light, Tanaka comes up with the working title: *The Big Monster From 20,000 Miles Under the Sea*. Special effects man **Eiji Tsuburaya** dreams of creating a giant octopus. Scenarist

Shigeru Kayama decides on a dinosaur. Screenwriter **Takeo Murata** and assigned director **Ishiro Honda** fine-tune the dinosaur into a radioactive mutant. The first script for Tanaka's production is called *Project: G.*: G for giant, G for *Gojira*.

1954. Joseph E. Levine steps out of the *Toho La Brea* theater in Los Angeles. He has just seen *Gojira*, which has done incredible boxoffice in Japan, and he knows without a doubt that the picture can be a smash hit for his employer, **Transworld Pictures**. After much wheeling and dealing, Levine finally purchases the film. The problem now is what to do with the raw Japanese product. English subtitles would do fine for the big-city art houses, but the potential market for *Gojira* is much bigger than that.... First things first: insert an American actor into the story and dub parts of the film into English. Also, the monster is going to need a name change. How does "Godzilla" sound?

1959. The entire world now knows two names via Japanese films: Kurosawa and Godzilla. The emperor and the monster, high and low culture. And yet there is an immense underworld, an *ankokugai*, of movies that never see international light: genre films made only for Japanese audiences. There's the ero-gro (erotic grotesque), sex thrillers, traditional ghost stories given new shades of Eastmancolor blood, tearjerking samurai pictures, the occasional judo movie, and genre-bending crime films with running times full of topless nudity and smoky jazz-nightclub scenes. Because Kurosawa and his contemporaries, **Kenji Mizoguchi** and **Hiroshi Inagaki**, start collecting awards and acclaim, this is called the Golden Age of Japanese film. For Japanese audiences, who love and support their native cinema to the extreme, it is indeed a Golden Age—but for entirely different reasons.

1964–1965. The latest production at **Daiei Studios** is canceled. The proposed film, *The Great Rat Swarm*, which was to have starred hundreds of real-life rats, has led to an epidemic of fleas on the set. The problem now is what to do with the completed—and expensive—miniature city that the "giant" rats were to have destroyed. Looking out of an airplane window, Daiei

president **Masaichi Nagata** suddenly imagines a giant turtle flying through the sky, an absurd, offbeat idea that he can't get out of his mind. The pack of flea-bitten rats has inadvertently led to *Gamera The Invincible*, the only serious challenger to the throne of Godzilla.

1966. Seijun Suzuki, a director for Nikkatsu Studios since 1954, is told that his recent film, *One Generation of Tattoos*, contains a number of sequences that are "unacceptable." Nikkatsu *does* release the film, but only after cutting out the odd non-sequitur touches that Suzuki added to alleviate his boredom with the pedestrian script. Warned to play his next film straight, Suzuki rebelliously directs *Tokyo Drifter* by breaking every rule he can. Suzuki next delivers *Branded to Kill*, which Nikkatsu president **Hori Kyusaku** considers even more incomprehensible than *Drifter* and *Tattoos*, and Suzuki is promptly fired. The visionary director turns around and sues Nikkatsu for wrongful dismissal and is embraced as a hero by the rebellious student movement. But he is blacklisted by

the industry and doesn't make another film until 1980.

1969. Helter Skelter, Altamont, *All Monsters Attack* (Kaiju Soshingeki). This is the last Toho monster film to feature the teamwork of producer **Tomoyuki Tanaka**, director **Ishiro Honda**, special-effects master **Eiji Tsuburaya**, and musical composer **Akira Ifukube**. **American International Pictures** prepares a quick stateside release. Their press book suggests selling the film not on its own considerable merits but by making "a tie-up with local council. These groups are always anxious to promote safety, etc. The title *Destroy All Monsters* lends itself to such a promo, i.e., safe driving, drinking, etc."

1972. Toei Studios contract director **Kinji Fukasaku** is sick and tired of the *ninkyo eiga*, or honorable yakuza, movies: the ones in which the criminals are always portrayed as tarnished angels with righteousness on their side. Raised in American-occupied postwar Japan, Fukasaku knows that, in reality, such men

are more often motivated by cowardice, impulsiveness, and violence. He pitches a daring new type of yakuza film to Toei, and they give him the go-ahead. A showcase for actor **Bunta Sugawara** and Fukasaku's hand-held camera work (inspired by documentary footage of student riots), *Modern Day Yakuza: 3 Rabid Brothers* changes the genre forever. With the aid of screenwriter **Kazuo Kasahara**, the director and actor go on to collaborate on numerous projects together, none greater than the *Jingi-naki Tatakai* (Fight Without Honor) series.

1974. Bruce Lee is dead, replaced by look-alike imitators like **Bruce Le** and **Bruce Li**. Now popular Japanese TV star **Shinichi "Sonny" Chiba** is being groomed as the next international Asian action superstar. America's **New Line Cinema** releases Toei's Chiba vehicle *Gekitotsu! Satsujin-ken*, renamed *The Street Fighter*. The film is a big hit on the drive-in and grindhouse circuit, in spite of the fact that some of its ultraviolence has been edited to avoid an X-rating from the MPAA. New Line releases the sequel, *The Return of the Street Fighter*, and, as an experiment, a Bunta Sugawara yakuza movie renamed *The Tattooed Hitman* (Sugawara's first name is inexplicably changed to "Bud" on the posters). While Chiba doesn't make anyone forget Bruce Lee, he *does* become a certifiable cult film star, thanks to New Line's efforts. Sugawara does not.

1974. The unimaginable. A world without Japanese monster movies. The energy crisis, known as the Oil Shock, and rising costs of movie-making have crippled the film industry. Producing more Godzilla movies has been deemed economically impractical at Toho. Multiple comeback titles—*The Resurrection of Godzilla, Godzilla vs. the Devil, Space Godzilla*—are announced, but never made. Daiei, despite its success with the Gamera films and several internationally acclaimed titles, has been closed for years.

1976. Japan. Things are tough all over, and domestic boxoffice is bad. No one goes to see Japanese films anymore, unless Romantic Porno movies produced by Nikkatsu Studios are on the bill. Even the once-durable yakuza genre is on its last legs. **Noboru Ando**, an actual gangster turned actor, shuts down Toei's "real document" series with his totally outrageous film *Noburo Ando: My Chase and Sex Journal*. Purported to be the whole truth and nothing but (and helmed by Nikkatsu porn film director **Noboru Tanaka**), the movie shows a young Ando on the run from the cops and a society-wide crackdown on crime and immorality. Realizing that the public considers him a social disease, Ando vows to become the most virulent disease he can, having sex with numerous women before the cops slap the cuffs on him…mid-coitus. Instructed to surrender quietly, Ando demands, "Wait until I'm done screwing."

The early '80s. Nikkatsu's Los Angeles branch publishes a little-seen English-

language booklet designed to sell its famed Roman Porno titles to Western film distributors. Despite the spirited synopses (a typical example: "Longings for beauty and love! Avarice and hunger for money! Rapturous sounds followed by sensuous scenes, then imbued with horror and cruelty!"), there are no takers for films like *The Beasts' Warm Bodies* and *Zooming Up on Rape*.

1982. A boom time in America for fan-produced magazines that cover Japanese film and television productions. There's **Damon Foster**'s *Oriental Cinema*, from Hayward, California; *Japanese Giants*, from Chicago, Illinois; and the very best of the lot, **Greg Shoemaker**'s *Japanese Fantasy Film Journal*, from Rossford, Ohio. Tiny print runs and indifferent distribution aside, these publications help to create and support a growing network of fans.

1984. The Japanese economy is an out-of-control monster. Toho at last produces a

new Godzilla film. Original director Honda and musical composer Ifukube withhold any contribution. Producer Tomoyuki Tanaka drums up publicity by showing off an eighteen-foot-tall, mechanically operated "Cybot" Godzilla, used sparingly in the actual film. New World Pictures releases the Americanized version, retitled *Godzilla 1985*. Within a few years, Toho is again producing new Godzilla films almost annually. Though they are seldom more than thinly disguised remakes of the older films, box office appears solid.

1988. Twenty-eight-year-old **Shinya Tsukamoto** is the new enfant terrible of Japanese cult cinema. Involved with nearly every technical aspect of filmmaking, Tsukamoto's artistically cluttered and visually arresting *Tetsuo: The Iron Man* is an impressive showcase for his do-it-yourself aesthetic. When it is released in the West, critics compare his horrific imagery to **David Lynch** and **David Cronenberg**; unbeknownst to them, Tsukamoto is also following in the tradition of Japanese 16 mm mavericks **Koji Wakamatsu** and **Sogo Ishii**.

1995. A resurrected Daiei Studios releases *Gamera: Guardian of the Universe*. Produced for a fraction of the cost of Toho's Godzilla films and created mainly by otaku who grew up watching the original Gamera series, it does only moderate business, but is warmly received by critics and hard-to-please fans for its dynamic, fresh approach. Two sequels follow.

1996. The Internet is connecting fans more directly than ever, but it's not a good thing. Anger and hostility in the Japanese cult film community is at an all-time high, and the **alt.movies.monster** newsgroup is a war zone. A post from God Erik Christ the Almighty has this to say about a fan-organized Godzilla convention: "**G-Con** is a lame excuse for a bunch of greasy thirty-year-old virgins to get together and exchange plastic vaginas and complain about their place in this putrid excuse for a planet. G-Con is a

disorganized gathering of maniacal losers who couldn't get laid if their lives depended on it!!!! ARGHHHH!!!"

1997. Toho producer **Tomoyuki Tanaka** dies at age eighty-two, his name on over 200 films. Comedian, actor, and filmmaker **Takeshi "Beat" Kitano** wins the top prize at the **Venice Film Festival** for his *Hana-Bi*. **Shohei Imamura**'s *The Eel* wins the **Palme d'Or** at the **Cannes Film Festival**. **Masayuki Suoh**'s *Shall We Dance?* becomes the highest grossing Asian film ever at U.S. box offices. The **American Cinematheque** presents the "**Outlaw Masters of Modern Japanese Filmmaking**" series, which brings a wide selection of Japanese cult films to the U.S., many for the first time. Now the president of the **Japanese Director's Guild**, Kinji Fukasaku attends the U.S. premiere of his classic, *Jingi-naki Tatakai*. While in Los Angeles, he is invited to visit the set of *Jackie Brown*, **Quentin Tarantino**'s latest film. **Toshiro Mifune** dies at age seventy-seven.

1998. A revival of two Nikkatsu Roman Porn films, *Wife to Be Sacrificed* and *Sada Abe Story*, plays to large, enthusiastic crowds in San Francisco. Seijun Suzuki's *Tokyo Drifter* and *Branded to Kill* are released on laser disc in the U.S. by the prestigious **Criterion** company. Sonny Chiba stars in the Hong Kong fantasy film *The StormRiders* and receives top notices from the critics. Takeshi "Beat" Kitano's films *Hana-Bi* and *Sonatine* do disappointing business in the United States. The American-made *Godzilla* movie, starring **Matthew Broderick**, ignites a tidal wave of interest and demand for Japanese monsters, but the movie itself bombs worldwide. **Akira Kurosawa** dies, aged eighty-eight. Japanese film is roughly one hundred years old.

Special thanks (as always) to August Ragone, the King of Kaiju and the heel behind the wheel.

Kagero-za (Heat-haze) Theater:

Growing Up Untranslated and Unedited in the Cryptic Flicker of Japanese Cult Films

Coming Attractions

Two layers of language trapped in a single frame of film: "*Anatawa dare*?" ask the Japanese characters. "Who are you?" say the English-language subtitles.

I am Mexican-American. An open-and-shut case of brown skin, black hair, and genetics based south of the border. Yet here I am, worshipping dutifully at the altar of Japanese cult film.

So I've never set foot on Japanese soil. Big deal. I've spent countless hours wading in its celluloid. Occupied territories of interest: giant monster movies, gruesome horror films, sublime ghost stories, yakuza gangster epics, skull-cracking martial arts movies, experimental art films, dirty-minded exploitation, and shocking sojourns into the badlands of sex and violence.

So this is who I *really* am, or at least a crucial facet of my identity that shouldn't go without some mention: an Indian-looking face with both eyes fixated on an Asian-populated silver screen.

Beyond ethnic identity lies the national self. I am American by birth. To watch and prefer Japanese films to modern multiplex fodder can feel like a vaguely traitorous act—like buying a Japanese car, leading to workers getting laid off at a Michigan auto factory. Japanese film in the U.S.A. is inherently *alternative* film. It's my feeling that it has, in some ways, given me an alternative identity.

But all of this comes more or less naturally in California, the Golden State, the source of so much American culture—a place where Asian influence is strong, carried on swiftly moving ocean currents.

Better than this, California is Ground Zero for new experiments in ethnic identity, new combinations beyond antiquated notions of color and class stratification. Taken from the honest truth: a girl born of African American and Mexican parentage identifies herself as "Blaxican". Someone else, a mirror reflection: a boy from California's capital city of Sacramento, born of Northern Mexican heritage, speaks no Spanish. Only English and the odd bit of Japanese and *yakuza* slang.

California is tremendous optimism and possibility. California endorses feelings of helplessness and alienation. There's nothing to really hang on to anymore, not even the comforts of your own birthrights and ethnicity. Instant obsolescence. Things will not, cannot, stay in their designated slots for very long. Blame an overabundance of media, an overpopulated planet, the diminutive size of the global village.

Blame change itself. The future is now the present; every passing second is like the encroaching steps of a giant monster, every movement forward a veritable earthquake heralding the subtle and overt destruction of old structures, leaving us only mysterious footprints to ponder. And pop cultures to excavate.

Now the feature presentation: a true document, a *jitsuroku eiga*, my life as a cult film, tied together by jump cuts, visible splices, crash edits, more enthusiasm than structure, a love of the imagination, and questionable, obsessive behavior—reminiscences no more charmed or meaningful than anyone else's. A life and work still in progress. The director's cut or defining work years away.

Reel One: SON OF GODZILLA

"Every boy needs a friend, even if it's a monster."–promotional copy for *Oru Kaiju Dai Shingeki* (Godzilla's Revenge)

Our eyelids are tightly closed and there is only a darkened space. Light? It comes flooding out of the projector.

One of my first memories of anything at all is of the sight of the animated giant in *Jack & the Beanstalk*, a film I would learn only much later was made in Japan.[1]

Despite its origins as Japanese anime, *Jack* came to my hometown of Sacramento, California, simply as a kiddie film set firmly in the **Disney** mold, i.e., inspired by a classic fairy tale with liberties taken for the inclusion of song and dance.

Through some mind-bogglingly inappropriate film booking, the kind that very much typified the early '70s, the cofeature was a killer snakes movie, *Rattlers*.[2] After *Jack*'s happy ending, this would-be Cinema Paradiso plays *Psycho*'s murderous shower scene with a devious twist. A woman taking a relaxing bath is nearly asleep from the warm water and a moist washcloth placed over her eyes. What she can't see is ours to relish: snakes slithering, one after the other, popping out of the faucet and into the tub. The thoughts of a screaming helpless victim: "Why is this happening to me? Why me? Why here?"

Other helpless victims: an auditorium full of young children and their outraged parents. It is pandemonium, but the snakes scare me less than *Jack*'s bizarre cartoon giant, who wore hearts on his underwear.

The adults go swiftly into action, dashing out of the theater and demanding a manager to punish. The kids stay with the snakes or are dragged or carried out. All in all, a great day at the movies.

But *Jack* and the *Killer Snakes* was merely the first of many memorable double features. Instead of leaving me behind with a baby-sitter, my parents would usually take me along with them to the movies, and frequently that meant the local art house.[3] Along with my first peeks at **Luis Buñuel** and **Ingmar Bergman** films there was master samurai director **Kihachi Okamoto**'s *Zatoichi Vs. Yojimbo*.[4] Already, at a tender age, I was forced to ask myself, who was stronger, **Shintaro Katsu**, as the preternatural blind swordsman, or **Toshiro Mifune**, as the poker-faced wandering samurai?

Across town, there was another battle to witness and judge, *Godzilla vs. the Cosmic Monster* on the bill with the American-produced *Giant Spider Invasion*.[5] There was no contest. The Godzilla movie, and thus Japanese film, was better. And believe me, it wasn't a tough call to make. Even at a young age I could recognize Godzilla for the man-in-a-suit monster that he was, but the Volkswagen bugs masquerading as giant tarantulas were utterly bereft of either stylish special effects or compelling personalities. Japanese monsters seldom had such handicaps...at least in my eyes.

Ever since Godzilla movies first emerged in the '50s and '60s, they had been held in contempt in the U.S. as eyebrow-raising signifiers of hideously bad taste. Sitcoms like *Gomer Pyle* and *Laverne and Shirley* sent their characters to Godzilla movie marathons, from which they brought back sightings of giant

1. Both *Jack & The Beanstalk* and its cofeature, *Rattlers*, were released in the U.S. in 1975. The odds are I was two years old at the time. It's likely that I had been to the cinema before—you know, Walt Disney and all that—but this was the first trauma worth remembering.

I've been playing hide-and-seek with *Jack* ever since, through various ages and mediums. It first showed up on television when I was nine or so, and I duly captured the entire soundtrack on audiotape. When it played years later on Cinemax, I recorded it, albeit in less-than-videophile quality. A few years ago, good old August Ragone bought the prerecord for me from a rental store that was going out of business. What's next for Jack and I? Rent-to-Own High Definition Digital Video Disc? The things we do for the films we love....

2. As if to prove that the line between our lives and the media we consume has become wafer thin, *Rattlers* was kind enough to show up on cable TV while I was writing this chapter. Hoping to plug into some inspiring cult movie memories, I eagerly began watching it for the first time since 1975...but I lasted less than half an hour. In my reminiscences, *Rattlers* was a balls-out, horrifying nature-gone-berserk movie, but it had aged poorly, become a dishwater eyesore with a color scheme leaning towards yellows and browns. Only the diabolical snakes-in-the-tub scene was good for a few chuckles and warm fuzzy feelings. But I've got to wonder—are there any young adults out there who grew up, by some freak of chance, totally ignoring *Jack & The Beanstalk* and now, instead, worship *Rattlers*?

3. This would be the Showcase Theater, which closed down, like a great many other repertory houses in the U.S., soon after cable TV and home video invaded our peaceful little world. The last film they ever screened was **Akira Kurosawa**'s *The Seven Samurai*.

4: What we refer to as samurai movies, the Japanese refer to as *chambara eiga*, a play on the sounds of swords banging and clashing together. Zatoichi, the blind swordsman, first introduced in 1962's *Zatoichi Monogatari*, is probably the genre's most enduring creation. To be fair, **Akira Kurosawa**'s *Yojimbo* came first in 1961, but **Toshiro Mifune** only played monsters who ate Tokyo (I've yet to see a Japanese monster who truly does *eat* a city brick by brick, block by savory block. It would be nice for a change). The mere mention of *Godzilla* or **Tohoscope** would ignite the laugh track or the much-touted live studio audience.

Even today, in our "enlightened" era of pop culture international, these Last Days of Planet Earth, who is going to resist snickering at the title *Godzilla vs. the Smog Monster* or the urge to ridicule its content: men in rubber costumes destroying miniature buildings? And yet the situation is probably worse than ever for fans and neophytes. No one has to make up the jokes themselves anymore. *Mystery Science Theater 3000* can do it for you wholesale, reinforcing laughter as a natural response and maintaining the status quo in which Godzilla and Gamera deserve nothing but smug, self-satisfied comedic beatings. Bad jokes: a denial of the imagination.

Yeah, I'm passionate about Japanese monster movies! Yeah, I'm liable to take any insult directed at them personally! I tell ya, it gives you one hell of a kinship with the underdog, having your true love forever be the subject of ritual humiliation. Example: everyone says your girlfriend is criminally ugly, breaks daylight with her morning face—but she's the light of your life, gives you hope to carry on, etc. Are you going to dump her, give her up just because she's been deemed socially unacceptable by the huddled masses? Or are you going to cling even tighter now, knowing that what you feel is right?

It could be as simple as talk show psychology. The Peter Pan Syndrome: a refusal to grow up and put away childish things (I'm plagued by thoughts of all the attics in the world full of abandoned toys and treasures). And yet who can blame me for staying tuned to *Creature Features* after all these years, especially when the process of growing up frequently reduces a sense of wonder to jive-ass cynicism?

But first there is the hook: a boy's simple love of mass destruction and monsters. The science-fiction imagery, the funhouse atmosphere, and the intense, if not overwhelmingly convincing, special effects sequences. These were the window dressing, the sheep's clothing that allowed the incursion of atom-age anxieties and nearly unconscious symbolic interplay.

It's no joke, man. The original Japanese Godzilla was conceived as a hibernating dinosaur, mutated and awakened by *atomic* fucking *testing*. The first Godzilla film, in 1954, implicates all of humankind for creating this radioactive and quite hostile behemoth.[6] From that filmic moment on, the horrifying reality of Hiroshima and Nagasaki would lurk just under the surface of every one of Godzilla's adventures, inseparable from even the most frivolous. To fully understand the saga requires an interdisciplinary outlook encompassing political and social trends, Japanese and world history. Over the years, viewers have seen Godzilla become a good guy (*Ghidorah: the Three-Headed Monster*, 1964), raise a son (*Son of Godzilla*, 1967), and even go back to his evil city-wrecking ways (*Godzilla 1985*). These greater narratives function on many levels, both as special effects extravaganzas and as mirrors of a postnuclear landscape with no end in sight.

Growing up in an era when **Ronald Reagan** and **George Lucas** were making two not entirely different kinds of "Star Wars" a reality, watching Godzilla films gave impending mass destruction a monstrous face. They were fun. They were weird. They were mythic. They tapped into an apocalyptic sense of wonder lurking just under the surface of everyday life. And they were my first great obsession, my interest today diminished only by overfamiliarity.

Located just outside Tokyo, Japan, **Toho Studios** had a faithful fan at the **Crossroads Cinema**, just off Freeport Boulevard, in Sacramento. (Now it's just an abandoned bank. I can't wait for the universe to stop expanding and start *contracting*. Existing scientific theory will be proven wrong and time will begin to flow backwards. Five-and-dime stores will transform into second-run theaters, and tract housing will be replaced by drive-in movie lots.) That's me with the rice bowl haircut (a **Beatles** cut, as I liked to think of it), third row center at the Saturday matinees, strategically placed just a few feet from *Monster Zero*, *Yog: Monster From Space*, and the eleven-creature strong tour-de-force of the genre, *Destroy All Monsters*. Little Kid + Big Screen = Major Impact.

But not all influences flowed back to the rising sun. Summer '77: *Star Wars* came out of nowhere, and quickly became the defining myth of the generation. To miss out on it would have been a tragedy. That was a long wait between *Star Wars* and *The Empire Strikes Back* (although countless would-be sequels were created with and without **Kenner** action figures during lunchtime recesses), and it was a perfect window of opportunity for foreign-produced space operas to invade U.S. cinemas.

1978 brought yet another impressive double-bill into town: Italy's *Star Crash* and the Japanese-produced *Message From Space*. It was a double-barreled sawed-off shotgun of gaudy eye candy consumed at the time only in the way that a child can eat pounds of Halloween loot or entire boxes of breakfast cereal without any signs of physical discomfort. My dad, who came along with me, simply went to sleep.

Despite a definite Mondo-Euro exploitation vibe, *Star Crash*[7] got the ribbon for the lesser film; directed by the infamous **Lugi Cozzi** (a.k.a. **Lewis Coates**), this low-budget *Barbarella*—featuring a bizarre cast that included **Christopher Plummer**,

David Hasselhoff, Caroline Munro, and Joe Spinell—was quick out of the starting gate, but ran out of steam halfway through, just as the money had run out midway during production.

Message From Space was the mind-blower. Spastic, loud, explosive, and playful: qualities that made it communicate and connect with an equally hyperactive child. *Message* retold the ancient legend of *Satomi Hakkenden* (The Eight Dog Soldiers) in a sci-fi setting populated by actors from the Japanese A list (and, conversely, the American Z list): **Sonny Chiba**, **Makoto Sato**, **Esei Amamoto**, **Estuko Shomei**, **Tetsuro Tanba** and confused occidental **Vic Morrow**. Everything was under the direction of **Kinji Fukasaku**, who had the good sense to create the film more in the manner of his period swordplay films and gangster movies than just as mere imitation of the Lucas juggernaut. Okay. *Message* stole like crazy too...coughing up "cute" robots, futuristic sword fights, and a musical cue that sounds preposterously close to Princess Leia's theme. But *Star Wars* had shown the way by swiping first. George Lucas quoted liberally, shamelessly at times, from **Akira Kurosawa**'s early filmography.

Even minus the requisite giant monsters, my heart was big enough to embrace both *Star Wars* and *Message* on equal terms, and later in life, while the world was drowning in crap from the *Star Wars Special Edition*, I would again find the uniquely Japanese cult-film elements of *Message* beckoning. And my life was to intersect in some small way with director Fukasaku.

Meanwhile, the glass teat of television was bringing Japanese fantasy films home. And technology was just on the verge of making them something you could actually own and collect. My

Starlog magazine, dated July 1979, ran an ad that screamed "VIDEO...the best thing to happen to TV!" predicting an era in which you would be able to "take control of broadcast TV...watching what you want to watch when you want to watch it" and "making home tapies...using instant erasable, practically foolproof videotape." Clearly, a great revolution of magnetic tape reels was about to occur. Only the future would have the sense not to call the finished product "tapies."

Japanese cult film and television were in heavy rotation on UHF channels back in those last great days before the dull uniformity of cable TV, infomercials, Fox, UPN, and WB (of course, cable can still be kind to Godzilla and Japanese genre films, but there's more of a predictable "marathon" mentality behind those broadcasts now). Programmers had to fill up the airwaves with *something*, and Godzilla movies, *Ultraman*, and all manner of Japanese fantasy and horror hoodoo frequently did the trick. But if I'm making it sound like they were ever-present and readily accessible, often they weren't. First of all, despite what *Starlog* magazine predicted, truly affordable home VCRs were still a few years away, so to find and capture Japanese monsters, one was continually up against a formidable enemy: time itself.

After spending Sunday morning searching the movie listings in the new *TV Guide* for signs of *any* Japanese monsters, one might find a true gem: say, *Godzilla vs. the Sea Monster*, scheduled for a dead-of-night three a.m. time slot. This meant serious sleep deprivation. In the morning you'd have to ask, "Was it all a dream? Did Godzilla and Ebirah the killer shrimp *really* play a game of baseball, tossing a giant boulder as surf-rock music warbled on the soundtrack? Was that the twin singing sensation the

that character in a handful of films. Zatoichi managed to appear in an astounding twenty-six films and a long-running TV series before actor **Shintaro Katsu** died in 1997, at age sixty-five. In addition to battling Yojimbo, Zatoichi also fought another icon of Asian action cinema, the One-Armed Swordsman, played by **"Jimmy" Wang Yu** (who also played an entirely different, but similarly disfigured, character called the One-Armed Boxer in many films, including *Master of the Flying Guillotine*). The novel sight of a blind guy fighting a one-armed guy must have inspired Hong Kong's **Shaw Brothers** studio to begin the *Crippled Masters* series, which featured real people with very real physical defects engaging in violent, acrobatic, revenge-driven kung fu. Exploitation, entertainment, or a little of both? You make the call.

5. *The Giant Spider Invasion* is often confused, both in reference books and in my own mind, with *Kingdom of the Spiders*, which starred **William Shatner** of *Big Bad Mama* fame. In *Kingdom*, tarantulas attack civilization, Shatner, et al., after exposure to a deadly poisonous pesticide. In *Invasion*, spider eggs exposed to high doses of radiation grow to proportions that tend to inspire laughter rather than terror.

All the same, in our current era, with an ozone layer poked full of holes and environmental-related illnesses ever-increasing, you've got to wonder, just what the hell ever happened to the nature-strikes-back movie? Is such a scenario just not fantasy anymore? I suppose I could have asked Shatner about his thoughts on the matter when I met him in 1995, but he wasn't about to actually *talk* to me. I was a ghost, probably the nine billionth person he had to give his autograph to.

6. To begin in a mode of genuine nuclear horror, only to abandon every drop of dread soon after, was but one of the many fatal mistakes made in the 1998 American *Godzilla*, which played like 139 minutes of missed opportunities and outright fuck-ups. The opening credit sequence is the film's best argument for existence: a seamless marriage of archival footage of atomic mushroom clouds and shock waves with newly shot inserts of hapless iguanas and eggs exposed to the blasts. It's a hopeful sign that the filmmakers know the origins and the purpose of a Godzilla movie and fully intend to deliver. Soon enough, though, it becomes what producer **Roland Emmerich** proudly calls a "popcorn movie." In other words, the product of grown men with raging hard-ons for mediocrity.

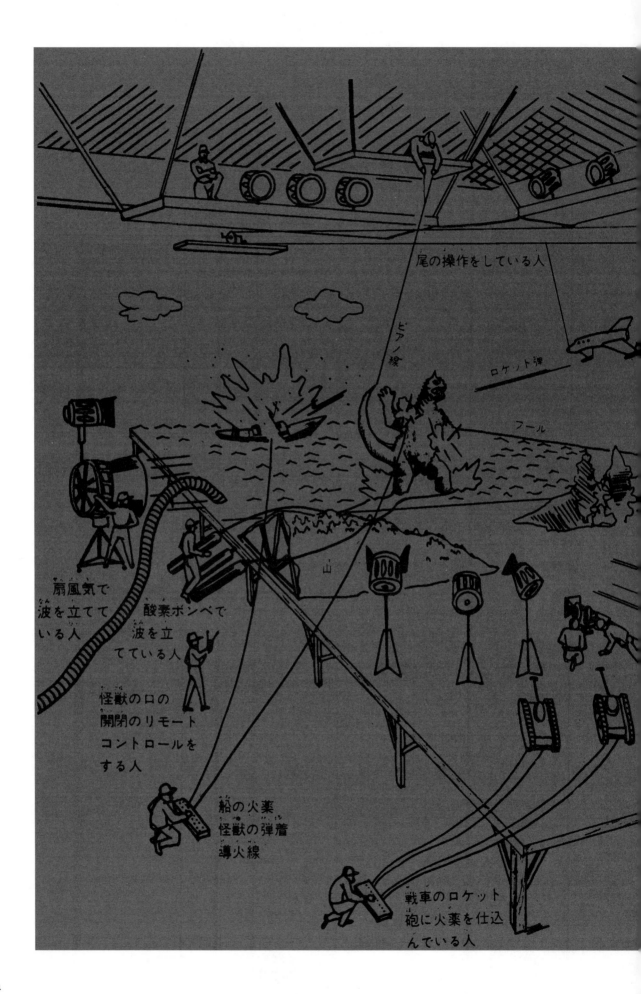

尾の操作をしている人

ピアノ線

ロケット弾

プール

扇風気で
波を立てて
いる人

酸素ボンベで
波を立
てている人

怪獣の口の
開閉のリモート
コントロールを
する人

船の火薬
怪獣の弾着
導火線

山

戦車のロケット
砲に火薬を仕込
んでいる人

ヒートルから
ロケットを発射する
導火線スイッチ係

ヒートルを操縦する人

ピアノ線

石膏板でビルを
作っている人

バックに雲をかく人

ABC

"You have your fears, which might become reality. And then you have Godzilla, which is reality."

—Ogata in *Godzilla, King of the Monsters*

怪獣映画はこうして生まれる

Peanuts who played Mothra's guardian fairies this time out?" (It wasn't. It was the **Bambi Pair**, but that's all academic now.)

And what was even stranger in those dark, unenlightened times of home entertainment before the "in every home, a VCR" era, was that the devoted fan would sometimes record movie soundtracks, dialogue and all, onto audio cassettes. Denied the moving image, the imagination would have to work overtime to re-create the film in the mind's eye. And most of the time, all one had to go on was the odd sound of English voice dubbing.

Here's a long and dishonorable tradition for you: rewording, recutting, and removing the Japanese origins of Japanese productions. It goes on today, on perhaps an even wider scale than ever before. On a current program, such as **Saban**'s *Power Rangers* or *Big Bad Beetle Borgs*, both originally *tokusatsu* shows from **Toei Studios**, the Japanese actors (save for very key players, such as **Machiko Soga**, a.k.a. **Rita Repulsa**, a.k.a. **Witch Bandora**) have been cut out of the action, replaced by miserably inadequate Western talent.[8]

When pioneering Japanese live-action shows like *Ultraman*, *Space Giants*, and *Spectreman* first aired on American TV in the late '60s and early '70s, they too were cut: the more extreme moments of death and violence were snipped, and so, too, were the odd bits of Asian culture too alien for Western eyes, like *kanji* newspaper headlines and Buddhist and Shinto religious rites. Space was also made for the sake of fitting in more commercials. All the same, those were Japanese faces that viewers had to look at between the costumed heroes and villains.

Despite efforts to obscure the truth, then as now, the feel of the original Japanese sources remained and endured, leaving a trail of clues behind. Take out the faces and you've still got the special effects: too optical and

pyrotechnic in execution to truly belong to an American kids' show. The monsters: otherworldly, seemingly conjured out of an entirely different frame of reference. Be sure to keep a close eye on those final credits, too; Japanese names can be found, even if they speed by in the blink of an eye. No doubt about it. Even when chopped up, surgically removed, and hidden away in the attic, the "Japanese-ness" lingers and can be detected by perceptive viewers every time. And when it's discovered, you are at a crossroads: ignore it or become obsessed with it.

I was a willing victim of the latter. Given the watered-down, incomplete versions of Japanese fantasy films, I demanded to see the genuine articles in their purest state, before the sloppy edits and bizarre voices. I loathed being denied anything.

Rumors abounded of incredible sights unseen by Western viewers. *Famous Monsters of Filmland* magazine and numerous reference books stated that there were *two* endings to *King Kong vs. Godzilla*; the American version, in which Kong is triumphant and the Japanese one, in which Godzilla clearly wins the battle of the century.[9] Mysterious film stills from Toho's *Frankenstein Conquers the World* showed an incredible giant octopus, absent from every version I'd ever seen.

So first there were the films. Impressive, provocative, cluttering a restless imagination and suggesting deeper histories and meanings. Soon after came the merchandise and a toy-strewn trail to a private ersatz Japan.

Returning from a business trip, my father had a gift for me. It was a die-cast metal figure of the monster **Gigan**, first seen in the 1972 film *Gojira Tai Gaigan*. Less a plaything and more an objet d'art, it hinted at something greater than merely watching a movie could supply. Here was a Japanese monster—actually from Japan!— via Japantown in San Francisco.

While it would be a serious exaggeration to say that Japantown, or Japan Center, or Nihon Machi is as declined today as ancient Rome, it certainly isn't the magic kingdom it was in the past. Even as nostalgia is a straitjacket, and warm and fuzzy childhood memories obscure objectivity, I recall toy stores of epic proportions: shelves full of soft-vinyl action figures and die-cast, transforming, missile-launching toys that collectors now pay hundreds for. Monsters were everywhere, and hints of a unique animation boom were beginning to peek out: a space ship made in the image of a World War II battle cruiser, heroes with bushy eyebrows and busy haircuts who, commanding giant robots, launched jet-propelled fists.

Stuck in a comparatively mundane America, one had to wonder what the grass was like on the other side. Could Japan itself be wildly different from Japantown? Were there *really* red and silver giants that protected Tokyo Tower from enraged radioactive mutants? Was the entire nation nothing more than just one big Monster Island? All I had to go on for now were the wayward cultural artifacts. I regarded the books and toys as precious moon rocks, evidence of some greater whole. Japan was my imaginary country. And one that was not legitimate at all. At worst, I was practicing a kind of cultural myopia, seeing only what I wanted to—not national treasures and cultures of the highest calling, but monsters, robots, and superheroes. Little kids' stuff. And I wasn't getting any younger.

If I was intoxicated on Japanese monsters before, then a Japantown-bought big-little book that obsessively catalogued seemingly every single hero, villain, and monster of Japanese film and TV made me all but blind drunk. Within an exhaustive 447 pages was a mythology I could step into and aim to master. The tiny pictures of super robots, transforming heroes, and endless monsters with exotic unreadable Japanese names were like coded messages from a more colorful world. Names

I could not read—Kamen Rider, Ultraman, Getta Robo G, Mirrorman, Henshin Ninja Arashi, Kikaida 01, Denjin Zaboga, Gaiking, Robocon, Mazinger Z—their images were devoted to memory.

At the time, since so few of these shows could actually be seen in the U.S., you had to create your own media constructs with whatever you had. The resulting private myths were interactive, subject to change at any moment. True pop culture chaos exists in a child's toy box: Ronald McDonald, Kamen Rider V3, Ultraman Leo, and Luke Skywalker team up to battle the Kraken from *Clash of the Titans* in a Cobra vehicle from G.I. Joe.

All toys were equal, but Japanese toys were clearly more equal than others. Die-cast treasures and soft-vinyl coolness. Another obsession. One that now led to inspiration.

Having Japanese monsters and a Super 8 mm camera readily at hand made me want to make Japanese monster movies. And what mentors there were for the task: figureheads torn from the pages of *Famous Monsters of Filmland* magazine. **Eiji Tsuburaya**: Toho Studios' special effects king, known as the "old man" among his staff, who breathed life into monsters and was such a driving perfectionist that he ordered entire miniature cities demolished if he was not one hundred percent satisfied with them, despite the fact that the monster would destroy them in only seconds on-screen. **Ishiro Honda**: the consummate Godzilla movie director, forever misunderstood and underestimated by foreign audiences, who saw his films in truncated forms. Producer **Tomoyuki Tanaka**: the man who dreamed up Godzilla in the first place and endlessly green-lighted works of fantasy, sometimes missing the mark or delivering subpar product, but always insisting on some form of spectacle.

In their image I made *Godzilla vs.*

Baragon, the top half of my own mini double feature. Synopsis: Godzilla emerges from screen left, Baragon from the right. Monsters fight. Godzilla wins and lives to walk away. Crude? You bet. Without the classic man-in-a-suit techniques of Toho Studios, I committed myself to painstaking frame-by-frame stop-motion animation, as detailed in *Famous Monsters* magazine. The remaining minute of the film reel was given over to simply following the family cat around the backyard. No special effects budget for that one.

Learning the fundamentals of filmmaking was a big undertaking—and so was pronouncing the name Tsuburaya with some degree of confidence. Plus, I was still visually studying the monster dictionaries as if they were the ABC's. From the get-go, I spent my time in elementary school classes tending to my own obsessions: perfecting pencil drawings of Godzilla, scrawling mysterious names in *katakana*, ignoring the schoolbooks for tomes in entirely different languages. I take full responsibility, but someone, one of those "counselors" for instance, should have warned me: your favorite hobbies will be your own worst distraction.

More tales from the suburban dark side. I was a kid who would rather stay up at night to watch monster movies and read movie magazines than pretty much anything else. This had to have concerned my elders a bit. I had plenty of friends, but preferred a shut-in lifestyle to social activities. (Hell, this is *still* my preferred mode of day-to-day living, with hopefully an hour or two of productive work spliced in there somewhere).

Then, as now, there's just too much going on to stay focused on one thing for very long. Eventually you discover your own orbit, which gravitational forces will attract you. Not only were Godzilla and his ilk foremost on my mind, but a whole world

7. As of this writing, *Message From Space* remains unreleased on home video in America. It's a shame, when you realize that every other Tom-Dick-and-Harry space opera from the '70s has gotten its due on tape, even Al Bradley's (Alfonso Brescia)'s ghastly *War of the Robots*, which manages to make *Star Crash* look, if not like *Star Wars*, then at least like the less than impressive moments of Dino De Laurentiis' *Flash Gordon* (1980). I suppose they all have their virtues. Flash has Fellini in-jokes and Queen's infamous soundtrack; *Star Crash* has *Maniac*'s Joe Spinell for a bad guy, a fine score from James Bond composer John Barry, and Christopher Plummer's glaringly *obvious* victory speech, which takes the time to point out things that other victory speeches take for granted (Example: "The stars are clear, the planets shine, we've won."). *Message From Space* ends on a high note with the late Vic Morrow turning his back on Earth, which he has just helped to save, telling his robot buddy, Beba 2, "Forget your medals...there are more beautiful dreams in space." *Star Wars*, of course, doesn't have a victory speech, just our heroes, some smiles, a matte painting, and some medals.

8. I must now profess a perverse fondness for both the *Power Rangers* and the *Beetle Borgs*. First of all, it's difficult to hate something that brings even a sliver of Japanese special effects into innocent people's living rooms. Even if it's crap. Second, given proper alchemical treatment, crap can be turned into gold. Just think, when today's TV kids grow up, they'll have nostalgia of their own to contend with. A *Power Rangers* revival is a sure thing. Maybe a revisionist sequel or rethinking of the storyline into something more adult and complicated. Endless possibilities: What *really* becomes of *Power Rangers*' cast members and their characters when they leave the show? What happens to children who grow up to realize intergalactic being Zordon has stolen their innocence to fight his own battles? And what of the messianic impulse of the Green Ranger? And the tragicomic fate of Skull and Bulk?

9. The truth: Only one ending to *King Kong vs. Godzilla* was ever scripted, shot, and screened. Here's what happens in both the American *and* the Japanese version. After mutually

of monsters and sci-fi history was slowly revealing itself, pulling me into them: the British **Hammer** horrors (think **Christopher Lee** and **Peter Cushing**), the elemental **Universal** monsters (**Lugosi, Karloff**, etc.), the **American International** B-movies (*The Ghost of Dragstrip Hollow, The Beast With 1,000,000 Eyes*).

Yet few of these films ever turned up on TV or at the local rep houses. (At least you could count on *Ultraman* every day on Channel 31 at 3:30 p.m. sharp.) Their very existence was chronicled mainly in the pages of the genre magazines: *Famous Monsters, Starlog, Fantastic Films, Cinefantastique*. A single article could ignite the imagination for weeks. Denied the possibility of seeing **Ridley Scott**'s R-rated *Alien* on its first-run engagement, I pieced together my own version from the now anti-quated filmbook format: a detailed blow-by-blow synopsis and starkly printed publicity and set photos.

But when it came down to the Japanese films, I had the advantage. Increasingly, I could spot oversights and errors in the TV guides and American reference books. I wielded the secret weapon in the war against misinformation: issue thirteen of the legendary amateur press zine, the *Japanese Fantasy Film Journal*.

Discovered by accident at a Berkeley, California, comic shop, it offered vivid proof that other people out there in the wilderness also took these movies seriously, to the extreme and beyond, to the point of utter devotion to the lore and arcana of *kaiju* and *kaijin*. Of course, the big hook was still the king lizard—specifically, a landmark cover story about the 1954 making of *Godzilla*—but the inside content was painted from a richer palate. Across thirty-eight beautifully printed and laid-out pages was an article on the anime movie *Galaxy Express 999*, **Shochiku Studio**'s *Demon Pond*, and a critical filmography entitled **"The Toho Legacy Part I"**. Running from 1960 to 1964, the article filled in the blanks and created new categories. There was now *The Human Vapor* and *Onibaba* to consider, alongside old faves like *King Kong vs. Godzilla*.

But the final frontier was surely a section, edited by one **August Ragone**, called **"Close Up: Far East Report"**: six pages in small type listing cast, crew, and plot information for hundreds of live-action and animated productions released from 1978 to 1980. My private Japan was slowly growing bigger than just the few square miles that made up Monster Island. I had to do a semantic rethink. I was interested not only in Godzilla movies, not even only in Japanese monster movies, but in Japanese fantasy films.

Increasingly, it became evident: some kind of golden age had gone and passed me by. Though it was the early '80s, the most recent Godzilla film, *Terror of Mecha Godzilla*, had come out in 1975, and to bad box-office returns. *JFFJ* did a great job of spotlighting the seminal works of yester-year, but it was losing the battle against the competition. *JFFJ* came out annually, and by the time 1983 rolled around, the writing was on the wall. The good-bye editorial read: "The Japanese fantasy film market has radically been altered by animation. It has become the dominant film medium, representing the SF, fantasy, and horror film genre in Japan, live-action movies having all but disappeared." A telling finale, accompanied by a final statement of purpose: the centerpiece of the issue was a giant retrospective on the 1962 Toho sci-fi epic *Gorath*.

Everything was coming up anime, and despite the lack of sterling new Toho product (*Godzilla 1985* was the sole big event during this era, but it was an overcooked disappointment on a par with *Star Trek: The Motion Picture*), I didn't mind it one bit. It was just another facet of Japanese fantasy film to collect and explore. While that old chestnut *Gorath* had yet to show up at all on local TV, anime had always been present: before school, after school, even in between meals. There was *Speed Racer* (Mach Go! Go! Go!), the fuel-injected alternative to *Sesame Street* when you were small; *Battle of the Planets* (Science Ninja Team Gatchaman) when you took the training wheels off the bike and dreamed of unrestrained, birdlike flight; *Star Blazers* (Space Cruiser Yamato) when you were old enough to watch your heroes die and consider the price of sacrifice; and the romantic *Macross* storyline from *Robotech* when your first crush on a girl was miraculously reciprocated.

While another section of this book is devoted to anime in all its primary painted-cel colors, there are some serious points of crossover with the cult film world. The anime shows and movies that *did* make it to the U.S. were usually dubbed in English, to odd-sounding results.[10] Unkind cuts and outright denials abounded: In *Battle of the Planets*, G-Force member Jason, a.k.a. Condor Joe, never made it to the final showdown, in which he gives his life to save his friends and planet Earth. The graphic deaths of key characters were also left out of *Star Blazers*, undermining an epic storyline that was adamantly mortal in its original form.

Live-action fans didn't have to adjust their point of view too drastically to appreciate the anime experience. The blueprints for the Yamato could have been taken from the flying battleship Gohten-Go, the centerpiece of Toho's *Atragon*.[11] And what were the multicolored five-member crew of *Voltron*'s Go-Lion series but reincarnations of Toei's long running *sentai* TV shows, soon to be better known as the *Power Rangers*?

I was still crazy for Ultraman, Kamen Rider, and Godzilla films when the word got out: a local martial arts supply shop was renting untranslated, prerecorded anime video tapes. The first rental: the first *Space Cruiser Yamato* movie (the faces of anime deaths at last!) and the 1984 *Macross* theatrical movie, *Do You Remember Love?* (first nude shower scene, c/o Lynn Minmay). As time went on, said store began to amass a good-sized collection of tapes, along with anime books and toys.

Anime was the means by which I began to truly *hear* the Japanese language. With no English dubbing, on-screen actors, or live-action elements, everything was just image and foreign sound. To watch without linguistic understanding was to free-fall in an untranslated void. But rather than fighting the lack of coherence, I gave in. Not understanding every little thing gave the imagination room to move around and interact with. At worst, you never knew what the hell was going on. At best, it became like walking a path between radio drama and silent film. You might never arrive at the director or screenwriter's intended meaning, but the possibilities were greater—what it all meant was up to you. Although many of my favorite anime films—*My Youth in Arcadia, Crusher Joe, Mobile Suit Gundam III, Megazone 23, Harmageddon, Adieu Galaxy Express 999*—have finally become obtainable in English, I still prefer my own private, personally understood versions.

Meanwhile, my family finally got a VCR, and I began cluttering up the living room with videocassettes, themselves clogged with the usual Godzilla and increasingly anime-related suspects. Recording, playback, re-recording, tape-to-tape dubbing all became daily functions like eating, sleeping, and dreaming. The future was but a litany of film titles to collect, study, trade. Well, wasn't it?

Sort of and not really. Either way, The son of Godzilla was soon to leave Monster Island for a life both more active and isolated.

Reel Two: Modern Yakuza

"This (film) will reveal cold and cruel modern violence with the color of blood."—from the poster for the film *Boryokudan Saibusou* (The Violent Gang Rearmed)

It happens with your consent or without it—the birthing pangs and the agony of growing up. High school crashes and burns in a holocaust of personal failure. For reasons not entirely clear, you cared more about sci-fi novels, pop culture crap, and sleeping in than achieving anything academically. To now enter college, night school, or even a room with a desk and a chalkboard would be a bad idea. You finally are the stereotype to a T: a Hispanic high school dropout.

While your peers study and graduate and smile with perfect teeth and every hair in place, you sit around the house for a year reading omnivorously, taking impossibly long baths, watching tapes, and playing with the home-video camera: making movies. Images, dialogue, and music edited together, gestures that will hopefully land like *I-Ching* coins, facing the direction of art.

One such video wins an award from a local cable station. Afterwards, a month of art school/summer camp seals the deal. I'm going to be a film and video maker. An ambition that is soon hijacked, but not too

destroying Atami Castle, giant ape and atomic lizard fall off a cliff together and plummet into the sea. We behold a volatile cauldron of bubbles and hear bellowing sounds from the deep. Only King Kong emerges from the fray, swimming calmly out of the picture, apparently the only surviving combatant. Popular perception says that Kong wins without question. But the next film in the series wasn't called *King Kong vs. Mothra.*

 10. While hilariously bad English dubbing remains one of the key appeals of Japanese cult film (something **Woody Allen** capitalized on when he turned a **Toho Studios** spy film called *Kagi no Kagi* into *What's Up, Tiger Lily?*), few fans seem to get off on atrocious anime dubbing. Except for Atlanta's **Corn Pone Flicks** collective, which makes compilation tapes of the very worst examples, spicing them up with live-action material, in an effort to show how anime has been mishandled by American distributors. Still, like me, they surely must maintain something of a love-hate affair with the practice. Now how about some simple sympathy?

An article by **Elliot Rank**, in the *Japan Times* (reprinted in issue twelve of the *Japanese Fantasy Film Journal*) conjures up a hellish vision of amateur *gaijin* actors stuck all day in a recording studio, subsisting on a diet of cough drops "in addition to bagfuls of Big Macs and gallons of coffee" while endlessly watching the same film loops over and over and repeating piecemeal the haphazardly-written English dialogue until it's nearly meaningless and *Twilight Zone* strange. The bottom line is, if you're going to watch a lot of Godzilla movies or Japanese cartoons, you might as well develop some affection for said voices and brilliant exchanges like: "This is Space Titanium." "Space Titanium? You mean it's from outer space?"

 11. Gohten-Go, or "10,000 Power Ship," was also the name of the space battleship in Toho's 1977 film *War in Space* (Wakusei Daisenso). The film itself is a desperate fusion of *Star Wars, Atragon, Battle in Outer Space*, and *Space Cruiser Yamato*, in which only hardcore Toho fans and indiscriminate space opera devotees can find merit. It too contains choice nuggets of bad dubbing, including "Hey, Jimmy! How ya doin', baby?" brought on by one too many Big Macs, no doubt.

 12. Sadly, as of this writing, only one Chinese theater in San Francisco's Chinatown tragically. While on an actual assignment to make a video in San Francisco, I meet the staff of a youth newspaper, who invite me to join them. Instead of becoming a struggling filmmaker, I am drafted into being an employed writer at age nineteen. Fine with me. I'm rescued from the stereotypical life: boredom, nothingness, premature failure. A clean-slate, a new beginning. Taking the job means moving to San Francisco; potentially infinite trips to Japan Center and Chinatown will be part of the deal.

Japan Center certain to be a regular destination, but Chinatown? How did that part of town wind up as a landmark on the map of obsessions?

Through a film, naturally, called *Tiger on Beat*, screened on local cable television and starring then-unknown-to-me leads **Chow Yun-fat** and **Conan Lee**. Graphic hilarious mayhem: a climactic sword duel conducted with chain saws, trick shotguns activated like yo-yos, stuntmen flying backwards through panes of glass. Ouch! Admiration. Amazement.

San Francisco's Chinatown was the local home to the new wave in Asian film: Hong Kong cinema. First-run Japanese films hadn't really been seen in Northern California since Japantown's **Kokusai Theater** closed down in the '80s. (It has since been converted into a Denny's. I'll admit that, while I never saw anything at the Kokusai, I have had some good times over dessert and "Moons Over My Hammy." Either way I'm still waiting for the time-space continuum to flip-flop.) But HK film was accessible if you wanted it.

At this point in the early '90s, Chinatown could boast of three theaters,[12] and dozens of Chinese video stores were scattered strategically throughout the city. Upon arrival, I drank deeply: **Tsui Hark** and **Ching Siu-tung**'s *Swordsman II*, **John Woo**'s *Hard-Boiled*, and **Jackie Chan**'s *Supercop*. Shrimp chips and soy

milk also devoured from the concession stand.

While some fans had been frequenting these theaters for years, more and more non-Chinese were catching the fever now. There was an energy, earthiness, and undeniable vitality in Hong Kong film that finally made it accessible to a mass audience—one that didn't need to understand a word of Cantonese or Mandarin. Unlike Japanese films, nearly all HK titles came with English subtitles, hilariously fractured though they often were. (A particularly fine example from **Jet Li**'s anti–Jackie Chan film *High Risk*: "Doesn't monster love eating pretty woman? Why bite my ass?").

Before Hollywood caught on and gobbled up its top talent, Hong Kong film was *the* foreign cult-film phenomenon in the West, and a new crop of zines were doing their part to encourage English-language exploration by disseminating information and adoring stars like Chow Yun-fat, Jet Li, **Maggie Cheung**, and **Michelle Yeoh**. One zine, **Asian Trash Cinema**, went even further in its devotion, wading into the uncharted seas of sleaze in search of a final frontier, good taste be damned.

"Dedicated to the Art of Action and Exploitation" was the *ATC* statement of purpose, and within its pages were reviews of dubious, frequently category III films such as the grisly *Human Pork Buns*, the murderously misogynistic *Dr. Lamb*, and the hyperactively violent *Rikki-O*. On the back cover, the inevitable photo of a topless woman. The zine has since cleaned up its act; it's more of a "proper" magazine now, with better distribution and a name change to **Asian Cult Cinema**, but it still remains controversial.

The sheer bulk of available Chinese product meant that it hogged a good majority of *ATC*'s pages, but peeking out from between the cracks was the occasional odd-ball Japanese film—not just the anime and

monster films that I now felt relatively familiar with but increasingly stranger things, things that could, conceivably, be found at the local Japanese video stores.

San Francisco's Japan Center has three main video rental stores. The oldest, **Japan Video**, is a stopover for old-time Bay Area fans of anime and live-action super-hero shows. Another store rents current shows taped right off the Japanese airwaves, a bit of a lost cause, really, if you can't decipher Japanese tape labels.

The newest store, **People Video**, which opened in 1992, quickly bested all neighboring competition. Japan Video, despite the implications of its catch-all name, in reality carried only a random handful of non-anime, non-*tokusatsu* tapes. People Video, on the other hand, had an overabundance of titles and genres: a whole section, thirty or so tapes strong, of **Tora-san** films; direct-to-video pachinko game comedies; a *chambara* section that spanned from the black and white era to the present; and an astonishing pornography section overflowing with unbelievable titles like *Black Jesus Clitoris Superstar* and *The Fuck! Fuck! Fuck!*[13] Non-Japanese films were there too, but in sometimes wildly different configurations, such as the *Captain Supermarket* edit of *Army of Darkness*,[14] a letterboxed copy of **David Lynch**'s *Dune*, and a longer alternate cut of **George Romero**'s *Dawn of the Dead* years before it was finally made available domestically. Cult film fans live for such finds, the perfect antidotes to the "new releases" worshipping **Blockbuster Video** nation that the U.S. is quickly, or has already, become.

Given new rooms to move and play around in, I found manga artist **Hideshi Hino**'s straight-to-video shocker *Mermaid in a Manhole*; **Nobohiko Obayashi**'s *House*, an all but indescribable lysergic teenage horror show from 1977; *Violent Classroom*, starring rugged **Yusaku**

なぜ吠える
なぜ暴れるか
野良犬文太！

現代やくざ

"Why do you bark?
Why do you behave violently?
You stray dog Bunta!"

—poster for *Hitokiri Yota*, from the
Gendai Yakuza series

Matsuda as an ex-boxer turned high school teacher at war with his students, a rumble-minded motorcycle gang called the *Sidewinders*. This and more just within the first weeks of store membership.

Running parallel to these individual discoveries was a single growing fixation, as momentous as when the monsters first arrived way back when.

The new breed first announced itself via garish pop art designs; titles smeared in feverish shades of red and yellow; scowling faces reproduced in high-contrast black and white, of hardened, yet impish, masculinity; killer tattoos; the Toei delta brand logo; everyone brandishing a gun or knife; fuzz guitar and Hammond organ just outside the range of human hearing. The yakuza movie section at People Video, about fifty titles strong.

Whispers in the air. Roughly around the same time, *Asian Trash Cinema* published a landmark, multi-part, A to Z of yakuza videos found by author **Chris D.** in L.A.'s Little Tokyo district. It proved invaluable as a guiding light for those first steps into the dark. **Ian Buruma**'s book *Behind the Mask* featured some photos of *Takakura Ken* purifying his samurai sword with sake and a rascally grin on his face, of **Bunta Sugawara** ignobly shooting someone pointblank in the stomach, his expression a **James Cagney** sneer. These pictures were the accompaniment to a chapter called *"Yakuza and Nihilist"*, which I read less as a thought-provoking essay and more as a video wish list of my dreams.

There ought to be a commercial jingle: "Dreams really do come true at People Video." My first yakuza rental was a jackpot: *Gendai Yakuza—Hitokiri Yota* (which luridly translates as "Modern Yakuza—Stabbing Drifter"). It was selected on the basis of box art alone. And who could resist graphics like this? In the upper left was a scrunched-up face clad in sunglasses, ready

to spit or take a punch: the countenance of a true punk. To the right was another tough guy, a cold laconic face with a deep scar running from chin to ear. Center left: the scowling face again, this time sans the glasses, about to throw a bar stool right at you. Bottom: a street riot, bad men running for their lives—maybe from the cops, probably from others just like themselves.

Someday book technology will evolve to the point where you'll simply touch the page and sounds and images from the film will appear in MPEG2 quality. You'll be able to enjoy, say, *Gendai Yakuza*'s dizzying opening montage: a flashback depicting the making of a low-life hoodlum who later slashes his way through a bathhouse, an act that gets him thrown into a hellish prison.

But we're a long way from this. A book is still just paper pulp. But take my word for it: it's one of my favorite movies ever—without English dubbing, without subtitles, without anything but *the film itself*. Ace scowler Bunta Sugawara plays a violent loser named Goro. Out of jail after a lengthy stay, his first new impressions of the world outside are culture shock—just look at the boys' long hair and the girls' short skirts! After a fight with the local gang at a Turkish bath house, Goro shacks up with a stray cat prostitute...a woman whom he and his crew previously gang-raped.[15]

While maintaining this jaundiced, uncertain affair, Goro the small-timer aims to ingratiate himself into the bigger gang under **Noboru Ando** (the cover box's scarface). Too bad. Goro is an ill-fated loser trapped on a downward trajectory. By the end of the movie, Goro and his collection of punks are told to chop their pinkies off: the classic yakuza beg-for-forgiveness gesture. They can't bring themselves to do it, yakuza code of honor be damned! It'll hurt too much to maim themselves, and there's no guarantee it will save them. So Goro grabs the

dosu short sword and starts chopping his gang's fingers off himself. But when brought face to face with Ando, Goro goes into a death charge, slashing his way through a horde of men until he's brought down himself. In death, Goro is simultaneously both the hero and the villain of the film...and nothing but another dead wiseguy. Ando shrugs. The (nihilistic "I-was-a-punk-but-at-least-I-never-backed-down") End.

The appeal? The technique. Every second of *Hitokiri Yota* is jittery, restless with energy. More than half the footage is shot with virtuoso handheld camera. Electricity. Bunta Sugawara superstar. He channels the essence of larger-than-life street-corner trash, so in love with being a violent asshole that your only response is admiration and respect.

Research turned up an astonishing fact: the film was directed by *Kinji Fukasaku*, the same guy who helmed childhood Japanese cult film fave *Message From Space*. Many other yakuza films at People Video bore his name too, and in time they would almost uniformly emerge as my personal favorites. But at the time I was consuming every old yakuza movie I could find, regardless of star, studio, or director. The slow and talky ones starring Takakura Ken in period settings, the ice-cold calculating Ando *gumi* (Ando's gang) films, the desperate cash-from-chaos ploys of **Hiroki Matsukata**, and everything spellbindingly explosive that starred Bunta.

I'd fallen hard for the *jitsuroku eiga*, the tough as nails and lurid as all hell "true-document" film. The titles that I regarded as slow and talky had belonged to another, more honorable, time. They were the *ninkyo eiga*, or "chivalry film." Tall tales of men adhering to gambler's codes of *jingi*, battling enterprising Westernized thugs who smoked Chesterfields, drove noisy foreign cars, and dressed like cut-rate **Al Capone**s. The good guys (a.k.a. **Takakura Ken**,

Kinnosuke Nakamura, and **Koji Tsuruta**) defied this obnoxious new breed by upholding the old traditions of Japanese masculinity: living in an antiquated world, embracing death with impartial samurai gusto.

That was all well and good, but the over-the-top true document methodology was more my thing. The language barrier still made the nuances of story and character obscure, but the dizzying violence—the prototype for HK movie gun battles—was hook enough. Then there was style. These films were cooked up with a funky, early '70s sensibility, but the setting was nearly always the '50s and '60s. Anachronisms and time periods clashed in self-proclaimed "documentaries" about an underworld that had never really existed.

But simply as gangster films, Japanese or otherwise, they were solid gold, fitting snugly alongside respectable company such as **Francis Ford Coppola**'s *Godfather* films, **Sergio Leone**'s *Once Upon a Time in America*, **Brian De Palma**'s *Scarface*, **Martin Scorsese**'s *Goodfellas* and its B-side, *Casino*—all of which used organized crime as a mirror image of the American Dream. In a similar fashion, the *jitsuroku* yakuza films revealed a uniquely Japanese underbelly: the sacrifices, compromises, and sordid truth behind the postwar economic miracle. Shorn of all fantasy elements, they still bore an ever-so-slight resemblance to the monster films. Both depicted the violent disruption of a mannered, well-ordered world by beings behaving in a bestial manner. Pure conflict, pulling no punches. The ritual elements of both genres leaned towards the fatal. Bad monsters and "I don't give a shit" gangsters usually end up dead by the time the end credits roll. Defeat becomes the greatest victory.

Things you could not possibly imagine in a major American film become standard

issue in a yakuza movie. Consider *Noburo Ando: My Chase and Sex Journal*, the "real-life" story of a Shibuya gangster who, in 1958, ran from the cops for thirty-four days, sleeping with seven different women along the way. Just imagine if mob boss **John Gotti** got financing from a major studio to make a movie about his sex life and spliced an active critique of the American Dream in between all the copulation. Couldn't happen, could it? That's where yakuza movies pay off, boggling the viewer on numerous levels: as social commentary, as scandalously sleazy entertainment, as fantasy for adults.

While the yakuza were marching in big time, Godzilla was still the king. Now my hero was helping me find employment. Following the death of director Ishiro Honda, who helmed numerous films starring G, including the very first one back in 1954, I was asked to give a lecture/presentation on both Honda and his work at San Francisco's experimental **Other Cinema**.[16] The idea was for me to put on a one-man show, but while researching and script writing, I got a phone call from out of the blue.

It was August Ragone. He was about to introduce himself when I stopped him. *The* August Ragone, contributor to the *Japanese Fantasy Film Journal* (he had put together the "Far East-Close Up" section) and copublisher of a legendary zine called *Markalite*? The same. He had heard through the grapevine about my upcoming show and was simply calling to volunteer his time and expertise to fact check my Honda script.

Sensing an even greater opportunity, I asked August to join me on stage. Our partnership led to successive Godzilla-themed lectures that took us to the **Northwest Film Center** in Portland, the **Festival of American Film** in Virginia, and the **Pacific Film Archive** in Berkeley.

remains open: the fabulously seedy **Great Star** at Jackson and Kearny. I went there once to see the action film *Zen of Sword* and found something called *Demon Wet Nurse* playing inside. "Exhibition" at its finest, but the prognosis for a prosperous future is bleak. Over the last three years, every time I've been to the Great Star, there have been about ten other people max in the audience, half of them asleep, half actually watching the film, and at least one gabbing on a cellphone.

13. *Japan Edge* coauthor and good friend **Carl Horn** tells me that such ripe titles would "make great band names." But I don't think that any form of music or performance can live up to a moniker like *Black Jesus Clitoris*. As band names, they would be misleading. Only movies about fucking can be expected to deliver such goods.

14. The alternate cut of **Sam Raimi**'s *Army of Darkness*, *Captain Supermarket* (now *there's* a band name!), concludes with **Bruce Campbell**'s character, Ash, taking one drop too many of a time-travel potion, sending him from the middle ages to a postapocalyptic modern city a la *Planet of the Apes*, but sans the apes or anything still living at all. This original ending was changed to something far less intriguing everywhere but in Japan—probably because, when it comes to entertainment, the Japanese tend to want their apocalypse now.

15. At this point a sensible person may want to ask, as a former girlfriend did numerous times, "How can you watch that stuff? It's sick!" Simple. It's make-believe. Fake. Imaginary. Just keep telling yourself, "It's only a movie, only a movie." No matter how you cut it, conflict is the essence of drama, and violence is conflict elemental.

16. Craig Baldwin, a brilliant director and champion of film—of both art and trash varieties—would make a great candidate for an American Dr. Who. We met immediately following a screening of his conspiratorial found-footage epic *Tribulation 99*, which used segments from Toho's *The Mysterians* and about 100 other found films. Craig had an agenda in making *99*—to expose CIA covert operations in Central America—but he did it with stolen scenes from *Blacula*, *Dr. No*, and *Godzilla vs the Smog Monster*. In essence, his films are

In our travels, August and I met regional Godzilla obsessives, did radio interviews to drum up publicity, and somehow got write-ups in local papers. But no honor was greater than when we made the front page of the Bay Area's *West County Times* newspaper, under the headline "Godzilla lives! Stalks Berkeley!" It's the sort of thing one expects to see exclusively in the movies, rolling off a printing press before a cut to a hollering vendor in the panicked streets.

August also helped me make another giant leap from fantasy into reality—a move away from merely reading zines like *Asian Trash Cinema* and *Oriental Cinema* to contributing to them.

My writing was already being published, but my work was mostly for **Pacific News Service**, which syndicated stories nationwide, and locally to the **San Francisco Examiner**. My function was to provide a young person's perspective on recent pop cultural events—**Kurt Cobain**'s suicide, the impact of ultraviolent video games like **Mortal Kombat**—but because I was writing for a mainstream audience, I was seldom able to rattle on about Japanese cult films at length.

Long a contributor to Asian film–related publications, August helped set up a dream date for me with the publishers of *Asian Trash Cinema*. My debut was a review of the straight-to-video production *Mermaid in a Manhole*, a mixture of wide-eyed romance and hardcore gore directed by manga artist **Hideshi Hino**. Our protagonist: an artist who borders on the insane. Like Alice, he takes a trip down a rabbit hole, in this case down a manhole and into the sewer. While sorting through debris and decay, which make up the inspiration for his fervid, macabre paintings, he finds a mermaid. A lovely, but very ill mermaid, with a gaping infected wound on her side. The artist takes her home, places her in his bathtub, and begins to paint her portrait. As the days pass, her wound and infection get worse. Much worse. Her hair falls out in clumps and worms erupt from her body. But it's love, true love, that keeps the painter painting, doing his work now with the aid of her multicolored fluids.

My piece was a more or less straightforward review that set up the context, relayed the story, and made a judgment. But it wasn't until years later when, looking back at the article, I saw something active underneath: a subtext, a hidden meaning. Most people piss on critics for reading too much into things—you know, Godzilla is a metaphor for the H-bomb; *Attack of the Mushroom People* is about the fear of losing one's identity in the modern world—but this time it was my own work in which I was finding meaning. I had turned Hideshi Hino's dying mermaid into a private reflection on a long drawn-out break up with a girlfriend and my mother's battle with cancer. Such was the power of writing and reflecting on Japanese cult film for me.

Soon I was contributing reviews and articles on a non-regular basis to *ATC*, *Oriental Cinema*, and several on-line publications. The timing was good. The film world was finally getting beyond the idea that Japanese movies had to be either Godzilla, Kurosawa, or **Juzo Itami** titles. Once again, Hong Kong was playing a key role. HK films were introduced to American audiences first in short runs in nearly academic settings or repertory houses. After a while, though, nearly everyone who was curious could see **John Woo**'s *A Better Tomorrow*, **Tsui Hark**'s *Peking Opera Blues*, or **Jackie Chan**'s *Drunken Master II*, as long as they lived in a major city or university town. Japanese films were the natural follow-up, at best because they had the artistic merit to hold their own, at worst simply because they offered more Asian guys blasting away with guns.

One of the first new "discoveries" was **Seijun Suzuki**, who had broken new visual and narrative ground in the late '60s, even as he inadvertently ruined his career at *Nikkatsu Studios*. A traveling exhibition of his films made the rounds, finally landing at the Pacific Film Archive in Berkeley. The shows did colossal business. Soon, the American Cinematheque in Los Angeles mounted the *Outlaw Masters of Modern Japanese Cinema* series, a major event that brought not only several Japanese films to the U.S. for the first time, but also their makers. One of them was **Kinji Fukasaku**, director of *Modern Yakuza* and *Message From Space*.

Using every means at my disposal, I nabbed a phone interview with Fukasaku. I was given only a half hour, a time frame that I knew would be too short given the time it would take to relay questions and answers both ways through a translator. We ended up talking for a full hour.

First I hit him with the basic questions: What are your filmic influences? (Italian neorealism.) How long did it take to produce a typical yakuza movie for Toei Studios? (A whiplash thirty days.) Gradually, Fukasaku began to shift the conversation to his own concerns. Foremost on his mind was the postwar era, specifically the U.S. occupation of Japan and **Douglas MacArthur**, head of the occupation forces.

Fukasaku began, "During the Korean war, MacArthur openly said that atomic bombs should be used against China, which had allied itself with North Korea. For that, **President Truman** had him demoted. During the occupation, MacArthur made a statement to the press that the average emotional age of the Japanese people was about thirteen years old.

"The politicians and the media were in no position to rebut a statement like that, made by the very head of the occupation forces. I was fifteen years old at the time and, when I heard the statement, I felt indignant, humiliated, and defiant. But since Japan had caused so much misery to the people of the world during the war, maybe we now had no choice but to accept those kinds of sentiments. However, I've always wanted to ask someone, 'If you think we are thirteen, how old do you think you are? How old are the American people? What is their emotional and intellectual age? Now MacArthur is dead and gone and I have yet to truly ask this question of somebody from the United States."

Fukasaku had completely turned the tables. The filmmaker had masterfully manipulated his audience. Now he was interviewing me, practically asking me the defining question of his life. How the hell was I supposed to answer? I paused.

Was I supposed to tell him that I was all of twenty four years old and in a great deal of doubt as to my *own* emotional age? How about telling him that I identified myself as Mexican-American first, and American second? Would that relieve me from the burden of having to respond on behalf of an entire nation? Could I say that my route to "maturity" wasn't a normal one? That I had progressed not from a hellish war into an uncertain era, or even from childhood into college and a nine-to-five workday, but from Japanese monster movies to Japanese fantasy films and finally to Japanese cult movies? Just how old was I emotionally? Just how old are any of us: Japanese, American, human race?

The audience withheld the final answer. For now, they sat in the dark, absorbing, wasting time, taking notes—the light from the projector providing brief bits of illumination along the way.

Final Shot, Freeze Frame

"My desire is to combine the imaginary with the real."–**Nagisa Oshima**, *Koshikei* (Death By Hanging)

In the future, all your dreams come true. And so do mine. In the future, time starts to run backwards. It's a side effect of the Big Crunch—a Big Bang in reverse—to come a hundred trillion years from now.

In the future...well, it's not *much* of a future, since it's only a selective replay of the past. But it has got its perks and it *is* a future. Movies once thought forever lost reappear, and this time we've got VCRs and recordable DVDs to capture them. The dead come back to life, but we're ready for it, and soon enough it's no big deal when it happens. We get to be children again, but now there's a context for it, and it's more enjoyable the second time around.

Expensive collector's items go back to being simple playthings again. The world wide web grows bigger, gets smaller. Race and skin color don't matter so much anymore. We go back into the ocean as a primordial lizard-fish-thing. Then the continents and land masses come together (Japantown is now located in Japan, the Showcase Theater on the Toho Studios lot). The Earth goes back to a molten state. There's a bright flash of *something indefinable* for a climax, and now the film is almost over. Are you ready for it? Here comes that scratchy black-and-white Film Academy leader you've seen a million times before counting down. And now it's counting back, counting forwards: 2, 3, 4, 5, 6, 7, 8....

a drive-in movie fan's wet dream, only effortlessly intellectual at the same time. I've never been to film school, but watching whatever was playing at Craig's **Other Cinema** became a great education. We also made annual summer pilgrimages to the **Geneva Drive-In** in San Francisco, another venue that has recently closed down for good. As of this writing, Craig is hard at work on his next film, *Specters of the Spectrum*, a narrative science fiction movie about one of my favorite subjects, time travel.

"This is the world of insects... the world of lower animals. Beyond this world lies death and darkness."

—Aki in *Moju*

future trend

99 AND $^{44}/_{100}$% DEAD

In a survey of the movie-going habits of 3,000 Japanese citizens, the newspaper *Yomiuri Shimbun* unveiled some statistics that no doubt made the Grim Reaper crack a smile. Of the 1,968 people who bothered to respond, 22% said they went to the movies only once or twice in 1998, while a whopping 59.9% simply did not go at all. A measly 13% identified themselves as regular filmgoers, meaning they went to the pictures once or twice a month—just as the majority *used* to in the '50s and '60s.

But this is all just a load of numbers, isn't it? With a wide margin of error?

Well, isn't it?

MOVIES FOR PEOPLE WHO HATE MOVIES

The prevailing idea that the Japanese don't like Japanese movies—and according to said newspaper survey, 38% explicitly said that they didn't—opens up some disturbing possibilities. Maybe the Japanese simply don't like movies anymore, period. And maybe the rest of the world is heading that way too.

The growing trend in *all* media is a movement away from *narratives* and towards *situations*. Maybe that's why video games, computers, television, manga, and karaoke have stolen the audience. Movies just aren't the great escape they used to be. Especially in places where the economy is down and ticket prices are up.

So give the people what they want—something without a set up, conflict, and resolution. Give them demons interactive.

EVERY MOVIE IS NOW A CULT MOVIE, INSTANTLY

Much has been made on both sides of the fence about the inferiority complex the Japanese supposedly have about their native cinema and pop culture. "Complex" or not, kids who grew up in the '70s and '80s certainly *did* go to the movies, and more than today's kids do. But they can hardly remember going to see anything besides foreign films like *Star Wars* and *Gremlins*.

Now, just as these kids have gone into the information-era work force, there's a whole new nostalgia market waiting to take their money. The logic goes something like this: it's cooler to catch things the second time around.

The last couple of years have seen cult cover stories in the trend-setting magazine *Studio Voice* and the recent sterling series of *Movie Treasure* books (two of which are devoted to Western films à la *Ed Wood* and *Bert I. Gordon*). And while the interest is certain to grow and wonderful things are certain to come of it, the revival is on video and satellite and cable channels, with theatrical engagements, *au naturel*, reserved for one-night-only bookings.

In the U.S., the gap between Japan, the international film festival circuit, and an American audience is getting smaller. Currently, there's talk of **Takashi Ishii**'s brilliant *Night in the Nude* and *Original Sin*, **Kaizo Hayashi**'s long overdue **Maiku Hamma** films, and **Masato Harada**'s *Bounce KoGALS* coming to stateside theaters and video.

It's a good time in Japan for these independents. The major studios seem more interested in multimedia and real estate than in production. But they still have to release *something*.

Meanwhile, in the tiniest of margins, with the aid of a consumer video camera or a hopelessly outdated Super 8 mm, some whiz kid is doing a **Kurosawa**.

OLD GENRES IN A NEW LIFE (BABY...)

These days, you can see old **Nikkatsu** star **Watari Tetsuya** hawking Takara sake on Japanese TV, with no legacy of shame carried over from his jitsuroku-era movies, such as *Jingi no Hakaba*, in which he slammed opiates and ate human bones.

Old Japanese movie stars only become more bankable as time goes on. Odds are we'll live to see a profile of **Sonny Chiba** in *People* magazine after he does a press junket for a new **Tarantino** movie.

And those most bankable of old Japanese movie stars, the giant monsters, only get more expensive. The toys made in their image, too. At **Toho Studios**, *Mothra 1*, *2*, and *3* are already past tense. By contrast, the proposed South Korean remake of giant monster movie *Yongary* still needs backers to complete production.

As of this writing, Daiei's *Gamera 3* has just opened. The buzz is that it will be to the giant monster genre what *Evangelion* was to the giant robot TV show. Never to be outdone, Toho studios has announced a new project called *Godzilla Millennium*, for 1999.

Meanwhile, in Hollywood, where even a box-office disaster can't ruin a hard-earned license, rumors run amok of a sequel to the 1998 American Godzilla film. Hopefully, it won't suck as much as the first one.

But what manner of beast is this now? Is Japanese film firmly a global franchise like Taco Bell? Or is it a monster due for a millennial makeover from its homeland?

As *Akihiko Hirata* put it in one of those old movies, "Two Godzillas? What does it mean?"

WHAT INDEED?

EASY TO FIND

1. **BRANDED TO KILL**
Koroshi no Rakuin, Nikkatsu, 1967;
Voyager-Criterion Collection VHS, LD, DVD

Director Seijun Suzuki's achingly beautiful and busted up black-and-white nominal hitman story is the sort of movie that can be defined only by comparisons to other films and filmmakers, such as *Eraserhead*, *Chinatown*, Roeg, Fuller, etc. Yet Suzuki's last genre pic proper is in a class by itself, not as a graduation piece, but as a sterling introduction to his filmic fever dreams.

2. **RETURN OF THE STREET FIGHTER**
Satsujin-ken 2, 1974;
New Line Home Video, VHS, LD

A sequel that bests the original by just a hair, a stray one from the eyebrows of Sonny Chiba perhaps, who is meaner and funnier this time around as "half-breed" killer-for-hire Terry Tsurugi. Events become random and disconnected. A weasely white guy is shot to death after walking out of a packed theater playing *Fight Without Honor* (see below). The Mafia plans to take over Japan through its judo schools. A portable 8-track player spits out clues. Bad guys spit teeth.

3. **BLACK LIZARD**
Kurotokage, Shochiku, 1968;
Movies Unlimited, VHS

As they say in *Velvet Goldmine*, a film with its own cast of androgynous jewel snatchers, "There's more to camp than just a row of tents." Sold in the U.S.A. as Japan's answer to John Waters, the *Liz* is actually an elegant cabaret act/tribute/parody spun from Rampo Edogawa's erotic-grotesque detective fiction, filtered through Yukio Mishima's stage adaptation, and given direction by Mr. Message From Space and Fight Without Honor himself, Kinji Fukasaku.

4. **THE LAST DAYS OF PLANET EARTH**
Nostradamus no Dai Yogen, Toho, 1974;
Paramount Home Video VHS, LD

It's 1999, and this is how the world ends: all at once. A crazed and cluttered canvas covered in giant snails, mutant children, crowded freeways on fire, food riots, nuclear warfare, radioactive mutants, and a blustery dual performance by Tetsuro Tanba as an understandably concerned citizen—Nostradamus. No doubt the real apocalypse won't be nearly as entertaining. Consider this incredibly dubbed literal "disaster movie" the alternative.

5. **GODZILLA VS. MONSTER ZERO**
Kaiju Daisenso, Toho, 1965;
Simitar VHS, DVD

The Lizard King, along with Rodan, travels to Planet X to battle King Ghidorah. What more do you need? How about a subtext-laden, tragic, star-crossed love affair "beyond all computation" between lady spy Kumi Mizuno and macho All-American astronaut Nick Adams? We can argue about its merits if you want, but this is my favorite Godzilla movie.

6. **TETSUO THE IRON MAN**
Tetsuo, Japan Home Video, 1988;
Fox Lorber VHS, LD, DVD

Love it or hate it, as *the* Japanese cult film of the last ten years (internationally speaking), Shinya Tsukamoto's quaint little 16 mm movie channeled numerous Western influences, the essence of the Japanese underground scene, and punk rock D.I.Y. energy. The sci-fi elements might bring it uncomfortably closer to something as predictable as "genre," but it's still vital and shocking. And if you can dig it, you're ready for a purer disease.

7. **THE FACE OF ANOTHER**
Tanin no Kao, Toho, 1966;
Columbia Tri-Star Home Video, VHS

The existential-horror elements of director Hiroshi Teshigahara's earlier *Woman in the Dunes* are recut with a harsh modernity bordering on science fiction. The theme of Kobo Abe's novel—the loss of individual identity in homogenized Japan—takes a backseat to brilliant cinematography and set design. A haunting lesson in style *as* substance.

8. **THE RAZOR-SWORD OF JUSTICE**
Goyokiba, Toho, 1972;
Samurai Cinema VHS, LD

Shintaro "Zatoichi" Katsu stars as a feudal-era copper who extracts confessions with torture and "hurts-so-good" sex. Katsu keeps the tool of his trade in shape by banging on his dick with a hammer and dry-fucking bags of rice. Depraved, delirious, and everything that was great about Japanese film in the early '70s. Helmed by director Kenji Misumi.

9. **LONE WOLF AND CUB: BABY CART AT THE RIVER STYX** Kozure Okami: Sanzu no Kawa no Ubaguruma, Toho, 1972; Samurai Cinema VHS, LD

Kurosawa begat the modern samurai bloodbath, the Italians cooked its essence into the spaghetti western, and the Mandarins made *wu xia pian* swordplay in its image. All the international influences come home to roost with this, the second film in the *Lone Wolf* series. With a screenplay by original manga author Kazuo Koike, the narrative is stripped down, leaving behind a brutal, sensual cinematic experience

10. **THE TATTOOED HITMAN**
Yamaguchi Gumi Gaiden—Kyushu Shinko Sakusen, Toei, 1974; New Line Home Video VHS, LD

In the only hard-line Bunta Sugawara yakuza film ever to make it to American screens in the '70s, nearly everything is, of course, lost in the translation and replaced by preposterous lunacy. The star of the show is sold as "Bud" Sugawara, pachinko becomes pinball, the yakuza talk like Chicago gangsters, and a narrator bravely attempts to give it all a useless moral edge. A perfectly unintentional *What's Up, Tiger Lily?*.

11. **THE WOLVES**
Shusho Iwai, Toho Video, 1981;
World Artists Home Video, VHS, LD

The Western world needs more English-subtitled Hideo Gosha films starring Noboru Ando (like his surreal modern-day yakuza pic *Boryokugai*), but this Showa-era gangster saga will do. Begins and ends on high notes of violence, and Masaru Sato's soundtrack isn't too far from his *Yojimbo* and *Godzilla vs. Mecha Godzilla* scores.

12. **THE GHOST OF YOTSUYA**
Tokaido Yotsuya Kaidan, Shintoho, 1959;
Hollywood Home Video, VHS

A ghastly video transfer can't ruin director Nobuo Nakagawa's definitive version of the eternal "weeping woman with child" ghost story. The pace is slow, keeping the supernatural at bay and tightening the screws until the walls come crashing down with surprising amounts of grue, scares that verge on the hallucinatory, and a final image that's both chilling and comforting.

13. **WAR IN SPACE**
Wakusei Daisenso, Toho, 1977;
Video Action, VHS

An elderly Ryo Ikebe wears a baseball cap with the name of his space ship, Gohten, written on it in English. The Earth is under attack from alien invaders known as Jigoku (Hell), who make trouble on the planet Venus with a laser-equipped seventeenth-century galleon. And they said this was a *Star Wars* rip-off? Like Obayashi's *House* (of the same year), a film that couldn't give two shits about logic.

14. **BODY SNATCHER FROM HELL**
Kyuketsuki Gokemidoro, Shochiku, 1968;
Sinister Cinema, VHS

Underappreciated horror director Hajime Sato knows that the world has already ended and we are but survivors of a mysterious plane crash who must now contend with both our baser nature and space vampires. Like a bad dream of genocidal pessimism (or a great episode of *Gilligan's Island*), made effortlessly worse by bad dubbing.

15. **NIGHT IN THE NUDE**
Nudo no Yoru, Argo Project, 1993

Erotic gekiga artist Takashi Ishii is my favorite filmmaker working in Japan today. Putting brilliant actors in everyday locations, he makes taut thrillers that gaze deep into the gulf that separates men from women, cities from nature. *Nude* stands out for its bleakness, alleviated by just the right jaundiced touch of hope. Not out on U.S. home video—yet. I heard a rumor, though.

16. **SONATINE**
Shochiku, 1993;
Miramax Home Entertainment, VHS

Takeshi "Beat" Kitano is one of Japan's greatest comedians. So why aren't we laughing at his films? Because his sort of comedy comes jet-black, drifting on gentle ocean breezes and punctuated by loveless violence. Superficially a "gangster film," this is actually a beautiful testimonial to the simple pleasures of nihilism.

WHERE TO FIND THEM

<RENTAL STORES>
People Video
1740 Buchanan St., Second Floor
San Francisco, CA 94115
(415) 292-5894

Recently dumped a lot of their old titles, but have a big selection of current titles. Legendary adult video section.

<MAIL ORDER>
Video Search of Miami
PO Box 16-1919
Miami, FL 33116

Notorious and dubious, but where else you gonna get a subtitled copy of **Jingi no Hakaba**?

Video Daikaiju
P.O. Box 185
Succasunna, NJ 07876

Subtitled, letterboxed, gourmet Japanese monster videos. Hope they haven't been sued out of business yet.

Cinema World
153 East El Camino Real
Mountain View, CA 94040
(650) 694-4677

Lots of yakuza movies and Nikkatsu Roman-Porno. Bonus points for a strong selection of Eurotrash zombie things.

And...a Japanese video store near you.

collection

HARD TO GET

1. ANDO NOBORU NO WAGA TOBOU TO SEX NO KIROKU
Noboru Ando, My Chase and Sex Journal, Toei, 1976

Peter Bogdanovich made *The Last Picture Show*, Dennis Hopper made *The Last Movie*, and real-life gangster Ando and Nikkatsu Studios porn director Noboru Tanaka made the last "true document" yakuza movie. It's a pack of filthy lies and censorship-observing fucking that ends with Ando masturbating in a cop car and feeling "like the emperor" after he's fired his last shot.

2. BORYOKU KYOSHITSU
The Violent Classroom, Toei, 1976

Supercool boxer Yusaku Matsuda has killed somebody in the ring; for penance, he takes up work as a high school teacher. His students: a blackmailing, glue-sniffing, bousouzoku motorcycle gang. With an eardrum-bursting, guitar-crazed soundtrack and sordid thrills a minute, this is yet more proof that Toei, in the freaky-deaky '70s, was the greatest film studio in the world.

3. HOUSE
Toho, 1977

Swerving between beauty and terror, art and crass commercialism, Nobohiko Obayashi attempts to revive the sleeping beauty of the Japanese film industry with a reference-filled scare film for the youth market. Godiego's finger-popping soundtrack reminds us that **"Cherries Were Made for Eating"**, while a haunted house and its wicked-witch inhabitant devour virginal little girls.

4. BAKURETSU TOSHI
Burst City, Toei, 1982

Japanese cult cinema offers several films equivalent to raging crystal meth binges. Sogo Ishii's second feature is a Japanese Jubilee with a killer selection of punk bands, action, youth rebellion, scum rebellion, and a terrifically shot 16 mm blown up to 35 mm look. Burn your calories and your corneas just trying to keep up.

5. GOJIRA
Toho, 1954

Without the inspiration of the American *Beast From 20,000 Fathoms*, it may never have been made. But Japanese cult film would have been denied its patron saint without the efforts of Ishiro Honda (director), Eiji Tsuburaya (special effects), Tomoyuki Tanaka (producer), and Akira Ifukube (music). Unlike motivationless American monsters, Gojira knows damn well where he's going every step of the way, leaving behind hospitals full of radioactive survivors and lifelong fans.

6. JIGOKU
Hell, Shintoho, 1960

A Buddhist horror film conjuring up a certifiably scary picture of Hell as not just a place of punishing demons and boiling cauldrons (though we get to spend the final third of the film relishing visions that put Hammer and Herschell Gordon Lewis to shame) but also a modern world of casual vice and eternal sin. A world-class religious horror film from world-class horror director Nobuo Nakagawa.

7. THEY RIDE AGAIN
Nikkatsu, 1982

It's just you and Jo Shishudo the Ace in a sleazy old theater watching reels of them dusty Nikkatsu movies from the '50s and '60s. There's lots of Yujiro Ishihara, Ruriko Asaoka, Akira Kobayashi and clips from both obscure and famous idol films, musicals, Westerns, and Westernized gangster films (but nary a frame directed by ousted Seijun Suzuki). And in the spirit of *That's Entertainment!*, the curtain goes down with Jo in a cowboy hat, riding the range one last time.

8. JINGI-NAKI TATAKAI
The Fight Without Honor series, Toei, 1973–1976

Just like the gangsters, cops, and businessmen who populate this eight-film series (the ninth, *World After The Fight Without Honor*, doesn't really count), each entry has its own vices and virtues. The consistency comes from explosive direction by Kinji Fukasaku and the modern yakuza archetypes played by a roll call of classic actors: Bunta Sugawara, Sonny Chiba, Akira Kobayashi, Hiroki Matsukata, Tatsuo Umemiya.

9. YUKE! YUKE! NIDOME NO SHOJO
Go! Go! Second Time Virgin, Image Forum, 1968

"Please don't commit suicide," reads the sign at the police station in the final shot from independent agitprop pornographer Koji Wakamatsu's own little Tate–La Bianca massacre. Too late. The kids are all dead, either murdered or having jumped from the top of a building after a sad, unfulfilling night of sex and violence. 1969 in a black-and-white-with-a-brief-color-sequence nutshell.

10. PEKING GENJIN
Peking Man, Toei, 1997

In the tradition of other major studio, big-budget, "What the hell were they thinking!" flops like *Sayonara Jupiter* and *The Great Spirit World* comes this pathetic Japanese *Jurassic Park*. Using outer space as his laboratory, mad scientist Tetsuro Tanba clones a family unit of unconvincing cavemen from the stolen cells of Peking Man. The uncredited, unfortunate actors run amok, get in trouble, and remind us how little entertainment and the human brain have evolved over the ages. Mediocre stuff now, but over time it will age like primo cult-film wine.

WISH LIST

1. CHOKUGEKI! JIGOKU-KEN
The Executioner, Toei, 1974

Under the command of Ryo Ikebe, modern ninja Sonny Chiba teams up with a hitman, a perpetually swollen sex addict, and a Bruce Lee imitator for sleazy, violent, steeped-in-funk thrills. God only knows why the hysterical English-dubbed version (overseen by the *Speed Racer* pit crew) hasn't been released on video yet.

2. UCHU KARA NO MESSEIJI
Message From Space, Toei, 1978

What began in pre-production under the title *Star Wars in Japan*, emerged as a space yakuza film, a futuristic period sword film, and an unrepentant *Star Wars* rip-off. As someone says in a better-known space odyssey, "My God, it's full of stars!" These include: Vic Morrow, street fighter Sonny Chiba, sister street fighter Etsuko Shiomi, Tetsuro Tanba (as "Ernest Noguchi"!), Makoto Sato, and Eisei Amamoto. United Artists was last in possession of the rights. So release the goddamned thing on tape already!

3. KOSHUKEI
Death By Hanging, Toho, 1968

A true story. The noose fails to kill a young Korean condemned for rape and murder. He awakes with amnesia and no memory of his crimes. So, to fulfill the legal requirements for his execution, various authorities act out his deeds in hopes of jogging his memory. The characters are drowning in their inane bureaucracy when director Nagisa Oshima begins throwing wild stylistic and conceptual curve balls. Only shown in the U.S. in cropped 16 mm prints, a far cry from its original VistaVision format.

4. SANADA FUNROKU
Sanada Warriors, Toei, 1963

Tai Kato's immeasurably entertaining pop-art *Seven Samurai*. An epic account of youth rebellion (rather than village preservation) that tanked when it opened, only to be rediscovered by rebellious youth audiences by the end of the decade. Politics aside, it's simply so good as to deserve its own line of collectable action figures. Just imagine, Kinnosuke Nakamura with glowing blue eyes. Never seen in the U.S. outside of the film festival circuit.

5. KURUTTA IPPEIJI
A Page of Madness, Kinugasa Pro., 1926

From the silent film era, a proto-horror film set in an insane asylum. Just as expressionistic as its German cousins, *Calagari*, *Der Golem*, and *Nosferatu*, thanks in no small part to cinematographer Eiji Tsuburaya, later the special effects architect of the Godzilla series. Forget about a U.S. release for this one.

BIO

PATRICK MICHAEL MACIAS was born in 1972, in Sacramento, California, but, nourished on a steady diet of action figures, film, books, video, and music, quickly traded in reality for an imaginary world.

Weaned on the *White Album*, *Swamp Thing* comics, New Wave science fiction literature, and after-school broadcasts of *Ultraman* and *Black Belt Theater*, he began a promising career in his teens as a videomaker, winning local prizes and a **California Art Scholar Award** for his video short *Vein*.

Upon moving to San Francisco at the age of nineteen, Macias became a published essayist under the guiding hands of the **Pacific News Service Youth Outlook Program**, which syndicated his writing to numerous daily newspapers, including the *San Francisco Examiner*, the *Arizona Daily Star*, and the *Baltimore Sun*. As a freelance writer specializing in Japanese popular culture, Patrick has contributed to *Oriental Cinema*, *Asian Cult Cinema*, *Video Watchdog*, and numerous on-line journals, including *Salon*.

Currently, he is an assistant editor at *Animerica* magazine, a regular contributor to the *San Francisco Bay Guardian*, and is working on an as yet untitled project for **Cadence Books**, to be published in the spring of 2000. That is, if the prophecies of Nostradamus don't interfere, as they do in Toho's *Nostradamus no Dai Yogen* (The Last Days of Planet Earth, 1974, directed by Toshio Matsuda).

Q&A

How big is your collection?

I have several hundred videocassettes scattered about without too much concern for organization, a couple of dozen laser discs of both Japanese and American origin, and steadily increasing amounts of DVDs. I can't really separate the wheat from the chaff or the Japanese cult films from everything else to give an exact count, but there seems to be an awful lot of them about.

What is the most expensive item in your collection?

That's the beauty of videotape. It's relatively cheap and reusable, so "expensive" seldom becomes an issue. Unless, that is, you become obsessed with picture and sound quality, in which case LDs, DVDs, and prerecorded cassettes *will* set you back some. The biggest single investment is probably my collection of **Toei Studio** yakuza videos. A local Japanese video store was dumping their older titles in order to make room for the new stuff, like *Jingi 8*, or whatever. I arranged an installment plan with the owners and picked up something like thirty tapes at ten bucks

each. A substantial investment; a lifetime of entertainment.

What is the most important item in your collection?

Actually, I don't think it's the tapes or the movies per se. It would have to be information, hard copy: Japanese language publications, books, magazines, American zines, press kits, international film festival catalogs. If you're going to write anything besides bad poetry, I firmly believe that you need solid files and good reference materials.

What is your favorite item in your collection?

A large format hardcover book called *Toho Tokusatsu Eiga Zenshi* (The Complete History of Toho Special Effects Films). I usually just call it the Gold Book, both in honor of its considerable price and the reflective color of the cover. Basically, as the title indicates, it covers in depth every special effects film from 1954 (*Gojira*) to 1983 (*Sayonara Jupiter*) with massive behind-the-scenes photos, blueprints, production sketches, sheet music, etc. I spent almost a whole summer as a kid mowing lawns, begging, and saving up enough money to buy that goddamned thing. It

was a real commitment. "A vow of faith," as TV evangelist Robert Tilton says. After that, there was no turning back.

What are your interests besides Japanese cult films?

As time goes by, following Asian film has become less of a hobby and more of a vocation, so now I've taken a big interest in European cult movies, with an emphasis on Italian cinema. The genres are the same—monsters, horror, gangsters, sex, psychosis—but I can watch 'em with my brain turned off and without having to take notes.

I can't write in stone silence, so there's always music playing in the background. My myriad tastes have basically whittled down to a love of power pop: heavy-on-the-melody songs of joy played with good production on bass, guitar, and drums. **The Move**, **Big Star**, the **Raspberries**, the **Scruffs**, **Redd Kross**, the **Vandalias**. **Cheap Trick**'s 1977 debut and *Funhouse* by the **Stooges** were probably the two records that I listened to the most last year.

Also, I read omnivorously. Some people take smoking breaks. I need reading breaks every couple of hours, or else I get itchy. Whatever's at hand will do: the paper, crime fiction, *Vanity Fair*, advertising copy; I'm not picky. But I am critical.

TOKYO

Yuji Oniki

DIARY no. 2

May 31

I have dinner with my friends **Shimamoto**, **Yakushiji**, and **Oya**. Shimamoto is what you might call a low-brow journalist, Yakushiji works at Shimamoto's office, and Oya lives with Shimamoto. We eat at a place called Tensato, a tempura restaurant so utterly devoted to the art of deep frying that they don't even serve rice. The killer discovery there is something called bone crackers, deep-fried fish bones. We munch them for appetizers.

Shimamoto is starting up a cyber-university with enrollment and courses that all take place over the Internet. He's not very specific about the subjects being taught; my suspicion is that the school is too risqué to exist in real space. This is one way to work around the authorities, at least until they clamp down on virtual space.

One of Shimamoto's business partners—I'll call him W.—is what you might call a yakuza computer whiz (a bizarre oxymoron). You wouldn't want to upset him. "But you know," Shimamoto protests, "the thing is, he's usually *right* when he's upset. Most people just keep it all inside." Shimamoto recounts the story of W.'s recent visit to a software company. Utterly frustrated with the continual revamping and updating of a piece of software, he went to the office of the manufacturer and proceeded to hurl threats at the employees, demanding that they make amends for their incompetence. The otaku employees were left pissing in their pants, having for the first time been confronted with something weirder in reality than in cyberspace.

"Not somebody you'd want to upset," Shimamoto agrees as he watches the foam settle almost immediately in his beer. He is convinced that the settling speed of beer foam has been significantly reduced, and longs for the kind that used to leave a white mustache on your upper lip. We experiment for a while with this

theory and conclude that it's true. The evolution of beer technology.

Shimamoto is working on another project, with the acclaimed Japanese photographer **Araki**, a series of nude photos of housewives. Do the husbands know about their wives' participation? "They have to get permission of course.... But sometimes they don't. And sometimes the women lie that they're married just so they can be photographed by Araki. Then Yakushiji has to do some detective work to make sure they check out. But even if they don't check out, sometimes we shoot them anyway. It's a popular series, and often there isn't enough supply for the demand. So we lie and insert portraits of single women. The real ones and the fake ones are mixed together so you can't tell the difference."

Oya and Shimamoto have just returned from Shanghai, where Araki had his first Chinese exhibition. Oya took videos of Araki working in Shanghai, and we watch some of them later that night. A European shoe designer appears in one. She and her boyfriend have flown in from Italy just to have Araki take promotional photos of her new line of shoes.

In the midst of crumbling mortar alleys, a Chinese model wears outrageously expensive Italian shoes and flaps her short skirt to achieve some kind of *Seven Year Itch* **Marilyn Monroe** effect, while subsistence-level comrades gawk at her and an odd bald Japanese man wearing round sunglasses darts around clicking his cameras. Capitalism seducing Red China? The giggling children and goggle-eyed adults in the background seem fascinated less by the model's sexual display than by the

juxtaposition of Italian shoe designer, Japanese cameraman, and assistants communicating in broken English. Unbeknownst to the observers, they're merely exploiting the Shanghai scenery to promote the sale of shoes.

Araki's reputation, like **Robert Mapplethorpe**'s, rests just as much on the extreme sexuality as the formal beauty of his photos. At the Shanghai exhibition, he has to lean towards the latter, restricting his photos to those of flowers and girls in school uniforms. Unlike Mapplethorpe's, however, Araki's vision blurs the distinctions between advertising and art, high and low culture. "What's really extraordinary about Araki is that he has somehow managed to nullify the difference between the things he wants to do and the things he has to do," observes Shimamoto.

Even more beguiling is that it's never clear which photos are done for money and which for art. For someone like Araki, it makes no difference. This detachment towards commercial culture turns out to be quite common amongst the artists I have encountered in Japan. Their attitude seems to be: it's hard enough to get by, and there's no way you're going to make it working strictly within the realm of high art. So even an ultrahip band like Buffalo Daughter contributes music to a Listerine ad without any qualms. There's no American anxiety about asserting one's economic/cultural independence. You'd have to be blind to think that you can support yourself independently in a city where culture and commercials are mostly synonymous. As oppressive as this atmosphere may seem, at times I find it strangely liberating, or at least realistic. I don't think a photographer like Araki could emerge from any city but Tokyo.

The tape abruptly ends with a night shot of Shanghai's neon-lit harbor: a little boy walks up to the edge of the boardwalk and nonchalantly pisses into the bay. This makes us giggle. It's a relief to see children acting like children. In Japan, it's become a crime for kids to look scruffy. These days they have what's called a "debut" for little children and their mothers in apartment complexes. The criteria for joining the other mothers' sorority is the proper behavior not only of the mother but of her children as well.

After downing a couple bottles of wine I brought from California, we start exchanging weird cabdriver stories. Shimamoto is one of the few friends I know who always travels by taxi. The cabbies keep him informed, so he kills two birds with one stone. Once a driver started playing him a tape of strange grunts and noises; eventually he giggled and explained that these were the sounds of him having sex. Another confessed to being impotent since being in a car accident. He had tried everything, but nothing worked. Now the miracle drug Viagra had appeared, but it was only available in the United States. In Japan, it's only available on the black market for $300 a pop.

If the law of supply and demand are correct, one might conclude that in Japan impotence is just as much a problem as (or a consequence of?) the recession. Shimamoto is convinced that the Viagra article in the *Asahi* newspaper (Japan's equivalent of the *New York Times*) that day was paid for by overseas drug manufacturers. "Articles veiled in ad copy," he says, shrugging his shoulders. The comment doesn't sound particularly paranoid coming from a journalist who has worked as a street reporter most of his life.

CUPID

BY: FURUYA USAMARU

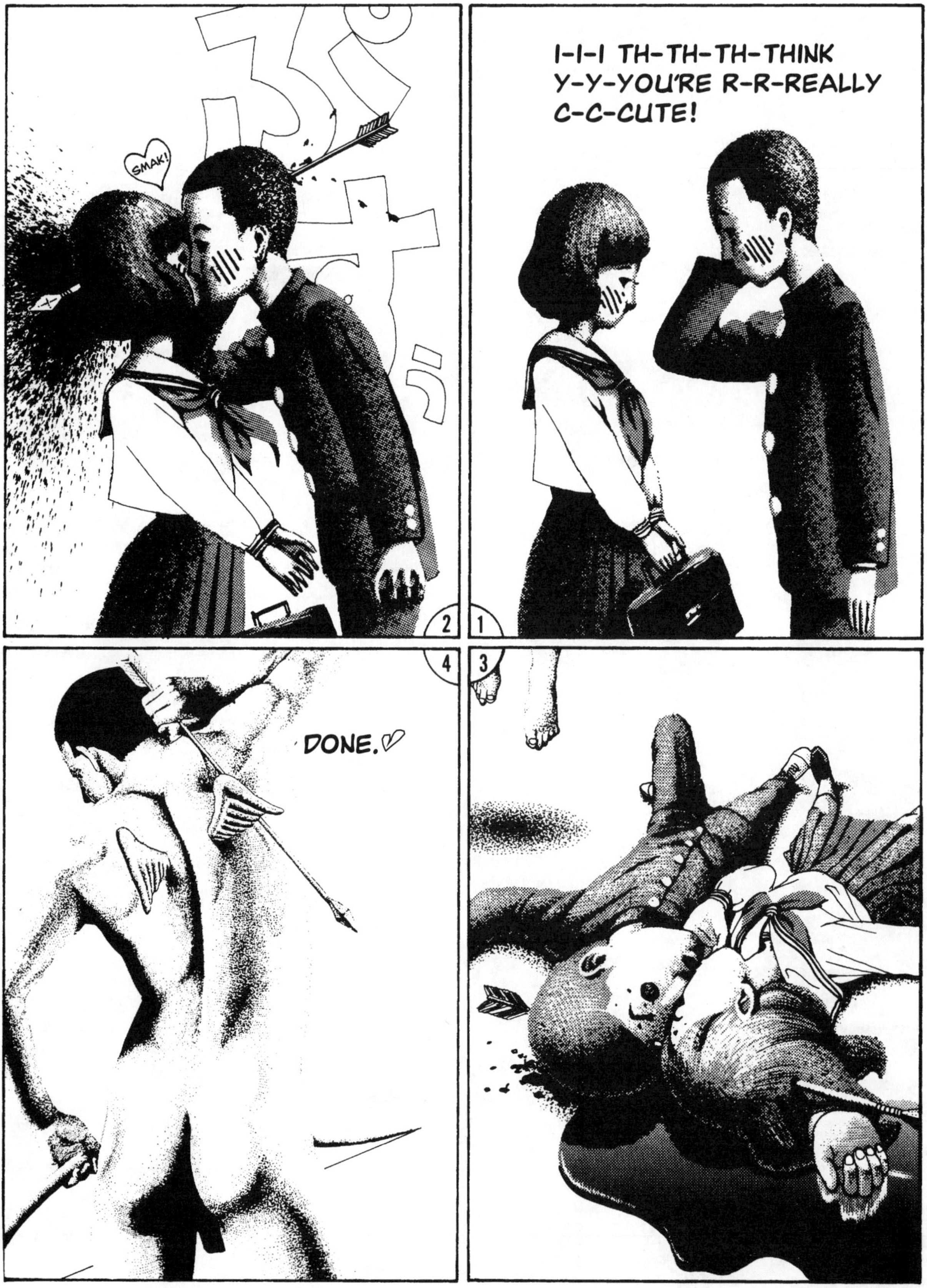
I-I-I TH-TH-TH-THINK Y-Y-YOU'RE R-R-REALLY C-C-CUTE!
SMAK!
DONE.♡

ノイズ

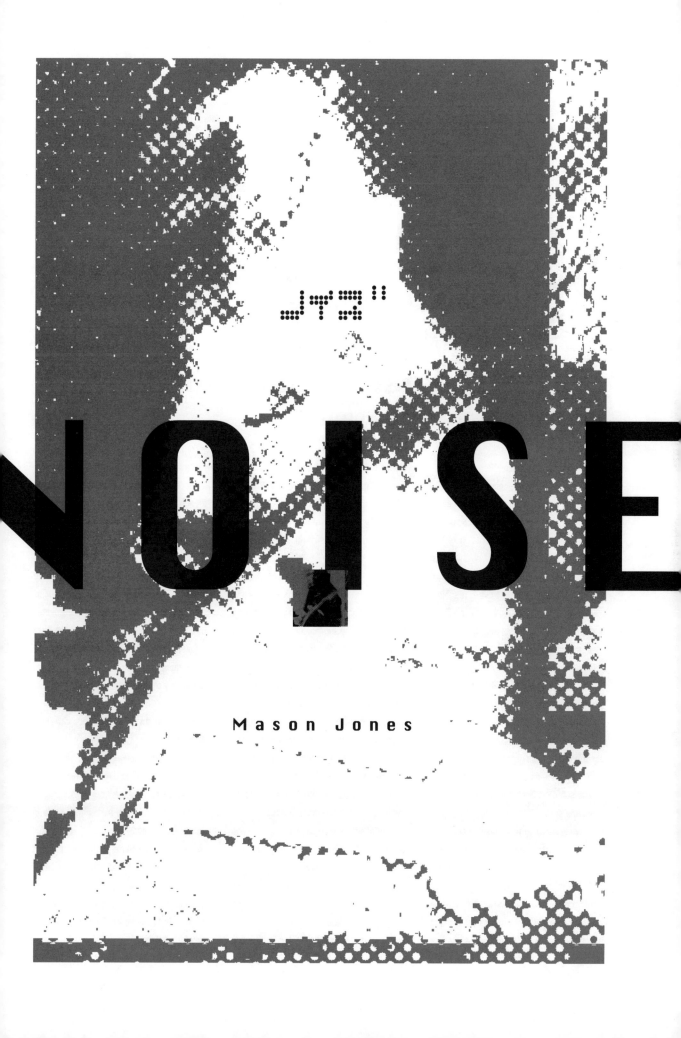

NOISE

Mason Jones

overview

The Noise Heard 'Round the World
The Japanese Noise Scene

Whaddaya Mean, "Noise?"

What exactly is "noise music," anyway? I suspect it's impossible to clearly define the boundaries of what comprises "noise" and what doesn't, but I'll take the risk of trying to draw a few lines. Always keep in mind, though, that noise can encompass a great deal, and that this is a subjective genre. Every guideline I mention probably has at least one exception, and in each case there will probably be at least one noise fan ready to quarrel with me about it.

At its most basic, noise is sound that doesn't have any melodic or rhythmic content. That said, there are artists considered part of the noise scene whose work does occasionally dabble in melody or rhythm.

Noise bands are almost never based on the standard "rock" formation of guitar, bass, and drums. In many cases, it's impossible while listening to a noise recording to identify the instruments or the origins of the sounds. Dominated by the widespread use of distortion and fuzz (effects which add an element of noisiness to any sound), a noise album washes over you like a tidal wave of sound composed of thundering sheets of hissing, distorted tones. Rapidly shifting

shards of sound collide and bounce apart; a heavy clanging may appear and then be washed away beneath rumbling, low-frequency tones; a warbling electronic hum may be cut apart by sizzling, high-frequency feedback.

The instruments or sound sources used to create noise are as varied as the people using them. **Aube**'s **Akifumi Nakajima**, for example, almost always uses a single sound source, processed through an array of electronics and effects. His albums have included the use of oscillators (to create a steady tone), heartbeats, flipping pages of the Bible, and water as original sound sources, which he manipulates to the point of unrecognizability. **Solmania**'s **Masahiko Ohno**, by way of contrast, builds special guitars for his recordings and performances, while the **Incapacitants** use a variety of sound sources processed through tabletops filled with effectors like fuzzboxes, delays, and pitch-shifters.

Clearly then, the definition of noise has little to do with the methods used to create the sound. Noise is noise, and perhaps that's all there is to it—you'll know it when you hear it. And when you do hear it, you'll

probably either be fascinated or repelled. Noise has a way of polarizing people, though, given the chance, it may grow on you, even if at first you're not sure what to make of it.

To my mind, noise is best experienced in live performance. Recordings can be exciting, intriguing, sometimes even trance-inducing, when played at normal volume. But it's in live performance that the best noise artists really shine, either by benefit of stunning, pummeling volume or the sheer physicality of their performance.

The Evolution of the Experimental Network

Make no mistake about it, the avant-garde music scene in Japan is a small one; in that, it's no different from similar scenes around the world. The bands and artists in Tokyo, Osaka, and elsewhere aren't unique to Japan: their counterparts can be found working in small but often influential enclaves in London, New York, San Francisco, and any other city active enough to provide them with clubs or warehouses in which to play.

The Japanese noise scene may be

said to have begun in the late '70s, when the earliest groups began to perform. The influences which led to their formation vary, of course, from individual to individual. Nonetheless, the strongest influences seem to have been twofold.

The first is the original industrial music scene, which was pioneered in the mid-'70s by groups including **Throbbing Gristle** and **Cabaret Voltaire**. These bands, while still operating to some extent within the boundaries of what most might consider "music," antagonized audiences with harsh, noisy performances that featured the use of homemade electronic instruments. Throbbing Gristle, while often featuring lyrics and vocals, played with notions of music and stardom while assaulting audiences with strange, harsh sounds. Cabaret Voltaire actually performed at least one live show that culminated in a riot and endangered the performers. Their cold, creepy, dark electronic sounds were created with early synthesizers and tone generators built by the band themselves. This industrial scene (so named after the **Industrial Records** label formed by Throbbing Gristle) was centered in England. These bands' use

of nonmusical sounds and their attitude, contrasted with the typical pop-star posturing of the time, were an inspiration to musicians around the world.

The second primary influence was a combination of free jazz artists, modern composers, and so-called Krautrock bands, such as **Neu!**, **Faust**, **Can**, and **Amon Düül**. The uncommercial, sound-first attitude of these artists and groups, in addition to the purity of the music itself, was an inspiration. While their music was based on the more established styles of rock and jazz, these groups pushed the envelope in terms of how they combined sounds, stretching songs to trance-inducing lengths and making no concessions to the music industry's desire for hit pop tunes. Whether spacebound rock, squealing saxophone, or minimalist electronic tones, in all cases these artists turned their backs on rock stardom.

The industrial music scene of the late '70s, together with the availability in the early '80s of affordable home-recording equipment, led to the development of a widespread network of experimental artists. Located around the world, these artists had no commercial aspirations; instead, they

sought to share their sound creations with others. To that end, they recorded cassette tapes which they sent to musicians with similar ideas. And some collected recordings from their contacts into compilation tapes.

This network, sometimes described as the "cassette culture" of the '80s, was an intriguing artist-as-fan community in which the fans—and thus the audience—of the recordings consisted of peers contributing recordings to the network. Essentially, this was the most do-it-yourself collection of musicians imaginable.

The first noise artist in Japan to participate in the network was probably **Masami Akita**, whose project **Merzbow** (named after a work of German collage artist Kurt Schwitters) began around 1978. The early Merzbow albums mixed a collage-style sound with heavy distortion and fuzz that seems to point to inspirations such as the industrial music scene, as well as electronic composers such as **John Cage** and **Stockhausen**. Akita's intense networking effort made Merzbow one of the first noise bands in Japan to come to prominence in the U.S. and Europe.

Around the same time, the group

Hijokaidan was founded by guitarist **Yoshiyuki "Jojo" Hiroshige**. Hijokaidan was based on live performances, while Merzbow was, at its inception, primarily a studio project. With its theatrical shock tactics, Hijokaidan was originally a mixture of noise and performance art, its sound mainly inspired by the spirit of free jazz.

Shortly after Merzbow and Hijokaidan appeared, other groups, like the **Incapacitants** (featuring a member of Hijokaidan) and **Hanatarash** came along. After an apparent gap of several years, the second wave of noise groups appeared, including **C.C.C.C.**, **Masonna**, Solmania, and Aube. More recently, a third wave has appeared, including **Pain Jerk**, **Government Alpha**, and **Yukiko**. No doubt younger artists are just now starting to make their own noise, perhaps in brand-new ways.

Japanese Noise in the World

The Japanese noise scene isn't unique—similar noise scenes exist around the world. However, Japanese noise artists have been extremely influential. Their uncompromising sound has made early bands like Merzbow and Hijokaidan respected members of the international noise community. More recent artists, such as Masonna and Aube, have also become influential.

Within Japan, the noise scene is very small and has existed primarily unnoticed by the mainstream music industry. Ironically, perhaps, the most notice received by native noise artists in Japan has come after American bands who are noise fans have invited a noise artist to open for them. For example, when **Sonic Youth** played in Osaka a few years ago, Masonna was the opening act. Later, when appearing as a guest VJ on MTV, Sonic Youth's **Thurston Moore** surprised viewers by playing a short Masonna video. And recently, Solmania opened for the band in Atlanta.

However, a few noise bands have made brief appearances in the mainstream. The founder of the **Boredoms**, Eye Yamataka, was a noise performer in the early '80s with Hanatarash, whose performances often teetered on the edge of dangerous chaos. Their sound, documented on early albums, was some of the most difficult listening ever committed to tape. Screams, distortion, power tools, stabbing feedback, and a whirlwind of unidentifiable sounds erupt into an inferno of noise. The moderate fame of the Boredoms, who have released albums on **Warner Brothers Records**, has given Yamataka the opportunity to re-issue some Hanatarash recordings at a more visible level than most noise artists have been able to achieve.

Violent Onsen Geisha, the project of a mysterious fellow named **Nakahara**, made a jump from independent to major label while still retaining some of the artist's uniquely peculiar aesthetic. His early recordings mixed noise with a surreal collage methodology, while his major-label work has emphasized the collage style and applied it to more mainstream musical styles. While less noisy, most of the work is no less strange.

The international noise scene isn't large, and is a relatively tightly knit community comprised as much of noise artists and labels as fans themselves. In many cases, in fact, people who start out as fans eventually turn to making their own noise, in much the same way that punk rock attempted (and largely failed) to inspire people to form their own bands and make their own music, independent of the mainstream.

Japanese noise artists, in the context of the international scene, have a very large presence. Many small noise record labels have started by releasing something by Merzbow or Aube, the two most prolific artists and networkers. For many noise fans, their first experience is hearing something by these artists. Thus, from the beginning, noise is almost defined by the Japanese artists. Compilations of noise recordings usually include at least one Japanese artist, and many singles have been released that are split between Japanese and Western noise artists.

Despite being a small, almost invisible scene in their home country, Japanese noise artists have managed to create a major presence for themselves among fans and other noise artists around the world.

Isn't Noise a Bad Thing?

People expend a great deal of effort avoiding noise in their lives, so why would anyone want to deliberately make it or listen to it?

To some, the appeal of noise may lie in its purity of sound. Not only is it instrumental and without lyrics, but it has no concern for traditional melody or structure.

Nonetheless, while it is true that anyone can make noise, a fan can differentiate between noise made by someone who wants to communicate and noise made by someone who is simply making a racket. An appreciation for and understanding of noise isn't as easy to come by as it is with pop music. At first, all noise recordings may sound the same. But after becoming familiar with the wide range of artists, a listener can easily distinguish between the different styles, methods, and sounds. As with any genre or scene, artists working to make noise in Japan are doing so as part of a group effort, albeit in their own unique, personal ways.

There is a great deal of support among members of the noise scene in Japan and elsewhere. Participants organize shows for each other, release tapes and albums by each other, and often write for and publish magazines about noise. This network of support not only demonstrates the personal nature of the scene, but can also make it an appealing, welcoming world to newcomers. Anyone can begin writing to other makers of noise around the world. And simply by recording homemade tapes of noise, anybody can become an active participant in the scene. Dozens, perhaps hundreds, of

people operate tiny cottage-industry labels that release tapes of noise by anyone who sends a recording that strikes their fancy. Almost every noise artist puts their address in their albums and welcomes contact from fans and other noise makers.

The strong ties between noise artists in Japan have no doubt helped to solidify the foundation of a scene which makes up for its small size with its integrity and support for its participants. Members of the scene take turns organizing small noise festivals and shows, including occasional all-night performances at which a dozen groups may play. The shows, with such names as "Gathering of Noise Galore" and "Pursuit of Noise," provide a meeting place for noise artists and their fans to truly participate in a supportive community.

Noise is a truly independent movement that is based on a love of sound and communication rather than any desire to become a star. Instead of encouraging passive consumption, the noise scene by its nature encourages participation and action. In a world filled with music and art that seems increasingly based on safe homogeneity and marketing surveys, this is a place where everyone is welcome. That is a rare phenomenon indeed.

Extra-Sensory Dispersion: My Years o Noise

In Which I Become Noisy

Sometimes I find it strange that I have become so involved in the music scene of a country about which, less than ten years ago, I was almost entirely ignorant. Since 1992 I have visited Japan four times to play shows with friends; I have released, on my own record label, Charnel Music[1], a number of albums and compilations of music by Japanese bands; and I have begun publishing a magazine devoted to the Japanese independent music scene. All of this sprang from an innocent curiosity about some musicians whose work I encountered in the mid-'80s.

At the time, I was fortunate enough to be in college in Ann Arbor, Michigan, a university town with a few exceptional record stores, so even in the American Midwest, it was possible to find the occasional musical rarity. Bored with the bands we already knew, my friends and I began buying albums almost at random. In our attempt to find the new and exciting, we chose based on artwork, band name, or anything else that caught our attention. Eventually, I took to mail-ordering albums and tapes from a variety of small outlets in the United States and overseas, which led me to what at the time was called the "cassette culture."[2] This was about as underground as it got: musicians the world over sending tapes back and forth.

There was a huge surge in home recording during the '80s, as recording equipment became affordable to the average person. Particularly inspired by the "power electronics"[3] scene, I bought my own 4-track recorder in 1986 and began making recordings, first under the name Dada Fish and then as Trance. After putting together my first tapes of guitar backed by cheap drum machine, I mailed them to people whose tapes I had purchased. I was very excited when I started getting replies. The responses came from all over the world.

Compilations of different artists were particularly valuable when it came to new discoveries; through them, I encountered musicians like **Controlled Bleeding**, **Master/Slave Relationship**, **Problemist**, **Hijokaidan**, and **Merzbow**.[4] The latter two—creators of some of the harshest, most unforgiving noise I had ever come across—turned out to be from Japan. Hijokaidan's recordings were like lightning transformed into sound, sheets of noise and static. Merzbow's work, while just as intense, contained more low-end rumblings, with quickly shifting chunks of distorted sounds, and was clearly more heavily edited.

Around that time, in 1988, a friend of mine found two volumes of a compilation album called *Dead Tech*, which, although released in Germany, contained only Japanese artists.[5] The bands made sounds so fascinating that I wrote to the person in Japan who had compiled them. His name was **Kazuyuki K. Null**. In addition to being in several bands (including the notorious heavy-rock group **Zeni Geva**), he ran a small record label called **Nux Organization**.[6] We began a correspondence.

In late 1990, Null visited San Francisco on a solo guitar tour, and we finally had the opportunity to meet in person. Contrary to my expectations, Null was very quiet. Given the intensity of his music and the wildness of the bands he worked with, I was surprised. As I was to continue to discover, there is often quite a difference between musicians' personalities and the character of their music.

The night we met, Null was upset and unsure about whether to play the show, because the previous night's show in San Jose had been interrupted by an audience member leaping onstage and unplugging his amplifier. Apparently, nobody in Japan had ever done anything so rude. That was my first encounter with one of the differences between Japanese and American noise-show audiences. Null wasn't sure he wanted to play for American audiences if they received him like that.

Thankfully, we convinced Null to go on with the show in San Francisco. His solo guitar set was very dramatic. Waves of distorted sound cascaded from the stage, layering feedback over harshly strummed chords and low, rumbling vibrations. His lone figure on stage bent forward, then backward, coaxing the sound of ten players from one guitar. He had very long hair, which flew around his head while he played, like headbanging in slow motion. At the set's climax, Null placed a circular magnet over the guitar's pickups and, holding the instrument over his head, screamed into it. His voice was amplified through the guitar and his effects, combining with the vibration of the strings in a chilling way.

The summer following that visit, my friend **Elden M.** and I organized a San Francisco show for Null's band, **Zeni Geva**.[7] While Zeni Geva has often been lumped in with the noise genre, that's really not accurate. To be sure, there is an intensity that may lead some listeners to claim it as noise, but Zeni Geva is really massively heavy rock pinned down by the weight of Null's low-end guitar playing.

Zeni Geva's show was well received and coincided with my record label's first CD releases. Naturally, when Null asked me if I would be interested in releasing the third volume of his *Dead Tech* series of compilation albums, I agreed immediately. The first two, released a few years earlier, had introduced me to the bands on the fringe of Japan's music scene. Having the opportunity to release a follow-up seemed fitting. Little did I know that I would continue to expand my musical world more and more across the Pacific in the years to come.

A Noise Epiphany via an Accidental Evening With the King of Noise
Fast Forward into...

'91

One warm July evening in San Francisco in 1991, I found myself carrying my guitar and amplifier up the stairs to a friend's loft space in the Mission district. Earlier that day, I had been there to interview **Yoshiyuki "Jojo" Hiroshige**, owner of Osaka's **Alchemy Records** label and leader of the infamous noise group **Hijokaidan**.[8]

I was familiar with some of Hijokaidan's recordings, and their pure noise focus fascinated me. As Jojo told me during our interview (for *File 13* magazine), "I'm trying to make this kind of pure emotional and psychological expression through noise."[9] After the interview, we somehow ended up deciding to play together that night. So, early that evening, I brought my equipment over, not quite knowing what I was getting into. A few friends gathered to watch the performance.

Hijokaidan is actually composed of three members: Jojo, his wife Junko, and electronics whiz **Toshiji Mikawa** (who is also the founding member of the noise group the **Incapacitants**). Mikawa, unfortunately, has a family and a job, which doesn't allow him much time off. Thus, when Hijokaidan plays outside Japan, the group is a duo. That night it was Jojo, Junko, and I, plus my friend Elden M. (of **Allegory Chapel Ltd.**).[10] Like me, Jojo plays guitar, while Junko is the most amazing screamer I have ever encountered. Once we started, I was taken aback to see the genial and quiet members of Hijokaidan transformed into raging noisemakers. I had never seen anyone use the creation of noise as such a pure means of expression before.

Normally, Jojo is quiet and studious; his sweaters and eyeglasses make him seem exactly like the golf-playing businessman he is. Back in the early '80s, he started the Alchemy Records

1. Charnel Music has released thirty-six CDs and half a dozen singles since 1988, including compilations of Japanese bands aimed at introducing American listeners to the sounds being created across the Pacific. Albums by Japanese artists have included noise work by **Flying Testicle** and Aube; psychedelic albums by **Kadura** and **Angel'in Heavy Syrup**; and avant-rock by **Fushitsusha** and **Mainliner**, among others.

2. The cassette culture of the 1980s was an amazingly vital scene connected by a few small magazines, such as *Sound Choice*, *ND*, *Unsound*, and later, *Electronic Cottage*, and an overwhelming amount of mail being sent back and forth (this before widespread e-mail access). A number of tape labels were key participants, and some of the most visible served as initial contacts for many people. **Sound of Pig**, **Cause & Effect**, **Ladd-Frith**, and the larger **RRRecords** were essential American hubs of activity. An equal number of labels in Europe and the U.K. helped to connect the international network. Anyone could record their own work onto a tape and get a few copies out for labels like these to distribute.

3. The term power electronics came to be attached to bands that were creating intense, noisy music using primarily cheaply available synthesizers, samplers, and other electronic noisemaking devices, often augmented by noisy guitars and distorted vocals. These bands included American groups such as **Controlled Bleeding**, **Haters**, and **Blackhouse**; European groups such as **Le Syndicat**, **Esplendor Geometrico**, and **Lokomotiv SS**; and Japanese artists such as **Merzbow** and **Hijokaidan**. The power electronics style wasn't necessarily pure noise, as it often included vocals and recognizable instruments like drums and guitars, but it was closely related.

4. I first found these artists released on the **Dry Lungs** series, curated by **Controlled Bleeding**'s **Paul Lemos** and released by the Arizona-based label **Placebo Records**. RRRecords, one of the most important (and still extant) experimental labels, also made available a number of cassette compilations that were valuable sources of information.

5. *Dead Tech* and *Dead Tech II* were compiled by K.K. Null and released by the

label, which grew to become one of the largest and most influential independent labels in Japan. In addition to releasing punk and rock bands, the label's Good Alchemy series has offered albums by many of the most infamous noise artists, including Merzbow, Aube, **Masonna**, Incapacitants, and of course Hijokaidan. Due to his work in Hijokaidan, people have nicknamed Jojo the "King of Noise."

Junko, Hijokaidan's "singer"–screamer, really–is ordinarily very quiet. Her relatively conservative dress hides her past as an art student. Her slight build and low-key demeanor give no hint whatsoever that when onstage with Hijokaidan, she transforms into a demon-possessed performer.

I had played noise performances for several years, but the night that I played with Hijokaidan, I realized that I had always concentrated too much on *what* to play, instead of allowing the sound to just happen. While that may sound like a good thing–obviously it's good to think about what you're doing–it's easy to get bogged down in self-analysis while performing. What Hijokaidan did was so direct and honest that it seemed as though they were channeling the sound from someplace else, rather than creating it. While playing with them that night, I found myself realizing that, in terms of noise, it's better *not* to think about it too much; one should simply *do* it. The more direct and pure it is, the more cathartic, exciting, and fun it will be.

When we started playing, I was taken aback at the instantaneous eruption of sonic assault. My previous live noise efforts usually built up slowly, in a manner that I considered graceful. Thinking back on it, I realize now that I usually performed that way both because I felt it was more artistic and because it was a chance for me to feel my way along, to get a grasp on my intentions and to gauge the audience's reaction.

Jojo and Junko didn't seem concerned about such things. They were there to make noise, and that's what they did. From the instant we were ready, Jojo's guitar exploded into static and fuzz and Junko's voice tore out of the speakers in a high-pitched wailing. In a split second, I actually found myself feeling dizzy from the intensity of the sound and the overwhelming density of the noise frequencies.

Junko's screams filtered through the wall of noise, since the human voice has a very distinctive character. I heard her words and extended vocalizing coming through the angular shards of notes, and in an odd way I think I grabbed onto her briefly as an anchor, a solid sound that I could follow and use as a basis for my playing.

Before we began, Elden had quickly sampled both my guitar and Jojo's into his keyboard, so that his noise blasts blended with ours. He leaned his full weight on the keyboard, pressing out shards of processed noise that mixed indistinguishably with the guitars.

At first, I held back a little, listening and responding and analyzing what was going on. I struck and held notes on my guitar, letting them vibrate and filter into the chaos until they began to feed back through the amp, becoming sharp frequencies that I detuned up and down using the whammy bar. Aesthetically, I was trying to feel where the holes were, and where I could lend my weight to the sounds being created.

But then I realized that I was thinking in terms of traditional musical improvisation–that, in fact, I was probably thinking too much, period. This sort of noise improvisation didn't require the sort of communication and calculated response that I was used to. Instead, it seemed best when I stopped thinking about it so much and just let myself play what felt right. Since then I've discovered that noise works best at an instinctual level based more on emotions than analytical methods. The purity of

expression needs to be allowed free rein.

Before that evening, even when playing noise performances, I had always worked with a more musical modus operandi. Improvising, to me, meant communicating directly and feeling out the holes where I could best add something; my goal had been to help complete the music that was being created.

That night, playing with Hijokaidan, I discovered that those ideas didn't work. Jojo and Junko together, just the two of them, effectively filled the sound spectrum (even more so with Elden participating). It wasn't a matter of me filling in holes, because there were none–instead, it was a matter of adding density to the sound. I thought of it not as adding breadth, but rather depth, to the noise that we were creating.

My ideas about performance communication also changed that night. Prior to that session, I based my performances on fairly direct communication–watching the other players, signaling, and making changes based on the signals. It was a conscious, planned communication. For pure noise shows, however, I changed my conception. Hijokaidan showed me that when making noise, communication can be an unconscious, almost telepathic link between players. Once I relaxed and fell into the spirit of the proceedings, all of the communication necessary happened on an emotional level rather than an intellectual plane.

Almost all the noise performances that I had seen before that evening were comparatively cerebral, with the artists seated behind a table covered with audio gear. While the sounds were often interesting, the performances usually left something to be desired.

Hijokaidan were something different. They spurred Elden and me to work harder in order to keep up. The physicality of the performance stimulated an amazing energy, a willingness to push as far as possible. Jojo and his guitar became one entity. He was clearly not paying much attention, if any, to where he was or even, in some ways, to what he was doing. (As I learned from him afterwards, during shows he communicates through noise itself. And years later he told me that for him, a noise show is like telepathy.) I watched as he pulled on the strings of his guitar, flailed around, and waved his instrument in the air, sweat pouring from him. The sound was high-end feedback and squealing noise, as if the instrument were being gutted and pulled apart. Tones cascaded from the amplifier at high-speed, changing so rapidly that it made me dizzy.

The basic lesson that I learned that night and continued to hone at future shows was to truly let go when playing noise. It's actually not at all easy to abandon yourself to a performance to the extent that you lose all self-consciousness. But I have discovered that the best shows are those during which I am able to fully disassociate myself from the activity of playing and put myself instead *inside* the noise, shows in which I am funneling the sound and participating in the flow with the other players. The shift doesn't always happen, but when it does, the results are always exciting.

Junko, for her part, sat down on a bed in the room holding the microphone and screamed incomprehensible words, pure intensity that conveyed no meaning but had enormous emotional power. The sounds barely resembled a voice; they made me think of the legend of the banshee. Speaking in tongues is nothing compared to Junko. That night, and at Hijokaidan shows since, I've discovered that this diminutive, quiet woman becomes an intimidating demon onstage.[11]

That evening set a standard for me to strive for. Jojo's chaotic abandon during

Hijokaidan performances has left an indelible mark on my own noise performance methods.

In Which I Meet Japan and its Noisemakers in Person

'92

During the summer of 1992, a pair of my friends, **Stephen Holman** and **Clam Lynch**, created a performance group called **Torture Chorus**.[12] To hold up the musical side of things, they enlisted Elden and I. The results were something along the lines of being trapped in a children's show in Hell emceed by two maniacal, costumed freaks. Their other, more theatrical group, **Theatre Carnivale**, had been asked to perform a few nights in Tokyo. Stephen thought, why not do some Torture Chorus performances as well? When Stephen asked Elden and I if we were interested in doing several shows in Japan, we of course said yes. Jojo proceeded to organize five shows for us: two in Tokyo, two in Osaka, and one in Kyoto. The performances put us on bills with some of the most notorious bands in Japan, thanks to the Alchemy Records roster and Jojo's friends.

The Torture Chorus shows, while somewhat noisy, consisted of equal parts calm music and chaotic mayhem. We used tapes and samples to create collages and loops of old cartoon music, over which Elden and I played guitar and keyboard noise. In front of this, Stephen and Clam ranted, ran around, and screamed like berserk kids' show hosts, using colorful props and wearing outrageous costumes designed by Stephen. Torture Chorus performances were equal parts cheery cartoon

Berlin-based label **Dossier Records** in 1986 and 1988. The first volume was subtitled "No Wave from Japan," and included Null, the Boredoms, **Ruins**, Hijokaidan, and **High Rise**, among others. The second volume featured Zeni Geva, **Leningrad Blues Machine**, the **Gerogerigegege**, and the Boredoms. As examples of the mid-'80s intersection between rock and noise, these compilations were extremely important, particularly as they were some of the first examples widely available outside Japan.

Null has been active in the Tokyo scene for many years as a member of diverse bands including the noisy no-wave influenced **Absolut Null Punkt** (a.k.a. **A.N.P.**), prog-rock trio **YBO²** (which also included Ruins drummer **Tatsuya Yoshida**), and the heavy rock group Zeni Geva (see below).

6. Null began the Nux Organization label in the mid-'80s as an outlet for cassettes by Zeni Geva and his solo work. At the end of 1990, he released the first of over a dozen CDs, *Sonicfuck U.S.A.*, which documented his solo U.S. tour. Later Nux CDs included the debut albums by **Space Streakings** and **Melt Banana**, both of whom went on to release singles and albums on American labels.

7. Zeni Geva is a long-running heavy rock trio founded by Null. The band's membership has changed over the years, but second guitarist **Mitsuru Tabata** (previously from Osaka's **Leningrad Blues Machine** and also a member, briefly, of the notorious trash-rock group the **Boredoms**) has been a participant for a decade. Originally inspired by the ultra-heavy sound of early **Swans**, Zeni Geva's powerful approach to rock has earned the band releases on labels in both England (**Pathological Records**) and the U.S. (**Public Bath Records** and **Alternative Tentacles**).

8. Alchemy Records is one of Japan's longest-running and most important independent labels. Jojo began the label around 1981 in Osaka and since then has released albums by **Omoide Hatoba**, Hijokaidan, Masonna, Merzbow, Angel'in Heavy Syrup, **Genbaku Onanies**, and many others. Perhaps most remarkable is the label's openness to a wide variety of styles: punk rock, noise, psychedelia, and more have all been given equal attention.

9. *File 13* magazine was published for several years, beginning in 1988, by **Mark**

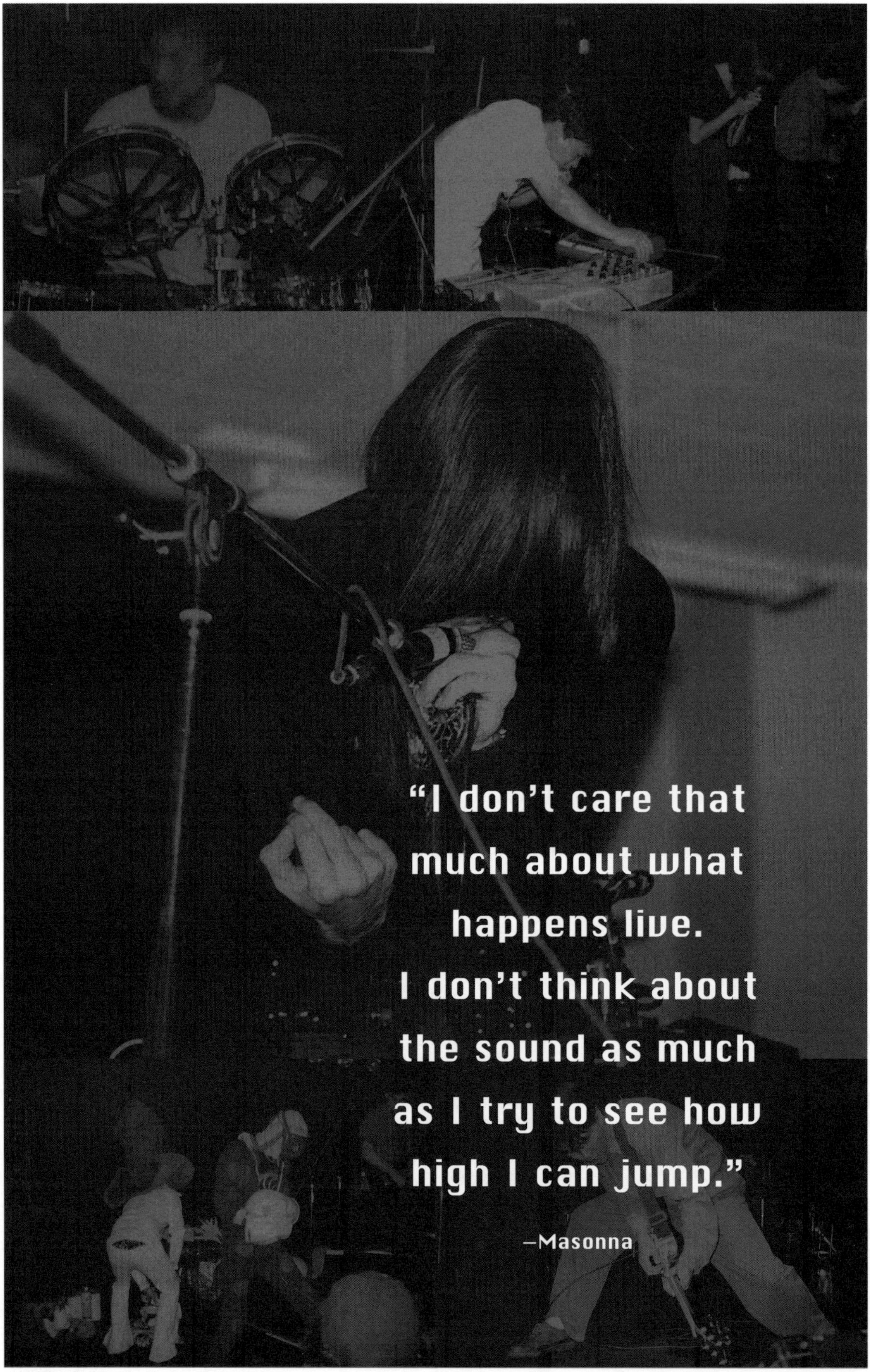
"I don't care that
much about what
happens live.
I don't think about
the sound as much
as I try to see how
high I can jump."
—Masonna

music, frightening morality tales, bursts of harsh noise, and incredibly confusing chaos.

When I look back at that tour now, I'm amazed by my ignorance. I didn't know a single word of Japanese beyond those adopted by the English language. I had no idea what to expect—from either the country itself or the bands we played with. I just knew the tour was an opportunity that I couldn't pass up. My intuition was more accurate than I could have imagined.

What I found in Japan was an amazingly supportive group of musicians, none of whom seemed to have any expectations about anything as prosaic as fame or fortune. Instead, they were true do-it-yourselfers, people who were making music and/or noise simply because they wanted to, and nothing more. Naturally, nobody like **Masonna**—who used a metal canister filled with coins connected to a string of distortion and delay pedals—could expect to become a top ten hit-making pop star. In a way, the huge distance separating these noisemakers from the mainstream consumer-driven music industry gave them the freedom to do as they wished without worrying about anything other than their own ideas. As an underground community, they were also able to help and support each other. There was no need for jealousy nor competitiveness, because there was really nothing to be competitive about.

That tour was my first opportunity to see noise bands like Masonna and **Solmania**, who have visited the U.S. several times since. They have also earned some notoriety overseas, which may or may not lead to more than a passing mention of them as curiosities in a few "alternative" music magazines. Nonetheless, I have been surprised at the growth of the Japanese noise scene's presence in the American independent music world over the past half decade or so. [13]

Masonna stunned us with a nine-minute performance that packed more energy into its short duration than almost any other show I have ever seen. With just a vocal microphone and a candy tin filled with ten-yen coins and a contact microphone, **Maso Yamazaki** whirled alone like a dervish through the tiny confines of Osaka's **Bears** club. [14] Of all the noise artists, Yamazaki has the most rock-star quality about him. As a big fan of psychedelic music (he is the co-owner of an Osaka psychedelic shop named **Freak Scene**), he dresses in flared pants and trippy shirts. [15] With his long, long black hair and eternal sunglasses, he projects a very cool image.

Throwing himself around the stage and even out into the audience, he screamed, roared, and stomped on effects pedals. On the darkened stage, he was no more than a shadow with hair flying about. Sudden bursts of silence interrupted the show occasionally as his gyrations unplugged a cord here and there, whereupon he would pause, breathing hard, and calmly plug the cord back in. After a moment of stillness, he would blur into high-speed motion again, the volume of noise from the oversized PA system physically pummeling the audience. [16] The sound alternated a pure vibratory distortion with hellish screams as he stepped rapidly on various effects pedals.

Talking with Maso, I was surprised to hear that he doesn't really like to listen to noise music much—he's a bigger fan of psychedelic music. But I later found that most noise artists have wide musical tastes, and in some cases only perform noise and don't listen to it very often.

The Incapacitants duo are sometimes affectionately called the Laurel and Hardy of noise by their friends. Physically, **Toshiji Mikawa** and **Fumio Kosakai** are complete opposites: the former (also a member of Hijokaidan) is a small, compact man and an

Lo, and I contributed many record reviews and occasional interviews. Issue 11, published in the fall of 1991, featured Japanese music and included my interviews with Jojo, Sekiri, and the crazy Gerogerigegege.

10. San Francisco–based noise artist Elden M., recording under the name Allegory Chapel Ltd. for over ten years, has released a number of cassettes and albums. He has been an important participant in the healthy exchange between the San Francisco experimental music scene and its counterpart in Japan. This has included organizing shows for visiting bands, as well as a long tenure at **Subterranean Records**, an important independent distributor of punk rock and experimental releases.

11. After the show, **David Hopkins** of **Public Bath Records** asked Junko what she was saying, because he had heard something about bats and cats. She answered that she couldn't remember what she said during the performance. This kind of disassociation from my surroundings, to the point where I don't remember all of the show, is the step that's hardest for me to achieve. At the same time, it's the key to really projecting myself completely into a performance.

12. Stephen Holman began his Theatre Carnivale project in New York before relocating to San Francisco and expanding his vision into the cartoon music–derived sonic nightmare of Torture Chorus. In addition to his theatrical endeavors, Holman works as an animator and is the creator of the series *Life with Loopy* for the Nickelodeon cable network's *Kablam* program. His noise group, **Poo Poo Bomb**, with collaborator **Josephine Huang**, has performed in both America and Japan.

13. The increased notice taken of the Japanese noise scene overseas is due to the interest of high-profile members of the American indie scene. For example, **Sonic Youth** have had Solmania, Masonna, and others open for them at shows both in Japan and in the U.S. In addition, some of the more open-minded music magazine editors have given coverage to noise artists. It's not nearly as uncommon now to read reviews of CDs by Merzbow and Masonna as it once was.

14. Bears is a tiny underground (literally and figuratively) club in the Namba section of Osaka managed by **Seiichi Yamamoto**, guitarist for the Boredoms and leader of **Omoide Hatoba**.

electronics aficionado; the latter is a tall, round man whose entire body, during performances, vibrates with energy.[17] Both of them stand behind tables covered with countless effects pedals, tone generators, and unidentifiable electronics. However, what could easily be a static performance—two people behind tables—is instead a visually engaging spectacle. The two mismatched performers throw themselves into the noisemaking, turning knobs, slapping switches, and letting their bodies channel...something. It's as if they are giving themselves over to an inner force that demands release. An Incapacitants show is possibly the densest audio experience I have ever encountered. Thick slabs of sound surround the audience, shifting and changing but always seemingly immovable. The weight of their walls of distortion is remarkable.

Along with Merzbow and Hijokaidan, the Incapacitants, founded around 1981, are one of Japan's longest-running noise groups. Also an active networker, Mikawa writes about noise and experimental music for several magazines, including **G-Modern**.[18] When I asked him what motivates him to make noise, he answered simply: "I sometimes feel a catharsis when playing noise, but it's not the only reason why I started to play noise and continue.... I think the main reason why I don't stop making noise is that I really enjoy the process. I can't tell you why it's fun to me, but I like it anyway."

Mayuko Hino, a noise artist from **C.C.C.C.** and **Mne-mic** who is also a dancer, once drew a parallel between butoh dance and making noise.[19] While I'm certainly no expert on the butoh style, I can see similarities in the attempt at pure expression. In most cases, noise performances are relatively straightforward and honest attempts at communication that convey emotions and feelings directly through noise.

Our Torture Chorus shows in Japan were well received, although at first we weren't sure, because of the differences between American and Japanese audiences. At most of our shows, particularly those in Tokyo, the audiences were almost eerily reserved. Noise audiences there are smaller and older than rock audiences. The way that they silently sit and absorb performances seems almost studious. Given the crazed nature of our shows, it was at first a little unnerving to have them received so quietly, almost respectfully. In America, audiences would shout, laugh, and enter into the spirit of things more obviously.

As it turned out, the more open nature of the Osaka area—known for its more carefree people, as opposed to Tokyo's reputation for a more reserved (even uptight) populace—complemented the Torture Chorus aesthetic more directly. Also, since the performance opened with a punk rock band, the audience was more energetic and younger than the Tokyo noise afficionados. At our show at Osaka's **Fandango** club, Clam ended up climbing above the audience on the club's metal pipes while they threw props back at us and even jumped onto the stage.

One of the openers was the death-rock band **Rapes**, whose singer, Shintani, was a heavily-muscled guy apparently renowned for starting street brawls and working as a low-level *yakuza* thug. With his numerous tattoos and shoulder-length, dyed red hair, he clearly wasn't an office worker. After the Torture Chorus set, we were called back for an encore, only to have Shintani grab the microphone and start singing in his guttural voice. I exchanged looks with my friend Sam, an American living in Osaka who had joined us on drums for the show, and we began playing. Elden joined in with keyboard noise. Afterwards we learned that Shintani had apparently been singing some particularly stupid anti-*gaijin* comments, though his vocals were pretty difficult to understand.[20]

In Which I Dig Myself in Deeper

After I returned from my first visit to Japan, I remained in touch with the noise artists I had met there and through them, I continued to make new contacts. I became fascinated by the growing noise scene in Japan and by the people I had met; they were almost all amazingly nice and distinctly lacking the ego-driven personalities I had often encountered elsewhere in the music world.

I was also intrigued by the challenge of learning more about the world of independent music in Japan. I think there resides in any fan of music, film, etc., a certain collector mentality that can kick in upon discovering, for example, a new artist or director. In addition, there is the not insignificant power of curiosity. I had stumbled upon a country that was completely new to me and filled with creative artists, most of whom were entirely unknown to me and everyone else I knew. I felt compelled to explore this new musical frontier.

Naturally, there is nothing intrinsically "better" about the Japanese music scene—there are just as many untalented, derivative bands, percentage-wise, as any place else. But the way the scene has developed has naturally been filtered through the entire history of Japanese culture and arts, just as the music of any country is shaped by that country's past. Thus, quite a few bands in Japan combine sounds in ways that appear very fresh and different to an American who has begun to tire of the often more predictable sounds of his native country's bands.[21]

One of the unexpected results of

93 exploring the world of Japanese noise and music was that I discovered that I enjoyed the Japanese take on certain styles much more than the American version. This holds true for styles like psychedelic rock as well as noise. In Japan, a band like **Fushitsusha** borrows influences from a band like **Blue Cheer**, which I never particularly cared for, and creates music which goes beyond any rock trio in existence. Likewise, Japanese noise groups draw influences from European and American sources (among others), but take them in very different directions.

I find the Japanese approach to making noise the most interesting and exciting, primarily because of their unique attitude towards creating noise—although I'm not sure any neat dividing line can be drawn. I think the lack of pretension most Japanese noise artists bring to their performances is due to the fact that they approach noise-making as play, as a way of expressing themselves unburdened by words, imagery, or a political agenda.

Many European and American noise groups I have encountered put their noise performances and releases into a context based on their political views. This sometimes has the effect of making the recordings serve as a mere backdrop to their philosophies. At the very least, it gives the noise an artificial air of importance, as if it carries some important message. It's difficult to determine whether the politics and philosophy came first and are being communicated via the noise, or whether the noise came first and is being focused via the political message.

For example, many Western noise artists have used crime and war photos and other horror imagery to illustrate their tape and record releases. Pornography and bondage images are also popular. It's as if the artists believe that because noise is anti-social and difficult to listen to, the imagery associated with it should be equally shocking. Quite a few American and European noise artists undoubtedly began making and recording noise as a way of intentionally shocking and offending.[22]

In contrast, much of the artwork on the noise releases from Japanese artists— like Hijokaidan, Incapacitants, and Masonna—has a playful feel and includes ironic or humorous titles and pictures. Several of Hijokaidan's releases, for example, are adorned with beautiful land-scape photographs or pictures of animals. The covers of Masonna's recent albums has an old-style, brightly colored psyche-delic feel.[23] Solmania's playfully named *Psycledelic* CD includes photographs of group founder Masahiko Ohno's motorcycle and the recording begins with the sound of its engine revving.

On the other hand, the use of porno-graphic and bondage photography on noise releases can be traced back to Merzbow's **Masami Akita**. Akita is renowned in Japan as the author of several books and magazine articles about *kinbaku*, or Japanese rope bondage.[24] Given that it's his field of study, it's not surprising that many of Merzbow's releases use related imagery. Why this led to other artists, mostly overseas, using this subject for their artwork (and usually with much lower-quality photography), I can only guess. I suppose in the beginning fans who were inspired by Merzbow's noise recordings to create their own recordings were inspired to adopt Akita's imagery as well. Personally, I find the connection between noise and that sort of imagery embarrass-ing. Hijokaidan's choice of beautiful, pas-toral photographs is far more interesting as a contrast to music that some people

The very open policy at Bears has made it an essential location in Osaka's music scene, since almost any band can play there, no matter how unknown. This is in stark contrast to many clubs in Japan, which are often pay-to-play, if a band can get a show in the first place.

 15. There is a rather large interest in the realm of psy-chedelia in Japan, resulting in a vibrant musical scene that includes bands like Angel'in Heavy Syrup, **Shizuka**, **High Rise**, **Acid Mothers Temple**, **Force Musick**, and **Ghost**. For some members of these bands and their audiences, the fascination with psychedelic music carries over into a taste for '60s-inspired clothing and accouterments. A few stores cater-ing to this niche specialize in these goods. Freak Scene, in Osaka's Shinsaibashi district, is managed by Masonna's Maso Yamazaki and **Fusao Toda** of Angel'in Heavy Syrup. The two have also formed a psychedelic band named **Christine 23 Onna**.

16. I'm repeatedly surprised to find that the smallest clubs in Japan (called live houses there) tend to have better and larger sound sys-tems than most medium-sized American clubs. The typical small live house in Tokyo is in the basement of a building—perhaps that makes soundproofing more feasible. They tend to have a narrow stairway entrance, small stages, and little ventilation. But the sound, even in the smallest, is usually far better than in their American equivalents—and often louder than I personally prefer!

17. In addition to his **Warm Garden** atmos-pheric project (mentioned elsewhere), Kosakai was a member of C.C.C.C. for several years and plays guitar in the noise supergroup **Bustmonsters** (also featuring Masami of Merzbow, Masonna, Ohno of Solmania, **Iwasaki** of **Monde Bruits**, and others), in addition to numerous other collaborations.

18. *G-Modern* magazine, published by P.S.F. Records, primarily covers the psychedelic and avant-garde jazz scenes. Issues have included features on Japanese artists like Fushitsusha, High Rise and **Kaneko Jutoku** (of **Kousokuya**), as well as international artists like **Neu!**, **Cluster**, and others. The magazine also features coverage of experimental and noise music, often written by Mikawa.

19. The *butoh* dance form was developed in Japan after World War II by **Tatsumi Hijikata** and **Kazuo Ohno**, and was first performed in 1959. Inspired somewhat by surrealism, dada, and German Expressionism, butoh aims to express the movements of the soul through the consider ugly.

As Jojo of Hijokaidan once said to me in an interview for *File 13* magazine, "I'm not really interested in appealing to the audience of people who listen only to noise music and collect abnormal photographs and things like that. I'd like those people to stop listening to noise and try listening to something more normal. They're making a mistake whenever they think of noise as connected with the abnormal.... I'd like them to be open."

Other artists give equally serious consideration to the packaging and design of their releases as they do to the noise itself. Aube's **Akifumi Nakajima** has carefully used his aesthetic sensibility to make his releases consistently elegant.[25] **Koji Tano**, aka **MSBR**, has made the packages of his cassettes, singles, and albums unique works of art, wrapping them within layers of thin papier-mâché, hand-painted newspaper constructions, or strange shapes made of hardened foam.[26]

One day I got a package in the mail from Koji that was notable for its dimensions: it was a cardboard box about three feet long and about a foot wide, but not very heavy. When I opened it I found his new seven-inch single inside, held, like the filling in a sandwich, between circular pieces of wood which were in turn attached to a long, skinny, wooden frame on wheels! This remains my favorite packaging design to this day.

April : Another Noise Trip

In April of 1994 I took another trip to Japan, during which I played three live shows with friends. The day after arriving in Tokyo, I played a guitar duo with Null (of Zeni Geva) at the Shinjuku Loft live house.

Our set was added to the bill at the last minute, so in the interest of keeping it brief we went straight into a powerful noise jam.

Playing with Null is very different from playing with Jojo, as Null's aesthetics are quite different. He doesn't view his guitar work as "noise" per se—it's more deliberate and, if not exactly composed, nonetheless more thought out and less ruled by chaotic abandon than the "pure" noise artists. Playing with Null, I found myself conscious of what was happening in the sound, and I took time to consider my decisions about what to play. I didn't reach the point of breaking away into freeform noise-making, but I nonetheless really enjoyed the performance. Null has developed a very atmospheric approach to his solo guitar work, often applying metal objects to the strings and creating loops of sound using sampler pedals, over which he plays additional layers.

I started by rubbing a small metal ruler on my guitar strings, which created a shimmering horde of notes. I then augmented them using a pitch shifter pedal that added duplicate notes shifted to higher frequencies. Null created his own vibrating carpet of textures and then I switched on my distortion pedal and started adding noisier scraping and squawking feedback. He responded with distorted sounds of his own making, and we quickly escalated into a raucous duet of most unguitarlike noises.

After the set, Null told me that he was surprised by how noisy my playing was. I told him that the rock feel of the club and the other bands on the bill, heavy rockers like **Def.Master**, **Cocobat**, and Null's own Zeni Geva, inspired me in an aggressive direction. He nodded and said that he had enjoyed it, although I wondered if he was disappointed that we didn't hold to a more atmospheric plane.

Live noise performances by Japanese

artists are almost entirely free of political preaching.[27] It's rare that they attempt to dress up the noise in terms of philosophy or pretension. Instead, in most cases a noise performance is just pure cathartic expression. The artists don't lose track of the fact that making noise is fun. I know of very few noise artists in Japan who do it because they want to shove their noise in people's faces to shock and offend them. But there can be some aggression to it, just as there's aggression in any honest outlet for frustration or emotion.

Jojo is infamous for getting out of control during Hijokaidan's performances. In fact, their earliest shows were part theater, and were intended to shock the audiences—which they frequently succeeded in doing.[28] But the idea of noise as the central goal won out over the theatricality.

I've seen Jojo throw his guitar to the floor and scream at it, shout at the audience, and scold his amplifier during performances. I watched a videotape of a show in a Tokyo University auditorium in which he became so enraged because the PA system wasn't loud enough that he used his guitar to smash all of the lights in the room. Once it was pitch black, the show was over. But the performances are undeniably fun, and certainly exciting.

The night after my show with Null, I played a guitar duo with Jojo at the Showboat club in Tokyo's Koenji neighborhood. After **Astro Black II** played, Jojo and I were on.[29] Of all the noise artists I've collaborated with before and since, I enjoy playing with Jojo the most. The sheer energy emanating from him while he performs is stronger than anyone else's. Each time we play together, I feel as though I absorb some power from him and can approach noise-making with a greater capacity and more to express.

As when I played with Hijokaidan for the first time, the moment we stepped on stage and turned up the amplifiers, the club erupted in sparks of cascading sonic mayhem. Jojo's fingers flew across his guitar strings—he plays without a pick—and he yanked on the strings to extract streams of skipping notes and wavering feedback tones. I chose to begin playing my guitar with my E-Bow, bowing to create extended, constant distorted tones and skipping it across the strings to elicit strange squeaks and metallic moans.[30] Then I changed to regular playing with a metal pick, which I used to chase hyper-fast notes around, echoing Jojo's chaotic abandon. I also used the side of the pick, which, since it was metal, clanged against the metal strings to make sharp, ringing sounds.

At one point, Jojo slumped down on the stage next to his amp, breathing heavily, and just let his guitar continue making noise, occasionally brushing the strings with his hand. I slowed a little as well. He jumped up again and his guitar roared back to full volume. Then he stood with his arms wide, his guitar feeding back on its own with strident high frequency tones. I used my E-Bow and, moving my slide up the strings, matched the tone so our guitars were singing together in a high-pitched chorus of distorted waves. It felt beautiful.

There are some noise artists in Japan whose shows are more "Western." Aube's Akifumi Nakajima, for example, sits behind a table covered with mixers and effects. As a more cerebral, less emotional performer, he has a more European attitude, and his recordings are usually more ambient than the harsh noise of Incapacitants or Hijokaidan. Indicative of his almost philosophical approach is the fact that in each of his releases he carefully utilizes only one sound source as his material. These sources have ranged from the sound of flowing water to the beat of his own heart. He has also made noise soundtracks for dance performances and gallery shows.

Playing noise music is clearly a form of release for many of its practitioners. It seems to be a good way to balance the desire for loudness and a certain amount of chaos with the need for everyday, even-tempered control. Perhaps just as some people need to go out and get drunk, others find a (more productive) outlet in noise.

I wouldn't define it as a cathartic release for me, and it's not an activity that I feel a compulsion to indulge in to escape. Nonetheless, I do feel somewhat cleansed after playing a heavy noise show. Maybe it's a combination of the adrenaline rush and a mental or emotional scrubbing, but I'm always alert and focused after a performance.

October : Noise Comes to America

Since I began meeting and corresponding with Japanese artists, I have organized a number of performances in San Francisco for Hijokaidan, C.C.C.C., Zeni Geva, and many others. Over the years I have watched the level of interest in these bands grow, but even at the beginning there was an obvious curiosity, particularly about the noise artists. Granted, San Francisco has a history of being home to a strong underground scene of experimental musicians, but even so, audiences have on occasion been surprisingly large.

In October 1994, some friends and I organized a noise festival, called "Kingdom of Noise," which included two artists from Japan during its three nights of noise shows. Masonna and Solmania came and we had the good fortune to find a well-known, local noise-rock band, **Steelpole Bathtub**, to headline the performance at one of the larger venues in San Francisco,

body in an attempt to achieve pure expression of the artist's soul. Additionally, the dance allows for a great deal of improvisation, rather than being strictly choreographed.

20. I actually thought the recording of that encore sounded great, so the following year I released it as the B-side of a **Trance** (my solo project) single released by the British label **Fourth Dimension**. I included comments about the xenophobic content. That was the only time I have ever personally encountered any sentiment like that in Japan, and I suppose it's not surprising that it came not from someone inside the noise scene but instead from the hardcore scene (and not from an exemplary specimen of that scene, actually).

21. One of the current examples of this fresh approach to combining styles is the so-called "Shibuya sound," spearheaded by **Pizzicato Five** and **Cornelius**. These artists adopt styles as different as **Beach Boys** pop, bossa nova, Latin rhythms, drum'n'bass, and punk rock to create a hybrid that sounds fresh again. The fact that both of these artists have been released in the U.S. to noticeable critical acclaim demonstrates that the American audience is ready for and interested in new approaches like this.

22. The primary example of this idea is probably the British noise group **Whitehouse**, founded by **William Bennett** in the early '80s. With songs like "My Cock's on Fire" and the early emphasis on pushing the envelope of pure white noise assault, Whitehouse was clearly begun with the express intention of offending as many people as possible. Ironically, early Whitehouse albums, now out of print, sell for large sums of money to noise collectors, while recent albums have found a relatively large audience (and one was recorded by noted engineer/producer **Steve Albini**).

23. The name Masonna was originally a pun as well, combining masochism and Madonna along with the Japanese word *onna*, or "woman." More recently the name was converted into an acronym for **Mademoiselle Anne Sanglante Ou Notre Nymphomanie Auréolé**. What that means, I don't know, but it's certainly an entertaining conglomeration of words.

24. There is a large community surrounding the art of *kinbaku*, or Japanese rope bondage. A number of

"Within art, music or whatever, as things move to the extremes, I think that they become noise."

—Masami Akita of Merzbow

the **Great American Music Hall**. It was quite something to experience the Japanese artists' massive noise assault in those beautiful, ornate surroundings (the club is reputed to have once been a brothel). When I brought them to the Music Hall, the Japanese were amazed. Masonna immediately decided to go to a music store to buy a wireless unit, which we did after the sound check. He used it to enable himself to leave the stage and run around the club through the audience while continuing to scream into his contact-miked canister. The show was a resounding success.

Solmania is usually the solo work of **Masahiko Ohno**.[31] On occasion, he enlists the help of others for live performances to fill out the sound—not that help is required. Ohno's noise is unique in part because he uses guitars which he has altered nearly beyond recognition. On one of his guitars, for example, he added a set of bass strings above the neck, parallel to the normal guitar strings. Then he installed a bass pickup and drilled the body to put in an output jack for the bass signal. Finally, he attached a microphone on a flexible neck and added an output jack for that as well. Thus he can play the guitar and scream into the microphone with three outputs into three separate amplifiers. Needless to say, this noise machine makes him more than a match for any three ordinary players. Another of his special guitars has two necks pointing away from each other, so it's actually two guitars in one.

Solmania performances are more like rock shows than most noise performances, partly because of Ohno's exciting onstage presence. With his long hair, tennis shoes, and t-shirts, he's like a punk rocker playing a guitar which just happens to be a noise monster. Ohno's Solmania T-shirts, adorned with cartoon monster drawings inspired by the **Big Daddy Roth** Rat-Fink style, perfectly embody his good-natured yet intense

manner. While performing, he struggles with the guitar, throws his head back, and "rocks" in a great balls-out noise manner.

The response to most of the noise shows I've helped organize has been good. It's clear that people are very interested in Japanese noise ideas. However, it's worth noting that avant-garde and noise scenes everywhere are much more participatory than mainstream music. That is, fans of mainstream bands attend shows to watch the bands, then go home: it's passive entertainment. That's usually not the case with noise and avant-garde audiences. These scenes are built around a core of people who are not only audience members, but also participants.

This is much the same phenomenon that I first encountered when sending tapes of my music out to people, taking part in an international network composed of doers, not consumers. People who were performing and making music were fans of their audience's music. Over the years I have found that this sort of participatory scene—at the risk of becoming too insular—helps to inspire members and fosters the energetic exchange of ideas and creativity.

After the first few San Francisco appearances by noise artists such as Hijokaidan and Merzbow, I observed that their live shows had inspired local artists, much as my impromptu performance with Hijokaidan had inspired me earlier. Prior to that, I believe that the rapidly-expanding list of releases by some Japanese artists, particularly Merzbow, had already begun to influence artists in the U.S. and Europe to explore the limits of noise recording and performance.

When I first became involved in the Japanese scene, only a couple of other labels in America were releasing Japanese indie bands. Probably the first was **RRRecords**, of Massachusetts. RRRecords' owner, **Ron Lessard**, was an early champi-

magazines, such as *SM Sniper* and *Kitan Club* (the latter in the 1950s), are filled with photographs and writings on this subject. Masami Akita has written for many of them and has contributed introductions and essays to books on the subject. Two of his albums, *Music for Bondage Performance* Vol. 1 and Vol. 2, are recordings for performances by the groups **Right Brain** and **Kinbiken**.

25. Akifumi Nakajima, in addition to his Aube work, has also operated the small, dedicated cassette label G.R.O.S.S. Releasing noise groups from around the world, every cassette has been presented with a carefully-designed cover, almost exclusively in the silver-and-black style that Nakajima has made his own. Some releases are nearly works of sculpture, such as the exemplary *Three Shrines* triple-cassette mounted in a triangular configuration. Nakajima, an industrial designer by trade, has also created artwork for other artists and labels.

26. Koji Tano has actually had art gallery exhibitions of his packaging designs, and his web site at www.msbr.com includes photographs of his work. Tano, who works a day job as a computer programmer, is also a talented manga artist whose twisted visions have appeared in the latest issues of *Ongaku Otaku* magazine.

27. I've seen quite a few noise performances in America with carefully-coordinated video footage of war atrocities, Nazi films, automobile accidents, and the like. I've also seen shows which mixed noise with political, spoken-word vocals or loud philosophical ranting. This sort of noise-as-message or noise-with-intent-to-shock approach seems to be almost exclusively Western, for some reason.

28. At a number of shows in 1981, Hijokaidan's members threw raw fish, seafood, and garbage, and an early member of the group, Semimaru, even urinated on the stage, as well as sometimes actually chasing audience members out of the venue. The group's ten-member performance at Shinjuku Loft in the summer of 1981 is legendary. A nicely-detailed history of the early exploits of Hijokaidan was published in *Opprobrium* magazine's fourth issue, in December 1997.

29. An offshoot of noise group C.C.C.C., Astro Black II consisted of **Mayuko Hino** playing a sheet of metal and **Hiroshi Hasegawa** playing keyboards. Their sound was like a psychedelic wall of noise, as if **Tangerine Dream** had on of experimental and noise artists everywhere, and some of his early releases in the 1980s included LPs by Merzbow, Masonna, and **Violent Onsen Geisha**. Compilations from RRRecords included contributions by a number of other early Japanese noise artists.

Another label, **Public Bath Records**, worked with a variety of styles. The company arranged U.S. tours for punk rockers **Sekiri** and Null's heavy rock band, Zeni Geva. They also released records by Japanese psychedelic bands such as **Subvert Blaze** and noise bands including Hanatarash, as well as the essential noise compilation of seven-inch singles, *Japan Bashing 3*. It was when they brought Sekiri to San Francisco that I first met Jojo and Junko of Hijokaidan, since Sekiri's releases are on Alchemy Records in Japan.

The interest from other foreign labels in Japanese artists (noise and otherwise) has grown considerably over the last few years. Witness, for example, the Boredoms signing with major labels and Merzbow releases on countless labels, large and small. I can't really say what the root cause of this change is. Certainly a cumulative effect is occurring as more and more people become aware that fascinating music and noise is being created in Japan. I think that this growth has only begun, and awareness will continue to expand among lovers of adventurous sounds worldwide, but it remains to be seen whether noise has an inherently small maximum audience.

Noise Is a Language

After my first two visits to Japan, I began learning the Japanese language, which seemed not only practical, but polite, as well. After all, when bands visit San Francisco, they do their best to use their English skills. While far more people in Japan can speak English than Americans can speak Japanese, it seemed wrong to rely on that. And I knew that learning Japanese would open more doors for me, albeit slowly. I didn't fool myself; I was well aware that learning Japanese would be a very long-term endeavor. But I also knew that it would be fun, rewarding, and would make my visits to Japan that much more enjoyable.

In retrospect, I find it amazing that it was possible for me to get so deeply involved in the noise scene in Japan without knowing the language. The truth is that English has moved a long way towards becoming a de facto communication standard. In my experience, this holds true for networking among the members of the international experimental music scene. But beyond that, I feel my ability to meet people and perform with them in Japan has been due to the combination of enthusiasm on both sides of the Pacific. It demonstrates the unimportance of language in this context. In my experience, people in the underground scene are very enthusiastic about sharing and making things happen. At the same time, since we're dealing with music and noise, language isn't as important as one might think. After all, the point of making music and noise is to communicate through those media. Recordings and performances don't require any language to make themselves clear—they are a language in and of themselves.

I returned to Japan again in the fall of 1995. Once again, I arranged to play shows with a number of friends. My first performance during that trip was another guitar noise duet with Jojo, at one of my favorite Tokyo clubs, **La Mama**, in Shibuya. Perhaps because the Incapacitants played right before us, I found myself inspired to create a particularly heavy noise sound, rather than my often spacier style. The two of us played for a fairly short time—perhaps only twenty minutes—but it was all very dense and thick. I could feel the sound almost more than I could hear it, or so it seemed. Instead of aiming for specific sounds, I concentrated on density, on combining with the sound coming from Jojo to help construct a barrier of sound, like the big rocks in a castle wall.

I asked Jojo what he thought about while performing and he compared the experience to ESP. "On stage, you play sound and I play sound; you give me your sound with images and I give you images. Maybe at the top of the trance, I can talk with the guitar and I can talk with noise and I can talk without words."

It is this communication that makes the best noise performances so enjoyable. This is also one reason why I have never enjoyed noise recordings as much as I do live noise shows. In person, there can be an energy that is impossible to fully capture on a recording. And obviously there is the visual aspect, which can be very powerful. Still, even a videotape can't carry the personal energy of the performers. At a show by Masonna, Incapacitants, or C.C.C.C., for example, the bands convey very different, powerful images and feelings. Masonna's aggressive, kinetic style is that of a person pushing himself as far as he can go before he collapses. Incapacitants positively vibrate with their effort to explode with noise, and they respond to each others' shifting sounds without even looking at each other.

Some of C.C.C.C.'s shows were the most theatrical of any I have witnessed in Japan. Leader **Mayuko Hino** was formerly an actress and model, and still works as a dancer. Her experience was obvious in C.C.C.C.'s live performance style. Now, with the duo Mne-mic, with performer Ranko Onishi, Hino stands up front playing a theremin with dramatic, sweeping gestures. Sometimes she holds a big sheet of metal and waves it, creating thunderous shards of noise. The members of the group emanate the calm feeling of the eye within the storm. It's almost as if, by creating this immense wall of noise from within, a peaceful serenity is left behind.

During some of C.C.C.C.'s early shows, Hino would perform a slow theatrical dance inspired by her past experience acting in bondage films. She would come out dressed in a kimono, then disrobe to reveal that she was wearing a rope bondage harness. While the other members of the group (at that time it was a quartet) created their ever-shifting wall of mind-bending noise, Hino would light a red candle and slowly, methodically, drip the candle wax on her arms and body.

This performance was meant to be beautiful and meaningful, and indeed it was. But she discontinued it because audiences (primarily outside Japan, I believe) misunderstood it. Due to the link between bondage/S-M imagery and some noise artists, her use of the ropes and candle wax was being taken out of the context she intended.

The key to noise, for me, is a wordless communication which is in each case unmistakable yet clearly open to different interpretations. No doubt every individual will see and hear something unique, but nobody can fail to come away unaffected. However, when the performance is expanded—whether to theater, politics, or philosophy—it changes the way in which the noise itself is understood.

When I asked Jojo about communication and noise, he summed it up like this: "We can't say everything with language; language is very limited. Also, music is sometimes limited. But noise is everything.

We can play noise that includes things that we can't say with language."

In Osaka, during my 1995 trip to Japan, I played a different kind of noise duet with **Seiichi Yamamoto**.[32] It was different in part because I played drums rather than guitar. I considered it a chance to do something unusual, and also to challenge myself; while I had played drums for a while, being the sole focus of rhythmic attention and filling the sonic space as half of a duo was a little daunting.

Before the show, Yamamoto and I talked it over briefly and agreed to begin very slowly and then speed up. We would make a sort of tribal-noise trance set. When we began, I was a bit nervous, but as planned, we started out slowly, leaving a lot of space. I hit the bass drum and the floor tom hard, then paused. Yamamoto was just holding the guitar cord. Instead of plugging it into his guitar immediately, he tapped the plug, which made a buzzing static. I slowly built up the rhythm until he plugged in his guitar and started flailing at it wildly, making a reverberating, multilayered chorus seemingly composed of a dozen fuzzy guitars.

Together, the two of us entered into a trance, blasting a full-speed psychedelic mass of rhythm and noise through the club. I quickly lost my nervousness, actually forgetting everything except the sound and rhythm. After about twelve minutes, Yamamoto had broken every string on his guitar, so he dropped it onto the stage and walked off. I met him backstage; both of us were breathing heavily, smiling and satisfied.

The following night, I played my last show for that visit at a Kyoto club called **Takutaku**. My performance was a very unusual duet with **Akifumi Nakajima**, a.k.a. Aube. As I mentioned earlier, all of Akifumi's work is based on taking a sound source and manipulating it beyond recognition. Water, heartbeats, and even the sound

added several distortion units to their setup. Hiroshi also plays solo as **Astro**, and has released some singles and contributed to compilations.

30. The E-Bow is a small, hand-held unit that creates a magnetic field over a string on the guitar, causing it to vibrate and create a constant tone. The effect is similar to the one derived from using a normal bow on a violin, hence the name.

31. Ohno is also the graphic designer responsible for the artwork adorning many of Alchemy Records' beautiful releases. Perhaps one of the best designs is his own Solmania CD, *Trembling Tongues*, which includes a beautiful transparent overlay in the front and a die-cut circle in the center of the back tray card that allows the back of the insert art to show through.

32. Yamamoto is one of the key participants in Osaka's underground scene. As guitarist for the Boredoms and leader of Omoide Hatoba, he has established a high profile. He also manages the small club Bears, and his openness to new bands has helped countless artists get their start there. Yamamoto is a member of many other groups as well—the count has sometimes stretched beyond two dozen projects at a time! These have included **Rashinban**, **Novo Tono**, and **Live Under the Sky**. Recently, he has founded the **Ummo** label, which, like Bears, is devoted to the exposure of unknown bands as well as strange side projects by more well-known artists.

33. Kosakai has a solo project called **Warm Garden**, which is full of beautifully dark droning atmospheres. He has also participated in a number of other projects, such as **Gun**, which has an amazing CD of minimalist drones on the **Pataphysique Records** label.

34. As Monde Bruits, Iwasaki released a few tapes and one CD, *Selected Noise Works '93–'94*. These recordings showcased a Merzbow-like penchant for incredibly dense, ever-changing noise. After that CD, however, Iwasaki turned to creating more synthesizer-based atmospheric work, inspired by the ambient wave of techno sounds.

35. Gunma is a small town about an hour outside Tokyo, which the store owners referred to as *inaka*, or "the middle of nowhere." But the store, of the turning pages of the Bible have all been transformed by him into mysterious soundscapes.

For that evening's performance, we arranged to take my guitar signal and split it, with one line going into my amplifier and the other into his mixer. He then took the sound from my guitar and processed it through all of his effects. The result was confusing to me, since I simultaneously heard my playing and my own effects, creating echoes and waves of filtered noises through my amplifier, as well as the results of his processing, which resembled my playing, but only in a vestigial form. The notes I played came back to me several seconds later, sometimes pitch-shifted into higher notes or flipped back on themselves in reverse and echoing as if from a deep well. I began to experiment by playing something and then waiting to see what parts of it would be familiar to me a few seconds afterward. It was a great deal of fun.

'97 Noise and Music Interbreeding

The combination of noise with other sounds—pop music, collaged recordings, electronic beats—has slowly but surely become a part of the mainstream. Partly thanks to the growing popularity of techno and electronic music, listeners have become accustomed to occasional bursts of noise or rhythms constructed from indistinct synthesizer blasts. Popular artists like **Aphex Twin** and even **Nine Inch Nails** have made use of noise elements. At the same time, some noise artists have developed an interest in more atmospheric, if not exactly ambient, work: **Fumio Kosakai** from Incapacitants,[33]

Shohei Iwasaki of **Monde Bruits**,[34] and others have done more textural, less noisy recordings recently.

Likewise, I have started to develop a solo style which takes the emphasis off the harsh "wall of noise" aggression and instead focuses on creating shifting waves of sound with the guitar. When I returned to Japan for another tour in 1997, my first show was a solo performance. Because I was still a little unsure about my ability to pull off a good solo show, I was glad that the performance was a small affair at a record store out in Gunma-ken.[35] Despite some technical troubles at the beginning, due to my attempt to use two amplifiers for stereo effects (in the small space, they kept creating howls of feedback), I was fairly happy with the results. I set up layers of delay-repeated tones which I used as a foundation for other droning sounds. The effect was perhaps like several people playing distorted violins in a cathedral.

A few nights later, I played another duet with Null, at the **Heaven's Door** live house in Tokyo's Sangenjaya neighborhood. This time, rather than creating a noise squall, we arrived at an unspoken agreement to focus on creating a dark atmosphere. Without even discussing our ideas beforehand, we each started with calm, textural passages. I scraped the strings softly with a metal rod and let my wah-wah pedal carry the sound up and down through the frequency spectrum. The delay pedal multiplied the sounds so that the high and low scraping noises overlapped, murmuring around each other. Null threaded something through the strings of his guitar and tapped it lightly, which set up a chiming that was repeated, ringing and

echoing, through his effects. Throughout the set, we occasionally took turns getting quieter, letting the other take over briefly with heavier sounds. It was a particularly successful, enjoyable, and satisfying performance.

Jojo stands by his philosophy that noise is intense and harsh, but he has indulged in some fascinating combinations of noise with music over the years. He contributed a brief piece of noise to the major-label and otherwise purely pop *Turbulence* CD by **Syoko**, for example. Most notable is the **Slap Happy Humphrey** project, which blended Jojo's guitar noise with gorgeous renditions of songs by **Morita Doji**, a singer-songwriter from Jojo's youth.[36] One would expect the sudden intrusion of intense noise in the midst of otherwise delicate melodies to be ugly, but somehow it works, and the whole remains beautiful and emotional. When asked about it, Jojo pointed out that the goal is to *combine* music and noise, not simply to add noise on top of music—a fine distinction, and perhaps not an easy one to navigate.

When I played another duet with Jojo in Osaka, I considered trying to figure out a way to actually be musical and let Jojo combine noise with me, but I decided we didn't have sufficient time to plan it properly. I hope to try it out in the future. Instead, I let the flow happen, and for part of the set I remained atmospheric, which occasionally led Jojo to slow down and allow feedback to blend with my textures. However, by the performance's end we roared into a fierce, heavier noise onslaught.

Today: Overseas Noise Popularity

A couple of years ago, I decided to

publish a magazine devoted to Japanese independent music in order to help disseminate information about the scene over there. I had discovered many different bands and small labels, which I continually updated my friends about. It seemed time to find a way to spread the information to more people. I named the magazine *Ongaku Otaku*.[37]

Although I am most closely connected to the noise scene, I endeavor to give the magazine as wide a scope as possible. In the three issues I have published as of this writing, I have encouraged others to contribute to help broaden the scope. Interviews and record reviews have covered noise, avant-garde, punk rock, experimental pop, psychedelia, and more—anything that is not predictable mainstream pop, since that is so easy to find that it doesn't require my support.[38]

Ongaku Otaku has been well received. I've been particularly pleased to get letters from readers saying that they have discovered bands for the first time in its pages. My concept was to aid in the quest for interesting music. I benefit as much as anyone else. I enjoy the act of discovery; when I buy an album in a Tokyo store and take it home, or when I get something in the mail and check it out, I'm always in suspense about what I may find. If it's something cool, I'm enthusiastic about reviewing it in *Ongaku Otaku* to pass the word along, share the experience, and make it easier for other people to find the album and enjoy it in turn.

Due to the magazine, I'm being contacted by ever more labels and bands. Recently, there seems to be so much going on that I wonder whether the independent scene has been growing by leaps and bounds or whether I'm

Comes Alive

simply better apprised of it now. I'm guessing that it's a combination of both.[39]

Oddly, the growing popularity of independent Japanese bands such as the **Boredoms**, **Buffalo Daughter**, and **Guitar Wolf** in the U.S. has been reflected back to Japan, increasing the popularity of these and other bands in their homeland. Perhaps it's the same mechanism that led Americans as far back as **Josephine Baker** and **Jimi Hendrix** to go overseas to earn the fame that eluded them at home.

In any case, this is also true, to a lesser extent, within the noise scene. In fact, some of the original Japanese noise artists have said that the younger generation of artists have started making noise only because they want to become famous, not because they really enjoy it for its own sake. I personally find that hard to believe. But if this is so, it's certainly a limited kind of fame—even Merzbow, the most infamous member of the scene, doesn't sell more than a couple of thousand copies of any given album. That's hardly the kind of success that dreams are made of.[40]

Whatever attention the noise scene has received hasn't seemed to make any real difference to the people involved. Since, by its nature, the audience is limited, the scene remains largely free of those seeking stardom. Some claim that noise may break through and become popular, but this seems very unlikely to me. The rewards in this tiny scene come only from participation.

Participants get their satisfaction from the act of expression. It's pure expression that matters most, not preaching or making statements. Ultimately, I think I appreciate the noise from Japan most of all because of its concept of expressing oneself through noise for which the only context is the personality and emotions of the performers.

called **Omega Point**, was very impressive. Although small, it was crammed full of obscure punk rock and even more obscure jazz and experimental records. I can't imagine finding a store like it in America outside a major city. One room of the two was set up for performing, with seats for a small audience and a video camera.

36. Slap Happy Humphrey included vocals by **Mineko Itakura**, singer and bassist for Angel'in Heavy Syrup, a marvelous psychedelic group available on Alchemy Records. Slap Happy Humphrey released a single and one CD (on Alchemy and licensed by **Public Bath** in the U.S.), but were then forced by Morita Doji's lawyers to cease production. Apparently she found the introduction of noise into her songs distasteful. This is ironic, since the project was intended as an homage to songs that Jojo had felt very strongly about since his childhood.

37. Literally, *ongaku otaku* means music maniac. The word *otaku* has come to be used as a synonym for fan, but can also have the negative connotation of someone with a truly unhealthy obsession. The magazine's name, though, always elicits a chuckle from Japanese readers.

38. On the other hand, a strong interest in J-Pop has grown in America. Despite the fact that most of J-Pop is candy-coated and carefully manufactured, it is different enough from American pop to stand out as an interesting phenomenon, if not as interesting music.

39. My Japanese friends have indicated that there has indeed been a huge surge in independent labels and underground bands in their country, despite the fact that Japan's economy long ago settled from the '80s bubble. It's quite possible that the economic downturn has caused the opposite effect in the arts, encouraging young people to experiment, rather than to simply buy the products that are offered to them.

40. The only noise artist on a major label that I know of is **Violent Onsen Geisha**, whose work is more based on a surreal collage aesthetic than true noise. By combining elements of noise with countless samples of all kinds of music, Violent Onsen Geisha spins out wacky, entertaining recordings. By no means a huge seller, some people have nonetheless muttered words to the effect that Violent Onsen Geisha's Nakahara "sold out" and softened his sound in order to get a record deal—proof that a certain amount of jealousy is always present.

"The performer comes out through the noise, so if I want to learn more about someone,

I'll listen to his or her noise."

—Mayuko Hino of Mne-mic.

future trend

Although the Japanese noise scene has been getting its share of attention recently, it certainly has a long, long way to go before it hits the mainstream—if it ever does. Certainly, some successful bands, such as **Nine Inch Nails** and **Prodigy**, have begun to integrate noise elements into their work. The recent incursions into the charts by electronic bands such as **Atari Teenage Riot** have begun to help listeners grow accustomed to sounds beyond those of standard rock bands.

But these events are not going to open the way for **Hijokaidan** or **Merzbow** to go gold or platinum with one of their upcoming releases. While Atari Teenage Riot and Merzbow have actually collaborated, the former's moderate sales success no doubt owes much to their vocals, rhythms, and presentation—qualities that most noise acts generally ignore.

The integration of noise with other forms of music will doubtless continue, and the results will be interesting to hear. However, noise purists will likely turn up their noses at these developments; their single-mindedness will keep the scene vibrant. But perhaps the cross-pollination will also help prevent stagnation in the noise scene.

The latest third wave of Japanese noise artists—such as **Government Alpha**, **Building of Gel**, and **Yukiko**—have already been contributing to the scene for some time now. But I haven't seen as many younger noise artists appearing recently as I expected. It may be that the noise scene has reached a point of growth such that there isn't room for new participants; however, I find that unlikely. More probably, we are simply undergoing a momentary lull during which current artists are redeveloping the necessary infrastructure to support future members of the scene.

In the early '90s, a peak occurred, during which there were comparatively frequent noise shows in which artists like **Masonna**, **Aube**, and **Solmania** made splashes. It is my hope that, thanks to the enthusiasm of the current movers and shakers, another peak is on its way that will include more and more performances by a variety of musicians. This energy will certainly encourage new activity and inspire younger fans to try their hand at noise.

Without a crystal ball, it's difficult (and dangerous) to predict what may lie in store for the Japanese noise scene some years from now. But if it echoes some of the scenes which inspired it, such as industrial and free jazz, we can make some guesses.

The industrial movement, after several years, was essentially co-opted. The label "industrial" was usurped by artists using emerging electronic technologies to create more beat-driven music, which later helped spawn the techno craze. However, other underground artists inspired by the industrial groups stayed with their original inspiration and continue to create intriguing, unusual music to this day.

The original free-jazz artists, on the other hand, have never, to my mind, affected or been affected by the musical mainstream. Perhaps simply by being a part—however much a fringe—of the jazz world, these artists have somehow been sheltered from being co-opted.

Perhaps noise will be so integrated into popular music that most current noise artists will either cross over or simply give up and find another occupation. Alternatively, noise may continue to be ignored by ninety-nine percent of the world and noise artists will happily toil on, unconcerned about what the music community at large thinks about them.

My bet lies with the latter, simply because I think the gap between "music" and "noise" is large enough to absorb the impact of the occasional contact between noise and the musical mainstream. Additionally, the sheer intensity of noise artists keeps the noise vision alive. In any case, I believe there will always be, somewhere in the deepest underground, noise artists at work, happily oblivious to the latest musical trends.

EASY TO FIND

1. 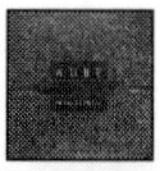
Aube
METAL DE METAL
CD, Manifold Records

Akifumi Nakajima always chooses a theme for his recordings and uses only one sound source for each. This time it's metal, primarily scraped and rubbed. In keeping with the theme, the CD is packaged in a beautiful steel folder. This is my favorite Aube release: the droning, buzzing sounds are truly hypnotic.

2. 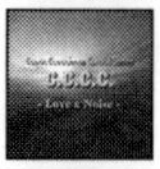
C.C.C.C.
LOVE & NOISE
CD, Endorphine Factory/P-Tapes

This 1996 CD from the trio formation of C.C.C.C. is a stunning noise release that sounds like the creation of our galaxy. Roaring static, hissing synthesizer tones, and rumbling bass combine to create a sense of what it might be like to be at the center of the maelstrom. It's more organic, slower to develop, and less heavily edited than many noise artists' work.

3. 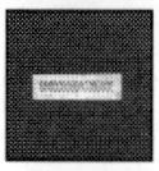
Contagious Orgasm
THE EXAMINATION OF AUDITORY SENSE
CD, Ant-Zen

Packaged in a beautiful corrugated black folder with a set of photo cards, Hiroshi Hashimoto's work straddles the boundary between noise and musique concrete. Over the years he has developed his own sound language, which tells unique stories. Combining synthesizers, distortion, voices, and more, each track is filled with a sense of purpose.

4. 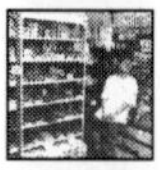
Hijokaidan
NOISE FROM TRADING CARDS
CD, Alchemy Records

Leader "Jojo" Hiroshige runs a successful sports-card business, hence the cover picture and title. Each of these three tracks, though all equally intense, has a distinct personality, due to the lineup. The first features the usual trio plus Merzbow's Masami Akita on drums, the second is only Jojo and Mikawa, and the third is Jojo and Junko live, with Mikawa joining them on tape. Powerful work, as always.

5. 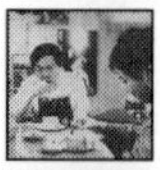
Incapacitants
AS LOUD AS POSSIBLE
CD, Zabriskie Point

This CD approaches the rewards of seeing their live performances. Particularly on the first track, **"Apoptosis"**, they throw in everything but the kitchen sink. While it remains as harsh and forbidding a listen as usual, the variety of textures and dynamics are extremely satisfying.

6. 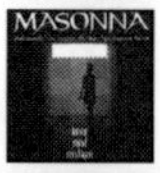
Masonna
INNER MIND MYSTIQUE
CD, Release Entertainment

"All Harshtronics and exclamation by Maso Yamazaki," say the credits, and that's truth in advertising. The tracks are simply numbered 1 through 7, and deal a more direct wall-of-noise assault than many other Masonna releases. At first it seems to lack dynamics, but after more listening, the details emerge, and as always, Maso's vocal exclamations are stunning.

7. 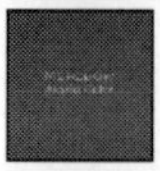
Merzbow
AKASHA GULVA
CD, Alien8 Recordings

One 73-minute track, recorded live in 1996 by the trio formation of Merzbow: Masami Akita, Reiko A., and Bara. This nice live document of Merzbow differs substantially from their studio work. The primary difference is the lack of editing, which allows the sounds to develop more slowly; the studio albums are always faster, cut-up experiences.

8. 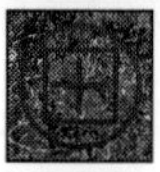
Monde Bruits
SELECTED NOISE WORKS 93–94
CD, Endorphine Factory/Charnel Music

The first CD released by Monde Bruits, this hour-long track splices together two years' worth of noise recordings. Mostly composed of fast-moving, ever-shifting squeaks, squawks, hissing distortion, and crackling electronic sounds, when played loudly, this can change your molecular structure.

9. 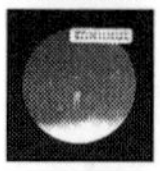
MSBR
DESTRUCTIVE LOCOMOTION
CD, Pure/RRRecords

Two long tracks of Koji Tano's distinct noise approach. MSBR's work tends to contain more low-end bass rumble than that of other noise artists. This is a fine example, with roaring distortion and slowly-blending synthesizer tones. At a high volume, it can collapse buildings, I'm convinced.

10. 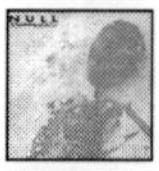
Null
TERMINAL BEACH
CD, Manifold Records

While Null doesn't consider his work noise, there's no doubt that many fans of the genre find his recordings very enjoyable. It's hard to believe that no synthesizers were used in this eerie guitar work. Late at night, this album will convince some listeners that unseen forces with evil intent are about.

11. 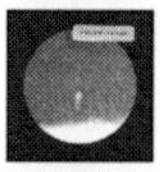
Pain Jerk
TRASHWARE
CD, Pure/RRRecords

Stuttering, chattering machines and whooshing laser blasts are followed by chugging mastodons and hovering extraterrestrial craft with loud engines and hostile intent. In addition, we get angry termites, frightened poltergeists, crystalline whines, underground nuclear tests, and much much more. Amazingly dense, hyperfast noise noise noise.

12. 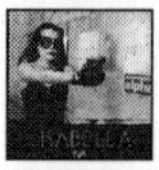
S. Isabella
POINT DE CAPTION
CD, Xerxes

This trio features Setsuko "Isabelle" Martin, Yoshiaki Funayama, and Yasutoshi Yoshida (a.k.a. noisemaker Government Alpha). This recording uses found sounds, collage, and contributions from numerous guests to create a fascinating experimental listen. It contains enough noise to satisfy those looking for that intensity, but changes frequently to incorporate many other sounds as well.

13. 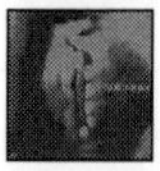
Solmania
TREMBLING TONGUES
CD, Alchemy Records

This Solmania release is a change from the past, as it's not a solo effort. Masahiko Ohno is joined by compatriot Katsumi Sugahara. Both of them play guitar (though Ohno's is so modified that it qualifies as a new kind of instrument). The five tracks are amazingly varied, from synthetic hums to the sound of the world cracking in half.

14. 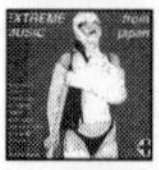
Various Artists
EXTREME MUSIC FROM JAPAN
CD, Susan Lawly

While sporting some truly unfortunate artwork, those who can ignore it will find a terrific collection of noise from Gerogerigegege, Masonna, Incapacitants, Merzbow, Government Alpha, Hijokaidan, and several others. A very fine introduction to many of the best noise artists.

15. 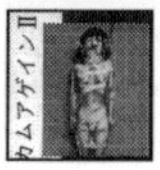
Various Artists
COME AGAIN II
CD, Furnace/Silent Records

This follow-up to the notorious *Come Again* collection perhaps suffers from having so many tracks that each is too short, but as an introduction to the noise scene, it can't be beat. Unfortunately, the artwork perpetuates the unfortunate association between noise and bondage/violence against women, but if you bypass that and concentrate on the sounds, you'll find a valuable resource.

WHERE TO FIND THEM

Anomalous Records, P.O. Box 22195, Seattle, WA 98122-0195 at www.anomalousrecords.com

Charnel Music, P.O. Box 170277, San Francisco, CA 94117-0277 at www.charnel.com

Manifold Records, P.O. Box 12266, Memphis, TN 38182 at www.vdospk.com/manifold

Relapse/Release Records, P.O. Box 251, Millersville, PA 17551 at www.relapse.com

RRRecords, 23 Central Street, Lowell, MA 01852

Self Abuse Records, 26 S. Main St. # 277, Concord, NH 03301 at www.mv.com/ipusers/selfabuse/home.html

Subterranean Records, P.O. Box 2530, Berkeley, CA 94702

collection

HARD TO GET

1. **Aube**
FLOOD-GATE
CD, Vanilla Records

This first CD displays the careful building of tension which Akifumi Nakajima perfected on his earlier cassette releases. Using only water as his initial sound source, through his processing he creates an almost frightening noise pressure. Rather than taking the sound beyond recognition, he preserves the essential liquidity and builds it into huge, mesmerizing walls of sound.

2. **C.C.C.C.**
COSMIC COINCIDENCE CONTROL CENTER
CD, Endorphine Factory

This first album by C.C.C.C. is a masterpiece of psychedelic noise. Using synthesizers, electronics, and bass, they create a thick noise onslaught that somehow manages to be intense without being incredibly harsh. It's possible to lose yourself more easily in these sounds than with almost any other noise album, especially during the mammoth last song, "**Sonic Machine**".

3. **The Gerogerigegege**
TOKYO ANAL DYNAMITE
CD, Vis a Vis

One of the funniest noise albums I own, this holds 75 ultrashort tracks with titles like "**Anal Bowling**", "**Kill Baby Kill**", "**Ass Morning**", and so forth, as well as covers of "**Satisfaction**" and "**Sheena is a Punk Rocker**", among others. Each song starts with a fast "1-2-3-4" count and then... sonic mayhem, randomly smashed drums, and guitar feedback. Over and over. A classic.

4. **Hanatarash**
LIVE!! 82 APR. 12 STUDIO AHIRU-OSAKA
CD, Mom'n'Dad

This weird release is one of a trilogy of live CD recordings from this peculiar record label. Each contains a live show and a collection of "incredibly strange music." On this one, it's "**The Exotic Mood of Chaotic Voo-Doo/Riot in Jungle**". The 25-minute live recording is composed of impenetrably chaotic banging, thumping, and feedback, but occasionally you can make out drums in the background.

5. **K2**
THE RUST
CD, Kinky Musik Institute

Perhaps the foremost metal-worker in the Japanese noise scene, Kimihide Kusafuka scrapes, bangs, rolls, and pounds metal junk, then processes these sounds through who-knows-what. This CD, with an impressive array of noise, is one of his finest moments. It feels like you're trapped inside a steel plant that's being demolished, or like you're in the biggest automobile accident you can imagine.

6. **Masonna**
SHINSEN NA CLITORIS
CD, Vanilla Records

When I first got this 32-minute album, I thought it was the most shockingly noisy thing I had ever heard. The combination of vocal screaming with hyper-fuzzed distortion took me aback more than purely inorganic noise. The super-fast editing makes it truly surreal. I snapped up this CD, limited to 499 copies, only by accidentally being in the right place at the right time.

7. **Merzbow**
CLOUD COCK OO GRAND
CD, ZSF Produkt

One of my favorite Merzbow albums, this was released in 1990 in an edition of 500 copies by Masami Akita on his own ZSF Produkt label as *Merz CD-01*. It's not the harshest Merzbow album; instead of concentrating on sheer intensity, it contains a varied collection of sounds, from metallic acoustics to reverberating scraping sounds and buzzing electronic hums.

8. **Pain Jerk**
GALLON GRAVY
CD, Creativeman Disc

The four tracks here display Kohei Gomi's ability to edit so intensely that he produces a new sound every few seconds. From the first moment of the CD (which is mastered extremely loudly), you are surrounded by crushing distortion and noise that is constantly shifting to throw you off-balance. There's no let-up until the CD is over.

9. **Various Artists**
NOISE FOREST
CD, Les Disques du Soleil

Released by a small label run out of an Osaka record store, this was one of the first compilations I got that covered many of the most infamous Japanese noise artists. With Merzbow, C.C.C.C., Solmania, Dislocation, Monde Bruits, Masonna, Violent Onsen Geisha and Incapacitants, it serves as an important introduction.

10. **Violent Onsen Geisha**
EXCRETE MUSIC
CD, Vanilla Records

Supposedly released after the death of the band members (shortly thereafter the sole member resurfaced feeling just fine), this 1991 CD starts with very quiet murmuring sounds, followed by literal explosions, feedback, rumbling, whistling, and weird voices coming and going. Later Violent Onsen Geisha releases delve more into collage and found sounds, but even on this album, his fondness for editing and cut-ups is evident.

WISH LIST

1. **Hanatarash**
HANATARASH
(LP)

This album stands as one of the most shockingly weird and noisy releases ever made, as well as one of the items most coveted by the hard-core noise *otaku*. Leader Eye Yamatsuka (now Yamataka) went on to some level of fame as the founder of the Boredoms, but this album demonstrates that back in the 1980s he went farther than most into the depths of insane noise chaos.

2. **Hijokaidan**
KING OF NOISE
(LP, Alchemy)

Alchemy's sixth release (it came out in 1985), this features five early tracks by Hijokaidan when they were still the duo of Jojo and Mikawa. It's a great document of these two noise stalwarts' process of learning about noisemaking.

3. **Masonna**
MASONNA VS BANANAMARA
(LP, Vanilla Records)

Limited to 290 copies, this 1989 release was Masonna's first nontape release. It was recorded directly with no mixing or overdubbing, and thus serves as a great example of Maso's original way of working. Each sound comes through clearly and harshly in the 29 tracks, each with a nonsense title.

4. **Various Artists**
COME AGAIN
(three 7-inch singles, Vanilla Records)

This infamous triple single collection was released sometime around 1989, and was limited to just a few hundred copies. It includes some early work by Masonna and others.

5. **Various Artists**
JAPAN BASHING THREE
(two 7-inch singles, Public Bath Records)

This double single collection, featuring one side each by Hijokaidan, Solmania, Hanatarash, and Masonna, was released in 1991 and was limited to 1000 copies, which were quickly snapped up by fans curious about these groups, who were just starting to earn some notoriety in the U.S.

BIO

MASON JONES was born in Ann Arbor, Michigan in 1964, but his family moved back and forth across the country several times during his youth. After graduating with a bachelor's degree from the University of Michigan, he and his partner swiftly moved to San Francisco.

Upon his arrival in 1988, he established the **Charnel Music** record label. Initially, it was simply intended as an outlet for his own music (mostly under the name **Trance**), but it grew out of control and accidentally became a "real" record label.

In the early '90s, as he was introduced to the music scene in Japan, Jones discovered that another benefit of living in San Francisco was its proximity to that country. While working from time to time doing computer programming (most recently internet/web development), he released CDs by Japanese artists and helped to organize shows in San Francisco by bands like **Zeni Geva**, **Hijokaidan**, **C.C.C.C.**, **Demi Semi Quaver**, **High Rise**, **Masonna**, **Solmania**, and others. Eventually, his enthusiasm got the better of him, and he began publishing the magazine *Ongaku Otaku* to help spread the word about the independent music scene in Japan.

Jones endeavors to visit Japan whenever he can to see friends, play shows, and discover more unknown bands by scouring the record stores and clubs in Tokyo and Osaka. Most recently he has been busy with his new band, **SubArachnoid Space**, playing improvised psychedelic space-rock here and there. He hopes to have the opportunity soon to introduce his bandmates to the Japanese scene in person.

Q&A

What are your main interests, aside from noise music?

Apart from music as a whole (I like psychedelic, hip-hop, avant-garde, and many other genres), I'm also a big fan of both art and literature. I draw and paint when I have the time, and my main inspiration comes from the dada and surrealist movements. **Ernst**, **Miro**, **Tanguy** and their fellows remain my favorites, since I can look at their paintings and always find something new and different in them. With literature, I'm particularly attached to the *fin de siècle* French decadent period, including the work of **Huysmans**, **Lautréamont**, and **Lorraine**. Their writing has such a dark, lovely feel. I've also been a long-time fan of **J. G. Ballard**, **William S. Burroughs**, **Paul Bowles**, **Angela Carter**...and so many others.

How large is your collection of noise music? What is its total value?

It's only a portion of my collection of albums, tapes, and CDs, but it's an important part of it, that's for sure. I've never really counted, but it numbers somewhere between three or four hundred pieces, I'd say. A lot of them are tapes, which are stacked up everywhere around here and hence hard to count. Quite a few noise artists are toiling away recording and sending out tapes to people and may never release a CD. The way I figure it, the format doesn't matter. But it's nonetheless true, unfortunately, that tapes won't get as widely distributed as a CD. Regarding the total value of my collection...I really have no idea! I'm afraid to calculate how much I've spent on it, but I've also gotten a great deal of it by trading my own releases with the artists. Calculating the value is probably impossible at this point.

What's the most expensive item in your collection?

If you mean which one cost me the most, well, I've never paid more than thirty or forty dollars for a release. If you mean which one is worth the most now...hm. Probably one of these: Masonna's *Masonna vs Bananamara* LP, which was limited to only 290 copies (Mine's autographed, too); Hijokaidan's *King of Noise* LP, which was limited, I think, to 500 copies; or **Merzbow**'s *Material Action 2* LP, released in a limited edition in 1982. Each of these is an important release by an artist who's now fairly notorious, and they were all fairly limited to begin with. But I haven't really kept track of what things are worth now, since I have no intention of selling them!

Which is the most important item to you?

That's a tough one. Maybe **C.C.C.C.**'s first release, the *Cosmic Coincidence Control Center* CD, which was also the first release from the **Endorphine Factory** label. It's a really great album, with a very psychedelic sort of noise, and after I heard it and met **Mayuko Hino**, the leader of C.C.C.C., we became very good friends.

What was your first Japanese noise music purchase?

I don't know if I can remember the first release by a Japanese noise artist that I bought, but the *Dead Tech II* compilation LP (though not really noise), which I got in the mid-'80s, was probably the most important in terms of introducing me to the exciting noise scene thriving in Japan.

TOKYO

Yuji Oniki

DIARY no.3

June 1

I visit old haunts in Takadanobaba in the Shinjuku district. The inconspicuous love hotels are still around and thriving despite the declining economy, but the public bathhouse I used to go to every evening has been leveled, replaced by the scaffolding for a new condo. I have to walk up and down the alley several times double-checking, as if I'm experiencing a slight disk error in my memory. When I realize that the bathhouse is really gone, I begin to doubt my memory of the place, of the middle-aged customers, the big-haired woman who worked behind the counter, the tiled floors of the wide open bath. What I remember seems no more reliable than a long-ago dream mistaken for a real event.

What would happen if all my favorite buildings (not too many, so it's not too unlikely) vanished from Tokyo? Would I, or could I, live in a place where the landscape lasts less than a lifetime? I'm learning that no matter how fond my memories of a place may be, my nostalgia, along with any assurance of belonging, can be demolished instantaneously. It's as if I'm being told, "Don't think you belong anywhere, because where you belong, along with you yourself, can and will be changed at any moment."

Through replication, suburbia creates brand new but identical topographies that annihilate unique crumbling old city- and townscapes. If we miss a certain place that no longer exists, it's because it's as irreplaceable as a friend. That something new can replace this place only heightens our longing. The identical tract housing of the suburbs thrives because it extinguishes the fear behind the longing and desire to belong some place *in particular*.

Revisiting the neighborhood in Takadanobaba, I don't really long for the bathhouse or the times I spent there. It isn't as if I had epiphanies while rinsing my back or hopping into the scalding water. I just feel slightly jarred, left with some weird aftertaste of doubt that makes me think I imagined the place, that it's just a piss-poor fantasy of Japan pastiched out of comics, TV shows, and movies.

Speaking of comic books, there's a noodle joint down the street that's frequented by one of my all-time favorite manga artists, **Kazuo Umezu**, creator of ***Hyoryu Kyoshitsu*** (The Exiled Classroom). I don't know if I've ever been there when he was, because I don't know what he looks like (and I kinda don't want to know, since he's drawn some of the scariest images in manga history), but I know he lives in the vicinity, and there's a signed drawing of his famous character, Makoto-chan pasted on the wall across from the noodle menu.

I want to go in and be reassured by the smell of fried soba noodles, the sight of this familiar snot-nosed cartoon-face and the piles of weekly magazines splotched with soup and beer stains. Unfortunately, the shop isn't open yet, which reminds me

that, despite the international image of Tokyo as a bustling city of salarymen and office ladies jam-packed into subways, the shops open relatively late, usually after ten, the moment marked by the rattling of opening metal shutters.

The only exception to this is the twenty-four-hour convenience stores sprouting up not only in this city but all over the country: the one lifestyle commodity successfully exported to Japan. What's amazing is how the convenience store has morphed into its own Japanese style. People actually hang out at these places, reading through magazines before contemplating which plastic-wrapped lunch or dinner they'll buy to wash down with their beer, **Pocari Sweat**, or canned ice coffee. When was the last time you hung out at a **7-11**?

At night I go to the **Milk** club in the **Ebisu** district of Tokyo to hear noise guitarist **Keiji Haino**. The DJ is playing ear-shattering house music while downstairs a bunch of kids gawk at a video projection of techno-acid cartoons. Lights spin around the floor, lighting up their stoned faces; they're not really talking much, just hanging out.

The lights go off upstairs and Haino's guitar begins to rumble in the dark. Then **Tatsuya Yoshida** of **Ruins** begins tapping on his drums. Haino swings his head in the air as he rushes to the mike screaming at a volume even more excruciating than his guitar. A burst of drums and then a wall of sound, less like the white noise from a TV set and more like the organic premonition of a natural disaster. Electricity is the last thing that comes to mind here. Within a half hour it's all over and the band disappears behind the stage. The DJ returns, the noise fans clear out, and the dance crowd comes in; one of

them, dressed in a Winnie-the-Pooh outfit, gyrates spastically.

As it turns out, **Enju**, Haino's manager, is a friend of mine. I go aboveground outside and find her, Haino, their friend Keiko, and Yoshida taking a break before packing their equipment into their cars. Haino is a bit frenetic because he usually plays two-hour sets and this one clocked in under twenty minutes. He jokes with Yoshida, "Hey, let's take the show somewhere else now!" A cop comes by to tell us that the neighbors are complaining about a disturbance outside. (If they call this a disturbance, God knows what they'd say about my neighborhood in Oakland, California. "Hey, there's a riot goin' on out there!") Yoshida leaves, and the four of us remaining decide to go get a bite to eat.

I have to admit, I'm really taken aback by Haino. I had this image of him, clothed in his trademark all-black outfits, as someone who takes himself a bit too seriously. I was proven wrong on all counts. He's super nice and funny, inserting humorous comments here and there. We hardly talk about music, concentrating instead on what to order, but occasionally he says something about the **Beatles** with just as much enthusiasm as when he mentions avant-garde gurus such as **Captain Beefheart** or **Mayo Thomson**. His most striking comment that night is about making mistakes in his music: "The best version usually happens around the second or third try. I get really mad at the other members of my band [**Fushitsusha**] when they try to fix their mistakes after making them; it completely messes up the flow, which is, in the end, all that matters." The stereotype that musicians—particularly those who play extreme styles like punk, noise, or industrial—are inarticulate isn't holding up very well with these folks in Tokyo.

TAKASHI'S FIRST FISSION

BY: FURUYA USAMARU

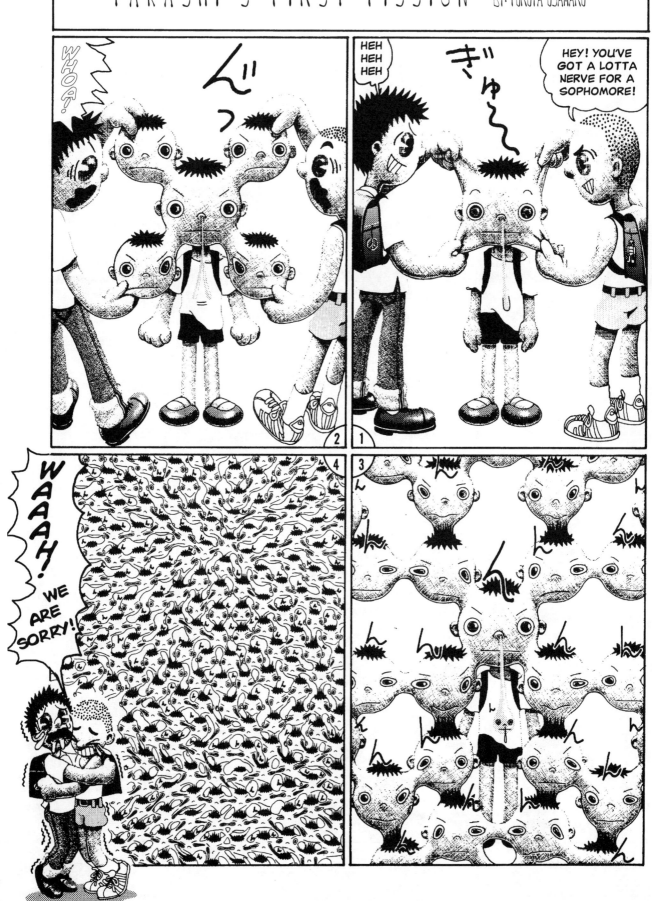

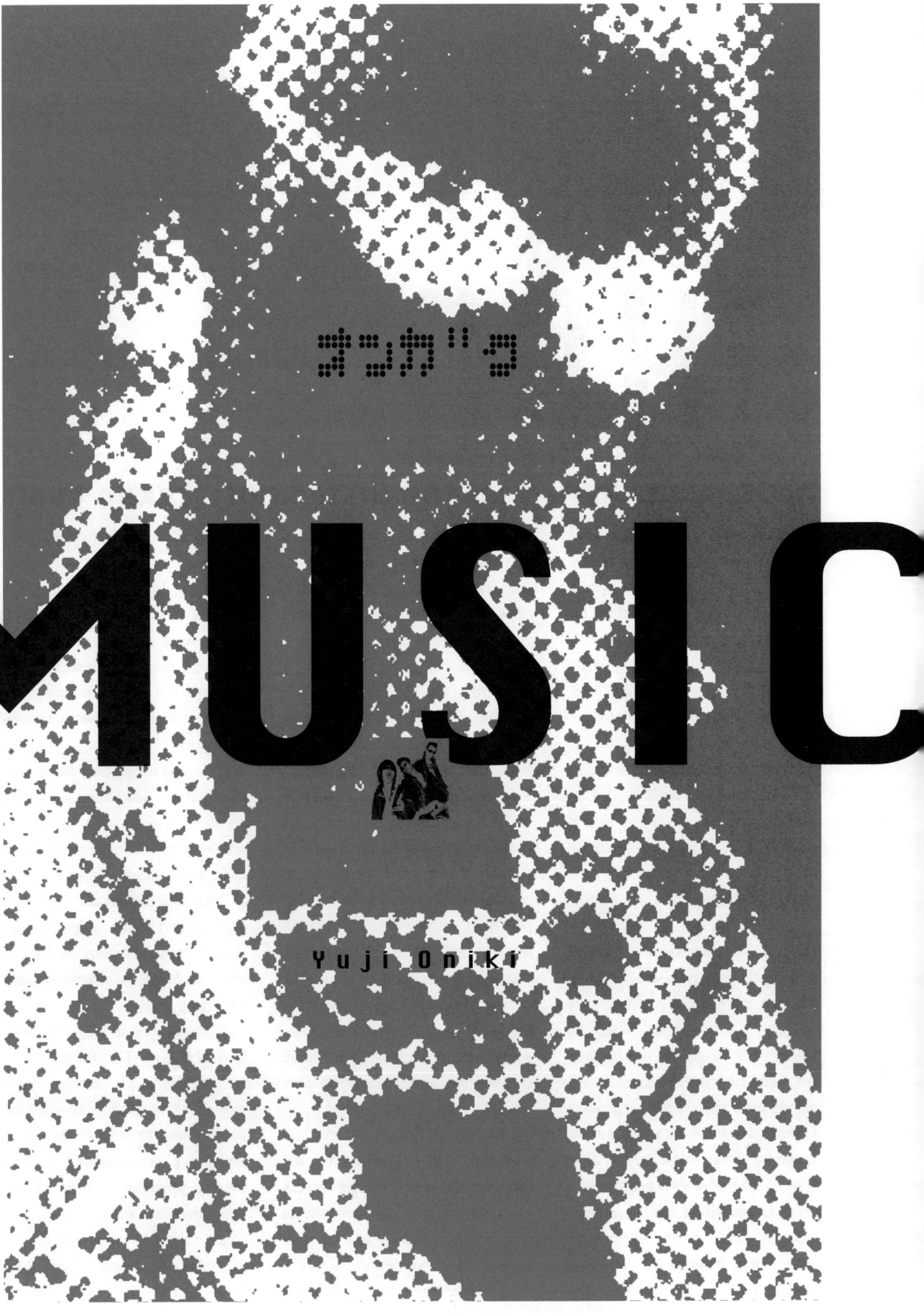

おんがく

MUSIC

Yuji Oniki

overview

Postwar J-Pop a.k.a. the History of "Lokun Loll"

Rock-'n'-roll came to Japan the moment the native rolling *r* became an *l*. Japanese musicians deliberately mispronounced the foreign words, spitting out butchered English. Similarly, rockabilly degenerated into *lockabiri*. For an updated version of this, just spin **Guitar Wolf**'s U.S. debut release *Planet of the Wolves*, in which singer **Seiji** yelps, "Lockun loll, yeah!" If language was a virus from outer space then the consonant "l" infected the Japanese tongue enough to give birth to rock and roll. But before the "r" turned into an "l" there were other detours to be made before Japan began to rock.

In the early '60s, the blueprints for Japanese culture were still being drawn in America. The folk revival taking place in New York and New England was a mass movement in which you sang along with everyone else. As with the contemporaneous student movement, you were supposed to meld into a single voice on your search for the Garden of Eden. But without a native Appalachia or blues-ridden Deep South to draw on, the neofolk scene in Japan often ended up producing a kind of simulated America. And when it came down to it, the populist ideals of **Woody Guthrie** or **Pete Seeger** didn't translate very well. How

natural would the *shamisen* folk songs of ghost-infested Japanese villages sound in the throat of an American folk singer? Folk music, for all its utopian vision, doesn't cross national borders well.

Before pop music could come to Japan, the guitar had to be imported into the culture. Right around when **Bob Dylan** plugged in his electric to offend American folk purists and in the midst of the period of high-growth economics that took place after the 1964 Tokyo Olympics, the group sounds genre emerged. For the most part, the bands that played group sounds were corporate creations and pale imitations of American pop bands, Japanese versions of the **Monkees**. Soon fed up with these syrupy bubblegum pop bands, a new movement emerged, one that gained momentum as angst-ridden youth were drawn to music as a medium for social protest. They knew all too well that politics had already been coopted by high-growth economics.

Acoustic performers like the **Folk Crusaders**, **RC Succession**, and **Nobuyoshi Okabayashi** emerged from this youth subculture. Instead of harking back to some imaginary pastoral America, these city poets lampooned contemporary life in Japan. Popular music—whether folk, rock-'n-

roll, or jazz—had to be in the present tense. Technology and electricity were on their side. The Folk Crusaders' million-selling single, **"Ora wa Shinjimatta da"** (I Kicked the Bucket), was a folksy song sped up until the singers sounded like chipmunks strumming frenetically on ukuleles instead of guitars; it undermined the folk movement's promise of authenticity.

Because the electric guitar and bass were postwar inventions, no one—even in the States—really knew how to use them yet. They were still outside the iron grip of tradition and national allegiance. Plucking out **"This Land is Your Land"** on the banjo might transport you back in time and space, but banging out three fuzzy ear-shattering chords would lead you nowhere else but to the present.

Mostly unknown, these underground bands of the early '70s stuck to the essential pop ethic: rip off other musicians to come up with a conglomeration of sounds that has never been heard before. Bands like **Jacks** reincorporated the echo-drenched garage rock of America into their slow strung-out tempo songs, creating spooky psychedelic sounds haunted by the dark folklore of premodern Japan. Barely remembered as *lokun loll* miscarriages, these sounds came and went because no one besides the youth generation of the time was interested. The nation was still geared towards importing rock-'n'-roll as a foreign commodity, which meant that rock as a way of life simply couldn't take place yet in Japan. Just because you could consume rock-'n'-roll didn't mean you were allowed to participate in its creation.

While a good chunk of second generation Anglo-American rock came from college dropouts, from Bob Dylan to **Syd Barrett**, the most interesting music in Japan came from those who couldn't get into college. Thousands of *ronin*, high school graduates who had failed their college entrance exams, were wandering around Tokyo unemployed, supposedly preparing for next year's exams. In the meantime, they inadvertently formed a slacker culture that couldn't help but get into rock-'n'-roll. One of these ronin, **Yosui Inoue**, eventually released the first rock album to sell over a million copies: *A World of Ice* (Kohri no Sekai). Rock-'n'-roll was now a national commodity.

The downside was that, by the late '70s, Japanese rock entered the dark decade of fusion rock and other hedonistic forms of California culture typified by overkill guitar solos à la the ending of the **Eagles'** **"Hotel California"**. Instead of creatively incorporating current technology and everyday life, rock music became commodified, reduced to a kind of muzak soundtrack for the narcissistic lifestyle promised by Japan's boom decade. The quantifiable

capitalist norms of technique and equipment became the fetishized standards of this era of rock.

Doing away with technique and advocating the automation ethic of technology, **Yellow Magic Orchestra** emerged with songs for the future. Their 1979 debut album of the same name finally broke the sound barrier that defined pop rock as American or Western. In retrospect, it should have been obvious that the first sonic innovations in Japan would be electronic. YMO managed to offend critics abroad, particularly in the States, by tapping into America's anxiety over losing its monopoly on consumer culture and technology. *The Washington Post* didn't take too kindly to YMO, calling their music "mechanical mush, an incessant drone which blurs any musical thought or substance" and accusing them of playing a part in the "technocrat invasion in contemporary music."

The fact that YMO's fashions alluded to both the Soviet Union and Nazi Germany didn't help. The other half of this technocrat invasion was **Kraftwerk**. Hmm... Do I smell a subconscious hostility towards techno as the postwar music of the defeated Axis powers? "Christ, they're not doing it with politics anymore, but just look what they're doing to our music!"

This was music of the future, closer to science fiction than rock-'n'-roll, although the two are never that far apart. Only the postwar paranoia of the Cold War could breed such bizarre twins. For many Americans, by the '70s, rock-'n'-roll had

regressed into a form of expression limited to girls, cars, and booze—you know, the concrete things around you that are as tangible as Coca Cola. In contrast, the futuristic landscapes evoked by YMO didn't even exist.

It wasn't until over ten years later, when the digital revolution did well for the American economy, that techno happily wedded to cyberspace optimism was, well, a-OK. As one reviewer put it in 1992, revising the history of techno with regard to YMO's re-released albums, "[This] pathbreaking synth band's 1978 debut album sounds as though it could have been recorded this year, its production values are so far ahead of their time...This Japanese trio crafted sophisticated, melodic tunes with sequencers, drum machines, and other electronic artillery before many of their European and American counterparts had ever laid their fingers on a synthesizer."

YMO was huge in Japan, but before they could make any impact abroad they called it quits. However, right around the time YMO was abandoned, three women working as "office ladies" in Osaka began making tapes of their threesome guitar rock. They called themselves **Shonen Knife**. Virtually unknown in Japan, they rapidly gained a reputation among American indie rockers like **Sonic Youth**. Their songs, partly due to their do-it-yourself sound and partly due to their lack of technical virtuosity, followed odd chord progressions—if you could call them that—laced with oblique lyrics about such mundane themes as cleaning liquids and other household products. If YMO

was rock for the cosmic future, this was pop for everyday life. Either way, these bands gained a cult following abroad that was big enough to plant the idea that American rock-'n'-roll was no longer a form to imitate but one to transform.

It's the strange sonic brew of the '90s in Japan that has most attracted worldwide attention. American indie rock bands hungering for something more than the incestuous post-rock sounds of their Oedipal Lolita nation have found inspiration in the local Tokyo and Osaka noise music scenes represented by **Keiji Haino**, **The Boredoms**, **Ruins**, and others. By mid-decade, the Boredoms were on the **Warner Brothers** label, and Haino and Ruins were consistently invited to tour both the U.S. and Europe. Without the hyperneurotic drive of punk and speed metal, these bands were just as much—if not more—of an assault on the ears. Indifferent to 4/4 time signatures, but not without their own signature grooves, their music was more like pulses and other bodily functions amplified over 1,000 watts. Soon other bands, such as **Melt Banana**, combined the noise ethic of Haino and The Boredoms with speed core and rap. Melt Banana blazed across the U.S., only taking a breather to record an entire album of twenty-four songs (each one clocking in under two minutes) with **Steve Albini** (producer of **Nirvana**).

But something stranger than noise came on the scene by the latter part of the decade. The past was being resurrected. Which was nothing new—fashions from past decades had already returned, but the clothes were international, not Japanese. What was strange and new was that for once Japan revived its *own* consumer culture from the '60s onward, instead of American and European styles. During the '60s, the average Japanese believed foreign fashions and singers were the ultimate in cool, but now the forgotten Japanese accouterments of this decade came back with a vengeance, assuring the Japanese consumer that their own culture wasn't just a poor imitation, but idiosyncratic in its own right and worthy of resuscitation.

The most well-known bands, such as **Pizzicato Five**, have delved into the archives to revive not only the sounds but also the fashions and photography of the times, so much so that their publicity photos look like stills from a series of '60s Japanese B-movies. The fact that they can pull this off on album after album reveals how rich the pop culture of Japan's postwar years turned out to be in retrospect.

There are others, though, who instead of reproducing glamour-magazine pop, went underground to give the buried sounds of psychedelia and garage rock a second life. The album *Second Time Around*, released by neopsychedelic folk band **Ghost**, heralded this return of the living dead, of sounds instead of souls transmigrating from the forgotten dark side of psychedelia to evoke otherworldly haunted mantras. Meanwhile, the leather-clad greasy-haired motorcycle trio **Guitar Wolf** revved up native posthumous garage-rock sounds to destroy any delusion that rock-'n'-roll can be progressive or modern. Sleeping through metal, new wave, and grunge, Guitar Wolf woke up and howled, "Gotta get more gas for my bike!" reclaiming rock-'n'-roll as something no less prehistoric than the dinosaur fuel feeding their bikes.

Even those '60s Tokyo bands wiped off the face of Tokyo's amnesiac map of pop culture were revived not by nostalgic over-the-hill middle-aged rockers but by twenty-something kids who found the music of their local former bands as evocative as any Dylan or **Rolling Stones** recording. Indigenous folk rock—so unhip just a few years ago—suddenly became a treasured archive, and young popsters like **Keiichi Sokabe** of **Sunny Day Service**, one of Tokyo's most popular indie bands, did their best to spread the new gospel.

Groups like **Demi Semi Quaver** and **Sakana** have managed to boil together a variety of influences from both here and abroad into one bizarre coherent sound, twisting their native tongue and foreign languages inside out, as if to remind us that rock-'n'-roll has always been about bastardizing languages, all the more so if they aren't ours.

The fact that all of this is taking place in a country slightly smaller than the state of California boggles the mind.

What seems most promising about this melting pot is the fact that the most interesting bands aren't attached to any particular genre. After establishing their kingdom of noise style, a band like the Boredoms can come up with a quiet record like *Super Roots 6* without giving you the impression that they're selling out. Instead, they make you wonder whether genres of music are really all that different from one another. The singer of the Boredoms, **Eye Yamatsuka**, says that when he first heard rock he wasn't able to distinguish between sounds he heard outside on the street and on the radio. The last time I saw Keiji Haino he was performing at the dance club **Milk**, where house music blared until Haino's thundering guitar and voice crashed in.

Allegiance toward one genre doesn't require betrayal of another. Displaying their communal link to the rave scene in Tokyo, **Sugar Plant** only took the layered droning guitars of **Galaxie 500** and the **Velvet Underground** as points of departure and then incorporated current techno into their second U.S. release, *After Afterhours*. **Cornelius** is Japan's reply to the worldwide obsession with **Brian Wilson**. Before naming himself after a character from *The Planet of the Apes*, he was a neo-folk rock singer. His first band, **Flipper's Guitar**, sounded more like Brit guitar-pop à la **Aztec Camera**. And if Buffalo Daughter's **DEVO**-like approach came out of a funk-oriented project pursued by **Sugar Yoshinaga** and **Yumiko Ohno**, it only goes to show how little your identity depends on the musical style you choose to pursue. In its most ideal form then, the New Rock from Japan has done away with borders between musical styles, gender, nationality, and language.

As opposed to history, the evolution of pop culture never seems to reflect progress. Instead of moving in a linear progression from the founding twins of country and blues to rockabilly to English pop and so on, the styles of postwar pop in Japan loop back and dissolve their original traces. They resemble less a family tree and more the history of electricity, wherein origins are irrelevant compared to what gets invented by accident.

"File Underground: Tokyo Transmissions"

Highway 74 Revisited:
The Grand Canyon to Tokyo

I heard Japan before I actually saw it. I was eight, coasting through the desert landscape of Arizona on the way to the Grand Canyon on a Thanksgiving weekend, when I discovered Japanese rock. We were crossing the state line with the radio stations drifting in and out, the DJ's accents unfamiliar, their music more local, less L.A. Besides the two plastic knobs our car radio didn't have any other controls, not even a half-inch slot for eight-track cassettes. So I clicked on the portable mono cassette player sitting on my lap; its trademark space-age speaker shimmered as the sunlight poked through my side of the car.

With the exception of a couple of John Denver songs stuck on the end, the songs were sung in Japanese, dubbed onto tape by the son of a friend of the family. Several years older than me and in the throes of Japanese teen adolescence, he was studying for the high school entrance exams he would have to take as soon as his father's corporation sent the family back. Along with many other teenagers in Japan, he had discovered what was called New Music (*Nyu Myujikku*)[1]. Taking the **Beatles**, the **Rolling Stones**, or **Dylan** only as points of departure, these emerging songwriters wrote lyrics which struck closer to home about everyday life in the cities of Japan. The notes and instruments no longer wrote the equation Modern = The West. But it would still be another twenty years before the borders between East and West and North and South drawn in terms of technology, pop culture, and politics would crumble.

So I'm sitting in this car heading for the Grand Canyon, and **John Denver**'s line "West Virginia, Mountain Mama" chimes in at the end of the tape. Like recovered memories fed to some amnesiac trying to reconstruct the origins of a baffling trauma, **"Country Roads"** is shooting through the airwaves and turntables of this country, feeding the public's greedy appetite for an America that can only exist in the mind. All I know is the song, though; I'm totally clueless about Watergate and its effect on the national psyche, just as I don't understand the war in Vietnam that has been broadcast on TV ever since I can remember watching. Nor do I understand why this word impeachment is such a big deal. The only things that matter are the things I see, hear, smell, and taste. Nothing else seems real. So the most real thing to me is the Arizona desert and the tape playing music from Japan.

If you listen to music while in motion, whether you're riding a train, car, or walking, you catch glimpses of another landscape besides the one you're passing through. You want to hear the same song over and over because you want to catch more than a glimpse of this imaginary landscape. With every hearing another detail is added to your image until the images become a series of still photographs in your head, and by the time you've memorized the song, you've got a motion picture loop that plays over and over in your mind. Years later you hear the same pop music (every song sounds the same, everyone has heard the song, the song has been repeated over and over on the radio) and you remember the associations you have built up around it. The film becomes a memory sifting through the landscape you imagined and the one you saw outside the car. The memory evolves, at times becoming ironic and jaded, at others times nostalgic. Television commercials exploit this film to the max, converting familiar songs into jingles for detergents, fast-food restaurants, and the like. But if these songs from the past matter even now after being so commodified as to obscure their visceral origins, it's because unlike the altered if not vanished landscapes we encountered years ago, these songs remain intact. They linger on, not because of their artistic integrity but because they are the scant means we have to claim a shared past.

I haven't been to the Grand Canyon since that long drive, but I still carry a vinyl copy of the recording we listened to over and over during the entire trip: **Yosui Inoue**'s *Kohri no Sekai* (World of Ice)[2]. And every time I hear the drum fills at the beginning I conjure up moments from the trip: the snowflakes drifting by, the overturned truck, the Big Boy Restaurant where we ate that night it snowed.

But more than these images of the trip, it's the double landscape that seeps through: my idea of Japan, a country that for me, despite having Japanese parents, only existed on paper, TV, tapes, vinyl, and nowhere else. Records and stacks of manga magazines provided me with the raw materials out of which I could construct another pop culture evolving on the other side of the ocean. But just because I could read and understand the hiero-glyphics of these contemporary sources didn't mean I had any idea what the place was really like. If anything, I started to concoct my own imaginary version of Japan because I couldn't taste, touch, or smell the real thing. So I listened to Japan on the cassette player, and when I heard it I was in both places, squinting out the window at the shiny suburban sprawl of Los Angeles while imagining what it was like to watch trains pass by more often than cars, cram every day for exams, and have relatives beyond your nuclear family.

Fast-Forward into…

I'm in Japan now. It's the late spring of 1998. John Denver's plane crashed into the sea sever-al months ago only hours away from where I live in the States, not in the ancient Appalachian Mountains, but off the coast of the gentri-fied Monterey Peninsula. Just like West Virginia in **"Country Roads"**, the country and city I imagined almost a quarter century ago on the way to the Grand Canyon seem suspiciously unreal, replaced by the pre-sent-day real Japan and Tokyo. Japan is no longer a figment of my imagination, and I no longer wonder what living here would be like since I have already done it.

When someone asks me about Japan or Tokyo, I tend to conjure up things besides economic circumstances, which, while allowing the circulation of these things to take place, don't account for that strange unique aura of another country. Whether it's described in terms of ideas, commodities, or trends, we end up calling the sum of these things culture, and in the

process of describing it we not only reveal the locale but, more importantly, ourselves. I can think of no other city besides Tokyo where the variety of experience is so multi-ple. You talk to one person and get one account of all the things that person con-sumed, all the events and incidents that person experienced, while someone else might not even know of the existence of these experiences, let alone occurrence. It's these variations that shape the landscape of Tokyo. But they occur at the lower fre-quencies, barely heard or noticed by most of the city's and country's inhabitants. Like a Tokyo without subway trains, Japanese pop music needs an underground. Without an underground culture, the city would not only be inconceivable, it would collapse.

A Brief Cross Countercultural History of the '60s

"The skies of America have had more changes occur under them in this century than any other country: assassinations, political wars, gangster wars, racial wars, space races, women's rights, sex, drugs and the death of god, all for the betterment of the American people."

—Ornette Coleman, notes to
Skies of America, 1972

I'm remembering a scene in **Beneath the Planet of the Apes** in which the crash-landed space pilot uncovers the tiled sign that reads "New York City Subway."[3] The message here is that the freaky outer limits of interplanetary travel are nothing com-pared to what's happened here at home: modern civilization has been taken over by our regressed ancestors! It doesn't seem such a bizarre message if you recall that

1. The term New Music was part promotional tag pushed by the music industry, part '70s trend advocated by singer-songwriters and bands. Asserting an integrity lacking in Japanese pop music and in search of their own domestic pop, New Music performers turned away from the anachronistic formula of repli-cating the most recent trends in Europe and the United States.

2. Released in 1973, *Kohri no Sekai* was the equivalent of *Frampton Comes Alive*, and sold an unprecedented million copies in Japan, prov-ing indisputably that rock-'n'-roll was here to stay whether you liked it or not. To me, even now, *Kohri no Sekai*, as evocative as **David Bowie**'s *Hunky Dory*, walks the fine line between folk and rock, and yet somehow man-ages to distance itself from both. When I was a kid watching a videotape of the Japanese Grammy awards, I was greatly impressed by these New Music stars' refusal to appear on TV. It seemed a gesture of artistic integrity in a time when any teen idol would have died to get air time. It made their music seem mysterious. Incidentally, you can find the same kind of integrity throughout manga culture as well. **Tsubame Kamogawa**, author of one of the funniest '70s manga, *Macaroni Horenso*, talks about refusing to license his work: "There was a lot of interest in making movies and ani-mation out of *Macaroni Horenso*, but the offers were always exploitative. In our manga coop, we were convinced that commercialism was ruining manga." *Macaroni Horenso* was certainly one of my faves; ridden with rock ref-erences from **Deep Purple** to **Led Zeppelin** to **Roxy Music**, it offered a kind of bridge between two cultures which books couldn't pro-vide. When asked about the basic concept behind *Macaroni Horenso*, Kamogawa replied, "I wanted to express the joy of rock through the medium of manga… I mean, there were a lot of strange bands back then. You'd never get bored by them. They'd wear outra-geous outfits and make wonderful sounds, dance around like crazy. Someone once com-mented on how the '70s were a decade when you'd bump into uniqueness at every street cor-ner.' That's what it felt like. In any case, what helped and influenced me most wasn't manga, it was rock."

3. While lacking the surprise ending of *The Planet of the Apes* (1968), in which **Charlton Heston** discovers that he has landed not on a freak planet galaxies away where apes rule and men are beasts, but at home, on earth, *Beneath the Planet of the Apes* (1968) paints an even bleaker picture of human evolu-tion. As it turns out, intelligence has squashed

this film was released during the Vietnam War around the time when Nixon unwittingly claimed he'd "bring the war back home." The subway in ruins not only undermined the grandiosity of America's million-mile effort to conquer space but also had the bizarre effect of making the present feel nostalgic. Revolution was dangerous not because it threatened our lives, but because it would throw history out of whack, making us regress into premodern times in which all memory of the good old modern world would be erased.

The story of the apes provides a strangely haunting allegory of the counterculture's increasingly underground and illegal status in America. Although the film series taps into the American paranoia of third world/black revolution, the fact that it was incredibly successful in Japan doesn't at all surprise me. Countercultures in Japan lashed out against mainstream America in terms of politics, consumerism, and lifestyle and chose other subcultures abroad as their allies. Outraged by blind imitation and adoration of the mainstream, everyone from black free-jazz musicians to PLO terrorists embraced an imagined underground. But by 1972 the marriage between youth and politics in postwar Japan had turned into a nightmare wet dream, fizzling out with the disintegration of the Red Army lynching of its own members in the infamous Asama Inn Incident.[4] Nor did free jazz's promise of liberation bode well; cafes blaring the weirdest harmo-melodic music available on vinyl quickly fossilized, with musicians and fans mimicking the drug habits instead of the music of **Coltrane** and other heroin-addicted musicians.

If you were part of some counterculture during this time, chances were you either left the country, became a drug casualty, got put away, or went completely underground. It wasn't so much that counterculture had disappeared but, even worse, that

its fundamental ideal of fighting against some mainstream force—whether it be the State, mass media, or The Man—had become an anachronism. By 1978, those who stubbornly opposed the construction of the Narita Airport were viewed as ghosts, recognized at best by the media as nothing more than evil spirits to be warded off. So you dropped out via drugs or by leaving your country or both; it didn't matter because, as a friend of mine who watched his friends leave Japan one by one remarked, it all boiled down to what he called "the annihilation of the comprehensible."

A lot of the ones who didn't leave or drop out, tuned out. As if leaving the radio dial stuck somewhere in between stations, they abstained, resorted to silence. It was this silence that would soon be split open in 1978, not by some new religion or terrorist movement, but by music verging on "the annihilation of the comprehensible," made by a band called **Fushitsusha** (The Unlost Ones) led by a guitarist named **Keiji Haino**. It was the year punk, both as fashion and music, invaded Tokyo. The two were often the same in Japan, Haino joked many years later.

Like Japanese cars from the '50s, Japanese punks were poor imitations. They weren't saying anything, only copying, doomed to be slightly out-of-synch anachronisms, always one beat behind in their aspirations to embrace both the lifestyle and the music. Haino had something more immediate to say, something that was beyond transcription; his lyrics and melodies were utterances and explosions in the dark. It would be almost another twenty years before this unprecedented music would be recognized not only by the rest of the world but by those who lived right next door to him in Tokyo.[5]

Tokyo Locale One: Goa Raves

For the longest time, I've believed that the sole purpose of pop music is to transport its listeners and practitioners somewhere inconceivable. Pop songs are like dreams, insofar as their landscapes are imagined. But like dreams they are all appearance and no reality.

I don't dream of Japan anymore. It's too real to me. What draws me to the country, to Tokyo, now are the layers—from the surface of a nation represented through mainstream media to the more subterranean local events you can only find by word of mouth, as both of these occur and unfold simultaneously. Magazines are useless not only because they virtually ignore the underground but because it's the accidental discovery, the unpredictable juxtaposition of sound and place, that I'm after.

"That was how we discovered Goa trance," says **Shinichi Ogawa**, **Sugar Plant**'s guitarist, recounting the band's first encounter with the rave psychedelic scene in Tokyo.[6] "Word of mouth. We heard about it through friends, tried it out, and really enjoyed it."

"That was about four or five years ago," chimes in **Chinatsu Shoyama**, Sugar Plant's singer and lyricist. "Now it's a completely different scene. We stopped going about a year ago. We sort of got bored with it."

They explained that the scene had changed, become more popular and diluted. "It's really big now. Back then only a few hundred people would show up, so everyone felt closer, more friendly. Now you'll see at least a few thousand at one of these events. It's even been covered in *magazines*," said Shoyama.

At the same time, Ogawa pointed out, the music itself had become more formulaic: "When we went, no one had any set ideas of what Goa trance was supposed to sound like. Now it's become codified."

"But I suppose those who are just discovering it now find the scene just as refreshing as we did," offers Chinatsu. Ogawa agrees and adds, "Back then there were middle-aged hippies from the '70s showing up, which was kind of cool."

Although their enthusiasm for the scene has waned, it's clear that their encounter several years ago with this instant community was more important to them than the rock bands themselves. Ogawa recounts, "Up until then, listening to music was a really internal experience. You'd sit in your room alone and spin a CD or a single. Goa trance was important because, for the first time, music became a communal experience for us."

Shoyama and Ogawa's enthusiasm for this recent scene reminds me of the explosion I encountered when I saw the **Replacements** perform at **Joe's Star Lounge** in Ann Arbor, Michigan. Retrospectively, their music would be labeled indie rock. The fall of 1984 was an eerie year, the reelection of **Reagan** signifying less an Orwellian world and more the victory of the myth of mainstream America over the reality of the marginalized majority of America. The myth had something to do with cowboys and the frontier while the reality was about what life was like when you haven't paid this week's phone bill and rent.

The Replacements tore through songs about the everyday loser, with vocalist **Paul Westerberg** screaming into the mike, "I'm a customer!" Even their name made you sneer against the dinosaur rock stardom of the late '70s, which ended with an abyss between performers and their audience that was less pathetic than the fact that everyone colluded with this separation. The stars wanted to place themselves above their followers, who in turn wanted to worship them. The stadium rock stars of the '80s, with their good intentions and world charity events, were only slightly different. From **U2** to the **Police** to **Peter Gabriel**, these charitable efforts expressed anxiety over the abyss between them and the rest of the world. Saving the world probably seemed easier than bridging this gap.

While moshing in a tiny club to the Replacements slaughtering the already butchered **Sex Pistols**' cover of the **Who**'s **"Substitute"**, I knew that something was changing. Music was no longer an exercise for teenage brooding narcissism or the expression of a longing to be somewhere else, but something more intimately connected with others. If the club scene was much smaller and therefore fleeting compared to legendary communal festivals like **Monterey** and **Woodstock** or all the variations on **Live Aid**, it only meant that our scene was that much more immediate (not to mention cheaper) and therefore more real. This moment in Joe's Star Lounge wasn't going to be documented on film or MTV because it was happening too fast. So fast that no one could legitimately claim its origins.

There's no point, though, in waxing nostalgic over these moments of discovery. I mention them only as a reminder that, however intense the seismic shifts of subterranean cultures might seem at the time as they spread across the country, these tremors come and go. People who bemoan the vapidity of contemporary pop compared to the more "classical" music of the '50s, '60s, or '70s, miss the essential point that, unlike paintings and other more "individual" works of art, pop was never meant to be permanent, and that is its strength, not

the emotions out of humans living in the caverns of the New York City subways. They don't speak, their faces are made of rubber, and they resort to the '70s passive aggressive tactics of ESP mind control to force other people to do their killing for them. ("We're too peaceful," they say blankly.) Their god is no longer Christ but the Bomb.

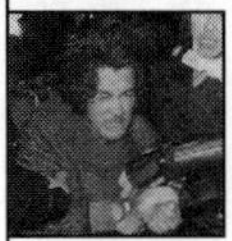

4. Fugitives on the run, these members of the **Japanese United Red Army** barricaded themselves in the Asama Hotel Inn. Televised consecutively for eight hours, this incident marked Japan's first marathon broadcast, perhaps providing an unprecedented instance of national surveillance conducted by an entire nation. Later, lynched bodies were found in the area, members executed by fellow members before their retreat into the inn. An even more unexpected bizarre incident occurred several months later when the Japanese Red Army, in collaboration with the Palestinian terrorists (PCLP), opened fire on tourists in the Tel Aviv airport, killing twenty-four people.

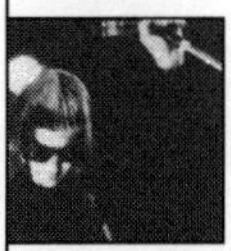

5. Haino and other "noise musicians" gained international recognition mostly as a result of word of mouth through European and American musicians, including **Sonic Youth**, in the early '90s.

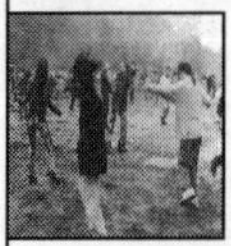

6. One of the major rave scenes in Japan, the name Goa trance comes from India. The music and fashion leans more towards the organic sounds and look of psychedelia rather than metallic techno. Events often take place outside of Tokyo in rural locations, where participants pitch tents to form instant communities, drop light doses of acid, and dance the night away.

7. This San Francisco folk rock band was led by guitarist **Jorma Kaukonen** during the early '70s. Kaukonen, an original member of the **Jefferson Airplane**, left the Airplane long before the band became the **Starship**, which, with a host of other California Bay Area bands, including the **Grateful Dead**, rose to extreme heights of commercial popularity. Meanwhile, Kaukonen retreated from pop stardom, following the obscure tradition of white acoustic blues a la **John Fahey**, to perform solo or with **Hot Tuna** in cafe-sized clubs.

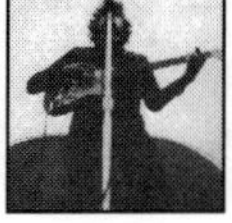

8. As the brightest new hope in the folk revival movement, Dylan outraged his fans at the 1965 Newport Folk Festival

"I'm sweet
Ha!
Tokyo-wido
Metaphysical Valentine
Metaphysical Chocolate"

—Demi Semi Quaver, from
"Metaphysical Chocolate"

its weakness. If there is a permanence to popular music, it's just barely discernible, lingering on like the echoes of speakers you can't see.

Mainstream culture convinces us of its importance by being excessively visible. This is why television is its primary medium (and surveillance its primary ideology). The more visible an event, place, or individual becomes, whether in terms of sales, casualties, or other excesses, the more likely it is to be forgotten almost immediately in the act of being consumed. If, by chance, we remember something from the past, it's the visibility, the hugeness we remember, not the significance of the event. Consumerism thrives off this blurry amnesia. Events and participants lose their unique contours, turning into a conglomeration of cultural excesses expressed in terms of sales, casualties, or other bland statistics. We all know there's nothing more forgettable than statistics. Hence the media's dependence on them.

Technology also provides us with the illusion that national, or at the very least cultural, borders cease to exist; information is freely exchanged. The fact of the matter is that "live" images, whether they're transmitted through the Internet or television, provide a distancing effect enabling the viewer, like a guard keeping watch over prisoners on video monitors, to confirm his or her separation from the televised location. We confirm the wealth of one nation by confirming the poverty of another. Like the spectacle of a national disaster, the bizarreness of a foreign culture gets exaggerated, justifying and reinforcing one's own culture, defined in visual terms by race, gender, and class.

The reasons I've ended up writing about music, and in particular about music that comes from a subculture, are twofold. I believe that the most interesting transmissions of culture during this century

have occurred in terms of sound. These transmissions interest me because they provide instances whereby culture distinguishes itself from nationality. Another way of putting it is that popular music sometimes engenders communal responses that are unrelated to adherence to singular notions of culture. However varied the music, the musicians and music scenes I've been exposed to in Japan all conform to this unstated principle. However, unlike in world music (a misnomer), no particular ethnic accent is present in Japanese sounds; it's as if the musicians are unwilling to make the sound of any one culture a priority over any other. The resulting melange of this coreless music is, to me, both strangely coherent and evocative.

It was this strangeness of the music that attracted me in the first place. And while I no longer have the delusion that writing about it clarifies anything, writing has forced me to rethink the ways I perceive not just popular music but the cultures it emanates from. This means I have to go back and forth between the two cultures, America and Japan, rewinding and fast-forwarding, following detours, getting lost, and dispensing with the notion of any map or guide to my experience. For all I know, these instantaneous communities may be gone by the time they're reported. The fact that they are fleeting doesn't haunt me anymore because I'm no longer convinced that the longevity of a situation, whether it's a relationship, a geography, or music scene, makes it real. In fact, as Reagan's and Clinton's reelections have proved, those who want to maintain their communities end up weaving myths, spending most of their time on covering up their tracks and obscuring what's actually going on in order to maintain their bland legitimacy.

So if there's been a rave scene, I

for two reasons: (1) he relinquished his solitary acoustic guitar/vocal performance in favor of an electric rock and roll band, and (2) his songs were no longer strictly (although they never really were) about social protest. The festival was no better off without Dylan, and no less dismal than the arena rock fundraisers to come decades later. One critic noted, "If the audience thought that the Dylan scene represented a premature climax to the evening, more was yet to come. A double finale saw hordes of singers, musicians, self-appointed participants, and temporary freaks take over the stage in a tasteless exhibition of frenzied incest. It seemed as though everyone wanted to make sure they were in on the big 'civil rights act,' and a moment that might have become the high point of the entire weekend was suddenly turned into a scene of opportunistic chaos, reducing the meaning of Newport to the sense of a carnival gone mad."

9. This British glam rock band was led by **Marc Bolan**. For influences, check out David Bowie's *The Rise and Fall of Ziggy Stardust*. Bolan's best known song is "Bang a Gong (Get It On)" from *Electric Warrior* (1971), because **Robert Palmer** covered it in the '80s. Bolan died in a car crash in 1977.

10. Postwar singer-songwriters of the French cool school of pop. **Serge Gainsbourg** (1928-1991), inspired by American pop music, whether by the lyricism of jazz (**Art Tatum**, **Dizzy Gillespie**, **John Coltrane**, and **Art Blakey**) or the emotion behind "le rock-'n'-roll" (**Screamin' Jay Hawkins**), combined both into his raconteur music revolving around city life in Paris, a world of drinking, women, adultery, fast cars, poverty, and miserable jobs. **Francoise Hardy** (b. 1944) provided the heavy dosage of '60s urban melancholia, as if anticipating the sadness rather than the exuberance of the decade; her melodies are reminiscent of the **Everly Brothers** and **Burt Bacharach** rather than Screamin' Jay Hawkins. Gainsbourg and Hardy ended up recording a duet on a single called *Bonnie and Clyde* later covered by **Luna** singer **Dean Wareham** and **Stereolab** chanteuse **Laetitia Sadier**.

11. Much to the chagrin of these nationalists, **Cheap Trick** and Dylan would end up releasing albums recorded live at Budokan in the '70s; the want to hear about it from someone who's been there but who also doesn't have to be there for good, because in a city that's been feeding off the fiction of monetary speculation told through visual cues—whether they be ads, TV, or magazines—the most subversive thing to do would be to communicate by means of something invisible that doesn't cost a cent: music by word of mouth.

Detour, 1966: The Year Pop Broke

"It's very complicated to play with electricity. You play with other people. You're dealing with other people.... Most people who don't like rock and roll can't relate to other people."

—Bob Dylan

When I ask guitarist **Nishiwaki** and **Pocopen**, the two halves of the band **Sakana**, "Where would you like to tour abroad?" they reply in unison, "America!" For the past ten years, they've been playing a kind of potpourri of folk and soul peppered with rock. Of all the bands I've listened to in Tokyo, they sound the most familiar to me, so their preference for American music doesn't surprise me. **Nishiwaki**'s tasteful guitar arrangements are on a par with **Jorma Kaukonen** of **Hot Tuna**, while Pocopen's vocals refute the stereotype that Japanese female vocalists don't have soul.[7] Sakana doesn't sound like any American band I've heard, but they do remind me of America. There may be bands in the States that have a similar effect on me, but they always remind me of a particular region. Listening to Sakana, particularly when I was living in Tokyo, reminded me of the

entire country—none of which either member had ever visited. A virtual America.

Nishiwaki has listened to a lot of American music, everything from the bad-ass southern rock of the **Allman Brothers** to the arty elegant ambient music of **Tortoise**. The juxtaposition of the two doesn't perturb him at all. He asks me what I've been listening to and I tell him about the Dylan bootleg series I just discovered before leaving for Japan. "Dylan," he smiles, "is it." He wants to know whether I've seen him perform. I haven't, but I tell him that my parents ended up seeing him at the 1965 **Newport Folk Festival**.[8]

My father drove to New England for the first time in his life, mistakenly thinking he was heading to the Newport *Jazz* Festival. Someone at his company had mentioned something about the Newport Music Festival. Such mistakes were not uncommon for him at the time. The first month he arrived in New York, he hopped on a subway train to see **Thelonius Monk** at the **Village Vanguard**. Not knowing what Monk looked like, he sat patiently in the basement club waiting for the opening black piano player to finish his set. When he asked when Monk would perform, the waiter pointed to the piano player and muttered, "That's him."

When my parents arrived in Newport, they were first puzzled by the folk music, then by the leather-clad man plugging in his electric guitar instead of strumming quietly on his acoustic, and finally by seeing everyone who had seemed so peaceful turn hostile, booing and yelling insults at the performer. When they asked a college student sitting next to them who the musician was, the young man sneered, "He used to be Bob Dylan, but now he's a sellout." Between Monk and Dylan, my parents accidentally

stumbled into both Americas, black and white.

By the time my parents moved to the States, the folk crusade brewing over the first half of the decade couldn't tolerate any other America besides the one that harked back to a mythical America. Folk music lovers passed over the noise of the streets for the pastoral harmonies of peace, love and understanding. The nation's psyche was assumed to be unscathed after World War II; this encouraged a childlike faith in nationhood, left, right, or moderate. And if this folk counterculture and mainstream America had one thing in common, it was their antagonism towards popular culture as a threat mocking their faith in America. Now the symbol of such faith, the American flag, was brush painted instead like graffiti onto the football helmet worn by **Jack Nicholson** in *Easy Rider* (1969).

What Dylan going electric and kicking the jams out with a band meant was that his portrait of America wandered in between these two realms of mockery and faith; he confused his most dedicated followers while picking up an odd assortment of fans as unlikely as the cast of characters described in his songs. The important thing for Dylan's band was that the music was *their* vision of America, one that no one was required to join, and that therefore risked being abandoned at any moment. And even if he and his crew in their songs and on tour wandered off to Europe, these foreign places, no less than those seascapes described throughout **Melville**'s *Moby Dick,* were seen through the American eye. Like the astronauts in *The Planet of the Apes*, Dylan was leaving America behind to crash-land back onto it. The country was somehow both stranger and more familiar, its tenants and wanderers in constant danger of both repeating themselves and reinventing themselves. This cycle of departure and return was in the end the inevitable contradiction embodied by a nation of amnesiacs that thrived and fed off lost memories.

Our recent past comes to us more clearly as a soundtrack of pop songs than as written history. Because it is ceaselessly jammed in the present, like some malfunctioning brake, America cannot help but flinch from what it faces, glancing back at the past and converting it into instant nostalgia. But sometimes the rearview mirror goes out of whack, there's a blind spot, and then the inevitable cataclysmic crash. The driver ends up losing him- or herself without knowing exactly what was lost in the first place. By revisiting the site of the car crash, maybe the rest of us can sort through the remnants and reconstruct this lost object. But like the word rosebud in the quintessential American film, *Citizen Kane* (1941), this lost object turns out to be as meaningless as the sled. The search for America for every American turns out to be futile from the start, and that's why it always evokes nostalgia.

When I hear a band like Sakana and some of Sugar Plant's earlier recordings, I'm reminded of America, but I'm not reminded of this search for America, which is another way of saying that their music doesn't inspire this feeling of nostalgia. What I like about Sugar Plant's sound is the way they draw on the traditions of American music (traditions that feel closer to me than French or German postwar pop) yet somehow don't make you long for the times of those traditions.

At the same time it's not as if all Sugar Plant listens to is American music. The band members also like the French techno of the **Reminiscence Drive** and **AIR**. Pocopen claims that she didn't stop listening to **T. Rex** during her high school years until the day she got her diploma.[9] Talking to them, I find they don't rank any culture's music above another—as long as

it's pop. Their sonic map branches out to Continental Europe and at times to obscure regions of India and other Asian countries. **Francoise Hardy** and **Serge Gainsbourg** were pop stars in Japan long before they gained their recent cult status here in the States.[10] If you want to see more foreign films, read more foreign books, and hear more foreign music, I suggest you go to Japan. It's the ultimate hub of world pop. This partly has to do with the lack of origins of pop music in Japan. Instead of being centralized, multiple pop universes thrive throughout contemporary Japanese culture, sometimes blending, sometimes colliding, sometimes passing by each other, but hardly ever being ignored.

Tokyo strikes me as a satellite city revolving around popular cultures from around the world. No matter how the images it transmits vary according to the climate of each country, every spot is covered. These pictures might not resemble the actual country on the ground, but they're just as valid.

Tokyo is to pop music as a satellite is to the weather, which is to say both help us predict the future. Tokyo records the surfaces of all other pop cultures. By now the visual and sonic cues of foreign countries have been so thoroughly imbedded in the city's cultural history that it is sending its own signals back to other metropolises. For me, Sakana is an unconscious America I found in Tokyo, one you can only see by hearing them.

But if they provide us with the sonic smells of the modern era by reminding us of our past, popular songs can also numb our hearing, our ability to listen to others' stories. Just as empires end up inciting unexpected rebellions or alliances or wars in foreign lands, popular cultures never migrate without losing something in the translation. Those who love these mis-

former's *Live at Budokan* turned the band into an overnight sensation.

12. One of the leading Japanese novelists to emerge in the late '70s. Not unlike the bewildered Midwestern narrator encountering Manhattan during the Jazz Age in **F. Scott Fitzgerald**'s *The Great Gatsby*, Murakami's narrator is no less perplexed and intrigued by life in Tokyo, where marriages, memories, and commodities are all equally disposable. The extent of Murakami's popularity was most apparent several years ago when a women's poll appeared in a national newspaper asking the question, "Who is your favorite male?" The top response was the narrator-protagonist in Murakami's novels. Instead of the syrupy *Norwegian Wood*, I recommend *Wild Sheep Chase, Dance, Dance, Dance*, or his most recent groundbreaking and disturbing *Windup Bird Chronicles*, in which Japan's wartime past is rigorously examined alongside contemporary humdrum life in Tokyo. Not to be confused with **Ryu Murakami**, whose first novel, *An Almost Transparent Blue*, reads more like **Jack Kerouac**'s *On the Road* narrated by **Syd Barrett**.

13. Formed in 1993, this trio made its U.S. debut with the 7-inch release *Legend of the Yellow Buffalo* and the CD *Captain Vapour Athletes*, both on **Grand Royal** in 1996. The two women, **Sugar Yoshinaga** and **Yumiko Ohno**, are in charge of the songwriting, while **Moog Yamamoto** volunteers as DJ and band philosopher. Without sounding anything like their predecessors, the band exudes an enthusiasm for rock from the **Ventures** to **Devo**: their hard rock fuzz chords strum through the chirps of Moog synthesizers and tight minimal beats more reminiscent of acid jazz than rock. Touring with American bands including **Luscious Jackson, Pavement, Jon Spencer Blues Explosion, Butter 08** and **Girls Against Boys**, Buffalo Daughter have also collaborated with Japanese musicians, including **Konishi** of **Pizzicato Five**, **Takako Minekawa**, and **Cornelius**.

14. As a performance artist, she performed with avant-garde musicians including **John Cage** and **Ornette Coleman**. As part of the experimental art movement **Fluxus**, Ono and others participated in what became known as happenings, in which the boundaries between audience and performers, performance and daily life, were obscured. Her book *Grapefruit* provided a series of instructions to make pieces happen, as if the work were in the hands of the translations claim that something is gained in the cross-pollination of pop culture. Those who deplore it advocate other, stranger forms of kitsch nationalism.

When **John Lennon** declared that he and the rest of the Fab Four were out to conquer the world, I doubt that he had any idea how literally this would be taken as the band embarked on their first and only tour of Asia, starting in Tokyo at **Budokan** auditorium the month I was born: July 1966.[11] Like Elvis, I think they were intent on having their music heard by as many people as possible. Unlike Elvis, however, they made an impact on a larger scale, if only due to the fact that they had the privilege of growing up in a world in which recordings could be made and distributed on a mass level. With the same insistent faith of missionaries exposing classical music to "savages" because they believed it to be universal, the **Beatles** set foot in Asia.

Which reminds me of the novel *Norwegian Wood*, written by one of Japan's leading novelists, **Haruki Murakami**, which sold several million copies in Japan during the late '80s.[12] The title comes from the opening scene, in which the narrator, after landing in Germany, hears a muzak version of the Beatles' song in the airplane and is thrown into a dizzy total recall of his youth during the '60s. The novel is less interesting than the phenomenon that this moment captures: the collective nostalgia evoked by a foreign song, in accordance with the myth that the Beatles are a group loved by everyone in the world.

The truth is, everyone in the world did not love the Beatles. Their Asian tour, marking the first attempt to test the sonic boundaries of rock-'n'-roll in the Far East, revealed that what they represented was not so universal nor so welcome. When local promoter **Tatsuji Nagashima** booked the **Nippon Budokan**, a sacred ground dedicated to

Japanese martial arts, for the Beatles, right-wing nationalists horrified by the prospect of the triple-whammy electrified Western pop invasion caused enough controversy through public demonstrations to force the police to employ 35,000 security guards during the groups' four-day stay. On their next stop in the Philippines, by refraining from having morning tea with the then First Lady **Imelda Marcos**, the Beatles infuriated the public enough to inspire telephoned bomb and death threats to the British Embassy and their hotel suite. At the airport they were chased down by an infuriated mob crying, "*Beatles alis diyan!* (Beatles go home)".

Even Americans from the religious South, where rock-'n'-roll emerged, were not all fans. The moment Lennon declared, "We mean more to kids than Jesus," they burned their records in public. The fact that this blasphemy came from an Englishman only rekindled their rebellion against their former rulers. The Southern Baptists were no different from Asian nationalists in this regard. Not only the Reds, but pop music too could betray their ideal of god and country. Southern Baptists and Filipinos were afraid of the same thing: the technology of pop enabling its listeners and practitioners to crisscross between geographies in ways unimaginable until now. As David Thomas of **Pere Ubu** triumphantly declares in *The Tenement Year* (1988), "We have the technology!"

The New Rock...

"Kore ga New Rock/Shibireru wa"
(This is new rock/It's mesmerizing)
—Buffalo Daughter

"I'm influenced by music that moves me, whether because of the sound, the tone,

or content; the musical style doesn't really matter to me. It's more about the background behind the music. For example, if it's hardcore music, I have the image of skateboarders going crazy over it, or if it's drum-bass-super-woofers-sounds, young kids are dancing to it. Then there's country music, which conjures images of big wide American cars and never-ending scenery. These images may not be correct, but what interests me most are the images evoked by the music. For me, because it's not a matter of seeing the truth behind the music, because it's about the music suggesting something more than the sounds, musical styles mean a lot less to me now than they used to. For example, the lyrics to Buffalo Daughter's **"Silver Turkey"** or **"Baby Amoeba Goes South"** were written from my imagination, they're not necessarily based on reality. I don't know what the reality of the images is, nor do I really care what that reality might be."

Such are the words of **Sugar Yoshinaga** of Buffalo Daughter.[13] When asked what a buffalo daughter is, Yoshinaga replies, "Buffalo to us is so American; it is a symbol of America. As for daughter, we wanted to have something that meant 'girl' in the band name." Like their band name, Buffalo Daughter's lyrics are filled with imaginary landscapes. The title track to their album announces "This is New Rock" and the fuzz guitar and bass hold onto C sharp during the entire song through the final lyrics "The familiar music born tomorrow."

While American rock bands even now try to simulate a Garden of Eden untainted by mass culture to evoke the nostalgia for "the real thing," the familiar music of Buffalo Daughter skids across various time zones, all of which are mediated through mass culture. Instead of inhabiting rock star personas, the band seems a lot more interested in landscapes beyond their egos. It's no wonder that they claim an allegiance with the techno wizards **DEVO**, who sliced and diced everything about rock into one creepy but funny scrapbook of America, leaving us with (depending on your taste) good or bad aftertastes of consumer culture.

Moog Yamamoto, the turntable member of Buffalo Daughter, espouses his philosophy: "I think that Japanese young people are rich. They have no ideology. Consumption is a form of self-expression for the young people in Tokyo right now. Basically, we have money, we are spoiled perhaps compared to other countries, and buying is a form of self-expression now. Consuming, wasting... There are no great philosophers in Japan right now, hence there is no one to follow. So rather than saying 'I am!' one says, 'I wear these watches, etc.'"

Yamamoto's statement is interesting in light of the fact that he speaks for a population that remains outside the jurisdiction of a Brand Nation. The musicians I've talked to in Tokyo have little regard for material objects, first because if they're going to spend any money it will be on music and, second, because in a space as cramped as Tokyo, the accumulation of material objects can suffocate you. However imaginative Buffalo Daughter's approach may be, it's fundamentally compact. An overload of sound might prove to be just as suffocating as riding the sardine-can subway during rush hour. Buffalo Daughter's songs, "written from my imagination, not necessarily what's reality," point toward a minimalist aesthetic of recycling instead of pure consumption and waste.

Is this minimalism part of the essence, the brush stroke aesthetic permeating even the remote caverns of Japanese subculture? Who cares? I, for one, don't. The more time I've spent in Japan and the more people I've met, the less I'm able to come up with an essential thread that binds everyone in the country together. It's no different from the States that way. The only things I believe about being American are the myths the country recycles over and over.

Subculture tends to reassemble those parts of consumer culture that have been junked and doomed to the garbage pile of our collective memory. The renovation of junk is akin to the process of amnesia—of remembering what's been forgotten. You can't remember without forgetting and perhaps, unlike enduring European metropolises, each Japanese city that sheds its past every year can only rebuild itself with recovered memories. That, to me, is what the end of the millennium is all about in this subculture of Tokyo.

The signatures of the past have vanished almost completely from Tokyo. Locations, participants, and events have all turned into fleeting media moments never celebrated as History; instead they are tossed aside for the next series of incidents like unsuccessful TV pilots. Better to leave the country if you're going to be remembered, to go to Europe or America where they still believe in history. Someone named **Yoko Ono** did precisely that and, in the process, slowly but surely wiped out the myth that only white men can rock.[14]

But there were plenty of others already wreaking havoc on the emerging mass culture in Tokyo. They would remain unknown for the most part, their ambitions and work disintegrating so instantaneously that twenty years later Japanese kids impatient to catch up with the **Sex Pistols** failed to realize that punk had already arrived around the corner and down the block in their own city two decades ago.

reader rather than the artist. Ono first established her reputation as a visual/conceptual artist, but she became increasingly interested in breaking down distinctions between disciplines such as music and visual art. She is a predecessor of performing artists including **Lauri Anderson**, as well as experimental rockers. Her reputation as an artist was completely eclipsed by the media, which identified her simply as John Lennon's partner. Ironically enough, art critics and historians were slow to pick up on her contributions, which were instead recognized by rock bands from **L7** to **Sonic Youth**. The latter set the record straight when they professed that Ono paved the way for their music.

 15. Groups including **Neo-Dada** and **Hi-Red Center** were primarily interested in taking art into the streets; their performances, called happenings, took place at station platforms, hotel rooms, and other public spaces.

 16. A former member of Neo-Dada and Hi-Red-Center, **Genpei Akasegawa** (b. 1937) eventually established himself as an essayist and novelist, writing on topics ranging from current pop phenomena to memoirs about art movements. He later coined the famous term Thomasson Object, derived from the American baseball player who, after being heralded as an one of the most important foreign players in the Japanese baseball league, turned out to be unremarkable and useless. A Thomasson Object then is any useless object or piece of architecture embedded in a city. In Tokyo, where every used thing gets disposed of, useless objects are not easy to find. Thomasson Objects include a concrete staircase that doesn't lead anywhere, a concrete tunnel with no hill over it, etc. Akasegawa managed to find enough of these to publish several volumes of images of useless objects. This pursuit of the Thomasson Object short-circuited the need for museums; the city streets became a kind of living interactive museum. All you had to do was take a stroll through the city to view them. It was the ultimate aesthetic response to the post-capitalist world of Japan.

 17. The first Japanese noise band to land a U.S. major label contract, this conglomeration of core members—**Eye Yamatsuka, Yoshimi, Seiichi Yamamoto, Hira,** and **Atari**—combined the orchestral dissonance of Sun Ra with the sonic assaults of noise-metal (**Black Sabbath** meets **Einstürzende Neubauten**). Their shows

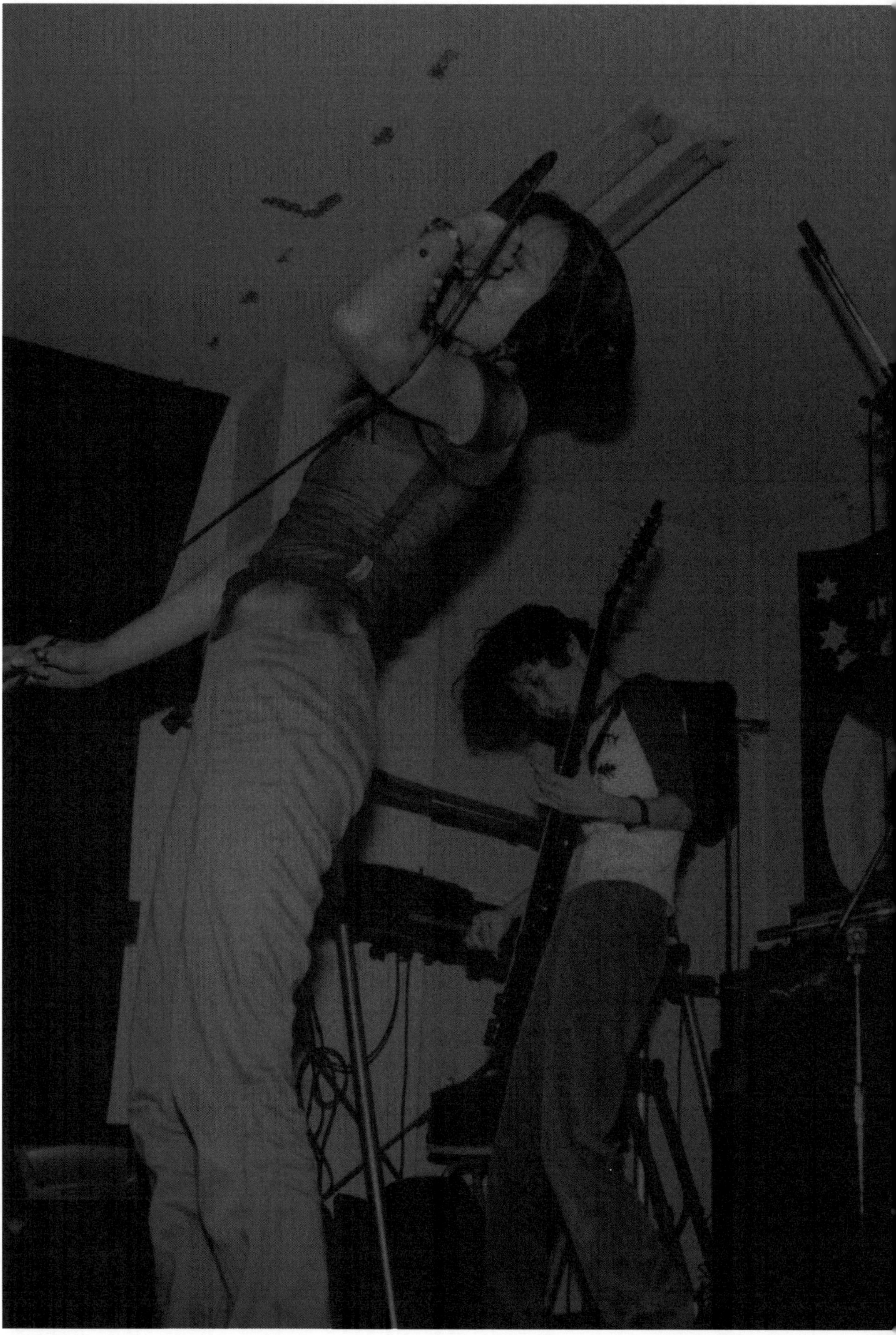

"Maybe yes, maybe no
Moody monkeys wearing laced shoes
Shoes squeak, 'Greed!'
(Take off your shoes, they lead you
to wrong way, you know!)"

—from Melt Banana's "Zoo, no Vacancy"

The Birth of Punk-Junk

The first mohawk cropped up not in the streets of London or New York circa 1976, but in Tokyo in 1958, on the head of starving artist **Ushio Shinohara**, who carved his hair into a mobile sculpture that did away with the need for galleries or materials. While the Sex Pistols and the rest of the punk scene would splash water on the faces of TV-fixated viewers for whom life without consumerism would seem artificial, Shinohara and other artists started turning commodities inside out in the late '50s because consumer culture was so bizarre as a new phenomenon.[15] Whether pissing on a cotton mattress and calling it the Imperial Hotel or pouring acid over metal panels and smashing them with an ax, this punk art built its fragile foundations on the first junked products of the nascent mass media culture. Commodities were misused, misapplied, and misrepresented by these artists not in defiance of mainstream culture, but because they had never learned how to use them in the first place. They couldn't afford the electricity, the housing, or the hundred other sources you need to make sense out of a single commodity. So they recycled the junk from this unaffordable consumer culture and called it art.

We're all familiar with **Andy Warhol**'s twist on commodities: the piles of Brillo boxes and silkscreened Campbell's soup cans. Warhol's statement was essentially American, a declaration of how indigenous art in the U.S. could only come from its postwar consumerism of cans and boxes. Europe was tossed aside as an anachronism in favor of a '50s suburbia sprawling endlessly into the future and other parts of the world. All great American art from this point on would be a commentary on this zone, which, like the Cold War, only existed for those who believed in it.

American commodities landed in Japan after the war, one by one, beginning with chocolate bars and canned foods and moving on to electrical appliances. But on the shores of another country, consumer goods often end up being unintentionally recycled, reassembled by foreigners to serve unforeseen purposes. The perfectly constructed Lego model of consumer culture became a miscarriage of commodities in the hands of these punk artists. **Genpei Akasegawa**, who would later be arrested for his hand copied blow-up reproduction of a 1,000 yen bill, had a work nailed to the wall called, **"Vagina Sheets: The Second Present"**.[16] This flattened pile of tire inner tubes included a bottle dripping sulfuric acid so that it would eventually melt down on its own.

Challenging the antiseptic utopia of consumerism, these artists made commodities bleed and rot. The works were never meant to last. Only a handful of these objects were preserved, because no one could afford to store their work, and because no one bought it. It ended up in the junkyard for good this time. If you wanted to know what it was like you had to have been there. Like pop songs on the radio, this art was available for free, and like radio songs all you had to do was be there at the right time and right place to encounter it. The art happened (it was even called happenings) and then, like the three-minute song, it was all over, gone without a trace.

The music I've discovered in Japan recently comes out of this short tradition of found music. You don't look for music, you stumble across it. And the person who accidentally discovers its sonic landscape is not at all like the person who purposefully seeks it out. Columbus would never have left Spain had he known of America's existence. On the other hand, the Puritans would have never bothered leaving Europe if they didn't know America existed. There lies the difference between accidents and pursuits.

Popular culture produced in Japan has attracted more worldwide attention than the country's literature or art ever did because the landscape embodied by this pop ethic of discovery and collisions has become a natural habitat for many of us. It has more to do with making something interesting out of trash than with following a tradition of grace. That which no longer seems relevant gets rehashed in another form, spat out with an immediacy and unpretentiousness that reminds me more of Elvis discovering rock-'n'-roll than the Beatles reinventing it.

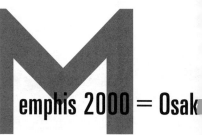

Memphis 2000 = Osaka

"In the early days, our sound was made up of every weird thing we could find... It might seem that we are anarchists, but we are dadaists. Or maybe we're Mickey Mouse... Osaka will be dissonant in 2025... We swing iron bats in medieval costume, but our hearts are always futurist. I think music can be that way."
—liner notes to **Omoide Hatoba**'s *Kinsei*

"In Osaka, there aren't as many rules in music," declares **Zak**, one of Buffalo Daughter's engineers, pointing out a crucial difference between his home territory and Tokyo, where he now lives. "You see, someone in Osaka might play Spanish flamenco guitar along with some computer percussion and it wouldn't be considered weird or strange; people would remark, 'Hey, that looks like fun.'" Zak has just returned from a six-month tour doing sound for Buffalo Daughter, and now he has a series of recording dates to take care of in Tokyo. When asked about contemporary music, he appears pretty indifferent to music from abroad, claiming that he prefers the bands from his locale, including the **Boredoms**,[17] **Omoide Hatoba**,[18] and "fifteen-year-old kids doing techno." Bands like Omoide Hatoba aren't driven by a single sound; they are constantly feeding on various genres to the point of mutating the genres themselves. "It's a lot like the jazz of the '30s in Kansas City where all these different styles of popular music formed a mishmash from which bebop eventually emerged. Musicians aren't very protective of their styles. That's why people like **Seiichi Yamamoto** (the Boredoms' guitarist and leader of Omoide Hatoba) have such an open approach," Zak elaborates.

A southern analogy seems more apt. I'm thinking about Elvis and Memphis in terms of how his locale encouraged him to bastardize his musical sources of influence. While America's most elaborate technology strove to break the speed of sound during the '50s, it took some local trucker recording a single in a tiny booth in Memphis called **Sun Records** to break the sonic barrier between blacks and whites. He did it with a song that was on neither side of the picket fence, singing **"That's All Right Mama"** as if that was precisely what the song was about, about it being all right to cross the line. But the real magic and grace about the recording was that Elvis didn't even realize how groundbreaking and breathtaking it would be.

When I used to listen to AM radio on the way to Japanese school after getting out of public school in the L.A. suburbs,

radio stations would happily play late Motown **Marvin Gaye** or the more aggressive **War** next to white syrupy **Olivia Newton John** (**"Have You Never Been Mellow?"**) and **Captain and Tennille** (**"Love Will Keep Us Together"**). At the time, it didn't strike me as odd to hear these songs side by side, because I had no concept of style; I only distinguished between catchy songs and not-so-catchy songs. And colors were invisible to my fingertips on the radio dial back then.

Whether pop songs are social barometers of race relations is debatable, but one thing I know for sure is that it's almost impossible nowadays to find a recording artist who occupies both R&B and Rock bins, now euphemisms for black and white pop. And regardless of your intention, the fact that you buy one instead of the other betrays your preference not only for one kind of music but the race associated with it. This isn't the time or place to write about race and pop music in America. I'm just wondering whether these Japanese musicians I'm meeting in Japan, from Sakana to the Boredoms, listen to jazz, soul, funk, and rap without the hang-ups that any non-black American musicians can't help but have when incorporating this music into their own.

Part of the appeal of cities like Osaka and Kyoto lies in the fact that there's no obligation to keep up with or imitate others, because if you really want to do that, you might as well just move to Tokyo. Unlike the latest flavor-of-the-month R&B music promoted in Tokyo, black music in Osaka survives fleeting trends. Outdated genres like '70s funkadelia (even before it became hip again in America) and dubhouse reggae survive, permanently embedded in Osaka pop history. The chronology is different here. Talking to Zak I get the impression that there are two kinds of Japans, one that lives on Tokyo

gained notoriety both in Japan and abroad; singers Yamatsuka and Toyohito Yoshikawa ran across the stage smashing into each other and at times bruising and spraining their respective bodies. Although the punk aesthetic has always been there, frenzied beats are replaced by loud regular thuds, as if to cancel out the obvious political agenda of punk. The lack of ideology behind their music might be what confuses reviewers abroad when confronted with the task of writing about the Boredoms. Nor does it help that their song and album titles are ridden with obscure pop culture references ("**Jah Called AC/DC**", "**Onanie Bomb Meets the Sex Pistols**") that confuse more than explicate.

 18. An ever-changing assemblage of musicians in both Tokyo and Osaka, **Seiichi Yamamoto**'s project **Omoide Hatoba** departs significantly from his work with the Boredoms. The tapestry of sounds and genres combining techno, rap, surf, folk, and noise is more varied, and despite the fact that the music tends towards instrumental, Yamamoto is committed to writing songs that can still be called (however loosely) pop. The music is less spectacle oriented but just as provocative and interesting as the Boredoms.

19. The major magazine *Studio Voice* covers the subcultural activities of Japan and other cosmopolitan cities in the U.S. and Europe. Issues are devoted to themes which aren't particularly local or domestic, ranging anywhere from fortunetelling to black identity.

 20. With the frenetic pace of speed jazz in **John Zorn**'s *Naked City* and the frenetic energy of the L.A. punk band the **Minute Men**, **Melt Banana** has been one of the more successful Japanese noise bands to perform in the United States. Both *Speak Squeak Creak* and *Scratch or Stitch* were produced by **Steve Albini** (Nirvana's *In Utero*) and released on an American label. Instead of providing harmonies and chords, the bass and guitar are as percussive as the drums; the entire ensemble creates a kind of mechanical syncopation of rumbles, squeaks, and spurts interlocked with vocals delivered with a rap artist's precision.

 21. Kramer is the founder of New York label **Shimmy-Disc** and the producer of bands including **Galaxie 500** and **Half Japanese**; his solo work includes *The Guilt Trip* and *The Secret of Comedy*. His collaborations include **Bongwater** (with actress/performance artist time and the others, which don't.

Tracing influences back from one source to another can be difficult when origins in terms of place and time are obscured beneath textures of sound. The sound can be so mixed up, you don't know where and when it comes from. This is what is so disorienting about the Boredoms, whether they're playing earsplitting noise or trance techno. It doesn't sound dated, but it doesn't sound new either. Along with ethnic and geographical origins, chronology has been thrown out the window here as well.

In an issue of **Studio Voice**[19] dedicated to dysfunctional kids (the cover reads "So Fucking What!" in big bold letters) **Eye Yamatsuka** of the Boredoms, Japan's only noise band available on a major American label, had this to say: "I'd like to do something really simple. Like tribal-folk music. The other day I heard some African music on the car stereo and it just blew me away. It's faster than hard core, it's ultratechno, and it's totally on. The rhythms are intricate and it never falls apart. Compared to that stuff, I can't believe how silly and pathetic the Boredoms are. Our rhythms are so infantile and gutless. I'd like to do something that only we could do, something special like that. I mean it doesn't matter whether others can do it. Tribal-folk music is meant to be played by these people and that's all these people can play but that's what they're best at. That's what I like about the tribal stuff."

When punk rock first reared its ugly head, offended critics claimed it wasn't rock, let alone music, because anyone could do it (of course, that was the same criticism leveled against Elvis). Now the same argument has been launched against the genre called noise. This hostility hides the anxiety over the obvious yet controversial fact that this kind of music can only be played by those who play it. You don't learn and then play. You play, period. Nothing can be more contrary to the manual-oriented Nippon modus operandi instilled in Japanese from childhood to retirement.

Unlike punk, instead of calling for a rebellion against this mainstream way of life, Yamatsuka and musicians like the Boredoms are quite content with the world they're in the process of creating and indifferent to the rest of the world. For those devoted to familial and national standardization and productivity, a world that does away with language, aptitude, and security might be regarded as antisocial. And to a certain extent it is. But rock-'n'-roll not only encourages you to undermine the community you come from, it also encourages you to conjure up another community with your imagination.

No other form of expression in this century has been so thorough in playing out this conflict between alienation and community. A sense of not belonging, however muddled, pulls you in and yet at the same time requires you to imagine something bigger than yourself *out there*. It's this kind of unspoken tradition which the Boredoms have inherited from the likes of Elvis and other pioneers of rock-'n'-roll. Musical styles only provide the facade of an invisible history too fast and elusive to be written. Whether the Boredoms are selling more records or are distributed on a major label is unimportant compared to how intensely they play out this contradiction between alienation and community. The Boredoms are still a pop band in my book, and in the best sense of the definition, for without the ability to inspire the creation of a community, however accidental and underground, music loses its force.

If you want to cut yourself entirely off from any community, you wouldn't even bother listening to the Boredoms, or music, or anything for that matter. You would seek the underground not to avoid the heat but because the light aboveground is too bright. In the dark you can stumble across, bump into, and what's more, hear rather than see things and people. There are no stars to worship, no rigid rules to define oneself, no solid lines of communication, only groups of people and sounds colliding. When asked why he played music, Yamatsuka replied, "It didn't come from musical influence. It wasn't something that came out of me. Even now I don't feel like it's something that I want to do. Nothing I do comes from some wish to do something. I mean, with music...it wasn't as if I did it out of some desire to. You wouldn't want to unless you were surrounded by magazines, records, and other sources of information, would you? So it's not something that comes out of me." It is as if Yamatsuka is tearing up any concept of individual expression. It's a myth, whether it's claimed in the name of rock-'n'-roll or America.

Texas Border Radio

"I miss touring America," states **Yasuko Onuki** of **Melt Banana**.[20] Crunched together with them in a back room that's a poor excuse for a fire exit while waiting for them to open for **Kramer** at **La Mama's** in Shibuya, I recall the last show they played on their previous tour, at the **Stork Club** in Oakland, California.[21] It's been almost two years since then, but their sound is as relentless as ever. **Agata's** guitar grinds over **Rika mm's** bass drills underneath the rumbling drums of new drummer **Oshima**. The whole thing is topped off by Onuki's yelping in machine-gun English. Like Yoko Ono's **"Why"**, unless you know the lyrics, you wouldn't know Onuki was singing in English.

"I like using the dictionary, finding words randomly to connect," she says. The other band members claim that they just stumbled across their instruments and made them their own, and Onuki sings her words as if they were found as well. Not that the lyrics don't matter. Their two American releases *Speak Squeak Creak* and *Scratch or Stitch* both come with lyric sheets.

"It's difficult to write lyrics in Japanese. You know how it's hard to rap in Japanese," Onuki explains. While their beats are a far cry from hip hop, Onuki takes her lyrical cues from rap, less in terms of rhyme schemes and more in terms of using language to layer rhythms. If she abstains from singing in Japanese, it might be because the patterns of her native tongue are already so ingrained in her that it would be too hard to come up with another set of crazier ones for her native language without being too self-conscious of the transgressions she's making. It's just a guess, but there does seem to be some common thread running through the bands fronted by female vocalists who sing in other languages besides Japanese; it's as if they can butcher the foreign words because they don't know what rules they are breaking.

Emi Eleonala of **Demi Semi Quaver** not only twists her language inside out but makes a career out of butchering the background from which she emerged.[22] Trained originally as a concert pianist, she turned her back on classical music and school, to the dismay of her parents who promptly kicked her out. She got herself hired as a lounge pianist in clubs without ever having learned a single jazz chord. The only thing

she had in common with jazz was her habit of improvising, making it up as she went along, mutating whatever happened to cross her path. **Yuji Katsui**, more established as a violin sideman for alternative bands including Omoide Hatoba, **Bondage Fruits** and Sakana (none of which remotely sound alike), explains how Demi Semi Quaver formed: "It's a very bizarre ensemble. The guitarist, bassist, and drummer are all very prominent studio musicians in Tokyo who are in heavy demand. Yet somehow she managed to draw them together without any credentials whatsoever. Then I was hired as a fourth. It's an odd assortment, a kind of meeting ground between the alternative and mainstream."

"Which is what we're trying to encourage," says **Masahiko Ogawa**, head of **dohb discs**, explaining the philosophy behind this subsidiary of Epic/Sony. We're crammed (once again!) into the hall of the studio where Demi Semi Quaver is recording. Zak, Katsui, and Eleonala are busy mixing down their new record. Artists on dohb's roster include **Super Car**[23] and **Tomovsky**,[24] as well as bands from abroad, such as the **Pastels** of Scotland and **Sportsguitar** of Switzerland. According to Ogawa, despite the current recession—which is even throwing the invincible megapublishing industry into turmoil—the music industry is doing comparatively well. "Sales might be tapering off, but they're not falling. You have to be realistic. After all, we're talking about music, not TV. Only so many people are willing to go out and buy CD's rather than watch TV."

Speaking of TV, according to Ogawa, even for indie bands, television is absolutely essential for gaining nationwide attention. There's no college radio or other word-of-mouth chain that extends beyond Tokyo. Magazine coverage is heavily monopolized by labels that pay for ad space for their

Ann Magnuson), Dog Bowl and Jad Fair.

22. You might want to call them cabaret rock, but then Demi Semi Quaver has added several new dimensions to the genre. Far from being complacent lounge, this band is tailored for the uncomplacent; the groove-oriented rhythm section of guitarist **Tell Assit!**, bassist **Hideki Yokoyama**, and drummer **Koichiro Naka** explode into free jazz improvs only to implode the outer reaches of their sonic horizons back into Led Zeppelinesque 4/4 beats. With lyrics that are untranscribable, otherwise known as Eleonolian, Emi sings a mixed bag of English, Japanese, and the product of some extra-linguistic dimension that goes on only inside her head.

23. Taking the baton of Brit pop first tossed off from the reverb-drenched bubblegum pop of **Jesus and Mary Chain**, followed by **Creation** bands including the noisydelia of **My Bloody Valentine**, **Super Car** is one of the best examples of noise pop coming from Japan. Oddly, they're not from Tokyo but from the northern prefecture of Aomori. Now the American equivalent might not seem like such a big deal. But to gain any exposure in Japan you pretty much have to create a scene in Tokyo. Osaka produces some exceptions, but most of its bands don't fall under the category of major pop. While in the States you can assert an urban identity provided you live in one of the many major cities, in Japan there is a century-long tradition of branding anyone located outside of Tokyo, Osaka, or Kyoto as an *inakamono*, or "country bumpkin." Things are beginning to change, though. Super Car's label manager, Ogawa declares, "Bands from anywhere in Japan should be able to make it here. Why not Aomori?"

24. Solo recording artist **Tomovsky** is part of the genre I call Diary Pop, which includes home-recording boy wonder **Kazuyoshi Nakamura**. These songwriters write pop gems filled with observations about their daily lives, a kind of anti-arena-rock attitude which exposes you to the artist around the street corner instead of the skyscraper penthouse glamour of the pop star.

25. A project led by drummer **Tatsuya Yoshida**. Yoshida's collaborations include **John Zorn**'s **Spy Vs Spy** performances (Ornette Coleman

bands. Like everywhere else in Japan, the market is not very free here. The only way to make it free is to go completely independent, like **Tatsuya Yoshida** of **Ruins**,25 who has managed to run his own label out of his cramped ten-by-ten room. Sakana's label, **Maboroshi no Sekai**, run by Katsui, is expanding its catalogue, which ranges from the art rock of **Bondage Fruits** to the experimental hardcore of **Bazooka Joe**. The number of pressings may be modest, but it's enough to get by and meet the needs of overseas distribution as well. Katsui gigs an average of twenty nights a month. Commenting on both his session work as a violinist and his Mabo label, he says, "It's my way of connecting all the different threads of interesting music being made right now in Tokyo."

But aside from these exceptions, even indie labels that were thriving until several years ago have closed up shop, with the result that their entire catalogues are wiped off Tokyo's sonic map. One of the most well-known independent distributors in Japan, **I.D.N.**, recently went bankrupt. Most of Sakana's material is now out-of-print. And the chances of major label reissues are a lot slimmer than with American bands.

Labels like Ogawa's dohb discs are striving for a happy medium between the almost instant obliteration of underground artists and the mass market consumption of Top 40 pop. In the end, though, what really struck me about Ogawa was how un-ideological he was about his support of indie music. What mattered most in the end was *sound* as the core of the indie ethic. The staff at dohb—and, come to think of it, everyone I talked to in Japan, from Katsui, Eleonala, Zak, Haino, Melt Banana, Sakana, to Sugar Plant—was in one way or another committed to this pursuit.

I'm at the **South by Southwest Music Festival** in Austin, Texas, to see several of the bands I've written about in my monthly column for **Pulp** magazine, **"Hi-Fi, Lo-Fi"**. This year, attending SXSW is like going to see the movie *Destroy All Monsters*. Instead of monsters from outer space, all your favorite bands from Japan are congregated in a single location. I'm beginning to catch a glimpse of what these bands from Japan might mean to me and other Americans who are waiting in line to see Buffalo Daughter, Demi Semi Quaver, or **Hoppy Kamiyama**26 instead of the latest indie band from Portland. We're here to see how pop music gets not only transmitted but *transmogrified* back and forth between East and West at a pace more uncontrollable than all other media.

We want to be reminded how weird rock can be. Which is nothing new. **Billy Lee Riley**, recording mates with Elvis during the heyday '50s at Sun Records, recorded "Flying Saucers Rock-'n'-Roll" with his band **The Little Green Men** before the decade came to a close. He was convinced that rock was so strange it had to have come from Mars. Upon hearing **"Get a Job"** by the **Silhouettes** in 1958, producer extraordinaire **Brian Eno** recounts, "I suppose people here [in the U.S.] might think it's strange to regard doo-wop as magical music, but I did, because in England we had no tradition of it whatsoever.... I had never heard music like this, and one of the reasons it was beautiful was because it came without a context. It plopped from outer space, in a sense." Or let's take one of the more well-known artists Eno has produced; only by reinventing himself first as space pilot **Major Tom** and then as an alien "like some cat from Japan" in *Ziggy Stardust and the Spiders from Mars* could **David Bowie** reinject some meaning back into rock during the '70s.

Every time I go see a Japanese band play in the States, I get this vibe from the audience that they're here to discover something about pop music without knowing what to expect, that their assumptions and associations with rock will be disturbed instead of confirmed. To the extent that most of us have been brought up on Anglo-American consumer culture, this disturbance will inevitably affect the way we imagine the landscape at home. The twisted pop sounds and culture of Japan get boomeranged back to us not to confirm how weird the Japanese are but to show us how strange it is where we come from.

It took a planet of apes to tell an American he's home and that this home is stranger than space's final frontier. Those were the thoughts that ran through my head as I stared at the video projection behind Japanese pop whiz **Keigo Oyamada**, a.k.a. **Cornelius**.27 On the screen looming above the bleached-blonde girl drummer **Yoshie Hiragakura**, I see Elvis in one of his schlocky Hollywood films, swaggering with hula-dancing gals in Hawaii, singing god knows what. In front of him, Cornelius waves his hand in vertical diagonals like a conductor testing out a baton, finding the notes on his space age **Theremin** (that eerie sounding instrument used in most Cold War era science fiction movies)28 as his band forms a wobbly version of **"Love Me Tender"**.

Which brings me back to the end of *The Planet of the Apes*. **Charlton Heston** and the other apes enter a cave, where they find a **Barbie** doll, a plastic fossil which proves, according to primate anthropologist Cornelius, the existence of an intelligent prehistoric human civilization. Time was thrown out of joint in this world. According to Cornelius, humans evolved into apes. Plastic dolls, not the fossil fuel from which they are synthesized, provide the relics to prove his theory, which may betray the horrible truth that modern human civilization will one day become one big dinosaurian flea market.

H ere Comes Everybody

Near the end of my stay in Japan during the summer of 1998, I rode Tokyo's Yamanote line, which forms a green ellipsis around the emperor's palace, with a photographer friend. She was taking random photos of passengers as we circled the city, marking the exact location where each photo was taken onto her map of train routes. A stop watch hanging around her neck gently beeped every minute, followed by the click of her shutter. Although the time and location for each photo was determined, who ended up in front of the viewfinder and how each subject was framed—all that was left up to chance. She had compiled over 200 thousand photos by that time, over a ten-year span.

This was less an artistic obsession than a necessity. She had been diagnosed with partial amnesia, a tendency to forget daily events. Despite Tokyo's miraculous transformation from the bombed-out ruins of World War II into one of the most expensive megalopolises of the world, for her it had become a city in ruins. She was born the year the Olympics were held there in 1964. All she could remember were the vanished buildings that had sprouted up suddenly like a movie set built to present a national image to the rest of the world. With mind-boggling accuracy she recalled the conversations between shop owners and customers that she had heard when she lived above them as a child. Now these people and buildings were gone, but to her they were ghosts more real than the Tokyo she knew now. She took photos of people around us to confirm their existence, which like that of the boom city they lived in, seemed tenuous at best. "The thing I can't figure out," she sighed, glancing up at the magazine headlines flapping from the roof, "is how I got here."

Photos tell us where we come from, but it's music that provides us with traces of how we got to here from there. No one could have predicted that some kid from Japan who named himself after an American sci-fi creature would be feeding one of the country's all time fave ballads back to us through an instrument that was invented by and named after a Russian émigré abducted by the KGB. Everyone—East, West, North, and South—plays a part in this unanticipated history of technological accidents.

Cause and effect doesn't have much weight in this world of music. You end up with something without knowing exactly how it all came about. History is bunk, as Henry Ford said, not because a single individual can reshape it, but because people don't make things happen, accidents do. Ancient mythology has it that Japan was formed by a bunch of mud-flinging gods; the updated myth is that the shifting subterranean plates that caused the islands to exist in the first place will also someday be the source of its demolition.

So in spite of the doomsday headlines flapping above us announcing political, economic, and social Armageddon, the vibe I got from the people while I was in Tokyo, whether they were making music, films, photographs, or just killing time, was pretty positive, as if it was the rest of the nation, not they, who had to be awoken from a deep slumber underground.

songs gone hardcore) as well as **Keiji Haino**. By recording and producing his recordings in his own cramped apartment, Yoshida has transformed the D.I.Y. ethic into a lifestyle.

26. Head of the record label **God Mountain Records** (Demi Semi Quaver's original label) and musician. His nickname comes from his favorite drink, known as hoppy, a mixture of nonalcoholic beer and shochu alcohol: the Japanese version of Jim Jones' punch.

27. Formerly a member of the neo-acoustic band **Flipper's Guitar** (a pastiche parody of Brit pop bands, most notably **Aztec Camera**), during the '80s, Oyamada began managing his own label, **Trattoria**. The label's catalogue, idiosyncratic to say the least, includes Omoide Hatoba and Boredoms' drummer Yoshimi's recent band **OOIOO**, but also rereleases **Bill Wyman** (Rolling Stones) records. After producing several albums by pop chanteuse Kahimi Karie, Oyamada decided to embark on a solo project, henceforth entitled **Cornelius**. Opting for an ethos of oversaturation, whether in terms of references towards pop songs or pop culture, Cornelius is the latest sensation in American imported Japanese pop; he twists the linear narrative of pop history inside out, making us realize that while anyone from all over the world can consume it, no one can predict how consumer culture comes out.

28. This predecessor to the Moog synthesizer is played by waving one's hand between perpendicular antennas. Mostly famous for producing sound effects signifying alien intervention in science fiction films from the '50s, the instrument reached its pop chart climax with the **Beach Boys**' "Good Vibrations"; you can hear it right before they start humming "I'm thinking of good vibrations." This instrument was invented by Russian enigma **Theremin**, who was later abducted by the KGB. For more info, check out **Steve Martin**'s documentary *Theremin*.

"I don't ever want to lose the world
Trying not to lose the sequence
Of the last moments so hard
I don't like the butterfly
It's trying not to lose the sequence
Of the last moments in vain"

—Sugar Plant, from "Butterfly"

"If I had been showered in gold blood
Wouldn't my prayer have been answered?"

—song title by Haino

future trend

We could, as historians, take a pretty dim view of the future in pop music. The catalogue of depressing phenomena pervading pop music can provide an easy departure point for recounting how things fell apart, creating a smooth analogy to the postwar politics of this nation. Back in the '80s, during the Reagan years, you could nail someone's musical tastes pretty much according to political persuasion. As **Michael Stipe** announced in the fall of '84 before REM began its set, "Let's get a new president this year," turning the message of a song that was otherwise obscure into a political position. **"Radio Free Europe"**, as we learned that night, was really **"Radio Free America"**.

But even at that point, the lines between music and politics had become pretty fuzzy. Reagan and an entire generation took **Springsteen**'s caustic critique of post-Vietnam America, **"Born in the U.S.A."** as a nationalist anthem. By the Bush years, the confusion was accepted by both sides. **"Losing My Religion"** was playing on *Beverly Hills 90210* and the **Grateful Dead** was blasting not through some hippie VW car stereo but the loudspeakers at Greek frat parties.

Historical dimensions entered a kind of *Deep Space Nine* when our first postmodern president turned back to a '70s single, **"Don't Stop Thinking About Tomorrow"**, to fuel some future optimism while waxing nostalgic over a decade that no one could define in any other terms besides hysterical excess. Meanwhile, Springsteen plucked away at his acoustic guitar, mumbling songs in the 3-D mode: Desolation, Despair, and Drinking. Driven nearly underground, he released the stark *Ghost of Tom Joad* as if the hope for polit-

ical change through music had been extinguished not by the country's representatives but by his millions of fans. Wherever America was, it could no longer be located in the present tense. Some claimed Nirvana's *Never Mind* (1991) relocated the ethic of independence—but if it did, it really was the last hurrah for music that could be called distinctly American in terms of the independence it symbolized and in the end (as good Americans do) betrayed.

I prefer to view the whole thing in a more positive light. A habitual amnesiac, I forget about the aspirations of these previous musicians, concentrating solely on their music, on the way it affects my ears *as if* it comes from nowhere. The more I talk to my Japanese musician friends, the more I realize that that's how they've always heard American and British rock. The national and social origins of the music are negligible compared to the visceral impact the sounds have on them. To put it bluntly, they couldn't care less what was going on in the U.S. or Britain, just as the **Rolling Stones** or the **Beatles** aren't busy meditating on the evolution of the blues in the context of racism when they're trying to howl like **Chuck Berry** or **Elvis**. If there was any political meaning to be retrieved from this relationship, it went something like this: everyone was forgetting politics as a tradition, refusing to be haunted by social imperatives handed down from generation to generation through family, god, and country.

So now and in the future, it is this practiced indifference, a kind of amnesia, towards social identities formed by language and nationality that is and may remain alive and well in the music that's coming from Japan. Everyone I've

mentioned in my chapter seems to have this symptom in common. Instead of being valued as kitschy, foreign bands are offering serious alternatives to the cul-de-sac of pop music only intended for domestic consumption. Being foreign is becoming less a novelty and more an incidental, subliminal fact that does little to explain what's interesting about music. Language may be taking a backseat, but that doesn't mean that these folks aren't interested in communication. It's precisely the opposite: by emphasizing the accidental semantics of sounds instead of words, these musicians are invested in the possibility of reaching a wider audience all over the modern world.

Bands like **Sugar Plant** have refused to sing in Japanese, even though, at times, such a move would have advanced their careers in their native country. "We're interested in reaching a wider audience," **Shoyama** of Sugar Plant proclaims. **Ogawa** adds, "We're not particularly attached to English or America, but we also don't want to be stuck solely within the confines of a Japanese audience." Which language a Japanese band sings in might matter more in Japan (what if an American band sang in Japanese?) than in the U.S., where some of us are beginning to accept the fact that a good portion of our population doesn't even speak English as a first language. But even if Japanese pop music sounds less and less "foreign," I don't think it will ever become mainstream. The future of alternative music, then, may be navigated not in terms of its value of counterculture "currency" (or the "hip factor") but according to an unforeseen web of simultaneous exchanges between multiple pop cultures. Such will be the privilege accorded to "nonnative" music. There's no room for prediction here.

EASY TO FIND

1. **Sun Ra**
WE TRAVEL THE SPACEWAYS
CD

A great introduction to the world of Sun Ra, in which music is less about mathematically precise chord progressions and more about the collision of sounds we encounter throughout our lives, whether we're from earth or (as Sun Ra claims to be) from Saturn. The chanting is exquisite: "If you find earth boring/that it's the same old, same thing/ C'mon, sign up with Outer Spaceways Incorporated...."

2. **Greil Marcus**
MYSTERY TRAIN
Book

One of the best books on the twin developments of 20th century America: pop culture and music. With a precise but not overly academic eye, Marcus traces the American paradox of various performers successfully transcending and at the same time doomed in their attempts to transcend identities assigned in terms of race, class, and history.

3. **Bob Dylan**
BOOTLEG SERIES VOLUME 3
CD

This was going to be on my rare list, but only two weeks after I spent big bucks on the unofficial bootleg, CBS records decided to put this out. For anyone who thinks that the punk explosion of '76 initiated the aesthetic of rude audiences, this recording, particularly when Dylan plugs in his electric guitar (one audience member shouts, "Judas!"), serves as a reminder of both how offensive rock has always been and how new the idea of "electric" music was. Dylan and the Hawks tear through this set with a vengeance (for what?).

4. **Philip K. Dick**
UBIK, A SCANNER DARKLY, VALIS,
THE TRANSMIGRATION OF TIMOTHY ARCHER
Books

These books make the X-Files look square instead of paranormal. In terms of capturing the weird surreal experiences evoked by pop culture—whether they're about autosurveillance, pink satellite beams sent into your head from God, or paranoia about commodities (the true "commies")—no one comes close to this postwar writer. Incidentally, Dick is immensely popular in Japan.

5. **Leroi Jones**
BLUES PEOPLE
Book

In a style that anticipates rap, Jones traces jazz as a visceral social history. Out to offend both white critics and musicians, Jones argues against idealizing the history of popular music as an easygoing miscegenation of culture, constantly pointing out the painful origins of jazz and its evolution as more furious than friendly.

6. **Martin A. Lee and Bruce Shlain**
ACID DREAMS
Book

A page-turner social history of LSD. Less a glorification of drug culture and more a report on how truly weird postwar American history can be. The hippies and the '60s counterculture pale in comparison to the CIA, far more intense practitioners of surrealism in its involvement with LSD.

7. **John F. Szwed**
SPACE IS THE PLACE:
THE LIFE AND TIMES OF SUN RA
Book

One of the few musical biographies that doesn't end up repeating the bummer trip of innovation-success-obsolescence (cf. Syd Barret). Not meant exclusively for jazz enthusiasts but for anyone interested in the evolution of one band as it spreads its vision over the course of postwar American history.

8. **Doji Morita**
MOTHER SKY
CD

The strangest folk phenomenon in Japan. An asexual Nick Drake, singer Doji Morita appeared on the folk club circuit in the early '70s when everyone was burnt out on the angry, frustrated politics of the '60s. Several years later, not unlike the political radicals who had gained notoriety a decade before, she disappeared. Out of print, her music was virtually wiped off the map of Japanese pop until the early '90s when one of her early songs, **"Bokutachi no Shippai"** (Our Failure), aired as the theme song for the controversial TV series, *Koko Kyoshi* (High School Teacher). As a result, all her records came back on CD.

9. **Thomas Pynchon**
GRAVITY'S RAINBOW
Book

I tried and tried over the years to get through this tome until I finally managed to romp right through it this summer while I was writing these pieces for *Japan Edge*. Less an account of World War II and more a meditation on trying to understand the multiple worlds of modernity with all its confusions and paranoia.

10. **Yoshio Hayakawa**
HANA NO YONA ISSHUN:
A Moment of Bloom
CD

The former leader of the much heralded '60s band **Jacks**, Yoshio Hayakawa left behind his music career for decades, running a used bookstore instead. Over twenty years later, he decided to come back. This solo piano vocal performance, which clocks in under twenty minutes, is my fave. Consider it the aural equivalent of photographer Nobuyoshi Araki's work.

11. **Jotaro Imawano**
GOTTA! KIYOSHIRO IMAWANO
Book

One of the best books I've read on Japanese music. The biographer traces the career of Kiyoshiro Imawano, leader of RC Succession. It's a rags-to-riches rock-'n'-roll story, filled with disgruntled high school kids who upset their parents and eventually mature into unhip, starving musicians strung out on cheap drugs, only to be met with surprise success one decade too late.

12. **Tetsuya Chiba and Ikki Kajiwara (art and story)**
ASHITA NO JOE: Tomorrrow's Joe
Manga

If the Rocky/Rambo series provided the American analogy to the Reagan years, this epic manga about an orphaned boxer named Joe provides the ultimate parable of youth culture self-destructing in postwar Japan. Avid readers of this series, the Japanese Red Army declared, as they defected to North Korea, "We are Tomorrow's Joe!"

WHERE TO FIND THE ABOVE

<Domestic CDs in print:>

Shin-ichi Ohkura Comfort
18-3 Tanaka Monzen-Cho
Sakyo-Ku Kyoto-Shi, 606 Japan
E-Mail: ohkura@mbox.kyoto-inet.or.jp; **Web Page:** web.kyto-inet.or.jp/people/ohkura/ENGLISH/main.html

<Japanese import CDs:>

DeoDeo.com
E-Mail: webdeo@deodeo.com; **Web Page:** web.deodeo.com

<Japanese books and manga:>

Kinokuniya
1581 Webster St.
San Francisco, CA 94115
(415) 567-7625
Web Pages: www.kinokuniya.com; Web Page: www.kinokuniya.co.jp

collection

HARD TO GET

1. **Duke Ellington**
THE ELLINGTON YEARS
LP set

One of the affordable vinyl compilations of Duke Ellington's big band. A revelation for anyone who wants to experience jazz as the pop phenomenon it once was.

2. **Bob Dylan**
HIGHWAY 61 REVISITED
Mono Version, LP

Mixed in true AM style, "Like a Rolling Stone" shimmers with Dylan's vocals and drums at the forefront. My other mono copy fave is *Bringing It All Back Home* with a kick-ass mix of "Subterranean Homesick Blues".

3. **Shuji Terayama**
SHO WO SUTEYO MACHI E DEYO;
Throw Away Your Books, Let's Go Out
Into the Streets, Book

Published in 1967, this compilation of essays by enfant terrible Shuji Terayama provides a romping critique of the pop culture flourishing through Tokyo and Japan. Kids all over Japan read it, threw the book away (or sold it to used bookstores), ran away to Tokyo, and attempted to reinvent themselves outside familial and national traditions. The original version, a parody of a Japanese weekly magazine, is filled with grotesque images by illustrator Tadanori Yokoo.

4. **Tascam**
TSR-8

An analog 8-track reel-to-reel tape recorder, this tank machine provides ultimate warmth unavailable in the digital sphere of sound reproduction. Cf. Elliot Smith's *Either/Or*.

5. **Canon Auto Zoom 814 Super 8 Camera**

My alliance to the "8" format branches out to visual technology as well. I shot hours of black-and-white footage in Tokyo with this camera.

6. **Koji Aihara, Kentaro Takekuma**
SARUMAN
Manga

Given to me as a gift by the members of Sugar Plant, this is the best manual about manga. On a holy grail quest to become manga artists, Aihara and Takekuma encounter the industry and culture that (in)forms contemporary Japan. Gut-splitting jokes and parodies on mainstream Japanese manga fill this rollicking roller-coaster ride through *the* medium of the bubbling '70s and '60s in Japan. Nothing comes closer to capturing the essence of manga.

7. **Big Star**
SISTER LOVERS
LP

The most inspiring and disturbing oeuvre of rock-'n'-roll pop, Big Star's three albums have haunted pop history ever since they ended up in cut-out bins in the '70s. This version has the original black-and-white cover and ultradepressing liner notes.

8. **Photo of Yoshiharu Tsuge**

Yoshiharu Tsuge is sort of the equivalent of Art Spiegelman insofar as they have both managed to elevate the status of comics to art. Given to me as a farewell gift by my friend Shimamoto, this original photo depicts Tsuge in his used-camera salesman phase. Trying to give up the depressing life of the manga artist, he sits in a small eight-by-eight room surrounded by dozens of outdated cameras along with his wife and child.

9. **Mikio Yamazaki**
A PORT IN VAIN
Film/Video

A first person documentary, presumably about Yamazaki. After a sudden premonition of his death, Yamazaki takes his savings out of the bank and deliberates how to use them. First he thinks of spending his cash on terrorism, or "tero," but then he decides to go for "ero" (eroticism). The narrator contemplates a kind of Oz-like story of Mickey and Minnie Mouse which crisscrosses between various contemporary pop cultures including Japanese, American, and Indian. This video copy is currently unreleased.

WISH LIST

1. **Brian Eno OBLIQUE STRATEGIES,**
OVER ONE HUNDRED WORTHWHILE
DILEMMAS Cards

A deck of cards developed by Brian Eno and painter Peter Schmidt modeled on the Chinese *I Ching*, or *Book of Changes*. When bogged down in his or her work, the user flips up a card that might offer an accidental hint. I could have used this deck for the chapters I wrote for this book.

2. **Bob Dylan**
BASEMENT TAPES
5-CD set

Filled with visions of blood, revenge, and displacement, these songs of Dylan, written and recorded at home while recovering from a long hiatus from fame and rock-'n'-roll, trash the optimism of the American dream with their landscape of nightmares, haunted memories, and lost communities. Actually, how would I know? I haven't heard the damn thing.

3. **Moog Synthesizer**

Accumulating dust in everyone else's garage, this analog electronic synthesizer, invented after the Theremin, has undergone a revival after the so-called digital revolution of the '80s when everyone woke up, smelled the coffee, and realized how organic outdated technology can sound. (Cf. Stereolab)

Since three is my lucky number, I won't wish for more.

BIO

Born in New York in 1966 while the Beatles' were performing in Budokan, **YUJI ONIKI** currently resides in Oakland, California. Oniki writes and performs music with other members of underground pop bands, including **Guided By Voices** and **Outrageous Cherry**, and has appeared on international compilations from Canada (**Back of a Car** label) to Sweden (**Yesterday Girl**). As an excuse (and economic means) to justify his life in music, Oniki writes monthly columns for the adult manga magazine *Pulp*. Oniki also moonlights as a manga translator for *Pulp* and the anime-related manga magazine *Animerica Extra*.

First exposures to pop music began in 1971 in the pre-FM (not to mention pre-MTV) days of AM car radio and ranged from one-hit-wonder Scottish band **Pilot**'s **"Magic"** to the **Jackson 5**'s **"I Want You Back"**. Dosages of commercial pop counteracted the half-hour bummer trip Oniki and his brother had to endure while traveling to Japanese school in Gardena, California. Japanese pop exposure occurred almost simultaneously via the annual New Year Kohaku Pop Music Festival broadcast by satellite on Japan's public network, NHK. Among the performances of cross-cultural plagiarism that made the greatest impression was the Okinawan Jackson 5 rip-off band, **Finger 5**, whose **"ABC"** hit was **"Kojin Kyoshi"** (Private Tutor).

After moving back to New York, Oniki got his hands on the best (**Yosui Inoue, RC Succession**) and the worst (**Masashi Sada, Off Course**) of Japanese rock and pop through the juvenile bootleg network at Saturday Japanese school known as "tape dubbing." After taking a ten-year retirement from Japanese pop culture (no TV, no manga, no nothing) during the Reagan-Bush years, upon seeing the Boredoms and a whole slew of noise bands from Japan, Oniki began writing about this scene because, he claims, "It baffled me. I always thought I understood pop music until I heard these bands who spat every musical/cultural expectation back in my face. That's how I started getting interested in Japan again. Every permutation of popular culture gets violated over there, for better or for worse."

For information on
recordings write to:

1 Plus 1 Rec'ds
2440 16th St. Suite #188
San Francisco, CA 94103
oneplus@sirius.com

Back of a Car
#4636 MPO
Vancouver
BC V6B 4AI
beeman@istar.ca

Yesterday Girl Records
Grusåsgränd 162, 4 tr
121 30 Enskededalen
Sweden
stefan@cyber.matteusskolan.stockholm.se

Q&A

Where did you live in Tokyo?

I spent about two years in the Takadanobaba section of the Shinjuku district. It's the student ghetto of Shinjuku, where college students and ronin live and get drunk on weekends out of frustration, boredom, or both.

What are your favorite shops in Tokyo?

The public baths rule—although they're becoming extinct along with youths who can deal with sharing baths. The baths have been disappearing over the course of the decade. Love hotels have replaced them as the national pastime for leisure and pleasure.

What do you recommend to visitors to Tokyo?

If you're a tourist, try spending the entire day on a shoestring budget of 1,000 yen and see what happens. If you have too much money in Tokyo, things can get too predictable, i.e. the people you meet, the things you buy, and where you drink and eat. Or if

you're living there, find the cheapest apartment possible and you'll meet some interesting folks. I certainly did.

TOKYO

Yuji Oniki

DIARY no.4

June 2

Although I'm no longer the cinephile I used to be, I finally get off my butt to go see a documentary called *A* at a theater in Nakano. It's the third-person video diary of **Hiroshi Araki**, a follower of Aum, who has been keeping the ship afloat since the leaders were arrested following the 1995 subway poison gas incident. The film covers a period of two years, beginning in the fall of 1995. Instead of joining the media witch hunt, these filmmakers turn the tables, treating the media's coverage of Aum as a spectacle more grotesque than the cult itself. No attempt is made to reduce the followers to profiles of criminal and abnormal behavior. Araki and other cult members are portrayed as remarkably articulate and level-headed, in sharp contrast to the hysteria of the public, authorities, and the media.

Hysteria only provides a minor cathartic relief to the Japanese from the current fear of political, social, and economic collapse. As filmmaker **Tatsuya Mori** puts it:

> The essential question shouldn't be asked in the past tense—"What caused the [poison gas] incident?"—but in the present tense—"Why, despite the incident, are Aum's followers still practicing?" What I realized was that the answer to this question can be found not inside Aum but outside, in other words, in the mentality of the Japanese people.

Under the twin banners of the emperor and economic development, Japan modernized at an incredible pace, doing away with ethics and religion. Wrapped in hysteria, most of the population has demanded vengeful retaliation [against Aum], but Aum's "darkness" is something that resides in our own subconscious. Any contact with this darkness is feared to an irrational degree. Avoiding any introspection into this darkness, the Japanese instead experienced catharsis through the ensuing media hysteria. Which is hardly surprising.... How can you continue to live your life the way you did once you come into contact with the darkness? This isn't the kind of darkness you can capture by wandering around Aum's vicinity. The camera can't capture something that doesn't give off any light. But if we examine what surrounds this darkness as accurately as possible, then perhaps the darkness will become clearer.

When TV reporters throng around the cult compounds, Araki confronts them on their invasion of privacy. A reporter repeats the same lame excuse over and over, that he wants to keep people informed, but it sounds more like a mantra that he automatically spits out under pressure. A woman from **NHK**, Japan's PBS equivalent, is rendered speechless during a special interview with several cult members, who point out that the media creates fictions by decontextualizing incidents into soundbites.

Bizarre incidents follow: after one cop, in the process of harassing a cult follower, trips over himself and sprains his ankle, the other cops arrest the follower. And one follower is arrested for returning a library book late.

The weirdest thing for me is watching the public go ballistic because the followers (1) left their family behind, and (2) are poor patriots. The patriotism issue strikes me as really bizarre. I mean, my immediate reaction to religious cults is, "What—are you *crazy*!?" not "You're a disgrace to our country!" Which just goes to show that many Japanese, despite having given up on politics, are still very nationalistic. Again, it's the same thing with family honor: "You're a disgrace to your family!" instead of "What—are you *nuts*!?"

My only personal contact with Aum came one evening in 1992 when I was living in Takadanobaba. The rooms were very small in my building, which was owned by the downstairs dry cleaner. The walls were so thin a thread of light came through a pinhole from the next room, which was occupied by a *ronin*. Ronin are high school graduates who, having failed Japan's college entrance exams, spend a year studying in anticipation of the following year's exam. It's a critical period during which they often begin to wonder what the hell the point of all their hard work is, making them easy targets for cults offering cheap and easy answers.

One night someone knocked on my neighbor's door and I heard him say, "About that conversation we just had…" I listened to the two having a religious jam session. About an hour later, the kid who lived there was beginning to sound really tired—it was past midnight—and finally mentioned his fatigue. His visitor didn't get it, so finally the kid spelled it out, "You have to leave *now*." I was getting tense myself. I heard the door open, followed by footsteps, a pause, and then more footsteps as the intruder continued down the wooden stairs and exited. Then I noticed a cartoon flyer he had slipped underneath my door. (Only after I returned to San Francisco a year later and was watching the Aum incident coverage on TV did I realize who the cartoon guru on the flyer was.) Ten minutes later, someone came upstairs and knocked on my neighbor's door again. The kid opened it and the cult

member said, "Look, I really think we need to talk…." I was too creeped out to sleep, so I went downstairs to take a walk and have a late-night bite at the small bar-restaurant run by the seventy-year-old woman who kept a subscription to the communist daily, *Akahata*.

I'm on my way to an event called "Arakinema," (as in "Araki's cinema") at the **Loft**, in Shibuya. At the Shinjuku train station, some women are approaching people at random offering to read their palms. Like most pedestrians, I ignore them. Then I realize I can use this occasion for a Tokyo Diary entry, so I turn back and wait to be approached. No one comes close to me, though. I'm getting a little upset now—I mean, c'mon, these other folks are giving you the cold shoulder and here I am making myself available! Finally I realize that they are only approaching women, not men. Damn, nothing to write about. Plus, now I'm late.

There are about 500 people in the Loft auditorium. All of a sudden, **"Shanghai Riru"** comes blaring through the speakers and photographer Araki, holding a wireless mike, strolls down the aisle singing the lyrics, karaoke style. Everyone bursts out laughing. After his brief introduction, his latest series of photographs are projected one after another onto the screen. It's a little photo documentary of his visit to Shanghai, but it's so different from Oya's video clips that it makes me realize how different the same place can seem through the eyes of different people. These diary notes on Tokyo must be subjective too, then.

TAKASHI'S FIRST FUSION

BY: FURUYA USAMARU

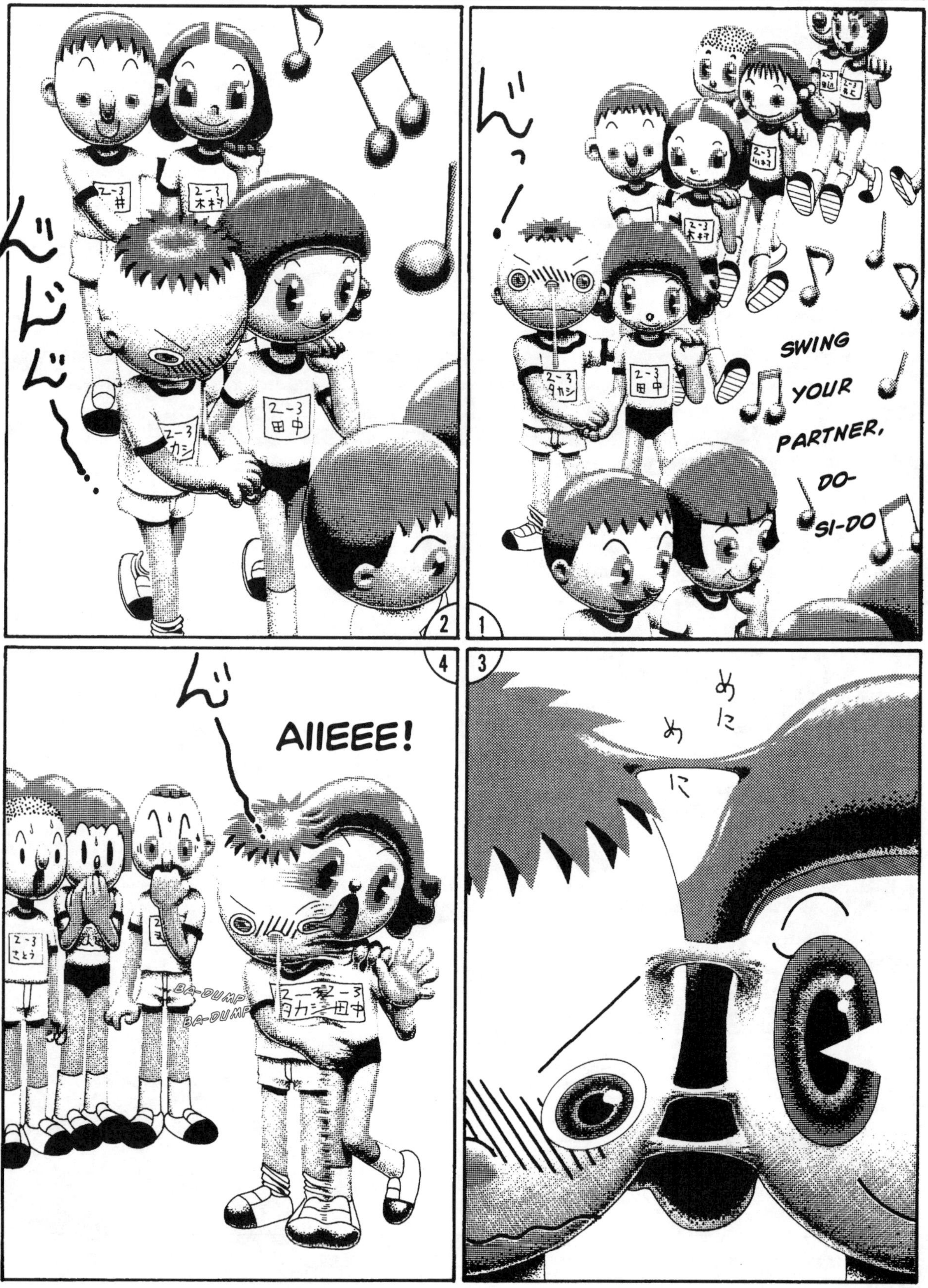
んっ！
SWING YOUR PARTNER, DO-SI-DO
んじんじ～…
めに
めに
ん～
AIIEEE!
BA-DUMP
BA-DUMP

マンガ

MANGA VIEWS

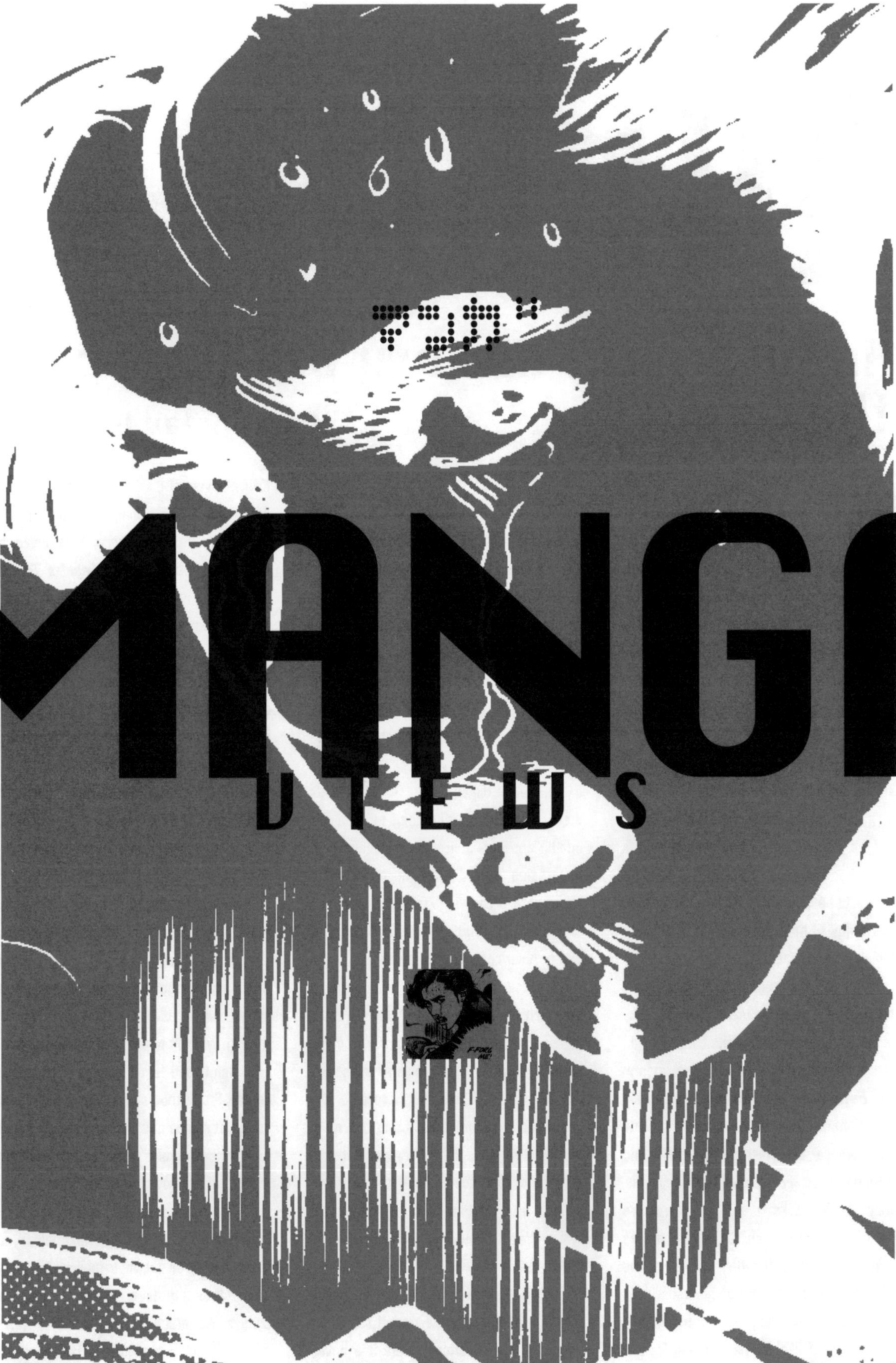

overview

An Alternate History of the Comics

Carl Gustav Horn

America, 1999 (and how futuristic that used to sound). The country is following a fiction bestseller entitled *Eagle*. Its provocative premise: in a not-too-distant presidential race, the nomination, and eventually the high office itself, is for the first time being sought by a Japanese-American: the ruggedly handsome Kenneth Yamaoka, Yale man and Marine veteran of Vietnam. *Eagle* is not a novel or TV series, but a black-and-white comic, one of ten different stories being serialized in a thick biweekly magazine appropriately named *Big Comic*. For the price of a mere two dollars (as it is printed on cheap newsprint and is no more meant to be kept around after reading than yesterday's newspapers), *Big Comic's* million-and-a-half strong audience, mostly men in their thirties and forties, gets a new twenty-five-page installment of each of its serialized stories when it hits the stands on the tenth and twenty-fifth of every month. But *Eagle* is the hottest story between the covers right now. And no wonder: a politician whose very identity provokes and intrigues a society wounded by race and history. Is Yamaoka the one to restore America's faith in itself? Or will he, like so many contenders for the presidency, be undone by a reporter hot on his trail?

Does this story sound intriguing? Maybe *you'd* like to get into *Eagle*, too. Unfortunately, as **David Bowie** said, "This is not America." Everything in the above paragraph is true, except for the first word, which should read Japan. No, that 1999 America is one of those alternate-history science fiction scenarios in which a change in the past leads to a very different today. An America in which *something* happened years ago to make *manga*, or comic books ("what your people call corn and my people call maize"), a form of entertainment competing for the gaze of millions of solid, well-established adults as well as kids, an industry with eight billion dollars in yearly sales that is only the starting point for spin-offs into billions more in licensed merchandising, advertising tie-ins, and an incalculable effect on a society's TV, movies, and even literature. Well, that's all *true* in Japan. But in an America in which so-called "mainstream" comics (which don't even begin to approach the sales figures of Japan's most popular manga magazines) are still dominated by suckers in blue-and-red suits, and any "alternative" comic that chooses a subject besides superheroes (or is drawn in black-and-white) is doing very well if it sells a few thousand copies—well, this scenario sounds as likely as a 1999 America in which Walter Mondale is finishing up a triumphant fourth term.

Eagle comes to mind because, on the face of it, it's exactly the kind of story that might intrigue Americans were it a novel, TV show, or movie. It's set in America and it's about Americans, after all. Its creator, **Kaiji Kawaguchi**, stirred up a bit of a buzz here when his '80s story, the equally political thriller *Silent Service*, was given a major profile by *The Los Angeles Times*. It's even drawn in a fairly realistic style, without that so-called big-eyed look often ascribed to manga (never viewed as strange on Fred Flintstone, but then, he was a *white* cartoon caveman). In short, *Eagle* seems to have no liabilities in its look or its story, only in its medium: the comic book.

Director **Kevin Smith** raised the point in his film *Chasing Amy* when **Ben Affleck** points to young lovers outside and tells struggling alternative comic creator **Joey Lauren Adams** that *they* should be the ones reading her stuff. Smith has called **Garth Ennis**'s **DC Vertigo** comic book *Preacher* "more fun than going to the movies" (and soon *Preacher* is to *be* a movie—a medium through which it hopes to reach the millions who don't read it in its original form). Of course, Smith knows that even though there are great stories and characters to be found in American comics, Americans are at the movies, like his own, instead.

The fact that comics here serve as the inspiration for mass entertainment, yet never get to be massive themselves, suggests that whatever makes American comics so much less successful than manga, it isn't a fundamental lack of merit. One can certainly argue, in fact, that since the comic book is one of a number of

American inventions, like the transistor radio and VCR, which was better manufactured and marketed in Japanese hands, manga as we know it today is as much a creation of business people as artists. Business needs opportunity or, as another preacher once said, the race is not to the swift, but a matter of time and chance. In Japan, the time was the late 1940s, and the chance lay in the postwar devastation. Back to the alternate history lesson. Such AH stories often revolve around the same concepts examined in the regular study of history: that is, history as determined both by the times—large social forces, such as wars—and by the chance appearance of important individuals—such as innovators. Both concepts were at work in the history of the manga world.

The great innovator was **Osamu Tezuka**, a medical doctor turned artist who, beginning in the late 1940s, introduced cinematic layout techniques that suddenly made comics as exciting to Japanese readers as movies. Equally important, Tezuka was a powerhouse both physically and intellectually. **Frederik Schodt**, author of the classic *Manga! Manga! The World of Japanese Comics*, calls him the human dream factory. Tezuka made his story comics work for every kind of story, from the charming animal kingdom of *Kimba* to an adaptation of *Crime And Punishment*. Yet the times were also receptive to Tezuka's genius. Innovation—progressive change—was the trumpet call in postwar Japan, as indeed it had to be, for a country that had lost everything. And having lost everything, it needed entertainment that was cheap to produce: comics, unlike movies, radio, or TV, needed no fancy equipment either to make or experience.

Indeed, Tezuka's example drew many of the same creative types into comics who, had they been living in prosperous postwar America, would have gone into movies, radio, and TV instead. By the time Japan completed its recovery in the 1960s, manga had established itself as a mass medium, a position it has never relinquished. Manga does what movies, radio, and TV do in America—like all of them, manga is a decades-old concept that remains relevant and successful by both reflecting the latest trends and providing something for every market.

"Time and chance" were different in America. Those who love comics here look at manga with wonder and regret. Yet it almost seems greedy to covet such success; after all, in the postwar years, America created the greatest film, radio, and television industries in the world. It says something about the power of manga that Americans successful in entertainment *do* covet the power of manga, and increasingly turn to it for inspiration. Nicolas Cage plays intense guys; it's this intensity that won him an Academy Award for his portrayal in *Leaving Las Vegas*. Yet *Variety* reports him determined to film a version of Tezuka's famous children's adventure, *Astro Boy*.

Manga is a world of strange attractors. In the articles that follow, you will only begin to touch upon its incredible diversity. It has been a medium advanced through daring, and it is that aspect, especially, that intrigues Americans who are both social scholars and fans, such as **Matt Thorn** and **Dan Kanemitsu**, who contribute their observations about the strange world of amateur manga, or *dojinshi*, in Thorn's "Girls And Women Getting Out Of Hand" and this author's "Sonoda's Eleven." **Yuji Oniki** explores the radical politics of manga in "Terrorist Manga," **Mason Jones** its avant-garde decadence in "Underground Manga Discoveries," and **Patrick Macias** the wandering souls of **Leiji Matsumoto** and the transgressions of **Go Nagai**, which changed Japan's view of comics forever in "Mainstream Outsiders: Prisoners of the Parallel Universe." Five faces of manga await you....

GIRLS AND WOMEN GETTING OUT OF HAND: The Pleasures and Politics of Japan's Amateur Comics Community   Matt Thorn

I was conducting research on the readers of *shojo* manga, or Japanese girls' comics, and had heard from several informants about amateur manga, or *dojinshi*, which focused on the theme of same-sex love between boys or men. This theme, known as *shonen ai*, or "boys' love," first appeared in commercial shojo manga in the early '70s but by the late '80s had faded to a narrow subgenre. In amateur manga for girls and women, however, it had apparently become the dominant theme....

The action [at a 1993 dojinshi convention in Osaka], I gradually realized, was at the *yaoi* booths. Yaoi is an acronym of sorts for the phrase, "*Yama nashi, imi nashi, ochi nashi*," or "No climax, no meaning, no resolution," a phrase coined in the latter '80s to describe this new genre of amateur manga.... At the event, I felt overwhelmed. There was a powerful energy in the air: this space belonged to these girls and women, and they were reveling in it. I envied the electric sense of community they shared, but I didn't have the courage to initiate many conversations....

In 1985, a group of young women artists began producing a series of spin-offs of the popular boys' soccer manga *Captain Tsubasa*, in which the two boy heroes were

Makaroni Horenso © Tsubame Kamogawa/Akita Shoten ● Captain Harlock © Leiji Matsumoto ● Violence Jack © Go Nagai/Dynamic Planning Inc. ● Wild Seven © Mikiya Mochizuki/Tokuma Shoten ● Otokogumi © Tetsu Kariya/Ryoichi Ikegami/Shogakukan ● Dame Oyaji © Mitsutoshi Furuya/Akebono Shuppan ● Seikimatsu Bansankai © Hideshi Hino/Tokyo Sanseisha

portrayed as lovers. This formula proved to be a stunning hit, and similar **Captain Tsubasa** take-offs began to appear in huge numbers, helping to rapidly increase the population of the amateur manga community. **Captain Tsubasa** was followed by take-offs of such boys' manga and anime hits as **Saint Seiya**, **Tenkuu Senki Shurato**, **Yoroiden Samurai Troopers** [shown in the U.S. as **Ronin Warriors**], and **Ginga Eiyuu Densetsu**. The term yaoi refers to the fact that many of these take-offs don't purport to be integrated stories, but are rather just scenes and snippets, *oishii tokoro dake*, or "only the yummy parts." What constitutes a yummy part is usually a scene in which the two male protagonists are in some way brought into physical contact with each other, there is an awkward moment, then one makes an aggressive move, perhaps initiating a kiss. The other resists, but it is clear that the feelings are mutual.

Some artists will end the scene here, preserving the tension between the two. Others will treat readers to several pages of skin, tangled sheets, sweat, and other bodily fluids. Many so-called yaoi manga, however, are genuine stories, often with plots stretching over many volumes, leading some fans to suggest alternative meanings of the acronym, such as "*Yamete, oshiri ga itai*" ("Stop, my ass hurts")....

In the summer of 1995, I attended the Tokyo Comic Market, which, with the introduction of yaoi, saw its attendance in the '80s shoot from five to six digits.... Yoshihiro Yonezawa, president of Comic Market, told me the event had grown so large and become so segmented that it lacked the overall sense of community it once had, and which can still be found in many smaller gatherings. But in spite of its segmentation, the Comic Market retains a festival-like character. Such events create a liminal space and time, in which participants shed many of the restraints of mundane society.

Many participants create and wear elaborate costumes, modeled on characters from favorite manga or anime. Known as costume play, or *kosupure* for short, this is so venerable a tradition in the Comic Market and other events that dressing rooms are provided. Kosupure often entails crossdressing, so one sees women dressed as the dashing uniformed heroes of **Gundam Wing** alongside men dressed as **Sailor Moon**. Erotic teasing is also common, particularly on the part of cross-dressed costume players, who will often make suggestive comments or fondle fellow participants of either sex, who are usually happy to play along....

When I ask fans why they like those genres, they tend to equivocate. One standard response is that stories of heterosexual romance, such as those common in shojo manga, are boring because they are predictable.... Another fan expanded on this, saying that a heterosexual romance is always limited by the fact that the heroine and hero, no matter what the circumstances, are ultimately following the socially prescribed norms of mating. In a yaoi story, the two male characters are inexorably drawn to each other, in spite of social proscriptions and their own desire to avoid such a taboo relationship. The problem with this argument is that it doesn't explain why the taboo relationship has to be one between two men, rather than two women or some other pairing or grouping....

Some readers have told me they enjoy the stories because they present an idealized masculine world. Some speak of despising femininity and even of wishing they had been born male, rather than female. For most such women, yaoi and shonen ai allow them to indulge in the fantasy of loving a man as a man, or, to rephrase it, as an equal, free of predefined gender expectations. Nonetheless, I think there is an undeniable voyeuristic element, because the readers and artists are in fact females.

Many fans also clearly take pleasure in seeing their male characters suffer. There is much eroticized violence. In one famous commercial manga in this genre, **Minami Ozaki**'s *Bronze*, the aggressor actually hacks his own arm off with a sword to demonstrate his love. This, too, suggests to me that, while readers may imagine themselves in the place of one of the male characters, they may also objectify them at the same time....

Perhaps you can begin to see why I characterize this genre and its fans as "queer." The women and girls in this community are not satisfied with mainstream norms regarding gender and sexuality. They may never display that dissatisfaction in front of their more conventional peers, but they give expression to it in the liminal space of the "event" and every time they read or draw or write a story in this genre. Fans acknowledge the subversive potential of their hobby when they jokingly describe it, as they so often do, as *yabai*, *abunai*, or *ayashii*, "dangerous" or "suspect."

But beyond the treatment of gender and sexuality in these stories, there is another subversive potential in this community. Feminists, both in Japan and elsewhere, have noted that the mass media tends to be male-dominated because of limited access to technology. Media require the capital of corporations because of the expensive technology and labor they entail, and women have limited access to such capital. Manga, however, like literature, is a medium that requires very little capital, which may be part of the reason why it has become a lucrative form of income for so many women artists.

Amateur manga, in turn, while providing income only for the most popular artists, provide women and girls with an inexpensive means of self-expression, utterly free of editorial restrictions.... The possibilities of such a community should make any feminist drool, yet there is a tendency to look on such popular culture with suspicion, to see participants as dupes of capitalist patriarchy. We would like to see these women identify themselves as feminists, but to try to make it into something "good for you" (*tame ni naru*) might spoil the fun and nullify the energy of this movement, if it can be called a movement. After all, the pleasure for most readers is the very fact that it is "naughty." Perhaps we should accept the progressive, subversive, and feminist potential in a community such as this that does not carry the "union label."

Excerpts from a paper presented at the annual meeting of the American Anthropological Association in Washington, D.C., on November 22, 1997. Mr. Thorn is a doctoral candidate in cultural anthropology at Columbia University in New York and adjunct lecturer of humanities at Kyoto Seika University, as well as an accomplished writer on, and translator of, manga.

Banana Fish © Akimi Yoshida/Shogakukan ● *Yume no O-saku* © Suehiro Maruo/Seirindo ● *Shunrei* © Tsukasa Kotobuki ● *Love Song* © Keiko Nishi/Shogakukan ● *A, A'* © Moto Hagio/Shogakukan ● *Chosen Ame #10* © Kenichi Sonoda ●
Ranma 1/2 © Rumiko Takahashi/Shogakukan

Sonoda's Eleven:
Sample the Dojinshi Scene With a Taste of *Chosen Ame*

Carl Gustav Horn

Chosen Ame # 10, published by Sonodaya

"**O**nce the cup is passed, no more superiors, no more inferiors, no restraint, no rudeness.... Condoner of improprieties, the jeweled rake to sweep away sorrows! Leveler of the high! Mixer of the low with the mighty...what a shame to turn it down!"

–Kazuo Koike, *Lone Wolf And Cub*

Kazuo Koike, one of manga's most famous writers, was speaking of sake. But he could just as well have been speaking of that potent homebrew called *dojinshi*. In its most common form, it is the moonshine of the manga world: untaxed mash from a small press sold directly from producer to customer, its contents an unfiltered travesty of the mass-produced brands, raw and crazy, and drunk straight from the jug.

In Japan, comics are a true mass medium, meaning the average Japanese would no more speak of being a fan of manga than the average American would of being a fan of television. In both cases, it is simply something they see every day. However, this does not mean that comics lack a cult aspect in Japan. And it is indicative of the strength and vitality of manga that the primary expression that manga fandom takes is to make their own. Dojinshi are an amazing aspect of Japanese media culture: a form of publishing as a hobby, practiced by fans in as many as 50,000 individual circles throughout Japan, representing any and every field of interest. While what these creative circles produce can in fact be anything from an original video to a tea mug, the vast majority of dojin consist of printed matter.

One could call them fanzines, but unlike the American fanzine, most dojin contain not articles but manga stories and illustrations. Another distinction between fanzines and dojin is that while many fanzines have a general satirical or ironic tone towards pop culture, those dojin which are not original fiction make unabashed use of copyrighted characters—usually from anime, manga, video games, and other otaku devotions—dropping them into situations of the authors' choosing with no attempt to alter their likenesses.

Because dojin are produced in limited print runs—usually from several hundred to several thousand—one could also call them small-press comics. Yet, as noted by **Dan Kanemitsu**—a translator, artist, and writer whose publication *Storm Front Journal #0* represents the most comprehensive study of the dojinshi scene available in English—in America, small-press comics go through much the same distribution process and are sold in the same comic book stores as comics from major publishers. By contrast, dojinshi are in a world quite distinct from Japan's manga industry, the juggernaut that puts millions of comics for sale on every subway platform in Japan. The manga industry comes to you, but *you* must come to dojin.

Shunrei from *Chosen Ame #2,* by Tsukasa Kotobuki © Tsukasa Kotobuki

And the most famous place to come and get them is Comic Market, Comike for short, a convention that, twice every year since 1975, has attracted hordes of otaku. The term horde is used here in the medieval sense of a great Asian wave of conquest; Comike has been known to have 300,000 attendees, making it one of the largest gatherings of *any* kind in the world. There are neither presentations nor panels at Comike. Its business, conducted at as many as 20,000 tables, is the sale of dojin. And Comike is only the largest. Kanemitsu notes that there are perhaps 100 dojin conventions in metropolitan Tokyo alone each year.

While some dojin are photocopied and stapled, offset printing is more common: the typical dojin for sale is a magazine-size booklet, thirty to sixty pages in length, perfect bound, with glossy covers and crisp black-and-white interiors. But the idea of dojin being works of craft rather than mass media means experimentation in format as well; odd-sized, hardbound, and full-color dojin are not unknown. **Hiroyuki Utatane**—known to U.S. fans through his **Fantagraphics-Eros** series *Temptation* and *Countdown* as well as his variant cover for issue #2 of Adam Warren's *Gen13 Bootleg: Magical Drama Queen Roxy*—even sheathed a dojin on the topic of leather in a *faux* version of same.

The most popular dojin at Comike will be sold from tables against the walls, so as to allow lines several thousand strong to snake around the perimeter of the event. At the front of one of these lines, you will find **Kenichi Sonoda**'s legendary dojin *Chosen Ame*. Sonoda named it for, and gave it the same logo as, the family business back in Kumamoto prefecture—not manga publishing but the manufacturing of *chosen ame*, "Korean candy," a sweet rice bonbon said to have been popular of old with the Japanese troops who attempted to conquer Korea in the late sixteenth century.

Sonoda is perhaps best known in America as the creator of the popular anime *Riding Bean* and manga *Gunsmith Cats*. At the Chicago convention Anime Central, as

the 1998 guest of honor, Sonoda was asked whether it was true that all dojinshi were erotic in style, because that was the impression American fans were beginning to get. "Oh, no," answered Sonoda, "Only about seventy percent." *Chosen Ame* speaks with the voice of that majority, and as a manga-style parody, or "paro," book, it represents a typical dojin in form. Where *Chosen Ame* is atypical is that most of its circle consists of well-known professionals, including many known to American fans. Besides Sonoda, **Hiroyuki Utatane** is a frequent contributor, as is **Tsukasa Kotobuki**, character designer for the game *Toshinden*; **Fumio Iida**, animation director on *Honneamise* and *Roujin-Z*; **Kenji Tsuruta**, creator of *Spirit of Wonder*; and **Hisao Tamaki** of the *Star Wars* manga adaptation.

A further distinction of *Chosen Ame* is its America-based contributors. Although *Chosen Ame* is directed towards a Japanese fan audience, Sonoda, who has set many of his stories in the United States, is a frequent visitor here and can list the names of American artists he enjoys. Besides Dan Kanemitsu, himself a longtime member of the circle, there have been appearances by **Adam Warren**; **Rick Mays** of DC's *The Arsenal*; **Robert deJesus**, a regular illustrator for *PlayStation* magazine; and **Studio Proteus**'s **Tomoko Saito**. As a brilliant retouch artist, Saito has smoothed the transposition of Sonoda and Utatane's

Otaku no Video + from *Chosen Ame #5*, by Kenichi Sonoda © Kenichi Sonoda

Tenshitachi no Kyoen (Angels' Crazy Party), by Adam Warren, from *Chosen Ame #10* © Adam Warren

artwork to America, but her own attractive, even elegant, manga style (as seen on the variant cover for the first issue of *Magical Drama Queen Roxy*) has won many admirers in her native Japan.

Saito, a veteran of rock music dojin who is capable of drawing Rob Zombie as a manga pretty boy, explains that for professionals who display fan spirit—the very sort found in *Chosen Ame*—dojin are an opportunity to "play house," to not only act like fans for a change but actually meet the fans themselves, at Comike. "Today's generation of manga readers in Japan aren't great letter writers," says Saito; the only feedback a manga pro might get is "when the editor says 'you suck, and you're fired.'" Although Saito says she has trouble keeping up with what characters are hot in Japan, the plus side is that her contributions to

Chosen Ame often inject bits of American culture, including psychic hotlines and the answer to the question why, in the words of the **Red Hot Chili Peppers**, "Catholic Schoolgirls Rule".

Sonoda did the character designs for **Studio Gainax**'s surrealist self-portrait *Otaku no Video* (available subtitled in the U.S. through **AnimEigo**), and the very first issue of *Chosen Ame* came out not long after, hitting the summer 1992 Comike with contributions by Gainax's **Hideaki Anno** (a four-page *Spirit of Wonder* story) and **Yoshiyuki Sadamoto** (two pages on *Nadia*) themselves. Sonoda's friendship with Gainax goes back to the '80s; it's a neighborhood thing from the streets, bars, and even the Denny's of Kichijoji, an urban center on the edge of Tokyo proper. The former locale of both Gainax and Sonoda, Kichijoji was then, and remains, a Greenwich Village for otaku in the industry. Kichijoji Station is not far from the offices of Gainax's **Hiroyuki Yamaga**, whose script for *Otaku no Video* features a nostalgic scene in which Kubo finds his college grounds invaded by dojin-selling otaku; while besieged with one circle's quality assurances for their "she-male" publication, another avers that they'll throw in the *Zambot 3* blueprints for free.

Gainax's association with dojinshi is no less strong today; *Evangelion* was specifically scripted as dojin-friendly by including scenes intended as points of departure, such as Shinji's first kiss, from which the fans could run wild. *Chosen Ame* in particular still features many artists associated with Gainax past and present. And as may be expected, *Chosen Ame* has had its way with *Eva* more than once.

The night-on-the-town ethic of the early Kichijoji days can still be found in *Chosen Ame*, but now that they're all famous, it takes on an almost Rat Pack–like atmosphere. As Frank, Sammy, and Dino jived on each other's routines, *Chosen Ame*'s artists commonly parody each other's professional work. And just like the Rat Pack, a whiff of mob violence is not unknown: in this case, the whiff of gun-

Cinderella's List, from *Chosen Ame #5* © Golden Lion Tamaki

powder whenever one of the dojin's artists portrays Sonoda "reviewing" an issue's contributions and/or contributors with a 9 mm.

This sort of ambiance was shown most literally in *Chosen Ame* #10, the theme of which (every issue has a theme) was booze. While three of the contributors made reference to the evidently much-beloved episode #44 of *Urusei Yatsura*, "Drunkard's Boogie," others described actual bar-hopping experiences with *Chosen Ame* friends in *Lost Weekend*–like detail. **Hizuru** "after H comes I" **Imai**, who typically draws herself in an inebriated state (in one comic waking up on a couch to quote *Eva*'s Shinji Ikari: "Another unfamiliar ceiling"), begins to recount the bender with Sonoda and Iida, only to have to resort to a blackout panel by page three. Coming to the next morning, she calls a friend, who phones in the rest of the story of the night before....

From an American standpoint, *Chosen Ame*'s wild satire—often topical, usually sexual, generally in extremely questionable taste—is reminiscent of the classic comics features of *National Lampoon*, which, like *Chosen Ame*, featured artists—such as **Neal Adams**, **Walt Simonson**, and **Howard Chaykin**—with credits in the straight world. Perhaps the height of outrageousness was Hisao Tamaki's four-page story **"Cinderella's List"**, from *Chosen Ame* #5 (theme: uniforms).

In June 1944, in Amsterdam, two

Jewish girls are holed up in a garret, one busily scratching away at a diary (*The Diary of Anne Frank* has been thrice adapted for anime, each time without approval from Frank's estate) when their fairy godmother—**Liam Neeson**—appears. Pointing his magic Oscar at them, their clothes, forced by Nazi law to bear the Star of David, disappear, only to be replaced by Wehrmacht uniforms, in which they hope to sneak out of the city to safety. (Oddly enough, they undergo this clothing transformation without a nude sequence of the type common to magical girl series; the reader may be aware that *Sailor Moon* was censored for North American broadcast.) The strictly relative restraint of the story thus far is quickly abandoned as the panicked girls, moving under cover of bombed-out buildings, attempt a tender moment with each other. In the midst of the tribadism, however, an advancing G.I. mistakes them for Germans and sweeps the rubble with his Tommy gun, but finds nothing left but a glass slipper. Cowering out of sight of the soldier in the darkness, the two girls are safe, but now—it having just turned midnight—presumably naked...

There's even a dash of politics. Shohei Oba's **"Godzilla Vs. North Korea"** was also in *Chosen Ame* #5, the issue published for the Summer 1994 Comike, during the height of fears about a renewal of war between North and South Korea. While cute girls (dressed in what **P.J. O'Rourke** has described as the Boy Scouts-gone-horribly-wrong outfits common to Communist states) spout word balloons filled with quotes from North Korean dictator **Kim Il Sung** written in dense, tiny script that fill up entire panels, Godzilla advances on Pyongyang. Not to worry, says the "Great Leader;" Kim has defenses ready that include a Gundam in North Korean People's Army uniform and the 105-story "world's highest" Ryugyong Hotel (a notorious pyramidal boondoggle said to be an empty shell with only one habitable floor), now retrofitted as a giant robot. When all these are stomped flat by Godzilla, the mad Kim threatens to use the nuclear-tipped IRBM North Korea has long denied building (and then launched in a test flight crossing Japan during this author's 1998 visit). That being too much for his people, Kim is tied up and given the heave-ho off the nearest pier. It's up to the North Koreans to save themselves—and so they do: the 1,500,000 gaunt, famine-crazed soldiers of the NKPA, chanting "Meat! Meat!" climb onto Godzilla in a swarm and eat him alive.

Chosen Ame's Robert deJesus is not the only American to express regret that something like the Japanese parody dojin scene cannot exist in the United States. The issue is often phrased in legal terms. In Japan, the fact that scads of dojin have been riffing on *Ranma 1/2* doesn't meant that someone can go into a Japanese court and argue that **Rumiko Takahashi**'s rights to her work should no longer be recognized. By contrast, an American copyright must be vigorously defended to avoid its loss. But when it comes to American otaku, the issue has remained largely theoretical. There simply aren't many who have bothered to try their hand at creating high-quality, Japanese-style paro-dojin that take familiar characters to what Bushwick Bill called "that other

level of the game," despite the fact that a handful of such—*Kimagure Orange College*, *Sailor Ranma*, *Nostalgia*, *Under The Influence*—have been manufactured in the '90s and sold here without incurring wrath.

Because printing costs are an issue, American fans are drawing original comics on the Internet; yet while dojin-style fanfics based on anime, manga, and games flourish online, regrettably few illustrated ones appear on the Web, let alone in actual print. It should perhaps be no surprise that the U.S. dojin scene remains minuscule, reflecting the proportions of the comics industry in this nation versus Japan; after all, Comic Market is a fan convention eight times the size of America's largest *professional* comics convention, the Comic-Con International in San Diego. Yet the genuine enthusiasm of American fans offers potential.

For the Western fan unable to travel to Comic Market or other Japanese dojinshi shows, there are still a number of options. The recent online sensation, **eBay** (http://www.ebay.com), a global swap meet where people sell everything from escrowed Dior gowns to bags of marbles, routinely features dojinshi (search under "doujinshi"). The would-be shopper is

reminded when coming across a dojin advertised as "rare" that dojin are rare by definition, and that the original price for most dojin in Japan was no more than five or ten U.S. dollars. Currently, anime conventions are held throughout the U.S. during the spring, summer, and fall, and larger ones may feature three or four dealers selling dojinshi. Unlike eBay, however, whose auction system makes a bargain possible, convention dealers routinely sell dojinshi at a markup of three hundred percent or higher. A recommended option is the rather alarmingly named **Ninja Death Graphics** (http://www.ninjadeath.com/); this web site features a selection of dojin at extremely reasonable prices, postpaid. NDG is also a dealer at certain anime conventions, at which times their stock is considerably larger, yet sold for the same low prices.

Enter the game of dojin with Dan Kanemitsu's *Storm Front Journal #0* (available for $10 plus $3 shipping and handling at www.tc.umn.edu/~kane0034/maingate.shtml, or write to Studio Revolution U.S.A., P.O. Box 13634, Minneapolis, MN 55414-5634). Kanemitsu, currently a graduate student in East Asian studies at the University of Minnesota, gives more than just his personal perspective as a longtime dojin creator; he goes into real depth about this incredibly diverse field, showing what dojin have to say about the historical tensions between free speech and legal restrictions—observations that are certainly as important for America as for Japan. No dry academic treatise, *Journal #0* features cover art and a preface by the notoriously talented **Yoshito Asari**. With encouraging remarks from Sonoda himself, Kanemitsu's publication may help do for the dojin scene what Schodt's *Manga! Manga!* did for the conventional Japanese comics industry: provide the English-speaking fan with their first detailed introduction to a culture often misunderstood in the United States.

Godzilla Vs. North Korea, by Shohei Oba, from *Chosen Ame #5* © Shohei Oba

Mainstream Outsiders—Prisoners Of The Parallel Universe

Patrick Macias

Captain Harlock, by Leiji Matsumoto, published by Akita Shoten

There is real love, real heart and soul to be found in the brush strokes of manga artist **Leiji Matsumoto**. Only his machines, his fabulous mecha, are ever given the practical consideration of rulers and straight edges. By contrast, his characters and faces are rendered in wayward strokes, pulsating lines with varying degrees of thickness. And just like a poet, more **William Blake** than **e. e. cummings**, Matsumoto constructs an entire cosmology one line at a time.

In 1977, in his peak period of artistic achievement, Matsumoto's ink was flying off his brush. A look back, even only a few years, to his 1974 *Space Cruiser Yamato* manga shows inconsistencies in tone. The work looks rushed, and it probably was. But everything had been perfected in time for *Uchu Kaizoku Captain Harlock*.

Scott McCloud, in *Understanding Comics*, calls putting cartoony characters in detailed settings the masking effect. Imagine **Charles Schulz**'s **Peanuts** characters at the rococo controls of a Zero fighter, or contrasted against the portals and scanners of space battleships. This is the Matsumoto style par excellence. But who wants to be reminded that we live in a universe populated by schlubs enslaved to machines? Not Western readers, even those who respond well to Harlock anime. They frequently grumble with complaints over Matsumoto's drawing style. Yet he has stubbornly refused to refine his technique any further. His magic brush strokes continue to unleash the lumpy potato within. Exceptions are made, however, for the exceptional: heroes and women.

Matsumoto renders the female form with a schoolboy's sense of inferiority and idolatry. Always lithe and long-haired, by turns maternal and cold, they have aptly been described by one Japanese writer as "prophetesses that link humanity with technology." Our hero, Captain Harlock, must contend with an entire invading army of such femmes fatales, vegetable in origin, hailing from the distant planet Mazone (read: Amazon).

Bushy haired, brooding, skinny as a stick, but in no way a French fry, Harlock is currently better known for his anime appearances than his uncompromised outlaw manga persona. There's the 1978 TV series, the 1982 tell-all origin film *My Youth in Arcadia*, the follow-up series, and plenty of cameos in other Matsumoto productions. Trouble is, most of these stories strip away the mystery and integrity of the character. Sometimes he smiles. Hangs out with children. That sort of thing.

Otaku bellyaching aside, I must admit that I don't read Matsumoto manga for the stories or their debatable affiliation with other titles. The appeal is narcotic. Analgesic. Again, it's those lines and a languid, hypnotic style of page layout.

Most of the time, Matsumoto sticks to five-panel breakdowns, alternating between extreme blacks and extreme whites. He punctuates with either stunning two-page spreads or nearly abstract closeups of the eyes. All of these conventions—which I know sound rather ordinary, but only until they are experienced firsthand—were refined to perfection in the original Harlock manga.

The '90s Harlock is much more the product of its times. Titled, diabolically

Captain Harlock, by Leiji Matsumoto, published by Akita Shoten
© Leiji Matsumoto

enough, *Der Ring Des Nibelungen*, it's available on the World Wide Web in both Japanese and English (the English version is located at www.webshincho.com/comics _e/index.html). A not entirely digestible stew of Matsumoto's sci-fi characters and **Richard Wagner**'s **Ring Cycle**, the vacuum purity of the space pirate is gone. And reading Matsumoto on-line also ruins the mesmerizing pace of a comic that's only interactive via your hands.

The original Harlock manga has been translated into a number of languages, sadly none of them English. Some Americans once tried to do an original Harlock comic, but like most Western attempts at the manga style, they got everything wrong except the licensing work. In an attempt to invoke the anime, the lines of the one true manga somehow wound up irrelevant.

A Universe Away…

Of course, as a citizen of the perfect, germ-free strip mall/apartment complex, you must remember how the world began/ended.

Back in 19–, a great earthquake shook down the entire goddamn planet. Civilization as we know it was destroyed. Tokyo was hit especially hard. The Kanto district separated from the Japanese continent and became an island unto itself.

Society was quickly rebuilt, not on peaceful utopian visions, but on brutal Darwinian terms. Roving gangs, warlords, and superhumans placed the weak, children, women, and the elderly firmly under their boot heels.

Such injustice commanded a response. And it arrived on page one fully developed. "His force is that of a gorilla! His teeth are those of a wolf! In his bubbling blood is the fire of prehistory!" He was the Incredible Hulk wielding a notched jackknife that gave him his name…Violence Jack.

It's an honest workmanlike comic book premise, rendered a hopeless cliché today by any number of postapocalyptic scenarios: *Mad Max*, *Fist of the North*

Star, and (God in heaven help us) *Waterworld* and *The Postman*. The difference is that Go Nagai's *Violence Jack* debuted in 1972, somewhere between numerous Japanese political scandals and the Bubble Economy and roughly a year before the ritualized combat of super robot Mazinger Z made Nagai's antisocial style profitable and, even stranger, socially acceptable. (His 1969 comedy series, *Harenchi Gakuen*, a.k.a. *Shameless High School*, received death threats from the Japanese P.T.A.).

But if *Mazinger Z* was for kids, then the first leg of the *Violence Jack* saga was for their older brothers, just on the cusp of teenage wild life. Here Jack befriends a gang of orphans menaced by a fearsome retro-samurai called Slam King. The action is mild, the artwork rough, and the Jack versus Slam King story relatively pedestrian, save for a few queasy touches—chief among them two pitiful creatures, Ryo and Miki, who, most of their arms and legs having been hacked off, are forced to move about on stumps in the manner of human dogs, their collar chains leading to the Slam King's clenched fist. This original series wrapped up in 1978.

In 1984, Nagai restarted the Violence Jack franchise, probably as a reaction to the success of *Fist of the North Star*, which was basically *Violence Jack* with the pretensions of martial arts. And it is in this second series that Nagai went as far into his obsessions as he would go on the printed page. And that's pretty far, considering the sex and violence in *Cutey Honey*, *Kekko Kamen*, and *Mazin Saga*.

For within *Violence Jack* lies a tapestry of 19– atrocities that evoke Nanking circa 1937, Bosnia 1993, and Rwanda 1994. While the original Jack was content with the occasional beheading and knife in the back, the new variety reveled in rape, mutilation, mass murder, cannibalism, kinky

Violence Jack © Go Nagai/Dynamic Planning Inc.

sex—name your poison in a lawless chaotic land.

Nagai's godless Kanto became a blasphemous mockery of Japan's isolated-in-the-ocean status. And it is surely what *Shameless High School* would have led to, had it escaped the notice of concerned parents. The überstory is again Jack versus the Slam King, but this central conflict isn't so important anymore. Jack hardly appears in most issues. Instead it is karate fighters, prowrestlers, honey commandos, jungle boys, and downright ordinary folk who venture up and down the circles of hell.

Violence Jack is the **Suehiro Maruo** aesthetic done in a mainstream manga style. It's not art, but entertainment. And it's therapy for both audience and artist, as Nagai graphically depicts every personal demon and evil thought he's ever had. As if to spell it out in big letters for everyone, the final panels of the 6,500-page story, which appeared in 1990, take place in an antiseptic futuristic city that has finally contained, or perhaps exhausted, the elemental and pure forces of nature. It is a world in which comics like Violence Jack are forbidden, but probably still kept by perverts, hidden somewhere in the sock drawer. Like the once-missing twenty-first chapter of *A Clockwork Orange*, it is exactly the sort of happy-sad justice that a juvenile delinquent deserves.

Underground Manga Discoveries

Mason Jones

Dotei Kanawanosuke from *Yume no O-saku*, by Suehiro Maruo. Published by Seirindo © Suehiro Maruo/Seirindo

Before my first visit to Japan, in 1992, I was dimly aware of the popularity of manga there, but knew almost nothing about them. I assumed that manga were simply the Japanese counterpart of American comics, albeit intended for more mature readers. My first introduction to them changed my conception immediately.

Since I was involved with the experimental and noise music scene, the friends I made in Japan were in touch with the underground in other media, including manga. The first manga artist whose work they introduced me to was **Suehiro Maruo**. I recognized his style immediately, because his work was on a CD cover for **Torture Garden**, a band formed by New York musician **John Zorn**. The cover caused quite a stir, as I recall, because Maruo's work is very uncompromising. His books of manga, such as *Q-Saku* and *National Kid*, contain explicit scenes of strange sex and weird violence, such as a striking image of tongues flicking out to lick an eyeball, or a young boy with a magical penis. Only one book by Suehiro Maruo has been translated into English, *Mr. Arashi's Amazing Freak Show* (**Blast Books**). This tale of a lost orphan girl and her encounter with a twisted traveling freak show is a fine example of Maruo's bizarre storytelling style. His gorgeous artwork makes the most unsettling scenes mesmerizing. His drawings are highly detailed and carefully shaded with painstakingly fine pen-and-ink work. Occasionally he'll experiment, for example, by blending in collage elements or emphasizing scenes by reversing the blacks and whites.

After I was introduced to Maruo's work, a friend gave me an amazing book, *Bloody Ukiyo-e*, containing work by Maruo and another modern artist, **Kazuichi Hanawa**, as well as nineteenth-century painters **Yoshitoshi** and **Yoshiiku**. The idea of this full-color book was to contrast Ukiyo-e paintings from 1866 with modern works by Maruo and Hanawa. Each piece is related to an act of violence, either the story of a historical event or a profile of a famous criminal, such as German murderer **Fritz Hahlman** or infamous sex killer **Sada Abe** (the subject of the cult film *In the Realm of the Senses*). Of all of the books I have from Japan, *Bloody Ukiyo-e* is the one that elicits the most comments. Some people are deeply shocked, while others are entranced by the book's beautiful depictions of violence and decadence. Whatever their reaction, nobody can put it down until they've looked through it in detail.

After receiving that book, I tracked down some manga publications by Hanawa, whose intimately detailed artwork is achieved with beautifully executed pen-and-ink drawings. His subjects—beautiful studies of samurai on horseback involved in sinister magic—aren't as modern as Maruo's and there's not as much bizarre sexual content, but his disturbing images—such as those of strange creatures bursting from a girl's body and tree roots attacking people in his

Bloody Ukiyo-e in 1866 & 1988, art by Kazuichi Hanawa and Suehiro Maruo, published by Libro-port

book *Suisei*—are nevertheless unlike what one would ever expect from American comics. Hanawa's art appeals to me the most of all the manga artists I know. The lushness of his black-and-white illustrations, shaded with intricate pen lines and combined with his supernatural subjects, really speaks to me.

Another artist whose dark visions I grew to like, **Hideshi Hino**, has had a couple of books published in English, including *Panorama of Hell* (Blast Books). His style is more American in a way, less detailed and more cartoonish; he works with a bold, firm line, very clean and strong. The black and white contrast works perfectly for his storytelling style. His subject matter includes nightmarish visions of sewer rats eating discarded infants and a man's stomach growing a face and eating dogs whole then spitting out the bones. His work is bleakly humorous, with images that you'll either chuckle at or turn away from in horror. I imagine he would appreciate either reaction.

A friend of mine in Nagoya took me to a bookshop during one visit to Japan to purchase books by Maruo for an American acquaintance. There he happened to spot

Seikimatsu Bansankai, by Hideshi Hino, published by Tokyo Sanseisha

works by one of his favorite artists, and showed me a book by **Keizo Miyanishi**, collecting his work from 1977 to 1980, called *Lyrica*. The drawings, whether depicting sex, violence, or a simple picture of a room, were so well executed that I bought the book on the spot. The pictures range from perfect, simple outlines to extraordinarily detailed textures, whether the shading of a tongue or the pattern of a snake's scales. His use of flowing clothing and tendrils of hair occasionally reminds me of **Beardsley**. I haven't learned anything since then about Miyanishi, but the spiritual quality of his work, depicting lovers' quarrels and sexual experiences, has made me a fan.

Oddly, I have become a fan of these manga artists despite the fact that I've actually *read* very little of their work. Few, if any, of their stories have been published in English. The books I've purchased in Japan are of course in Japanese. Having studied Japanese for several years, it's only recently that I've

Mazushiki Flute from *Lyrica*, by Keizo Miyanishi, published by Atelier Peyotl Co.
© Keizo Miyanishi/Atelier Peyotl Co.

begun to decode the written word. Like a child with picture books, until now I've enjoyed the manga solely from the stories I've decrypted from the drawings.

I've been able to derive a great deal of enjoyment from manga without being able to understand the text; I don't need to grasp one hundred percent of the meaning, as I would with a novel. In any case, the books of sufficiently talented artists such as Maruo and Hanawa qualify as art. I can stare at a two-page spread by Hanawa and get as much out of it as I could from most paintings at the local museum.

Recently, I've begun to find and enjoy some of the more mainstream manga available in English, such as *Battle Angel Alita*, *Nausicaä of the Valley of Wind*, and *Domu*. Some of the underground manga have begun to make appearances in translation as well, particularly thanks to Blast

Books, but the mainstream titles, of course, are still much easier to find. I recommend Blast's *Comics Underground Japan*, as it includes stories by Maruo, Hanawa, and Hideshi Hino, among others. Drawn from the extremely influential underground manga magazine *Garo*, this book covers both the serious and silly sides of alternative manga.

Light-hearted manga—including both silly alternative manga and the romantic love stories that are a staple of mainstream manga—don't appeal to me (neither do light-hearted Western comics). I continue to scour the underground for darker, more personal visions. And I find myself returning to Maruo and Hanawa, the ones who first convinced me that there was something very special here, something completely unlike the illustrated stories I grew up with. Unfortunately, unlike manga, it's very rare that Western comics, even in the underground, match impassioned, bizarre stories to mesmerizingly accomplished art. I hope that eventually someone will discover these Japanese artists and make their works fully available to English readers. In any case, as I continue my studies in Japanese, I'll slowly read them in their native language.

Until then, I'll just look at the pictures.

Suisei, by Kazuichi Hanawa, published by Atelier Peyotl Co.
© Kazuichi Hanawa/Atelier Peyotl

Terrorist Manga

Yuji Oniki

One country's mainstream can be another country's underground. For example, the **Plastic People** were banned in their native country, the former Czechoslovakia, from playing rock in the '60s. Every time the Plastic People kicked out the jams, they'd get put away in the slammer. Meanwhile, back in the States, rock-'n'-roll provided equal opportunity to pursue the right to gluttony and maximum happiness. The only way you'd get busted in America was to make it clear that the excess in rock was more about sex than money or happiness.

Anyway, over the course of writing these chapters for *Japan Edge*, I got to thinking how the popular media gets framed in each culture, and how certain kinds of media get censored in one country while they proliferate in another. The closest thing we have in the U.S. to the Czech pop underground is comic books. While few have gone to jail for what they illustrate, American comic book novelists, particularly those who depart from the superhero genre, have remained an underground phenomena. The reasons for this ghettoization are above and beyond me, better left to the task of the cultural historian. What interests me more is how marginal comic books are in the U.S. compared to Japan, and how this status turns virtually every translation of Japanese comics into a cult phenomenon to a varying degree. Because translation takes time, there's always a lag, so few of us have access to Japanese manga in the present. Unlike pop music, we don't get immediate exposure to current manga in what the Japanese call *riaru tymu*, or "real time." Everything is slightly delayed.

But that delay is nothing compared to the fact that popular manga preceding the appearance of English translations, circa 1985, will probably never be translated. What bothers me most about this is that readers here will eternally miss out on the most revolutionary manga, published between the late '60s and late '70s, before manga become a cultural staple which most natives couldn't do without. That there was a time when it wasn't so commercial (nor so censored) may seem unimaginable to anyone who's only been to Japan since the '70s. There once was a time, though, when manga was not so mainstream, or even if it was, its practitioners were so fascinated with the art form that they couldn't help but weave incredibly strange stories, albeit set in the context of daily life in Japan.

"Burn your manga!" **Takeo Udagawa** announces in his *Manga Zombie*, an encyclopedia mostly about manga published during the '60s and '70s. Udagawa continues, "Especially your '80s manga, the programmed manga that's become commercial, the manga that lacks all originality, the calculated manga made to sell…and those interactive manga whose plots are determined by the readers' polls." Udagawa calls for a revival of out-of-print manga from the '60s and '70s, drawn by artists living at ulcer-inducing subsistence levels while they "expressed such extreme experiences they traumatized their readers." Instead of waxing nostalgic for the good old days of manga, Udagawa urges the revival of forgotten manga so obscure or extreme that they haven't been reprinted or collected.

I was surprised at how many of the manga mentioned in this book were familiar to me. Having grown up in America, as a kid I didn't get to read these stories from cover to

Shonen Sunday, published by Shogakukan

cover, issue after issue, but only managed to get sporadic glimpses of them. They appeared in the *shonen* (boy's) weeklies ranging from *King*, *Jump*, *Sunday*, *Champion*, to *Magazine*. Despite the perky boy-scoutish names, the content of a lot of these weeklies was pretty extreme, so traumatic sometimes that they would make me wonder what kind of psychological price I would later pay for reading them. Reading the "Trauma/Marginal" section in *Manga Zombie*, I couldn't help but recall these memories of manga that, rather than being suppressed, had simply gone out of circulation. Here are some examples from that period:

1) *Astro Kyudan* (Astro League) (story and art by **Norihiro Nakajima**): Ostensibly a baseball story about nine super players who, as it turns out, are transmigrated souls originating from Japan's famous baseball hero **Eiji Sawamura**, who was killed in action in the Philippines during World War II. Gradually, each game turns into a death match instead of a competition for points. In order to survive through the nine innings, each player engages him/herself in the most masochistic, scientifically preposterous training sessions (practicing batting in the

Astro Kyudan, by Norihiro Nakajima, published by Shueisha

middle of an active volcano, for example). Because they're so extreme, they finally get banned from the Japanese pro baseball league, but upon hearing about some mysterious tribe that excels in baseball, they depart for Africa. Not unlike the Japanese Red Army, they decide Japan's not ready for the revolution (...in baseball?).

2) *Damé Oyaji* (Loser Father) (story and art by **Mitsutoshi Furuya**): This topsy-turvy story of domestic violence depicts not a father wreaking havoc on his wife and kids but the reverse. Oni-Baba (Devil Mama) and her children devise new lynching techniques to punish the mundane salaryman, Damé Oyaji, in every episode. This serial wouldn't have lingered on in my memory had it not been for its weird New Age twist towards the end, in which the father meets a young woman, Himiko, who confides in him her dream to create a utopia. The father learns how to enjoy life and the rest of the family, in turn, learns to love and accept him (even Devil Mama). Without knowing anything about Scientology, even as a kid I was creeped out by this radical narrative shift,

Damé Oyaji, by Mitsutoshi Furuya, © Mitsutoshi Furuya. From *Shonen Sunday*, published by Shogakukan Inc.

no matter how positive. The antiseptic utopia only seemed like a grotesque compensation for the dysfunctional family.

3) *Wild Seven* (story and art by **Mikiya Mochizuki**): A kind of synthesis of *Easy Rider* and the *Magnificent Seven* (derived from **Akira Kurosawa**'s *Seven Samurai*), the Wild Seven are seven former death-row convicts now working for the chief of police to stamp out corruption in Japan (and, in one story, Vietnam during the war!). In the end, the seven get finished off one by one due to the rise of a Hitleresque (he's got the same mustache and hairdo) defense minister preparing a coup d'état against Japan.

4) *Gaki-deka* (Brat Detective) (story and art by **Tatsuhiko Yamagami**): This is one of the strangest manga I have ever read. Gaki-deka is a boy cop who wears an imperial Japanese police cap while wreaking havoc by displaying his body in perverse poses and imposing his S&M impulses onto bourgeois girls and boys. The political message behind this depiction of authority coupled with sado-masochism was, to say the least, obscure.

I could go on and on about serials as twisted as the above four. Consider them just a sample of the hundreds of equally deranged

Wild Seven, by Mikiya Mochizuki © Mikiya Mochizuki/Tokuma Shoten

Shonen Champion, published by Akita Shoten (cover by Tatsuhiko Yamagami)

narratives I consumed way back when. Even though these artists clearly had some pretty extreme issues to work out, what's really odd about these manga is how incredibly popular they were at the time. *Manga Zombie* isn't so much an archival project reviving the underground as it is a series of flashbacks on popular narratives too incoherent to gain cultural recognition but weird enough to leave a stamp on the memory of every kid born during the Vietnam War.

What does the Vietnam War have to do with Japan? Well, quite a bit. The Japanese student movements pretty much revolved around the U.S. military presence. Critics from both the right and the left charged the government with either being a Western puppet state (right wing) or immersed in bureaucratic apathy (left wing). Meanwhile, U.S. military ships and submarines were passing through Japan, turning Okinawa into a launch pad for missions over North Vietnam. It didn't help that the relatively "backward" Vietnam won the war over a country which had defeated Japan only a quarter-century ago. No matter how you sliced it, the people's political faith in the nation was at an all-time low.

What does this have to with manga? Bear with me. Basically, the Vietnam Era youths felt profound disgust and confusion towards postwar Japan. Student activism was the popular mode of expression for altering the course of the country, but without much success. By the early '70s, you

Japanese vertical text in the manga panels:

砦の上に我らが世界
築き固めよ勇ましく

立て兄弟よ
行け戦いに
聖なる血にまみれよ

Otokogumi by Tetsu Kariya and Ryoichi Ikegami, published by Shogakukan © Tetsu Kariya/Ryoichi Ikegami/Shogakukan

either dropped out by joining an alternative community or reentered the mainstream nine-to-five (nine-to-nine?) working world. The focus centered on insulated communities such as the nuclear family, while the investment in national identity shifted towards the collective effort to increase the GDP. And the more Japan pretended not to care about its nationhood (other than in monetary terms), the more demand there was for alternative communities. This was, for better or worse, the cultural space manga filled. Whether we're talking about sports, comedy, Armageddon science fiction, or the family sitcom, some of the most memorable manga of the period depicted the dystopia of contemporary Japan contrasted with idealized, imaginary communities.

It's only in a context like this that **Tetsu Kariya**'s twenty-six volume epic, *Otoko Gumi* (Men's Gang), could have become so popular. Zenjiro Nagaré leads a teenster gang of juvenile delinquents against Goji Jinryu, the heir to an increasingly totalitarian Japan. Jinryu believes in the totalitarian ethic of the few ruling over the dumb, subservient majority, while Nagaré fights for equal brotherhood. One of the things they share is a distaste for the present state of Japan, immersed as it is in bureaucracy. Some of the dialogue is truly numbing in terms of pomposity, arrogance, and naiveté, not to mention fascist overtones, but the blend of the '60s student movement ("We must fight the Power!") with the cynicism of the Nixonian '70s paints a pretty compelling picture of the mounting frustrations Japan was accumulating at the expense of economic growth. The last episode features quotations from the Bible as lone terrorist Nagaré approaches the palace of the "Shadow Prime Minister" to assassinate him and save Japan (from…?).

What was it that drew us kids towards these stories of social transgression, whether through terrorism or the breaking of sexual taboos? Implicit in every social regulation is a taboo. One might even say that the manner each taboo is dealt with defines the contours of a particular culture more than its regulations. For example, while it's not hard to find similar taboos within most modern countries, it's a lot harder to find common strategies in enforcing them. Children are less interested in breaking taboos than they are in sniffing one out as it drifts by them; they don't know that a taboo is inherently wrong, just that it somehow doesn't fit into the patterns of thought they're being forced to learn. Manga broke the sound barrier of taboo by deforming the official manipulation of both language and images. How it ever managed to become so popular and so weird at the same time is completely beyond me.

Of course, just as a band of revolutionaries must eventually end their revolution, the reign of these manga terrorists had to come to a close. They bade farewell either by moving on to young men's instead of boy's weeklies, retiring, or, in the worst cases, burning out. **Tsubame Kamogawa** paid a heavy price. Staying up five nights in a row to meet the deadlines for his masterpiece '70s comedy manga *Macaroni Horenso*, Kamogawa not only stopped going out, he became completely agoraphobic. In a recent *Quick Japan* interview conducted by **Cornelius**, Kamogawa recounts, "At the time I had to complete three serials in five days, everything from the plot, drafts, drawings, and colors, so I couldn't afford to sleep.… I was willing to die for the sake of *Macaroni Horenso*.… When that ended, I knew I was finished. It was horrible. I was on the verge of going insane. I was really close… It's a miracle I'm here speaking to you. For a long time I couldn't face anyone, it was as if I were in a coma…"

To suggest that comedy has any revolutionary potential may be stretching the point (in fact, maybe it's the opposite; after all, revolutionaries aren't known for their sense of humor), but reading *Macaroni Horenso* was the closest experience I had of manga as rock-'n'-roll. When asked what the basic concept behind *Macaroni Horenso* was, Kamogawa replied, "I wanted to express the joy of rock through the medium of manga… I mean, there were a lot of strange bands back then. You'd never get bored with them. They'd wear outrageous outfits and make wonderful sounds, dance around like crazy. Someone once commented on how the '70s were a decade when you'd bump into uniqueness at every street corner.' That's what it felt like.… In any case, what helped and influenced me most wasn't manga, it was rock."

It wasn't just the style but the ethic of rock-'n'-roll that Kamogawa emulated in order to carve out a less assembly-line approach to manga. Essential to his craft was the idea of artistic, as opposed to commercial, integrity. Unlike most manga artists now, Kamogawa generally refused to license his work. "There was a lot of interest in making movies and animation out of *Macaroni Horenso*, but the offers were always exploitative. In our manga co-op we were convinced that commercialism was ruining manga."

The subsequent work of those manga revolutionaries who, unlike Kamogawa, continued their work into the '80s and '90s, isn't necessarily less interesting. But what's missing is the extremity of their previous manga. Gone are the days of rock-'n'-roll manga. Gone are the days of abstract ideologies extolling utopian communities, the background drawings of the protagonist's poverty-ridden neighborhood, the bizarre displays of sadomasochism alternating with absolute love and camaraderie. What we have instead, to put it bluntly, are the more nuclear, private fantasies of a generic middle class.

Which came first, though? Did manga just represent the growing *heiwa boke* (peace senility) of Japan during the '80s, or was it also complicit in brainwashing its readers into enacting more passive narratives in their own lives? (A Japanese friend of mine commented how Pokémon (the game/anime/comic phenomenon) isn't nearly as popular as *bokémon*, or "senile beings.") This is always the inevitable question we end up asking about pop culture. Rather than untangle the complex web of consumption and representation of pop culture, I think terrorist manga might be more interesting in terms of its delayed ghostly resonance in contemporary culture.

A lot of critics, including Udagawa, frequently comment on the relevance of this earlier manga to the contemporary underground; they point out how certain artists, such as **Joji Akiyama**, anticipated the Aum Shinrikyo religious cult and other incidents

of terrorism in everyday life. As members of the Japanese Red Army went into exile in the early '70s, they paraphrased not Marx but **Tetsuya Chiba**, author of their favorite manga, bestselling *Ashita no Jo* (Tomorrow's Joe, drawn by **Ikki Kajiwara**) with the declaration, "We are Tomorrow's Joe!" The Armageddon narrative plotted out by the Aum was a pastiche of bestselling science fiction manga from the '70s. I won't make the facile claim that these folks ended up as poor parodies of the culture they consumed, but I do think that the revolutionary impulse behind a lot of the early manga carried enough resonance for its readers to pursue lives that wouldn't have been conceivable without their exposure to manga.

I also don't want to make a reactionary statement blaming manga for being a bad influence on kids—but there does seem to be

a correlation between the nature of the crimes these folks commit and the kinds of manga they grew up on. There was, after all, a time when literature was acknowledged to have such effects on its readers. You would have pairs of adolescents leaping into oblivion, committing double love suicides after reading **Goethe** or **Dazai** and the urban intelligentsia living off the land a la **Tolstoy**, and so on. But these cases tended to revolve around individual simulations of the stories they read. The manga I'm talking about has had a more social and subliminal effect, not only because its readers were much younger. It was so extreme in its social outlook that in order to emulate its narratives you'd have to lose a good chunk of your grasp on reality; having been brought up on the mainstream terrorist manga of the '60s and '70s, you'd have to go underground in the '80s and '90s.

Macaroni Horenso by Tsubame Kamogawa, published by Akita Shoten © Tsubame Kamogawa/Akita Shoten

WHAT'S YOUR MANGA TYPE?

If you're a true otaku, you already know what manga lights your fire, floats your boat, runs your engine. If not, this handy flowchart will lead you down the optimal primrose or prickly path. The results may not be absolutely accurate, but fun pages like this are de rigueur in Japanese magazines. So enjoy this mini Japanese pop culture trip—on us!

The Editors

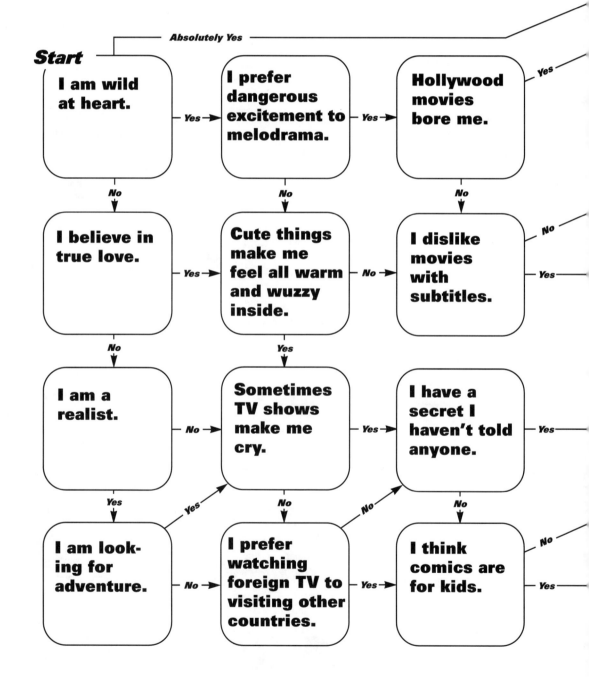

Absolutely Yes

Start

I am wild at heart. — Yes → **I prefer dangerous excitement to melodrama.** — Yes → **Hollywood movies bore me.** — Yes

No ↓ · No ↓ · No ↓

I believe in true love. — Yes → **Cute things make me feel all warm and wuzzy inside.** — No → **I dislike movies with subtitles.** — No / Yes

No ↓ · Yes ↓

I am a realist. — No → **Sometimes TV shows make me cry.** — Yes → **I have a secret I haven't told anyone.** — Yes

Yes ↓ · Yes ↗ · No ↓ · No ↗ · No ↓

I am looking for adventure. — No → **I prefer watching foreign TV to visiting other countries.** — Yes → **I think comics are for kids.** — No / Yes

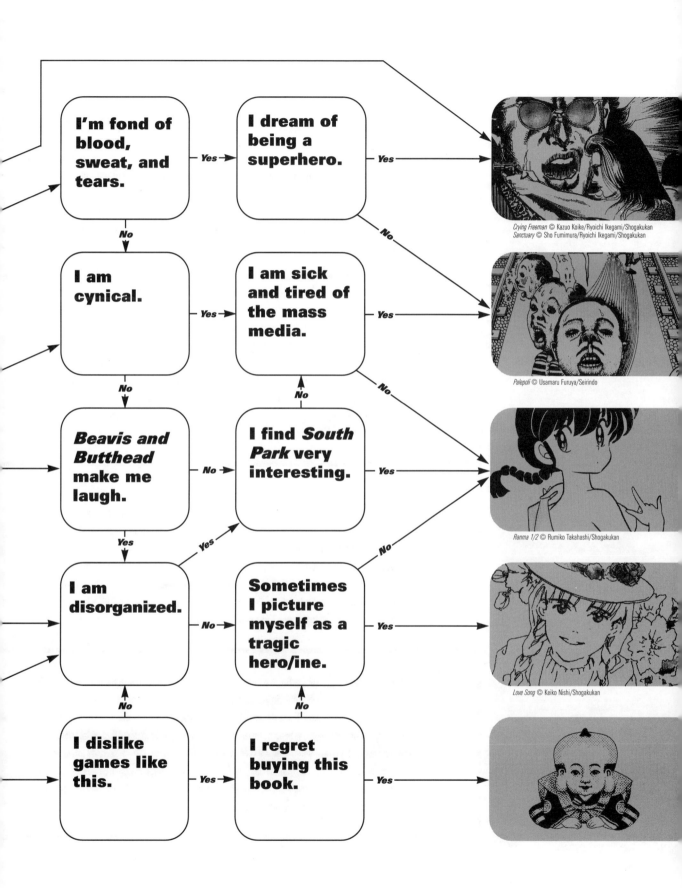

I'm fond of blood, sweat, and tears. — *Yes* → **I dream of being a superhero.** — *Yes* →

Crying Freeman © Kazuo Koike/Ryoichi Ikegami/Shogakukan
Sanctuary © Sho Fumimura/Ryoichi Ikegami/Shogakukan

No ↓ ... *No* →

I am cynical. — *Yes* → **I am sick and tired of the mass media.** — *Yes* →

Palepoli © Usamaru Furuya/Seirindo

No ↓ ... *No* ↑ ... *No* →

Beavis and Butthead make me laugh. — *No* → **I find South Park very interesting.** — *Yes* →

Ranma 1/2 © Rumiko Takahashi/Shogakukan

Yes ↓ ... *Yes* → ... *No* →

I am disorganized. — *No* → **Sometimes I picture myself as a tragic hero/ine.** — *Yes* →

Love Song © Keiko Nishi/Shogakukan

No ↑ ... *No* ↑

I dislike games like this. — *Yes* → **I regret buying this book.** — *Yes* →

155

TOUGH

You who leapt into this category are undoubtedly a man's man. You may think, "No I'm not!" or "But I'm a woman!" but deep in your subconscious you have a burning desire to grow more powerful, cut loose, and accomplish something *big*. It could be just a small spark inside you that you're barely aware of yet. But with the right fuel, it could explode into something truly scary. Wow! But you're lucky. There are lots of manga titles published in English that model constructive ways to channel all this excess energy. After reading them, you'll be able to run the Ironman, go wild, cry like a man, and battle the world's injustices!

WEIRD

You're weird. It's impossible to explain to weird people how they're weird, but you're weird anyway. However, you're lucky. There are lots of manga artists in Japan who are weirder than you. There are many degrees of weirdness, from a little weird to considerably weird to extremely weird. Not to mention varieties of weirdness: sexual weirdness, narcissistic weirdness, and anarchistic weirdness…the possibilities are endless! So don't worry, you're bound to find manga to satisfy your twisted desires and obsessions. I recommend you develop and polish your weirdness by reading them. How lucky you are that this world is full of weird comics!

MAINSTREAM

You are in the mainstream—for now. Normal people fall into this category, supposedly. But…I have to warn you. This personality test is created from data sampled from countless people—"countless" meaning "a few"—data that has been input into the latest supercomputer—one with two megabytes of memory. Moreover, to be more accurate, we refused the cooperation of NASA. *Battle Angel Alita*, *Dragon Ball*, *Gundam*, *Gunsmith Cats*, *Neon Genesis Evangelion*, *No Need For Tenchi!*, *Oh My Goddess!*, *Pokémon*, *Ranma 1/2*, *Sailor Moon*, Bean Bandit, Belldandy, Doc Ido, P-chan, Pikachu, Ryoko, Son Goku—you can name all the stories and characters. But what is mainstream manga *really*?

SHOJO

This is the world of fantasy, the one Tinkerbell described when she softly whispered in your ear. Birds are singing, a breeze gently caresses your cheek, girls' waists are wasp-thin. This is the world of dreams. Those faces are the faces of Japanese, no matter how hard you look at them, but their names are Andrew, Stephen, Alexandria. Welcome to this Wonderland. I'll give you wings. I'll give you stars in your eyes. (Three seconds later: Oh no! I forgot to put a million roses on your back!) (Thirty seconds later: That's it! Comic panels look so much better with all those roses. We just can't do without roses in shojo manga.) (One second later: Open up this forbidden drawer with me. My name is Princess Gossamer.)

Abandon hope, all ye who enter here.

FIST OF THE NORTH STAR
Story by Buronson
Art by Tetsuo Hara

STRAIN
Story by Buronson
Art by Ryoichi Ikegami

CRYING FREEMAN
Story by Kazuo Koike
Art by Ryoichi Ikegami

COMICS UNDER-GROUND JAPAN
Various artists

PULP
Various artists

AMAZING FREAK SHOW
Story & Art by
Suehiro Maruo

RANMA 1/2
Story & Art by
Rumiko Takahashi

AKIRA
Story & Art by
Katsuhiro Otomo

DRAGON BALL Z
Story & Art by
Akira Toriyama

LOVE SONG
Story & Art by
Keiko Nishi

A, A' [A, A Prime]
Story & Art by
Moto Hagio

BANANA FISH
Story & Art by
Akimi Yoshida

Shopping for Manga Online

Amazon
www.amazon.com

GraphicNovels.com
www.graphicnovels.com

Fujisan.com
www.fujisan.com

j-pop.com
www.j-pop.com

Kinokuniya Bookstores
www.kinokuniya.com
www.kinokuniya.co.jp
(800) 59-JAPAN

Sasuga Bookstores
www.sasugabooks.com

Asahiya Bookstores U.S.A., Inc
www.asahiyausa.com
www.asahiya.com

The Place
www.the-place.com/manga.htm

Nikaku Animart
www.nikaku.com/

eBay Inc.
www.eBay.com

Anime Web Turnpike
www.anipike.com

Newsgroups
rec.arts.manga
rec.arts.anime.marketplace
rec.arts.anime.misc
rec.arts.comics.marketplace

TOKYO

Yuji Oniki

DIARY no.5

June 3

I visit film maker **Mikio Yamazaki**, who lives in Higashi-Murayama. We start drinking as soon as we're seated on the floor around the *kotatsu* table. I mention the film *A* and he frowns, then smiles and tells me that a former friend of his from college, now a such-and-such minister of such-and-such a religion, once asked him to film their leader flying in the air. He wanted the scene shot on film instead of video to make it look "more authentic." Yamazaki, who'll pretty much photograph anything provided it's interesting, accepted the request. But the following week, when his friend informed him that the leader would instead be submerging himself in water for a prolonged period, Yamazaki bailed. "I mean, with flying there are cinematic possibilities, but diving? *Bo-ring*."

"As it turned out," he continued, crushing out his cigarette, "This leader was Asahara of Aum."

It's only been a year since I last saw Yamazaki's most recent film, *A Port in Vain*. Since he won a special prize for it at the **Yamagata International Documentary Film Festival**, he has been getting requests to submit the film to various international venues, including the **Pompidou Center**. The film is a first-person documentary, presumably about Yamazaki, who, after a sudden premonition of his death, takes his life savings of 100 thou-

sand dollars out of the bank and deliberates how best to spend the money. He films himself flipping through the bills to prove he's not inserting white sheets in each stack. The movie has a gritty look because it's shot on cheap 8 mm film. This is because he prefers to spend the money on something other than the film itself, which will only serve to document his actions.

First he thinks of spending his cash on terrorism, or "tero," but immediately realizes that wouldn't be terribly cost effective, so instead he opts for "ero," or "eroticism." Somewhere in the middle of this pursuit of eros he ends up with a woman who calls him by his old nickname, Mickey. The film flashes back to old 8 mm footage of Yamazaki from the '80s, while the narrator's commentary on the ensuing bizarre Oz-like story starring Mickey and Minnie Mouse ends up as a meditation on sex, love, and pop culture. I can't put my finger on why exactly, but it's one of the few films about popular culture that actually moves me, perhaps because it bridges gaps between the contemporary pop cultures of such disparate nations as Japan, America, and India.

Yamazaki has also published several books on yakuza gangster films, RPGs (role playing games), computer and video games, and canned coffee. The latter called *The Landscape of Canned Coffee* is no joke, nor is it PR for the canned coffee industry. As it happens, Yamazaki has collected coffee cans since he was in junior high school. Ten years later he has amassed a collection of over 900 different brands, all stored away in cardboard boxes like toys in the attic. The fact of the matter is that Japan didn't have its own original consumer product until the invention of canned coffee, and Yamazaki wanted to know what the story was behind this national commodity.

We always react towards things that have never existed until now. Adults tend to dismiss them automatically while children feel an odd attraction to them, as if identifying with the open-ended future of a new product. Yamazaki was born in 1959. He was ten years old when canned coffee came into existence. The product, available in constantly new and emerging brands and packaging, was invented during his childhood.

The preceding generation at one time had a similar affinity for glass Coca-Cola bottles, first introduced to Japan through red refrigerated soda machines. That generation rejected the innovation of the six-pack tin can format. The old Coke machines and bottles fed the imagination of postwar Japanese adolescents yearning for America, but almost twenty years later, Yamazaki and his generation scoffed at their fantasy as they watched it shrink away like plastic wrap soaked in hot water. "As far as we were concerned, America was inept. They beat a hasty retreat from Vietnam."

As the last American helicopter fluttered above Saigon, Yamazaki was caught up in the tail end of a student movement that envisioned a country that would do away with American influence completely. Yet this movement was itself rapidly reaching its demise. As Japan's postwar inferiority complex evaporated with the oil crisis of the '70s, the last of the radicals began fighting amongst themselves, disillusioned as they were with a nation which hypocritically proclaimed absolute pacifism while silently promoting wars in Korea, Vietnam, and more obscure theaters of Asia. By the time Yamazaki and his contemporaries graduated, the movement had died out and its most radical survivors were thrown into jail, exiled, or in hiding.

Unlike otaku, Yamazaki is interested not so much in accumulating data as in figuring out how and why we can't help but construct narratives out of the technology we consume every day. In his book *Electric Hero Marches in the Naked Emperor's Dungeon—A Radical Essay for the Sibylline Computer Game Culture*, he is fascinated by the role computer games play in the stories we construct around our daily lives, whether we play the games or not.

Bestselling games like *Dragon Quest* have been criticized for their depiction of human apathy towards a collapsing world, but Yamazaki quotes one avid player who points out, "Don't these inhabitants of the game world resemble someone? That's right, us earthlings—particularly the Japanese. Critics of this game can't see how complacent real people are in the face of Armageddon."

Instead of pointing out how RPGs encourage fantasies and antisocial behavior, Yamazaki points out how often these games represent real life in Japan: "When you get tired of playing the role of the fighter-hero and try to bow out, the response [from the game] is, 'You fool, you cannot!' No matter how many times you try to quit, it's always the same, 'You fool!' Ugh. This is the same as those times you'd like to quit school but can't, those times you'd like to quit the company but can't. If pachinko is a game that simulates investment and profit returns, then RPGs might be called simulations of contemporary social life cloaked in a narrative of swords and magic."

The rest of the book covers the subversion of this simulation of real life and how one might apply this RPG sensibility out in the streets through a kind of homespun terrorism. It's a long twisting discussion involving Zen drawings, religious cults, left- and right-wing terrorists, and even the emperor.

C'EST LA VIE

BY: FURUYA USAMARU

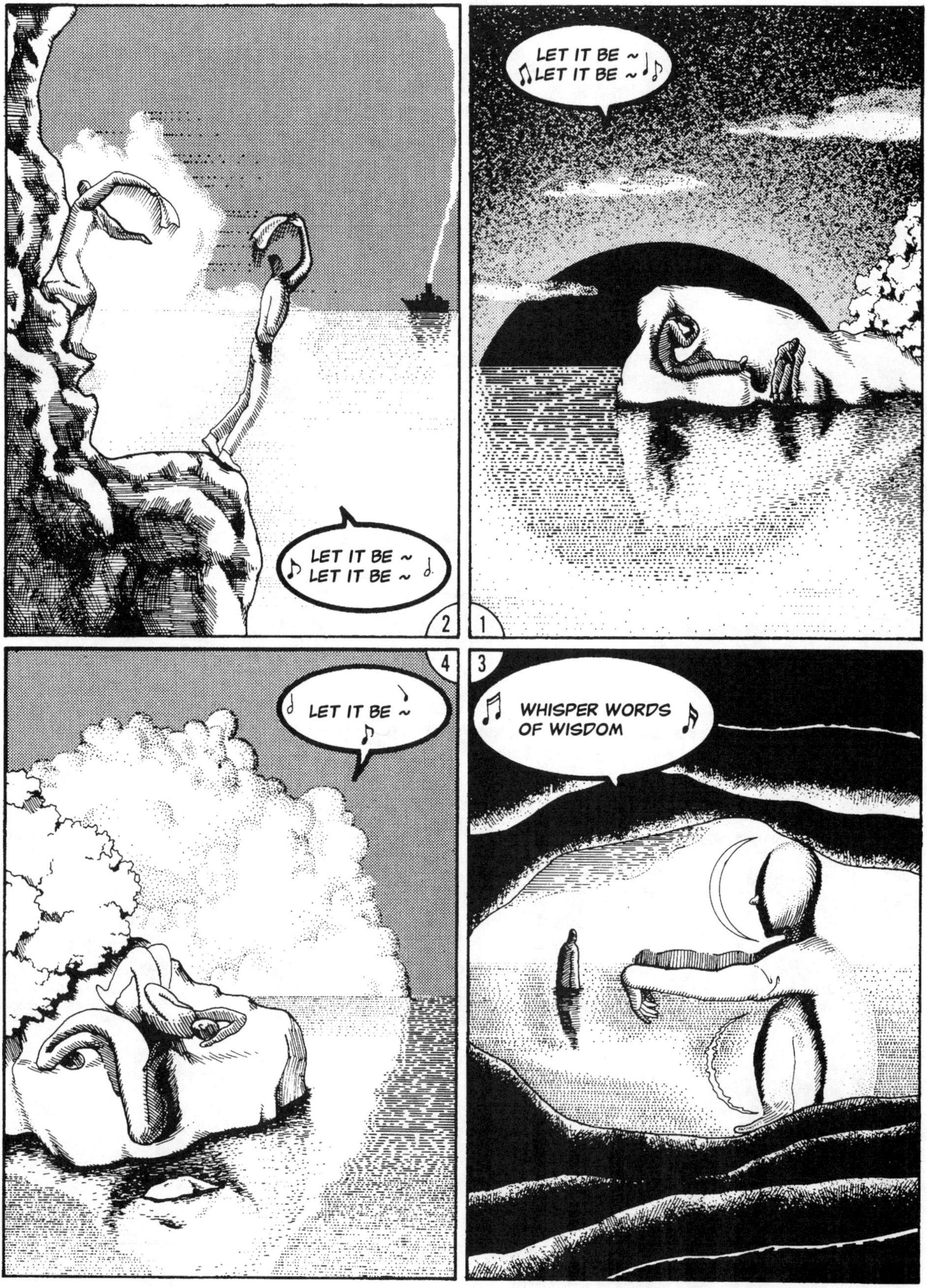

LET IT BE ~ LET IT BE ~
LET IT BE ~ LET IT BE ~
WHISPER WORDS OF WISDOM
LET IT BE ~

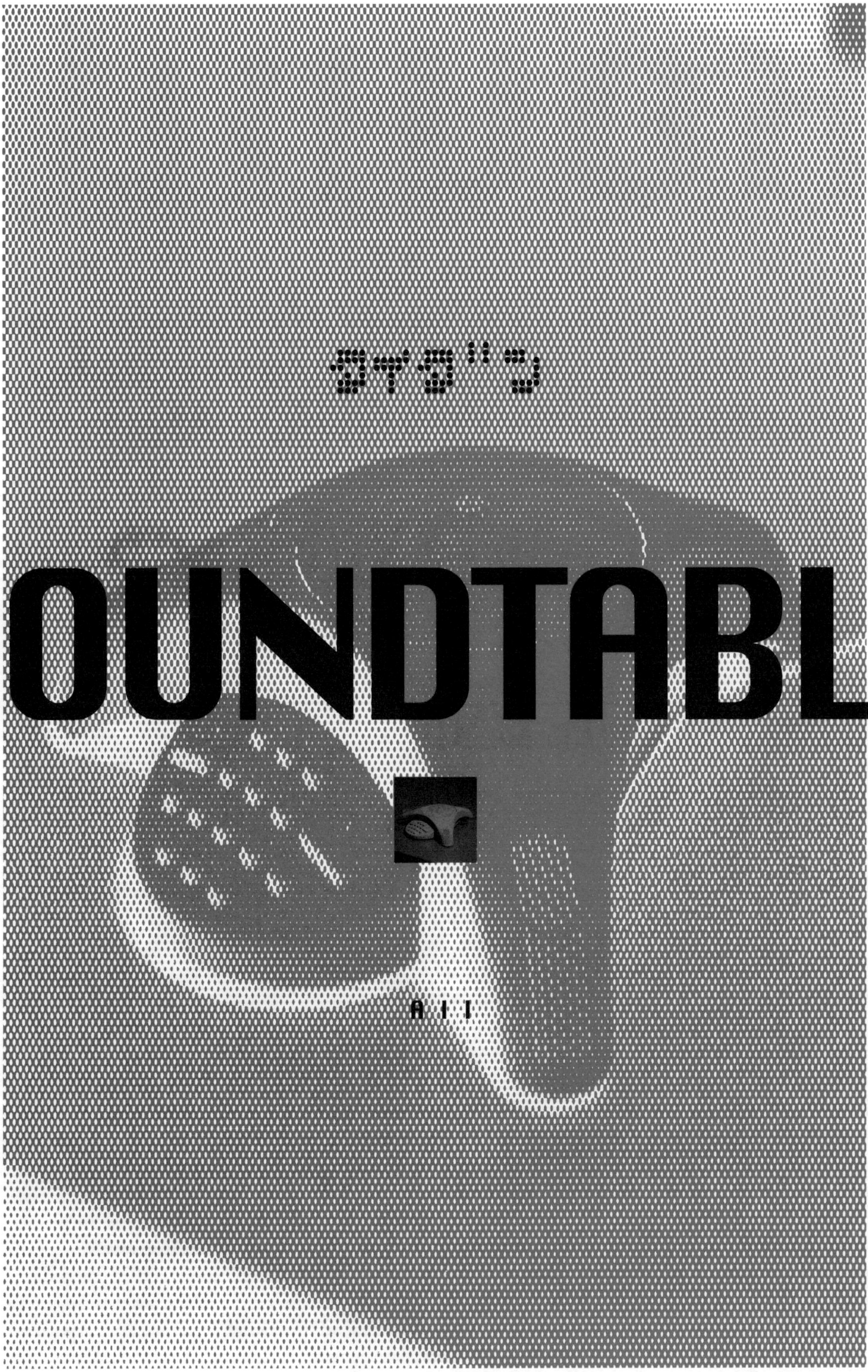

ROUNDTABLE

All

Roundt

The following is a transcript of excerpts of a discussion complementing the main chapters of this book held in January 1999 between the writers of *Japan Edge* and Editor-in-Chief Satoru Fujii, cofounder of **Cadence Books** and **Viz Comics**. In the course of the dialogue between these writers—each an expert in a specialized area of Japanese pop subculture—a variety of fascinating new insights emerged....

Photo by Kiyo Hayashi

JAMMING ON
THE THEMES

THE LIFE OF AN ANIME OTAKU

SATORU: First of all, since we're discussing this in America, everything that's Japanese is going to be subcultural from our perspective. But in the context of Japan, some of what you discuss is mainstream there, while some is also subcultural and underground there. I want to make this distinction. Also, for example, in the case of the yakuza movies Patrick has written about, they were mainstream at the time they were *released* in Japan, but now, for those who get into these old movies in Japan, they've got a subcultural atmosphere. I'd like to consider each of these subjects with that in mind.

Let's talk about anime first. As we know, it's basically a mainstream thing in Japan: it's shown on TV; it's sold on video; it's in the movies. But it's a subcultural scene in the U.S., and in Japan the subcultural aspect of it is the fandom associated with it.

CARL: It's been my impression that, historically speaking, while anime may have been a mainstream thing for the young, it has generally not been among older viewers. Once you get beyond college age, I wouldn't say it's a mainstream thing. Certainly **Ghibli**'s films—which, like **Disney** films, are often thought of as something to take your children to—are very popular

Pokémon: The hottest anime of 1999
(Viz Video/Pioneer)

with all ages, but that particular level of popularity doesn't carry over to the rest of theatrical anime.

MASON: Although, every year it seems several of the top-grossing films in Japan are anime.

CARL: Sure. But those are, again, films designed to draw in the children's audience, like *Doraemon*.

SATORU: This year's number one is *Pokémon*.

CARL: A lot of the Japanese film industry in general is directed towards children and teenagers. And, of course, that's

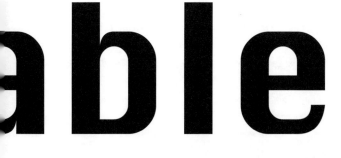

[Osamu Tezuka's *Astro Boy*] and the Toei films, so it would make sense that there was this gigantic, hidden community of anime fans in the mainstream, as it were, and that *Eva* could be the liberating moment for them. *Eva* contained a number of references to the anime someone of that age had grown up with; moreover, in its writing, it was the kind of show that an ordinary older person could look at and say, "There's some consideration for life in here beyond age fourteen."

true of America as well. But anime has hardly any *You've Got Mail*s or *Saving Private Ryan*s, movies, shall we say, intended for twenty-five- to fifty-year-olds. It's long been the case that a Japanese person in their thirties who's not an otaku may think, "I'm going to see an anime movie," but he's not likely to boast about it.

SATORU: Could you talk about some of the older fans in Japan?

CARL: It seems to me that in Japan, if you're not an otaku, you either keep quiet about it or you try and find a "respectable" outlet by working in the industry or by writing a postmodern analysis of some anime for a journal or book.

SATORU: *Evangelion* is an example. There were a lot of people in the Japanese media who we never knew were anime fans. But once *Eva* became a phenomenon, everyone started writing about it. They found out they actually *were* anime fans, right?

CARL: Right, and there were books published to help you fake your way through a conversation about *Eva* at a party, for example. *Evangelion* may have done a great service by revealing the shameful secret of how many adults are anime fans. They then started to ask, "Well, why *do* we like this?" and started to examine what's good about it.

SATORU: There's no shame any more about being an anime fan, about being an

Neon Genesis Evangelion: A big hit in Japan in 1997 (A.D. Vision)

Neon Genesis Evangelion: The controversial ending fueled the fire (A.D. Vision)

otaku. People's perceptions have really changed.

CARL: Do you think in part it's simply that money talks, causes people to pay attention, and *Eva* made so much of it?

SATORU: Well, it's not just that...it's that people's values have become liberated. There's much less of a central sense of how people should think any more in Japanese society.

CARL: It's been argued that *Evangelion* was a Trojan horse of Mr. Anno's—that supposedly he was making it for the core fourteen-year-old anime audience, but in reality he was making it for people his own age, who had grown up watching anime. I brought up the idea that his generation—now around thirty-five—started with *Tetsuwan Atom*

SATORU: I guess you're right; *Evangelion* was epoch-making when it started and received that heavy, heavy coverage in all kinds of magazines—general interest magazines, art magazines.... Now a lot of people feel free to just let people know, "I like anime."

CARL: Right. But I'm curious how a Japanese would answer this question. I'm an otaku, which means I like all kinds of anime. For example, I can enjoy a show for kids, like *Pokémon*. But I also would like to see more things like *Evangelion*, which offer something to an older audience. Does this new acceptance of being an adult and an anime fan mean it's okay to like these silly, frivolous shows or does it mean, "I like anime, and I'd like to see more anime that I can relate to as an older person?"

SATORU: It means both, I guess. There's this one guy in particular, **Hiroki Azuma**—he's basically a guy who had been writing books about Derrida...

CARL: **Jacques Derrida** [founder of the literary theory of deconstructionism]?

SATORU: Yeah. And Azuma has been writing several articles for *Quick Japan*, as

Quick Japan: The best subculture magazine in Japan. Published by Ota Shuppan (cover: Hideaki Anno, director of *Evangelion*)

well as other books and magazines about being an anime fan...he's a disciple of **Kojin Karatani**. I read two articles of his; he's phenomenal. So, for *him*, there's no shame in doing that. It's just letting people know what kind of person he is. Things have changed so much that I have more respect towards him now, knowing that he's an anime fan. [laughs] This guy must be very interesting!

CARL: It's a complicated issue. I think this kind of "otaku-ization" that **Toshio Okada** predicted is wonderful, but I also agree with what **Hiroyuki Yamaga** says: "Come back in twenty years, see what we've accomplished." I think he's right. If you look at the development of American feature-length film over the past century and then compare it to the mere forty years of theatrical anime, there's many places for it still to go, beyond the handful of great works it's already achieved. When **Hayao Miyazaki** was **Hideaki Anno**'s age, he was making *The Castle of Cagliostro*: a classic in and of itself, yet every one of his films with **Ghibli** still lay ahead of him.

SATORU: What's the context of being a Japanese animation fan in America? Is there any stigma to it?

CARL: To be honest, I think that not only is there no stigma anymore in being a fan of Japanese animation in the U.S., but even the term anime is becoming familiar to everyone. When you have people like **Nicolas Cage** praising the wildness, the weirdness, the strangeness of it, and people like **James Cameron** praising it for its film-craft and the skill of its directors, you're getting recognition for both sides. The stigma that remains may be self-assigned.... Having a stigma attached to it can be cool, too, even inspiring: "the otaku against the world."

But the other side, which can happen in any subculture, is the underground that goes sour and starts to stink. It goes back to what I said in the overview about my highly

ambiguous feelings about anime clubs. After my experiences as a kid, I never wanted to form one, and I didn't join one again until I was twenty-three and hooked up with **Cal-Animage Alpha**, the club at the University of California at Berkeley. And that was because they were the complete opposite of what I had earlier associated with clubs. Alpha struck me as a large, public-oriented, vital group of young people. A lot of the staff of the largest U.S. anime convention, **Anime Expo**, came out of it. I can't help but think that if Alpha had been around in the early '80s, the history of the U.S. anime industry might have had different names.

NEW TRENDS IN JAPANESE FILM

SATORU: Let's look at movies now. Patrick has talked about *yakuza eiga*, which were

Gonin: Director Takashi Ishii is a violence expert. (Phaedra/Shochiku)
Hana-Bi was awarded the Grand Prix at the Venice Film Festival (Milestone/Shochiku)

among the biggest movies of their time in the '60s and '70s, but as I said earlier, Patrick, and even the people in Japan, are trying to grasp these movies from a different standpoint. And that's also part of the subculture: the way in which you grasp these movies. But right now, in Japan, there's a new wave of independent movies, although I'm not sure we can call **Takashi Ishii**'s films independent anymore....

PATRICK: What's interesting is that a lot of Japanese directors began their careers working for major studios. In America, the path of the independent is that you start out

small and you either stay that way doing your own thing or you become **Quentin Tarantino** or get swallowed up by Hollywood to direct *The Beverly Hillbillies*. In Japan, it seems that people often start at the top and then go down the ladder to do more personal work.

MASON: Are they doing more personal work under the auspices of the studios they were working with before?

PATRICK: It seems that many Japanese films are produced independently and then released through the studio's channel of distribution.

SATORU: Japanese studios hardly have any money, so for each project, they have to get funds from all kinds of people.

CARL: What we call a "major studio" in America is of an entirely different order than a Japanese major studio.

PATRICK: A studio is really whoever controls mass distribution. Theater chains, video, dedicated satellite channels, that sort of thing. They're not really production facilities anymore.

CARL: Remember that scene in *Heartbroken Angels* in *PULP* magazine where the couple is deciding on a movie to rent and it's like, "A Japanese movie? Give me a break!" Is that common among Japanese audiences—they hate their own movies, think they're lousy?

YUJI: No, they don't *hate* them, it's just that they rent movies for entertainment, and the average Hollywood blockbuster is more fun.... That's pretty much the attitude.

Takeshi Kitano: One of the most fascinating figures in J-Pop culture today.

SATORU: Patrick, can you

give some examples of directors who fit the context of a subculture?

PATRICK: Takashi Ishii is a good example. His films like *Original Sin* and *Gonin* have a strong basis in the crime and suspense genres, but his approach to them is radically different. The narrative is broken up. The

Junk Food: Drugs, violence, and alienation in Tokyo © Junk Food Connection

message is ambiguous. And there may actually be a message buried there, as opposed to just entertainment. He's bringing experimental techniques into traditional types of stories.

SATORU: How about **Takeshi Kitano**?

MASON: Is he at all underground now?

PATRICK: That depends on where you are.

SATORU: He's a major, major comedian, and that's separate from the independent nature of his movies when he started making them.

PATRICK: In America, he's probably the most recognizable and visible of the new Japanese filmmakers. He's not someone whom we've been watching forever, like **Kurosawa** or **Imamura**. Takeshi sort of erupted out of *Merry Christmas, Mr. Lawrence* scenes, and suddenly he's smiling with a gun to his head and a bullet in his brain.

CARL: I gather the Japanese still think of Takeshi first and foremost as a comedy star.

PATRICK: He's really a pop Renaissance man. He does manga; he paints; he's a constant presence on Japanese TV.

SATORU: He's really a comedian. He started as a stage comedian, doing his stuff in between strip shows.

CARL: But we have a very different viewpoint on him in America. [laughs]

PATRICK: What's interesting about Beat Takeshi is that, while his films are acclaimed and written about in hip magazines, they don't do very well in the United States. Last year, there was a small release of both *Sonatine* and *Fireworks* and they performed poorly wherever they played. I think the problem is that Western audiences want something specific from an Asian person with a gun. And if the film doesn't live up to those expectations...

CARL: They expect Hong Kong?

PATRICK: Yeah, I think people expect—and demand—**John Woo** every time.

MASON: They probably expect either a Japanese art film or a Hong Kong action film, and it's neither.

SATORU: Even in Japan, his films receive a lot of publicity, and you can read all about

them in the magazines, but very few people are going to see them in the theaters or rent them on video. In that sense, it may be mainstream in terms of publicity, but it's subcultural at the box office. [laughs]

CARL: Isn't it true that *Sonatine* was a commercial success, as these things go, in England?

Junk Food: The daily life of foreigners in Tokyo © Junk Food Connection

PATRICK: Yeah, it was successful over there, but I don't know the exact boxoffice or number of prints struck. You would think these films would be solid gold, because they've won so many awards and we've seen Beat Takeshi in all these cool magazines. He's Mr. Japanese Film right now. Yet no one goes to see his films when they open in America.

CARL: The "Asian Robert Mitchum," that's my favorite thing they say about him.

SATORU: What's your impression of where these Japanese films are going in comparison to other Asian movies?

PATRICK: The Hong Kong film industry is in a very bad depression right now. They only had one box office hit in 1998, *The StormRiders*. But it starred **Sonny Chiba**, so I'm optimistic. The Asian economy is in bad shape right now and Japan hasn't been

Sonatine: Yakuza war in Okinawa and the fate of one hapless gangster © Shochiku Co., Ltd.

spared. But economic depression can sometimes bring out the best in popular culture. I don't know if this is going to create a situation where people are going to crave entertainment or if it's going to be a situation where the industry simply can't produce anything—which seems to very nearly be the case in Hong Kong right now.

CARL: Like the '30s or '70s in American film?

PATRICK: They have a fondness for genre. And there is a lot of nihilism. *Junk Food*, for instance, is a film about nothing. It's about trying to preserve a single moment in time. Whether this sort of thing is successful or not, I don't think we'll really be able to judge for another fifteen or twenty years.

SATORU: Do you feel a distinctiveness between art films from Japan compared to those from other Asian countries, like Korea or Taiwan?

PATRICK: They all have a certain fondness for genre and youth, you know. I don't know what it is. There's a lot of guns, there's a lot of death... There's something not very serious at the heart of them. Like *Junk Food*, it's a film that's about nothing.

But it's trying to get its hands around what it's like to be a person in the late twentieth century, I think.

SATORU: One of the senses I get from other Asian art movies is that in those

countries they can still talk about society, about family, about love. But in Japan, they just can't do that any more [laughs] unless it's a movie for entertainment. So what I see instead is the frustration of people in the big city and in the modern world, alienation, and a sudden blast of passion or anger.

PATRICK: Not being able to articulate anything other than that.

MASON: You saw *Tokyo Fist*? That's quite an example.

EXPERIMENTAL JAPANESE FILM

PATRICK: Yeah. It could be that people are just going crazy from living in the cities and that these are the only people with the access to produce feature films.

SATORU: I'd like Yuji to talk about the other scene: experimental filmmakers and amateur filmmakers using 8 mm cameras.

YUJI: There's one scene which is sort of like the

Guiding Star (1987): A 75-minute 8 mm movie, directed by Mikio Yamazaki

institutionalized version of experimental films in Japan, in Tokyo. It's called **Image Forum**, and it's just an archive and film festival organizer. They create or are in charge of what you would consider your real independent film, experimental artworks with no outside funding. They're pretty interesting, but they're kind of stodgy. Every year there's a certain angle they'll stress for work and anything that doesn't fit under that rubric gets disposed of. And then there are scenes that are more local, that are like dojinshi in some ways. They're made by people who are attracted to each other's films. But anyway, the medium is pretty much Super 8 or 8 because it's Fuji film

8 mm. I mean, this is pretty much a superficial distinction, but...

CARL: You mean, reel-to-reel 8?

YUJI: No, it's different from Kodak Super 8. But in any case, they don't use 16 mm, because they can't afford it. It's way too expensive. Compared to here it's like three times more. So the films tend to be really, really low budget. And even though video is

A Port in Vain (1996): directed by Mikio Yamazaki, director of the 1994 35 mm film *Pu*.

getting more and more popular, people still insist on making films in the 8 mm format.

CARL: Is 8 better supported by the industry in Japan than it is in the United States?

YUJI: No, it's worse. It has virtually disappeared, but people are still making these films. Actually, **Yamazaki**, he's from this scene, and there are people in it who make these feature length, hour-and-a-half Super 8 films...and they would win some awards, and maybe they might get some money to make an independent film that could then get major distribution, which is pretty much what happened to Yamazaki. But most people, they just do exactly what they want. And the stuff they come up with is, I think, more fascinating than any of these other, more established independent filmmakers.

SATORU: Aren't there contests for the 8 mm filmmakers?

YUJI: Yeah, there's the **Image Forum Contest Festival**, and there's also one that *Pia* magazine sponsors, called **PFF**. With that one, you win the equivalent of U.S. $10,000 to make a film.

MASON: In America, in the really independent films, they're often just more personal stories...

PATRICK: But that can lead to narcissism...

MASON: Yeah, that can lead to films that aren't interesting to anyone but their makers...

PATRICK: Turn the camera on yourself in the bathroom and think of a movie...it's easy!

SATORU: But these films are really based on the director's passion...they have to come up with the money themselves...it's just like a home recording, no one wants to watch it! [laughs]

CARL: You've talked about the question of dojinshi people going professional.... Do you think there's real talent, another Kurosawa, another Ozu, to be found in the ranks of these 8 mm filmmakers?

YUJI: The thing I like about this stuff is that it's totally indifferent to making any films

Nekoyoru (1992): Director Mikio Yamazaki made this movie by editing 8 mm film shot by the actors themselves.

like that. It sort of comes up with its own art form, I think. That's what was weird when I first started watching these films; I thought that I knew what experimental films were, to the extent that I knew what they were here, in the States. And then I realized that in Tokyo they were making experimental films that had nothing to do with any genre or style I'd ever seen. And that's what was really intriguing, that it was occurring not on this big pop culture level, but on this really, really, localized level, where the images and ideas were unique.

SATORU: Not just Yamazaki. There's already several directors who came from that scene.

CARL: Could you mention a particular film from this scene that you found memorable?

YUJI: There was one that had a notorious reputation. It's called *Memory by the Seaside*, or something, and it's just a close-up of a guy's hand as he starts cutting it.

MASON: Is this narrated or purely visual?

SATORU: Is this like a snuff film?

YUJI: No, it's just the filmmaker cutting his own hand.

PATRICK: Performance art.

CARL: It's not snuff; it's more like "ouch" film. It's not as severe. [laughs]

YUJI: But the fact that it was shot on 8 mm made it all the more gritty...

PATRICK: Intimate, raw...

CARL: Was this an individual scene or was it the main subject of the film?

YUJI: It was the main subject...there were two alternating scenes. The other

was a guy in a faraway shot just whaling on someone with a bat, and those two scenes intercut. And that's a three-minute film.

Anyway, the more interesting film I saw recently was called *A Port in Vain*. [described in further detail in the "Tokyo Diary" chapter]. It's sort of a long meditation on pop culture and these little venues we have in the city. It did really well at the **Yamagata Documentary Film Festival**. It won a special prize. It was going to be shown at the **Pompidou** in France. Also, there was talk about U.S. distribution. But one of the main problems—and this actually gets back to what you were talking about with dojinshi, about parodies—is that there's this whole thing about "Mickey and Minnie," this little weird narrative about Mickey having been exiled, kicked out from Disneyland. It just couldn't be released; it would get slammed with a lawsuit. But it's essential to the film. And that relates to something I think is interesting about experimental film, but also music as well: it's that they're really interested in American pop culture, and the way they manipulate it is really interesting.

One last film which I should mention is called *Marilyn*. Each frame in it is a different photo of Marilyn Monroe; it's got something like a thousand photos of her. And you just sort of watch them in rapid succession, and it's really jarring.

Thee Michelle Gun Elephant's *Gear Blues*: regarded by many as the best Japanese CD of 1998

MAIN-STREAM VS. UNDERGROUND MUSIC

SATORU: In Japan, there is of course mainstream music and indie music. And the noise music Mason wrote about is part of a small, subculture scene. In the mainstream, there's idol singers and stupid rock bands [laughs], imitation hip-hop groups, and things like that. And then there's a lot of serious, good music now in the mainstream that came out of the indie scene. **Thee Michelle Gun Elephant** and **Supercar** are some really good bands like that. But what's good and bad about the mainstream music scene now in Japan? Of course, eighty percent of mainstream music is going to be bad....

We mentioned noise music and some of the independent musicians Yuji was associated with. But there's definitely other subculture music scenes. For example, if I go to a record store in Japan, there's hardcore punk, skapunk, reggae, the techno rave scene.... Could you talk about them?

YUJI: I think Mason probably has more to say about hardcore punk. But I heard that skapunk was the happening thing in Tokyo right now.

SATORU: I recently read that the better punk bands are in Osaka.

YUJI: And then the techno scene, the DJ scene, sounds really interesting. One thing I think that's kind of different, that I like, is that they'll incorporate bands that really have nothing to do with the techno scene. A

Keiji Haino: One of the most respected noise musicians in Japan. Photo by Hiromi Wakui

show I saw with **Keiji Haino** last summer was at this place called **The Milk Club** in Ebisu...

MASON: It's one of the hip places now.

YUJI: There was sort of this DJ thing going on, and then downstairs, there was this...all this psychedelic, weird...I don't know how to describe it, because I'm not very familiar with it.... Anyway, this psychedelic projection and stuff. And then the music stopped and **Keiji Haino** and the **Ruins'** drummer, **Tatsuya Yoshida**, they did a show with this DJ. Anyway, it was a rock show, for all intents and purposes.

SATORU: The same audience?

YUJI: That's what was weird. There were definitely people who were there for Haino. The stage cleared out immediately after the show was over, but then it was filled again. And it seemed like half of the previous audience was still there, although I wasn't really paying attention to who was there and who wasn't. But just the fact that you could have a show that could include those types of music together....

MASON: That's one thing that I've always noticed. I mentioned it in my chapter. Ever since I've been going to shows there, there's always been more of a willingness to mix genres during the same show than in America. So I'd go to a show and I'd see a noise band and then a psychedelic pop band and then a punk band. And they would mix them completely, which never happens over here.

SATORU: So is there a friendship between the musicians of different genres?

MASON: Yeah. A lot of the time there is. And a lot of the time a person who's doing noise will also be in a rock band or also be doing something else. **Masahiko Ohno**

Tetsuya Yoshida of Ruins. Yoshida owns his own independent label.

from **Solmania** has been in a lot of other bands, too.

SATORU: So do you feel that's kind of different from the U.S. scene?

MASON: Yeah, yeah. It is.

CARL: I like the sound of that. There's so much pressure here.... I'm more familiar with '80s punk and hardcore scenes, but if you played too fast or too slow it often seemed back then that you weren't going to be friends with that guy or you weren't going to be playing in that club.

MASON: Yeah. It may be that *because* the difference between the mainstream and the indie scene is so strict in Japan, there's not so much of that thought in the back of your head, "Well, if I do this one thing right, then I might become successful." I think that even here, people don't necessarily *plan* that, but the thought might always be in the back of your head. Whereas over there, it's even more difficult to make the jump to real mainstream status.

CARL: Is that because mainstream Japanese music is so much more conservative?

MASON: It's much more manufactured than the mainstream music scene is here.

YUJI: This ties into it, but also, legally, it's much harder for you to assert your independence. The contracts...

CARL: Musicians don't have as many rights over there?

SATORU: They have rights, but there's a certain system. There's a certain talent agency that you have to belong to. Show business is very close knit. It's really changing now; there's a lot of new bands, and they're going to do what they want, and they're going to pick the show they're going to play and what style they're going to play in and what's going to be the appearance of their CDs. But there's still this whole industry system where everybody knows each other, and if you don't have some connections you can't do anything. For the most part, if you want to get into the mainstream, you have to sacrifice something. Not necessarily musically, but your time, or your lifestyle.

MASON: It has changed some in recent years, but before, it seemed that you couldn't become a successful mainstream band if you started as a band *first*. More often, a management company would assemble people, put them together as a band with a certain style....

Pizzicato Five, *Made in the U.S.A.*: mixes and remixes of pop music from all eras

CARL: The **Spice Girls** thing was much more common in Japan.

MASON: Yeah, yeah, it was. But it has been changing, with the success of bands like **Cornelius** and **Pizzicato Five**.

SATORU: It's really been changing for the past five years, since some indie bands started to get major contracts.

CARL: Do you know what made it change?

MASON: Probably the same thing that made major labels here start to pick up punk rock. Someone suddenly realized, "Ohhhhhh...these bands *could* actually make us money."

SATORU: They have to catch up to their audiences eventually.

THE COMIKE (COMICS MARKET) SCENE

SATORU: Let's look at manga. As you know, there are all kinds, but most of those published here in the U.S. are big, mainstream comics in Japan. But shojo manga—it's sort of mainstream, but there's a lot of Japanese fandom in shojo manga who are in a subculture, in terms of the way the readers form associations about the manga...

CARL: Yeah, I hear that the women's day at Comic Market [Comike], is much bigger than the men's.

SATORU: I would like to discuss subcultural underground comics in Japan. Most of you have read **Blast Books'** *Comics Underground Japan* and know about the Comike scene. Some of you are familiar with the Japanese underground comics magazine *Garo* [stories from which have been collected in English in *Comics Underground Japan* as well as Fantagraphics' *Sake Jock*]. And also, there is a special fandom in the comics scene, the people who organize Comike.

CARL: First of all, it's probably a curious thing from the standpoint of the American reader, because there are lots and lots of things in Japanese mainstream comics that here in America you would only find from the small presses. I'm not just talking about what would be considered in the U.S. to be offensive or shocking material—although that's certainly to be found in mainstream manga—but the more radical idea—radical in American comic books, at least—of stories about ordinary people and familiar situations, which mainstream manga are full

Heartbroken Angels: Creator Masahiko Kikuni is also the leader of a rock-'n'-roll band. © Masahiko Kikuni/Shogakukan/Viz Comics

of, too. So Americans are probably very curious to know what is "underground" to a Japanese, and by underground I mean noncommercial, not sellable. It's an aspect of manga I really don't know too much about. I look at *PULP*'s *Heartbroken Angels*, for example, which appeared in a mainstream magazine in Japan. What separates that kind of satire and humor from the satire and humor you'd find in *Garo*?

SATORU: I guess that, more and more, there are no such distinctions. It used to be there were definite distinctions, but a lot of big talent in manga today started off in the underground or in small publications. Editors are always looking for new talent. The competition in the industry is really intense and the tastes of readers are always changing. Even Masahiko Kikuni, who does *Heartbroken Angels*...he started off in those smaller magazines.

CARL: But he's in his forties, isn't he?

SATORU: Yeah. But he still plays rock-'n'-roll. [laughs]

A horde of costumed otaku and other fans at Comike. Photos by Chikao Shiratori

SATORU: Let's talk about the Comike scene. Could you talk about what kind of people go to Comike? Who is a part of this subculture of dojinshi?

CARL: It's hard to say. There are many different kinds of people who go to Comike. The difference lies, perhaps, between those who would admit they go and those who wouldn't. There's another director who told me that he would never admit that he went to Comike—he feels that he would lose respect in the industry and be seen as unprofessional. As you know, it's not always considered a good thing to act like an otaku in this industry, because you may be accused of not caring enough about what *this* company is doing now on *this* project and of having an idle and frivolous viewpoint. Companies *like* fans, but they like them to buy things, not necessarily to work for them.

SATORU: So the purpose of people who are creating dojinshi and selling them at Comike.... There may be a lot of money involved now, but it originally started as just something for themselves, right?

CARL: Yes. And it has to be remembered that it still is that way. The big money is only for a very few titles out of the thousands that might be sold at any given Comike. And even very successful dojinshi full of big names are made by big names who are *friends*.

YUJI: One thing I was wondering, though, is that the people who are doing these dojinshi...

do they usually have aspirations to make it into the big time?

CARL: That must depend on every individual. I'm sure there are people who are perfectly happy in their jobs and who simply like to draw on the side, like people who doodle. And then there are those who want to follow the lead of so many other artists who have gone professional.

UNDERGROUND COMICS & GARO

SATORU: Let's talk about underground comics, such as those in *Garo*, and the influence they've had from the '60s and '70s to today.

CARL: One question I'd like to ask is: if, as you say, big publishers are always looking to the underground for fresh talent, why is it that same talent could not make *Garo* succeed on its own level?

MASON: Wasn't there a management change? I thought someone else took over *Garo*.

SATORU: Yeah, and most of the editors got rebellious and left to start a new magazine. *Garo* tried to keep on publishing [after being bought out in 1991 and after the death of founder **Katsuichi Nagai** in 1996], but it's gone for now. But there are plans to start the magazine again.

MASON: I always thought that *Garo*

Garo: This magazine, synonymous with Japanese underground comics, will soon be reincarnated.

vanished because it never really recovered from that change.

SATORU: Those things happened because the sales had become so low.

CARL: But it seems odd, considering how dojinshi manage to go on—some, at least, for ten years—with very low print runs.

YUJI: Yeah, but that's not a particular company, it's based on a phenomenon, right?

CARL: And unlike *Garo* [which did not pay its contributors unless the individual's work proved popular enough to later be compiled in graphic novel form], people who do dojinshi might make *some* money with each issue.

YUJI: Well, I don't know how *Garo* came about, but I think one of the important things about that magazine in the '60s was that it marked an occasion when college students were reading manga quite regularly, not just as entertainment, but as something instead of **Sartre** or **Dostoyevski**. They would claim it was just as significant. So already the balance gets changed in terms of what's important about culture. And I think *Garo* was really important for that.

SATORU: In the counterculture movement in the '60s, there was a lot of theater going on, and of course music. And underground comics such as *Garo* were a major cultural power at that point.

YUJI: Yeah, it wasn't so much that it was underground or experimental material. One of the most popular comics in *Garo* was about ninja: **Sanpei Shirato**'s *Kamui*.

SATORU: Viz published Shirato's *The Legend of Kamui*, which was a side story of *Kamui*, but that main story, which has Marxist tastes in terms of its themes, was published in *Garo*.

YUJI: *Kamui* was very heavy on plot, and the kind of serial you wanted to keep on reading. It wasn't very experimental in terms of doing away with linear narrative. It seems that *Garo* was accessible in terms of attracting a mainstream readership, whether you were interested in the subculture or not.

CARL: Do you think that *Garo*'s readers in the late '60s were—like a lot of student radicals in the United States—into a more fun, pleasure-oriented, individualistic type of rebellion as opposed to the earlier, more serious, labor movement—oriented types?

YUJI: Actually, I think there was a lot of

crossover. These were students who were reading the ninja rebellions of *Kamui* as an allegory for the student movement. There was politics in the comics...

SATORU: Yeah, like hippies in the U.S. read [**Gilbert Shelton**'s] *The Fabulous Furry Freak Brothers*. It's the same kind of people. [laughs]

CARL: In Japan, the high point of social unrest was not in the late but the early '60s, specifically 1960. And, yeah, I have read that some of the people involved considered *Kamui* something they could relate to.

PATRICK: Something I think happened in the '60s was that the counterculture who grew up with popular culture like comics and rock-'n'-roll didn't want to stop enjoying it. So, in order to justify their continued interest in pop culture, both the audience and creators had to take a step forward in sophistication.

CARL: Stuff like **Robert Crumb** and **Gilbert Shelton**'s, though, was very different in tone from that historical stuff about peasant rebellions.

PATRICK: But there was still narrative and an appreciation for the art of the gag. While their subject matter was revolutionary, they weren't wildly changing the medium itself. Whereas if you pick up an issue of *Garo* from, say, five years ago, you would find things inside that totally demolish traditional ideas of storytelling and page composition.

CARL: I was just suggesting the difference between the so-called New Left and Old Left, which we had in America, too. In Japan, the Old Left—which was more serious and all about the labor movement and the U.S.–Japan Security Treaty—versus the newer generation of student radicals who basically wanted to be liberated from social constraints...

PATRICK: ...and still listen to their rock-'n'-roll and read their comics. It's not responsible to pick up a comic book and enjoy a moment's escape from reality. It must have relevance. Suddenly, *Kamui* is not about ninja anymore. It's really about class struggle.

SATORU: In terms of *Kamui*, it's not really concerned about class struggle, it's more about people being oppressed by authority and rebelling against them. It's got a certain background; it's not *really* about ideology.

PATRICK: I'm curious about whether *Kamui*'s author was aware of what he was creating. Was he consciously manipulating all these political themes or were people reading what they wanted into it?

SATORU: Sanpei Shirato, who created *Kamui*, was at one time a member of the Communist, so he had the ideology which is reflected in his

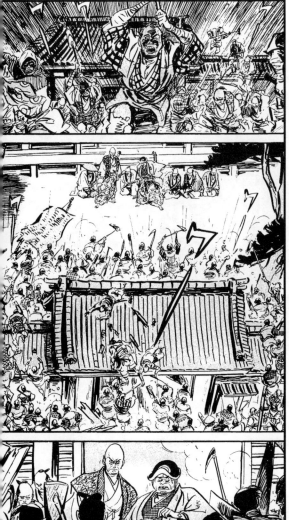

The Story of Kamui: Ninja Kamui aids peasants rising up against their masters in Japan's feudal era. © Akame Productions/Shogakukan

The Legend of Kamui: Kamui's life as an apostate ninja

Akai Hana: Artist Hino transcends horror. © Hideshi Hino/Hibari Shobo

work. The readership and atmosphere of that whole era was more receptive to those kinds of stories.

YUJI: Yeah, his father was involved in the proletarian movement.

CARL: When I look at the stuff from *Garo* that's been published in the U.S.... *Planet Of The Jap*, by **Suehiro Maruo** [reprinted in *Comics Underground Japan*], was probably the most political, but most of the stories seem to be more satirical, nonsensical, taboo-breaking rather than really "political." I'd like to know.... Do you know if *Garo* changed its balance over the years to less politics, more sex and satire?

SATORU: I guess at first, in the middle and late '60s, *Garo* had a variety of titles, including story comics. And then, when major publishers started publishing comics for older people, a lot of talent, artists who worked for *Garo*, went to the majors. Actually, what I think was happening with *Garo* was this: in the '70s and '80s, major publishers started publishing material for all different ages. So talent began going to the major publishers directly, rather than through *Garo*, as in the old days. And many of *Garo*'s editors couldn't see how the subcultures were changing and just stuck to their old, '60s counterculture audience, whose numbers were dwindling and dwindling. And some new magazines, such as *Studio Voice*, began picking up some of *Garo*'s artists who were part of today's subculture.

OTHER GENRES

NEW-WAVE NOVELS

SATORU: Let's talk about the other subculture genres which we haven't talked about in this book. Let's start with literature.

CARL: Hideaki Anno has now gone from anime into what you might call cult film with the live-action *Love and Pop*, based on the **Ryu Murakami** novel.

MASON: That's one of his that hasn't been translated into English. I'm a big fan of Ryu Murakami.

CARL: I've only read the other Murakami, **Haruki Murakami** [*The Elephant Vanishes*].

MASON: Ryu Murakami's *Coin Locker Babies*.... It's not a very pleasant book, but it's very powerful.

SATORU: The two Murakamis... [laughs] Of course, they're not mainstream in Japan.

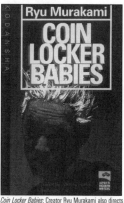

Coin Locker Babies: Creator Ryu Murakami also directs movies and is a big fan of Cuban music and soccer.

But literature itself in this country is subcultural. [laughs] And of course, Japanese literature is sub-subcultural.

MASON: That's actually the problem. I talk to friends from Japan who can recommend great authors, but I don't read very much Japanese, so I have to depend on things being translated. And obviously the authors who are translated are the ones that the publishers decide are big sellers. So we're never going to see very many of the real Japanese subculture or genre authors here in English.

CARL: Are you saying that Japanese read "serious books" even less than Americans? I had the opposite impression.

YUJI: They *read* more, but *what* they read can be questionable.

MASON: Every country's gonna read their own equivalent of **Stephen King**.

YUJI: Right. Someone like Haruki Murakami is really exceptional because he's considered literary yet is widely read, but somebody like Ryu Murakami—he's definitely had his ups and downs in terms of sales.

CARL: When I read Haruki Murakami, there was nothing particularly obscure in his style. He writes about today.

A Wild Sheep Chase: In the '80s, Haruki Murakami taught at various U.S. universities.

MASON: He's got that "pop" aspect.

SATORU: It depends on which of his novels you read. Some of them are realistic, but *A Wild Sheep Chase* is very abstract. Now I've found out that people like you who are into Japanese subculture also read Japanese literature.

CARL: Haruki Murakami's been published in *Playboy*, so I'm not sure how subcultural you could call him here any more. It was the story about the husband and wife who rob the McDonalds ["**The Second Bakery Attack**", January 1992].

SATORU: He's been writing about the Aum Shinrikyo incident recently, interviewing ex-cult members.

YUJI: That's one that'll never be translated either.

CARL: Why not? You'd think it would be of interest…

YUJI: It's this *tome*; it's huge. It's great, but it's not going to get translated. I think Murakami's audience here is made up of people who have some relationship to Japanese culture. But those who are "literary" and interested in reading foreign literature will at times end up reading Murakami also.

Kitchen: Writer Banana Yoshimoto's father, a literary critic, was the idol of students in the '60s.

MASON: And Banana Yoshimoto [*Kitchen*]…

SATORU: She's been much more popular in this country, too.

MASON: And she's been publicized in a different way, to a different kind of audience.

YUJI: Right, the Gen-X thing.

CARL: Hasn't Haruki Murakami himself translated American stories? That sort of suggests that when he writes, Americans might have an easier time relating to it…

YUJI: Yeah, **Raymond Carver**.

SATORU: Yes. When Murakami first became accepted in Japan, his writing style was known as "translating style." His writing read like something translated from English. He's of my generation, and when the student movement was going on, he was reading nothing but **F. Scott Fitzgerald**…so he's kind of a weird guy. [laughs]

MASON: But then, Ryu Murakami wrote about the '60s generation in *69*.

SATORU: He's of that generation, too. So he wrote about when he was in high school and the student movement.

FASHION & THE MUSIC CONNECTION

SATORU: Let's talk about fashion. I guess Japanese fashion actually came about during the late 1960s through people like **Hanae Mori** or **Kansai Yamamoto** who had something to do with the glam-rock scene and were actually chosen by **David Bowie**, who started wearing their clothes. They became very popular in London, and Yamamoto had his first fashion show there in the late 1960s. He became popular in Europe before Japan. Today the Tokyo collections are as important as London or Paris. I'm not actually that familiar with the current scene, but there's still a connection to the music scene through labels like **Hysteric Glamour**, **X-Girl** [part of the **Beastie Boys**' X-Large line of clothing], and bands like **Sonic Youth**.

HYSTERIC GLAMOUR

Hysteric Glamour T-shirts: The members of both Sonic Youth and Primal Scream wear this brand. © 1999 Hysteric Glamour

MASON: Was there a connection to the music scene with Hysteric Glamour?

SATORU: Yeah. Actually, **Sonic Youth** started wearing the T-shirts and they're wearing them in a video. And Hysteric Glamour was using that video at the fashion shows. Hysteric Glamour is the name of the factory that makes the fashions. There's one guy, named Nobuhiko Kitamura, who is the major designer. I think it's part of the subculture because it's not high fashion. It was the street kids who started wearing those clothes, and eventually it became very expensive, but...

YUJI: What kind of people buy these clothes, the ones you're talking about?

SATORU: People who like Sanrio stuff, I guess?

CARL: So, are these cooler and bigger than foreign fashions? Or are Japanese fashions still minor compared to...

SATORU: How can I explain it? Okay, there's this Japanese mall called Maruei. In the 1980s, the economy was good in Japan. Most young people had lots of money to spend on clothes. When you go to the mall, the lower level is more for junior fashion. When you go up, that's where you'll find the high fashion. But actually, none of those clothes in the mall are cheap—they're actually all very expensive. It's not so much about the style of the clothes; it's more about the brand name.

Because the yen was very strong, it gave energy to those Japanese brands over those of other countries. But now—this is my own, personal opinion—I think that the Japanese fashion scene and the music scene are really linked. Not with the music scene in *Japan*—but with American bands like Sonic Youth who started to wear those brands and appreciate them. That in turn gave the brands a new value for Japanese people who like clothes. That link has made fashion more of a subculture than it was before.

YUJI: Why do you think bands like Sonic Youth like these clothes?

SATORU: With Sonic Youth, I think it's that Hysteric Glamour is one of the craziest Japanese brands. I can't speak about the whole scene, but Nobuhiko Kitamura, the designer of Hysteric Glamour, personally loves music—the whole New York underground scene. He had connections with them and also with **Russ Meyer**. He did a video clip with him, with one of Russ Meyer's women dancing around with one of those tiny Japanese T-shirts. [laughs]

MASON: When it comes to Sonic Youth, **Kim Gordon** has a big collection of Hello Kitty stuff. She's apparently a huge Sanrio fan.

CARL: In Japan, have teenage girls always worn Sanrio stuff like they've been doing here, or is it more for young kids over there?

SATORU: In Japan, Sanrio is high school and younger. Little kids wear them, but high school students wear them too. Even some college students.

I want to add one thing. Japanese society is really fashion conscious; they spend a *lot* of money on clothes. "What to wear?" is a constant question, and it makes a statement to wear a certain brand. A certain brand carries a certain meaning to the people who wear it and the people who look at it. So someone who chooses the kind of brands I've described is making a statement by wearing them. And also, in Japan you have to be conscious of somebody's eye. You don't travel by yourself in a car, you travel with a crowd in a train or elevator. Nobody *likes* to spend all that money on clothes, but you kind of have to.

PHOTOGRAPHY SUBCULTURE

SATORU: Let's talk about photography. It's really part of the arts scene, but...

YUJI: Like **Araki**?

Cosmosco: Araki's book of photographs of a seventeen-year-old girl
Published by Shogakukan

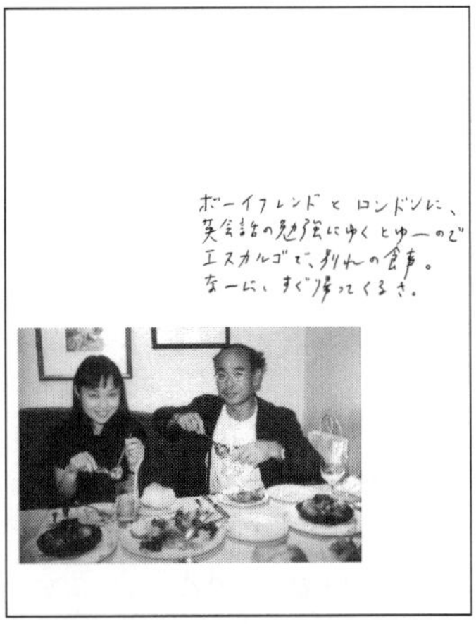
ボーイフレンドとロンドンに、
英会話の勉強にゆくとゆーので
エスカルゴで、別れの食事。
なーに、すぐ帰ってくるさ。

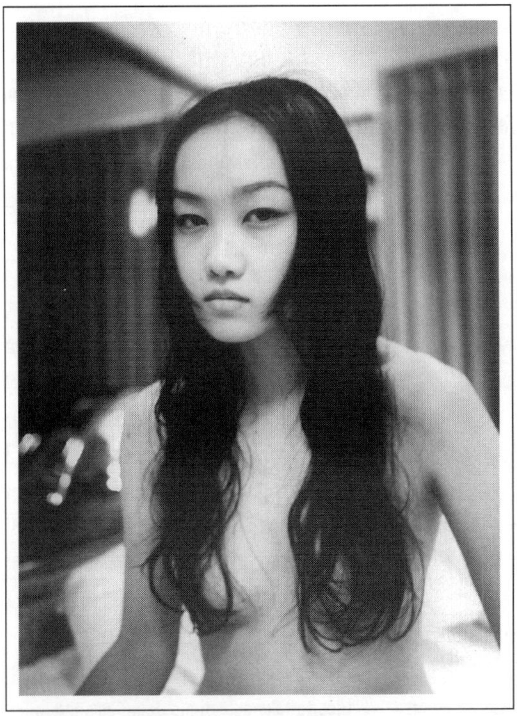

From *Cosmosco*: Araki knew his subject since she was nine.
© Nobuyoshi Araki

SATORU: Araki is part of the arts scene, not the subculture scene...

YUJI: Well, he *depicts* the subculture.

SATORU: Yes, right.

YUJI: You find his books everywhere. He's sort of...well, one could compare him to **Mapplethorpe**, but I think he's really different. The thing that's really interesting about him is that he does these very formal photographs and then he has the really raunchy photographs, content-wise, of Tokyo's subcultures.

SATORU: A lot of photographs about sex and S&M.

CARL: You mean he has some photos which are staged and formal and others which are just...

PATRICK: ...documentary?

YUJI: Yeah. But the weird thing is, he's not like, "I do this just to make money, just so I can pay for my high art." It's all mixed up. It's a really weird combination.

SATORU: Yeah, he's very interesting as a person. He's highly respected in the art world. But at the same time, he's a big figure in the media. He's got a lot of exposure, and he's interesting because he's not afraid to talk about anything.

CARL: Does he show his work through magazines or galleries? How does he get it out there?

SATORU: Every way. There's tons and tons of books, and a lot of them have been printed in this country and Europe.

MASON: Does he do advertising photos?

SATORU: Yeah. He started that way.

YUJI: Now he's doing some video documentaries, things like that. He's a lot bigger in Europe than he is here. But I think that's got something to do with his content.

SATORU: We should talk about **Hiromix**. It was Araki who discovered her. Her name is Hiromi, and she named herself Hiromix. She brought her work to him as part of a contest and she won an award. She was an everyday amateur photographer. She used a Konica and developed her pictures at the mall and then she copied her pictures through a copy machine and made her own picture book, ***School Days***. That book got an award when she was only nineteen and had just graduated from high school. She didn't have any experience as a photographer, but her work was really powerful. She changed the photography scene in Japan. Music magazines started using her as a photographer.

It used to be that photographers in Japan wanted to work for either fashion or art magazines, but because of people like Hiromix, music magazines are getting the avant-garde work now. And photography has become available to anyone with things like Print Club everywhere. For a young girl, photography doesn't have to be this art far away from your reality. Last time I went back to Japan, I saw a couple of girls taking pictures in the station. It's become very common, and that's something that happened just a couple years ago.

You can say that Araki is also an artistic photographer, but Hiromix really has subcultural tastes–she'll present out-of-focus work. You can say it's amateurish in some ways. But at the same time, it's opening up new possibilities and raising the idea of subcultures taking over the art world.

Studio Voice, March '96 issue: Just after graduating from high school, Hiromix and her work became the cover story of this well-respected art and subculture magazine.

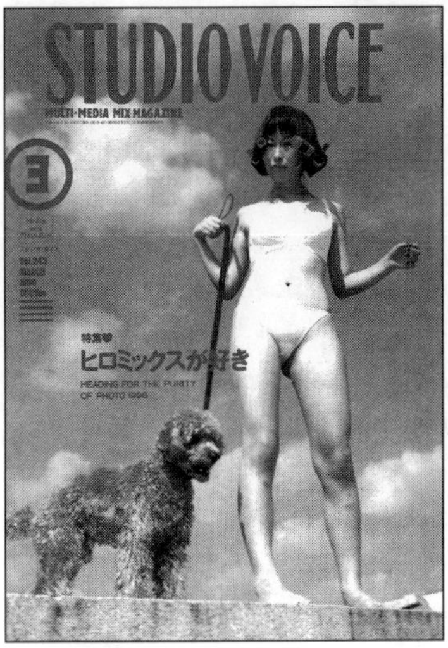
STUDIO VOICE
MULTI-MEDIA MIX MAGAZINE
3
特集号
ヒロミックスが好き
HEADING FOR THE PURITY OF PHOTO 1996

HOW THE WEST CHANGED JAPAN

SATORU: Let's talk about how the acceptance of Japan's pop subculture has affected Japan. Of course, Japanese producers know about the possibility of selling work to a foreign market, but creators tend to focus on the Japanese audience. In anime, there have been some exceptions to this, like *Ghost in the Shell*, made with a worldwide market in mind from the beginning—which is why they used U2 in it.

CARL: They used U2's *drummer*. [laughs]

SATORU: Manga Entertainment [then a subsidiary of **Island**, U2's label], when the movie was created, paid some money for that. In terms of music, there's definitely Pizzicato Five and **Shonen Knife**, who have some popularity not just in the U.S. but in Europe. And that's changing the attitude of some indie labels in Japan. In any of the genres you're interested in, do you see the existence of American fans affecting the awareness of Japanese producers or creators? *Ghost in the Shell* was created for a worldwide audience; *Akira* wasn't. Yet it was just as, if not more, successful. Of course, the films had different creators, but what do you see in the different approach?

CARL: An interesting thing happened with *Ghost in the Shell*. When the director, Mr. Oshii, was asked by American fans at Anime Expo '96 whether the characters were changed for the international market to look more Western, he said no. On the producer's side, when this same question was asked on a radio show I was on in Salt Lake City with **Marvin Gleicher** from

Manga Entertainment, Mr. Gleicher said yes. But I have to say from my perspective as a writer, Westernization appears to be a nonissue where *Ghost in the Shell* is concerned.

It seems Manga, as co-producer, left the director alone. Oshii even remarked on how they were nicer to deal with than some Japanese producers he'd known. And that's saying something, because they must have been aware that they were giving their money to one of the most idiosyncratic people in anime. There was no "extra" shock value inserted for the film that wasn't in the original manga. As for the perception of "Western" character changes, *Ghost* truthfully seemed little different in approach from the pale and unadorned characters of Oshii's previous film, *Patlabor 2*, which had no Western financing. No, the irony is that *Ghost in the Shell* was treated as a Japanese film even when it really *did* do something Western.

Oshii has long used biblical epigrams in his films, and when *Ghost*'s famous quote from I Corinthians 13, "When I was a child, I spake as a child..." shows up in the dub, it's barely recognizable in English. Why? I was told that the studio had dutifully *re-translated* the quote from Oshii's Japanese translation of the *King James Bible*. No, I don't think there are real examples

yet of Japanese animation being twisted out of shape, made something it isn't, to reach the Western market. How it gets translated and promoted here is another matter, but the originals remain Japanese.

SATORU: How about movies? Of course, **Ozu** and **Kurosawa** won major Western film festival awards. But how about more recent films?

PATRICK: And Kurosawa was always being criticized for being "too Western." Films like *Swallowtail Butterfly* and *Junk Food* have a very international flavor. They deal with different types of people in what was previously a homogeneous Japan. I guess another subculture there would just be other people: foreigners, their lives and their stories. As far as the Western market goes, it's very telling what happened when Hollywood tried to make an American Godzilla movie. It's awful when the U.S. tries to take something Japanese and make

Ghost in the Shell: This internationally produced anime was a hit worldwide. (Manga Entertainment)

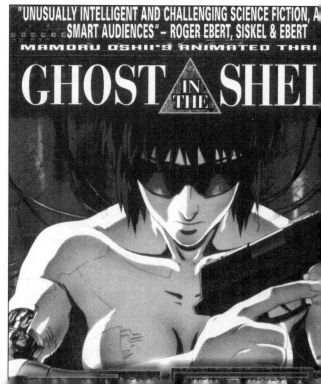

"UNUSUALLY INTELLIGENT AND CHALLENGING SCIENCE FICTION, A SMART AUDIENCES" – ROGER EBERT, SISKEL & EBERT

MAMORU OSHII'S ANIMATED THRI

GHOST IN THE SHEL

Speed Racer: It's hard to believe that more than thirty years have passed since the creation of this internationally popular anime series.
© Speed Racer Enterprises, Inc.

it presentable to a mass audience. Thank god it was uniformly rejected.

CARL: Of course, an anime director would say the issue is complicated because Western films, from **Disney**'s to **Tarkovsky**'s, from *My Darling Clementine* to *The Terminator*, have been a constant influence on Japanese animation. They might well re-phrase the question: how are American influences twisting what is made for a *Japanese* audience?

PATRICK: So…what if **Spielberg** and **Katzenberg** did try to do an anime film? How horrible that would be.

CARL: But I don't think they would make a film like *The Prince of Egypt* in Japan, either.

PATRICK: Yeah. And I don't think the Japanese would make a film like the American *Godzilla*.

HOW THE WEST CHANGED JAPANESE MUSIC

SATORU: How about music? Of course, noise musicians are really conscious about international appreciation. Does that in some way influence their music?

MASON: There's definitely an influence, but I don't think that it actually affects what they're doing. I think they're doing it with the consciousness that it's such a small scene *worldwide*. The scene in Japan itself is really small. And because it's small everywhere else, too, there's a constant communication going on. Anything they do is done with a knowledge that their audience consists of people everywhere. But I don't think it affects the *content* of what they're doing.

SATORU: How about other, more regular music? [laughs] Like with **Shonen Knife**, when they have a new album, there's an English version released in America and a Japanese version released in Japan. So, definitely, they're really conscious about it. And of course, they probably sell more CDs in America and Europe than in Japan.

MASON: They do. But bands like Pizzicato Five and **Cornelius** are reusing elements of music from everywhere. That doesn't mean they're doing it in anticipation of it being heard in New York.

YUJI: I wonder whether Cornelius made *Fantasma* knowing it was going to be released in the U.S.…

MASON: No…he was going to do a different version of the single **"Starfruit Surfrider"** in English. But I asked the person who was working on the American release and he said he tried it but wasn't happy with the result, so he just released the regular version here. I think the licensing was worked out after it was recorded.

SATORU: Is there ever a sense among the American fans of Japanese subcultures that they're being catered to?

MASON: Sometimes, I suspect, like with fans of Japanese punk bands, because punk is so inherently British and American, and because of the fact that it's very easy for Japanese punk bands to hook up with bands here and come over and tour. There's

an established support system in the punk scene around the world. And I kind of wonder whether some Japanese, when they start a punk band, sing in English because that's just the way they think punk's supposed to be.

SATORU: A lot of Japanese indie bands sing in English, not because they're thinking about an English-speaking audience, but because to them it's cool.

MASON: It's some of both. I've asked that question of a few bands, and sometimes they just think that English is easier to sing in; they say it fits in better with the music than Japanese.… Especially some of the newer rap groups…

CARL: There are Japanese painters who have worked in the anime subculture, like **Nobuyuki Onishi** and **Yoshitaka Amano**, who have made a very conscious effort to market themselves in America. But a common thing you hear from anime and manga artists who come here to U.S. conventions is how pure-hearted the enthusiasm of American fans is compared to the jaded scene in Japan. And you even hear them say they take new inspiration and energy from hanging out with American fans. Now, I don't know if they're just being polite to say all this…

YUJI: I wonder if that isn't also in part the fact that, being a manga guy in Japan, you have to deal with so much of the business bullshit. And there, readership and business, it's all like this [locks fingers together]. But when they come over here, there's no

Fantasma: Cornelius is the one-man band Keigo Oyamada.

performed by CORNELIUS produced by KEIGO OYAMADA matador incvu. OLE 300 compact disc digital audio stereo business, only their fans.

CARL: So manga artists feel that their American fans appreciate them on a purer level, because they're not a factor in their daily business?

YUJI: I think in manga that might be what's going on. When it comes to music, for the indie bands that tour here in clubs, I think it's kind of inspiring to see people come out in Michigan, everywhere in this huge country, for a band that in their own country can't even tour outside of Tokyo because they're virtually unknown. I'm thinking of the example of **Melt Banana**. They can tour all these cities here and find a pretty good following that would be unthinkable for them in Japan.

MASON: The scale here is so much bigger for a band—you can do a full tour of Japan in probably six shows.

SATORU: Yeah, I remember ten years ago, when the **Blue Hearts** were big in Japan. There was no reason they had to come here, but they wanted to do it for the experience. And they got a great inspiration from playing here to a totally different kind of audience.

CARL: I remember—their video made MTV's *120 Minutes*.

PATRICK: I think some of their shows were free.

SATORU: Yeah. I saw them at the DNA Lounge. I think their singer, **Hiroto**, was really into it.

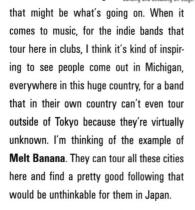
Meet the Blue Hearts: Lead singer Hiroto has a reputation for wild dancing and streaking on stage.

CARL: They were promoted here as a kind of Japanese version of the **Clash**.

YUJI: There's just one thing that I've noticed a lot about some of these bands in Japan. They don't really—especially those people around my age or younger—have this thing about America any more, this complex about American pop culture or about touring in the States. When I asked the sound guy from **Buffalo Daughter** what he thought about touring here, he was like: "Oh, America's just this kind of backward country…" [laughs] And I thought that was kind of interesting, because I'd never heard anything like that from a Japanese, until this generation.

MASON: I'm less surprised to hear that from a sound person, since he's accustomed to the Japanese clubs. Theirs are far better outfitted than the ones here. [laughs]

CARL: Conversely, I know this guy, **DJ Kino Senshi**, who spins at this club in San Jose. He's nineteen, and for him, being able to spin in Tokyo would be the high point in his life. It's where the action is.

YUJI: Yeah, **Emi** from **Demi Semi Quaver** said, "Tokyo is where it's happening for me." She likes New York, but to her it's just another city. It's not a big deal for them to play there. They don't have that kind of inferiority complex.

CARL: Do they consider the Japanese expat community in New York to be kind of an extension of Japan?

YUJI: They don't really care. Besides the language barrier, they don't really care whether the people they play to there are Japanese or American.

JAPAN & THE WEST: COMMON EXPERIENCES

SATORU: That's related to something I wanted to talk about—my generation is really different. When I came over here, I had a hard time convincing Americans that I had the same experiences as they had, that I'd heard the same music and seen the same movies and TV shows. It was, "Oh, this is America, big America." But the younger generation doesn't have that; there's this sense of worldwide common experience, at least, you could say, among the most industrialized nations. As Yuji said, there's the language barrier. But do you guys have any particular ideas on this? Do you feel different when you look at the Japanese of your generation?

MASON: It's the same *and* different. Consider **Cornelius**, who's taking all of his influences, his pieces and styles of music, from many different places, including a lot from America, and then putting them into his work. What he comes out with is familiar to an American listener *and* familiar to a Japanese listener. But I have the feeling that the conclusions that might be drawn from his music will be different for each. What a piece of music from Cornelius reminiscent of the **Beach Boys** might mean to a twenty-year-old here could be very different from what it would mean to a twenty-year-old in Tokyo.

YUJI: Or a thirty-year-old.

MASON: You could say that each individual piece is recognizable to both, but put all together, they spell out a different message.

Demi Semi Quaver: Emi Eleonola sings in "Eleonolian," a mixed bag of English, Japanese, and something else going on inside her head. Photo by Yoshio Ozawa

In recent years, director Seijun Suzuki has made many TV appearances as an actor.

CARL: I think we live in a worldwide sampling culture in which things are constantly taken out of their original context.

YUJI: Yeah. I think maybe one way to explain the difference in context is to say that there *was* no context for the Beach Boys in Japan to begin with, no consensus as to what they meant. Instead, it was a conglomeration of curious sounds and images from American pop culture. *Here*, depending on the generation, if you have any relationship to the Beach Boys and then you listen to Cornelius, it will feel that it's been taken out of context. That's why his sound might be thought of as weird over here, but in Japan, it's not so weird.

SATORU: How about filmmakers? We know that Kurosawa took a lot from **John Ford**, but when regular movie fans see a Kurosawa movie, they're thinking, "Wow, this is Japanese film." They're not observing what particular things he took from John Ford...

PATRICK: I think as *The Seven Samurai* went on to inspire films from *The Magnificent Seven* to *Battle Beyond the Stars*, the original work became more "Japanese," more "Kurosawa." The John Ford stigma began to vanish as the reputation of *The Seven Samurai* grew. It really seems that Japanese film has had only a handful of international success stories over

the years. For so long, only a handful of films and filmmakers have represented everything. And I'm not sure that this situation has changed much today. Once people get the idea of the "classics" into their heads, there's not much room left for new arrivals.

SATORU: So when you interviewed **K inji Fukasaku**, did you talk about his favorite American movies?

PATRICK: He was very big on Italian neo-realism. He didn't say much about American films. Everyone has their own set of influences, but the impression I've gotten from Japanese filmmakers is that they are more interested in foreign cinema than Japanese film.

YUJI: It's funny; the people I talk to in Japan who are involved with experimental film seem to have much more attachment to their own national cinema. But when I read articles about or interviews with Kurosawa, Ozu, and Oshima, it's clear that they were more attached to European and American influences.

MASON: Right. But I assume that, nowadays, if someone goes to see a film in Tokyo, most people of the younger generation—even if they're watching a Japanese film—are going to have most of their film experiences with Hollywood. Odds are, a sixteen-year-old in Tokyo is more familiar with Spielberg films than he is with Kurosawa films.

YUJI: Yeah. That's why to some college students in Japan, discovering the B films of a **Seijun Suzuki** is really refreshing. They didn't know that they existed.

PATRICK: But at the same time, you have to wonder how much they are reading into these films.

Again, it's a case of an audience that still wants pop culture, but only on sophisticated terms. Was Suzuki really this brilliant B-movie auteur, or was he just bored with the kind of films he was assigned to grind out? Either way, you're expected to refer to him as a visionary nowadays.

MASON: In the interviews I've read with him, he doesn't think they're anything that special.

PATRICK: But years later, after leaving Nikkatsu, Suzuki came back with a series of independently produced films. They were the personal works he had been longing to make. And they aren't nearly as popular or as widely seen as his studio B-movies are. I'm unsure at what point pop culture becomes, if not high culture, then at least something worthy of academic-minded scrutiny and praise. **Koji Wakamatsu** is also someone who's enjoying newfound interest and popularity for films that he did in the 1960s.

HOW JAPAN CHANGED THE WEST

SATORU: Let's talk about how Japanese

The *Voltron* anime series wasn't a big hit in Japan when it came out fifteen years ago, but the series is fondly remembered in the U.S. © WEP 1984, 1998

Video clips from the Beastie Boys' music video
"Intergalactic"; Tokusatsu goes mainstream?

subcultures are influencing America. Well, one example is these TV commercials now which show some kind of taste for Japanese subcultures.

CARL: Although I think that sometimes people draw the wrong lessons from these examples. Going back to *Evangelion* and the idea that it brought out all these adults in Japan who can now say they're anime fans.... I became very interested in the existence of such fans in America, not those who ever went to clubs, but those in their thirties or forties who grew up watching anime on television here in the '60s, '70s, and '80s.

I don't think the multimillion ad campaigns you're referring to are necessarily based on the traditional American anime

subculture. *Voltron* was a popular show among young black kids; a few years back, **Warren G.** mentioned in his hit **"This D.J."** that his friends used to call themselves the Voltron Crew. But from anime clubs back then you would rarely know that people liked this stuff in the 'hood. It's like, maybe some Hong Kong film fans today don't know that martial-arts films were always very popular among black kids in the '70s; that's part of why they resurfaced again in hip-hop, with **Wu-Tang Clan** and the **Fugees**.

So, yeah, to a certain extent these commercials might be coming out because anime is seen as a "now" thing, but just like Wu-Tang is sampling '70s films and not the latest Jackie Chan, look at that Sprite ad using *Voltron*, a fifteen-year-old anime. It's not like they're selling the anime look as something that's got to be super slick, like *Ghost in the Shell*. It's not just a surface thing; they're appealing to the memories people had, what they grew up with.

PATRICK: Yeah. But they're preying upon those memories in order to sell to them. Not necessarily to sell them a culture and a future, but to sell them nostalgia and a soda.

CARL: Yes, but it is interesting that the *Voltron* commercial was subtitled in Japanese, which the original broadcast wasn't. They're playing up the Japanese origin.

MASON: What's with all these clothing ads these days that have Japanese text in them? Have you seen those?

CARL: It's only fair; the Japanese have been putting English on their clothes for years!

SATORU: Last year, on the MTV Awards, they had all this Japanese text on screen. And then there's the PlayStation ad with the Japanese accent and the Beastie Boys

video in the *tokusatsu* style. What's your opinion about that? Or about Disney studying Miyazaki's movies in order to assimilate some of their aspects? Or in terms of comics, we know a lot of American comics artists are taking influences from manga.

PATRICK: I like the idea of the influences going around the world and there being no barriers; the products of people's imagination taking root in other people's imagination and inspiring new things. The idea of them being used in mass-marketing campaigns has less appeal to me; it's the product of demographics instead of genuine culture. I'm very suspicious of that sort of thing.

YUJI: But what I'm wondering is, when *is* it a genuine cultural trend, and when is it marketing?

PATRICK: I don't know. I guess when it's not selling something actively. I don't want to sound so reactionary, to say that making money is bad....

CARL: But isn't advertising part of our culture?

SATORU: You feel like something important to you has been taken away.

CARL: Like the objections when Nike used **"Revolution"** for a commercial—or was it **"Instant Karma"**?

MASON: The advertising industry, however, is a lot more forward-looking than the record industry or the print industry in this country. They're a lot more willing to take risks and a lot more willing to grab onto something that seems like it may be the cool thing at the moment, whereas books and films and the music industry will take another year to get something that the ad agencies already noticed. You can hear a lot more unknown bands in commercials than you'll see their albums being pushed by the major labels. The current

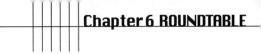

Volkswagen campaign—the songs that they're using… a lot of them are from unsigned bands. Whoever's handling that ad campaign is a music fan.

SATORU: I think there are two levels. There's the people in advertising who like the creativity in these subcultures; they like anime, manga, and music. And then, what they do will be interesting, because they like what we like. But then, there's this other aspect, which is how this is being exploited. So you always have ambivalent feelings about it.

CARL: My primary interest is to see that the people who *made* the stuff get recognition, that people know their names. So if anime or manga or a band gets used in a commercial, Americans come to know who

Kirin Beer TV commercial featuring Godzilla and Mecha Godzilla: "No! Not Mecha Godzilla, Mega-Kirin!"

made the images, the sounds. That's what I care about, more than any other issue. As far as someone using it to sell a product, that isn't so important.

MASON: I think some people have the feeling that it's great to know about something that not too many people know about. When it starts to become a mainstream thing, there's both this gratification that more people are getting into it and a little bit of sadness that it's not going to be their private thing any more. So there's always some of that. But I think that, overall, what we might, unfortunately, see happening—especially with anime and manga—is some of the surface style being adopted without really going beyond that.

CARL: That's already happened. But to talk of culture war: culture *is* war—it's always shifting. In terms of Disney studying anime, I've heard that there, the key animators or animation directors are king and they don't understand this concept in anime in which you have a director who doesn't actually get in there and draw. That wouldn't be a problem with Miyazaki, who is literally hands-on. That's why he's retiring from Ghibli, to make films at his own pace, because it's been starting to affect his health. But it might be a real artistic divide between Disney and an Oshii or Yamaga.

MASON: Once anime starts being released more to theaters, rather than just directly to video, then there'll start to be more recognition of the director behind it.

YUJI: One thing I did notice about this difference between having an "individual" relationship to pop culture and being more commercial…most of the bands I've talked to in Japan really don't seem to care if their song ends up in a commercial or not. **Buffalo Daughter** and **Sugar Plant** haven't been in that situation but, judging by the way they talked about their friends who *were* used in commercials.…

It was weird…

PATRICK: They were just nonchalant about it?

YUJI: Yes. They were just indifferent.

MASON: But that's probably part of growing up seeing these commercials that always had music and which identified the bands.

CARL: When **Toshio Okada** was asked about the Volkswagen commercial using *Speed Racer*, he said the main concern should be seeing that the studio who made the animation gets paid.

SATORU: I feel that recently, looking at the Japanese people in their twenties in Japan, pop culture, subculture, and commercialism have sort of melted together…it's not as clear as in the United States. Most Japanese kids don't feel self-conscious about it. What they want to do is have fun, and it's not more than that or less than that. That's one of the things we talked about at the beginning of this project and it's one of the unique things about subcultures in Japan: the constant mix between the mainstream and the subculture, the commercial and the underground.

YUJI: Bands don't get accused of being sellouts in Japan; they get accused of being boring. It's not an ideological issue; it's more formalistic. It's not where their music is playing, but whether people think their music is interesting anymore.

SATORU: What Yuji described is that Japanese music doesn't have the concept of the sellout. Some bands get big and they become boring. But some bands get big and they keep making interesting music. Even if they get famous, it's fine. I think that's a healthy attitude.

YUJI: It's just that the chance of them *making* it big is slim. [laughs]

GETTING PERSONAL

HIGH SCHOOL DAYS

SATORU: Whether you call it being an otaku or a cult film or music fan, what's your personal experience as one, and how do you feel it's different from that in Japan?

PATRICK: It's a little strange for me because Japanese film started off as my hobby and over the last couple of years it has slowly become my profession—something I write about for a living. I'm not sure if I'm still a fan anymore. I'm now very into Italian trash films, which I'm able to enjoy just as a hobby, without having to take notes.

SATORU: We talked earlier about how, in Japan, the stigma of being a cult film fan is going away. As an American, do you still feel isolated for being into cult film?

Patrick Macias

PATRICK: No. There is a growing feeling of global community. I hate to sound like Al Gore, but I think the Internet has really connected people. It's given trading and sharing ideas and information a very big shot in the arm.

Photo by Kiyo Hayashi.

SATORU: But do you feel that there's a definite distinction between mainstream people and you?

PATRICK: Hmmmm… [whispers] I think that's kinda *secret*.

CARL: I never felt any automatic sense of friendship or fraternity with other anime fans. As a matter of fact, as I said, the first clubs I encountered—and I think Patrick would agree—were actually kind of scary. There were only a few people that I felt I could really relate to. This may signify something, but my closest friends in the world are not otaku; they don't even particularly like anime. In America, though, these days—and again, this is also an advertising gimmick—we're an "otaku-ized" culture, too. It's like, "Oh yeah, this is like that episode of *Gilligan's Island* where—" Or it's *The Brady Bunch*. The exact kind of thing an otaku would say, relating a real-life situation to something that happened on TV in the 1970s. [laughs] That's the stereotype of this generation; that we have this culture that's made up of little bits and pieces.

PATRICK: Pop culture has *become* culture.

CARL: **Quentin Tarantino** made that sort of thing respectable for films. So it seems to me that what an otaku does is not unusual anymore in America. I realize the name has had its social connotations in Japan, but I was never an otaku in Japan;

I've been one *here*.

SATORU: So you guys are adults, and this is now established as part of your *professional* lives. But when you grew up, in high school—Yuji's experience is different, because he belonged to two cultures at the same time, but—I'm really curious. I personally don't have any experience with American high school life. My stereotype is that it's the quarterback on the team who's the hero. But you weren't part of that? Did you hate high school?

CARL: I was a politician in high school: student council…. [laughs]

YUJI: First politician to become an otaku. [laughs]

CARL: I ran a strong second for student body vice president when I was a sophomore, and then managed other people's campaigns. I never took any pride or pleasure in being part of some subculture where I'd say, "Okay, I've got me, I've got those few friends who understand me, that's it, I don't need any more." I was never happy that way. I never wanted to cut myself off from others or cut what I *did* off from others. I was lucky because *Robotech* was on

Carl Gustav Horn

television then. Anyone could see it after school at four in the afternoon. So if someone asked me—and they did—"Why do you watch those cartoons if they're in Chinese?" I could say, "Well, check it out after school, see what you think."

I was always fiending to show some anime during that precious lunch half hour. But it would be wherever I could find a TV/VCR cart that had been left in a class; I'd ask around where there might be one. I'd put something in and make sure the doors and windows were open to carry these strange sounds. The idea was to be fluid, no club or anything, just show it and hope to hook the passerby.

To me, it's even *more* sincere to try and make a living out of it. I decided in 1996 I was never again going to earn another penny except through this field, and I've stuck to that. I've committed my life to this. It's not particularly *easy*, but it gives me an incredible sense of energy and adventure. And why shouldn't it be an adventure? There is still a lot of uncharted territory for anime in the United States.

SATORU: Patrick, how were your high school days?

PATRICK: I dropped out of high school. I utterly failed scholastically. It wasn't because I wanted to watch Godzilla movies or anything terribly subversive like that. It may come off like a big statement years

later, but at the time I was just being lazy. But I suppose I had some sort of outsider status. I don't look like the captain of the football team or Mr. Popularity.

CARL: Were you smokin' in the boy's room?

PATRICK: There was some smoking in the boy's room. I think in California there is a lot of space to move around in, particularly if you are a minority. You still have your roots, but you're also open to other cultures and influences.

CARL: Do you mean that if you're already an outsider, it's easier to take an interest in outsider culture?

PATRICK: The door is just open.

SATORU: You made a decision to go with your own lifestyle?

PATRICK: I wanted to follow my own interests. I hated school; I just wanted to do what I wanted to do. It's something like the decision Carl made. There were things I wanted to read, things I wanted to do, so that's what I did. And now I'm here, havin' coffee.

MASON: With me, it's hard to say. Junior high school in Michigan, high school in California, in Davis…except for my last year, when we moved back to Ann Arbor again.

YUJI: Mason and I went to the same college.

CARL: I always think of a place like Ann Arbor as being more progressive.

MASON: It *is*—but not as progressive as it would like to believe itself to be. But it tries. [laughs]

SATORU: Your interest in noise music grew

after college, but in high school…?

MASON: In high school, I guess I was sort of an otaku in other ways. In Davis, I got into reading science fiction, into gaming. But my last year of high school, back in Michigan, I got involved in writing and publishing an underground newspaper. The high school administration wasn't very fond of it, but they couldn't stop it really.

SATORU: So did you feel uncomfortable in high school?

MASON: Oh, yeah. I hated sports, always have. I don't even know what other things tend to get ordinary high school students together. The people I did make friends with were those I had something in common with, but they were definitely the minority in the school. I wasn't really alienated per se, it was just that most people seemed to be interested in things I couldn't care less about.

SATORU: How about you, Yuji? Your case is a little different…

YUJI: I grew up in a suburb of L.A. and then

Mason Jones and Yuji Oniki

a suburb of New York, in Westchester, Mamaroneck, home of Matt Dillon. [laughs] I don't know; I think it's the same thing, not having mainstream interests. I mean, I played sports, but the majority of students

were either WASPs or Jewish—there were hardly any Asians there.

I was into jazz, not pop. I got into things that didn't seem that interesting to my friends. As far as Japanese school went, I was going every Saturday until I was thirteen or fourteen. That was a different scene from being Asian-American. People were there because their parents had been sent to work in America, so they didn't stick around very long. By the last year, there were only three or four kids left in my class, so you're having this existential dilemma: "Why am I here?" [laughs]

SATORU: In your case, it seems like you established your own space, your own world, and whatever went on outside didn't affect you too much.

YUJI: Yeah. But in terms of exposure to J-pop stuff, you know, I just digested it as a kid. And then in high school, I just stopped completely, because most of the contemporary culture came through manga which we'd just pass around. And after high school I wasn't hanging around with anyone Japanese any more, and it just started up again about six or seven years ago. So there's a big gap, a kind of cultural amnesia.

Mason Jones

MASON: What got you interested again?

YUJI: I was studying

Japanese literature in college and then I made my way back to pop culture. That's not exactly right. It was when I was in Japan, between '92 and '94, and I learned a lot from these friends who showed me how interesting everyday pop life in Tokyo was.

MEDIA-MIX EXPERIENCE

SATORU: In Japan, there's what they call a "media-mix strategy." A lot of anime is based on manga and there's a lot of sales of CDs based on anime... Anyway, so there's a big promotional strategy that takes in anime, manga, music, and games as well. Of course, there's the natural development where a director gets interested in a manga and wants to make a movie. The director of *Shall We Dance?* made several movies based on shojo manga: **Reiko Okano**'s *Fancy Dance* and that one by **Akimi Yoshida**, who did *Banana Fish*, the adaptation of that **Chekhov** play, *The Cherry Orchard*. Of course, on the subculture level, there is an unintentional media-mix: creators are friends with each other, people are interested in two different areas....

Looking at the Japanese subculture scenes, do you have a sense of this? And what are your personal experiences? Have you gotten into one subculture through the other?

CARL: Even though it doesn't seem to follow logically, my experience of being an anime and manga fan has made it more natural for me to go and see a Beat Takeshi or an Ishii film. An interest in one kind of Japanese pop culture leads to another—despite the fact that it's in an entirely different medium. The fact that it's Japanese

means you'll at least give it a try.

PATRICK: There is a lot of crossover. I watch Japanese TV; I listen to Japanese music. I take an interest in all of it. But I've never been to Japan, so I've got this partially real, partially imaginary country in my head. That's one of the problems with being a person who is not Japanese but who has an interest in Japanese pop culture. You wind up sort of privatizing what really is a mass culture.

CARL: You should build your own private Japan underground, like in *A Boy And His Dog*.

PATRICK: You could do it! With just a VCR and a CD player. Just pipe in Japanese movies and Japanese music twenty-four hours a day. Who needs the real world? That's the danger of living vicariously through media. You become myopic and disconnected from real people and real experience.

CARL: I wish anime had some of those interesting Japanese bands on their soundtrack.

SATORU: Yeah, anime music is...I think part of it is the budget; you've just got one guy on his synthesizer...

CARL: I think, unfortunately, that there's been a real firewall between anime and

Akira: The English version colorized the original black-and-white manga. (Epic/Marvel Comics)

Banana Fish: It's rumored that Ash, the main character, was modeled after River Phoenix. © Akimi Yoshida/Shogakukan

times the anime is made by a major record label in Japan which is looking for a way to promote their latest idol. I got impressed with an anime soundtrack when someone progressively finally came in with **Ryuichi Sakamoto** doing *Honneamise* or the **Geinoh Yamashiro-Gumi** doing *Akira*, which is my all-time favorite anime music. And, in both cases, they, and no other, were the musicians the directors wanted.

MASON: Yes, *Akira* was incredible. Although the *Ghost in the Shell* soundtrack was pretty good, too.

CARL: Yeah. Someone told me how when they were mixing down the English dub of *Ghost* they were using a three-hundred-year-old female choral style on the soundtrack, one that's almost died out in Japan. Personally, though, I would love to see someone like Cornelius on an anime soundtrack.

SATORU: I was reading a Japanese music magazine where people were asking that too: "How come Japanese animation is so high-quality, but they don't care about the music?" But there's time and money constraints, plus an industry that often feels that they can sell otaku anything.

CARL: But about what Patrick was saying: I didn't really have a *fantasy* image of Japan when I went there in 1987, when I was sixteen. My favorite anime was *Megazone 23*, which was trying to capture an image of Tokyo in the mid-eighties. So I tried to go to every place I'd seen in the anime: Café du Rope, Studio ALTA. In other words, I was trying to get a sense of the real, contemporary Japan through the anime.

MASON: Well, I got into noise first, and *that* doesn't carry any image of what Japan is like with it. And then, the first time I went to Japan, in '92, to play there, I didn't really know anything about it at all, so I learned firsthand. But from the noise music and the other music I slowly started to learn about the manga and anime and everything else as well. There's this manga artist who has done album covers for people in both Japan and America, **Suehiro Maruo**, and the first time I found out about him was because he'd done an album cover for **John Zorn**, for the *Torture Garden* record. [laughs]

other Japanese subcultures. There aren't any noise bands on any anime soundtrack I've ever heard. I'm a real partisan of Western music, and generally I've never been blown away musically by anime soundtracks. I might be very fond of a certain theme because I liked the show, but it's not like I'm going to forget about **Desmond Dekker** or **Soundgarden**. Of course, many

CONCLUSION

JAPAN'S CONTINUING INFLUENCE ON U.S. SUBCULTURE

SATORU: I want to talk about one last subject. The way I see the state of pop culture

in the U.S. is that there is an increasing consolidation of entertainment companies. One huge multimedia entity is putting out movies, TV, music.... A lot of mainstream things are boring to begin with, and it's going to get worse and worse. It's just inevitable with these monopolies. That means an interest in subculture is becoming

more and more important in this country. Major record labels have been unable to release anything interesting for some time, so indie labels have become much more prominent. That kind of thing has been happening in other media as well. So, in that context, how do you assess the state of subculture in the U.S.A., and how does Japan contribute to making it a little more interesting? [laughs]

CARL: Well, one of the things I touched on in my chapter was the idea that *Evangelion* and *The Princess Mononoke* were acquired by very different companies here. For anime fans, especially, there's this temptation—and I indulge in it myself—to bash Mickey Mouse and say that Disney is the antipode to anime. But then, Disney owns **Miramax**, and there was never any insistence that *Pulp Fiction* be like *Pocahontas*. Simply because a lot of things are owned by the same company doesn't imply that some kind of common taste will be imposed on everything it owns.

If you want to put it cynically, a company might want to own every last subculture niche, but it can't make money off of them if it eliminates the spirit of that subculture. Japanese animation still seems unpredictable and strange enough to be a shot in the arm, just like that Miramax heroin is for American entertainment. I don't think it will be co-opted or homogenized, at least for the foreseeable future. At least for a while, anime is going to surprise people here and make them think.

PATRICK: I'd like to see people take an interest in older Japanese films, like the pink films and yakuza movies, if only to finally erase the blind spots. We've looked at Kurosawa and Ozu for so long, but there are thousands of other things to see and discover. As far as the future goes, it's very disappointing to see Beat Takeshi's films do well critically but not really work for an audience. I don't know where that's going to lead.

I don't know where *anything* is going to lead except that everything is going corporate and digital and it's hard to say what sort of climate that's going to create. People may want more entertainment options, and that may drive them away from typical Hollywood productions. This can make culture either more localized or more global. Maybe we'll all be watching anime because it's the only thing on the one network. Or maybe there'll be a million options—an infinite past and a future where everyone is making their own media.

SATORU: But now, for a lot of people in the world, a movie means a *Hollywood* movie.

PATRICK: Yeah, but filmmaking technology and language isn't just in movies anymore. It's in television and, increasingly, in video games.

CARL: For much of the world, yes. But India and also Egypt have large and vital film industries and they don't necessarily take their cues from Hollywood. And it's not only Bollywood in India; regional cinema is alive and well there, too. Very few Americans like all that singing and dancing in their movies. Although, oddly, American *animated* films feel they have to contain musical numbers—but 800 million Indians think it's just their own style.

PATRICK: But if life was miserable here, we'd all want to go to the movies for three hours every day, too.

CARL: Certainly it gets people's minds off their poverty for a little while, but that doesn't mean there aren't interesting films being made. Look at the 1930s in America, when people went to the movies for the same reason; that was also a classic era for movie making.

MASON: I have to admit, given that Japan is practically where the video camera came from, I can't figure out why there aren't thousands of people making films on video. There are a lot of American underground filmmakers who have been making things on video and distributing them themselves; there's a couple of places where you can mail order them...

CARL: Well, *Love and Pop* was shot on video. Anno took every advantage of the format. The cameras are so small that you can shoot from inside a microwave oven—so he did.

MASON: It's an exception, though. I haven't come across that many video films from Japan.

SATORU: I guess maybe the medium is so common that people don't think of it for anything more than shooting vacations....

MASON: But that's exactly why people *should* use it!

YUJI: I think it's just that these movies aren't available here. There are a lot of amazing video movies from Japan. They just never make their way to film festivals here.

PATRICK: Yeah, those worlds are small. I mean, there's not a lot of places to see experimental video, even in North America, because it's limited to galleries and other marginal venues that only attract those in the know here.

MASON: Yeah, like the ATA. [San Francisco's well-regarded **Artists' Television Access**].

CARL: Even *Love and Pop*. Why do I know about it? Because it's the same guy who made *Evangelion*. It hasn't been in any festivals here.

MASON: Of course, film, no matter what it's

shot on, has the problem of language. It's not so easy to go about the task of dubbing or subtitling a homemade video.

SATORU: It's time for your conclusions. [laughs]

MASON: The noise music scene has flattened out a bit. But it has definitely had an influence on more mainstream music. Sonic Youth is a good example; they had **Solmania** open for them at their show in Atlanta. There's more accessibility here than ever before; more places where people can find out about noise and get their hands on noise recordings. From a fan's point of view, things are better. Sonic Youth is very influential here, and they've helped to serve as a conduit for ideas from noise, not just to American noise groups but also to rock as well. As for where it's going in the future, I don't know. [laughs]

SATORU: Okay, it's Yuji's turn.

YUJI: To continue on Mason's train of thought, it also seems that bands like Sonic Youth have helped introduce Americans to what's going on now in contemporary Japanese subculture. But I also think that they've helped reevaluate and show a historical significance for it as well. Someone like **Yoko Ono**, who's been repeatedly bashed for two or three decades, is finally being recognized as an artist—and I think that's connected to the interest in Japanese noise music. You can listen to Yoko Ono and

then listen to some noise music and you can hear the connection.

MASON: And then she actually turned it around and lent her support to bands like **Cibo Matto**.

YUJI: Right. I think that kind of historical reevaluation, of recapturing the past, is just as important a consequence as appreciating present Japanese subculture.

SATORU: In the case of Yoko, she was never part of the scene in Japan; she became an artist and musician only after she moved to New York. I read this interesting conversation between Yoko and **Beck**.... Beck's grandfather was friends with Yoko...

MASON: Right, they were both in the **Fluxus** movement.

YUJI: So, taking that perspective, Japanese pop culture has come a long way here. But I don't think that any of the Japanese pop bands that are here are ever going to become mainstream, so there will never be this *problem* of it becoming mainstream. Which I kind of like. I could be wrong, but I think that if Japanese music continues here, it will be able to assert a kind of independence that isn't necessarily political but that won't be co-opted the way American indie bands get co-opted in the States.

MASON: Yeah. There's always going to be a language barrier to being a truly mainstream artist here in the States.

PATRICK: What about "Sukiyaki 2000"? [laughs]

CARL: Yes, but people don't mind the language barrier so much if it comes across more as sampling. They may not want to hear an entire verse or chorus sung in

Japanese, but if it's a few lines here and there, that may sound cool.

MASON: Right. I think that Cornelius or an electronic artist like Ken Ishii could reach a reasonable level of success but never compete with **Celene Dion**.

CARL: Again, things may be distorted because we're living in California in the Bay Area, but Pizzicato Five's **"Twiggy vs. James Bond"**, which is sung entirely in Japanese, was the number-one most-requested song on Live 105 for three weeks in a row. That says something, anyway.

SATORU: It can be on top of the college charts, but it'll never be on the top of *Billboard*. I've been working in Japanese comics here at Viz Comics for thirteen years. When we started, we had these desires, of course, that it would become part of the mainstream here and have big sales and be everywhere. Now I'm more realistic; that's never going to happen. Of course, it's going to get more exposure; our graphic novels will get in more bookstores and we'll get more readers, probably. But it's not going to take over from *Batman* or the *X-Men*.

One thing we can be proud of is that manga has influenced a lot of people in this country, including comics creators. I'm not sure that it has improved American comics, but at least some creators took inspiration from what we released. It's not just creative; when people heard about how manga artists own their own characters, that had an influence too in changing the DC/Marvel-dominated industry. I believe that when **Image Comics** came about, they took a strong interest in seeing how creator ownership worked in Japan.

SATORU: Does anyone have anything else to say?

YUJI: [wearily] Well, it's been great working with you. [everyone laughs]

SATORU: Thanks a lot!

TOKYO

Yuji Oniki

DIARY no. 6

June 4

As an architect imagines the blueprints for Tokyo Tower, as a writer I pick up on the hidden ideologies and motivations behind Japanese texts. The last time I lived here, I didn't pay any attention to the media. I never read the paper or watched TV. Partly due to spatial economics; there wasn't enough room in my eight-by-eight-foot room for a television. But mostly because I wanted to cultivate a nearsighted view of Tokyo in which every person, place, and thing was unmediated. Everything had to come in direct contact with me. So my exposure to current events came with month-long delays, whether it was the much hyped engagement of Prince Hironomiya or the end of the LDP single-party system. And then these events all seemed like fictions conjured up by the papers, television, and radio to create some elaborate myth of the nation. These fictions, especially the one about a prosperous economy, were already falling apart by the time I left in 1994. If, four years later, I am scanning headlines and channel surfing through TV news bites, it's probably because I'm interested in sorting through the wreckage of a recent past.

Unemployment isn't the only issue these days that has the unlucky number four attached to it. The voting rate has plunged to the forty-something percentile as well. What does it mean to have a

government run a country that hasn't ever bothered to vote for it? The entire population's attitude towards the government seems to fluctuate between frustration and apathy. While it's clear to me that the largest group of nonvoters in the U.S. are those who are so oppressed they feel completely disempowered, in Japan, people of all classes, genders, and ages are apathetic: the only thing that's democratic here is the apathy. But everyone's fed up for their own idiosyncratic reasons. One student: "There's no one famous in the House." A twenty-eight-year-old computer programmer: "I can only protect myself. The nation won't protect me. There's no point in elections or the government." A thirty-something retail clerk: "I'm going on vacation."

It's not just disillusionment with one particular party, but with the government in general. Having maintained a single party system over the last forty years, it seems hardly surprising that the public doesn't differentiate between the party and politics itself. One political analyst has been urging citizens to abstain from voting. Only if threatened with imminent collapse will the government institute effective reforms. A small minority are already casting blank ballots in protest. What would it be like to have a majority cast blank ballots—to have a faceless, faithless nation?

Depending on the newspaper (ranging from national equivalents of the *New*

York Times to something like the *Enquirer*), the front pages are dominated by headlines about either the deployment of nuclear weapons in Pakistan or the miracle impotence drug Viagra. Just as the current Clinton-Lewinsky scandal reveals the American public's anxiety about sex, the Japanese fascination with Viagra suggests that impotence is enough of a preoccupation in Japan to influence ratings and sales. After all, we're talking about a drug that you can't even obtain in Japan.

The media's unwitting juxtaposition of Pakistan's nuclear missiles as a national threat and impotence as a domestic threat reminds me of *Gravity's Rainbow*, **Thomas Pynchon**'s anarchic meditation on the technology of the V-2 rocket and sex. Viagra is only available in the U.S., where the coverage of the president's private life is becoming increasingly pornographic, tapping into the nation's Puritan fascination with sex as sin. In the past, nuclear bombs and space rocket technology effectively repressed the American libido. Now that these technological sexual metaphors have been exhausted, the nation is left to deal with original sin. Although the seeds of bomb and rocket technology were sown by European scientists, they could only come to fruition in a nation both fascinated and disgusted by sex as an extreme metaphor for annihilation (as in, the nuclear bomb) and excess (as in, let's see how far this rocket goes, or, let's make a drug that will induce erections). In America, everything encourages this preoccupation with sex and yet at the same time everything smothers it with disgust.

Later that evening, after several shots of whiskey, I share this view with a right-wing journalist who joins me and Shimamoto. For this journalist, the simultaneous appearance of the two headlines is not at all coincidental. He puts a different spin on it, tracing everything back to Japan's unconditional surrender: "Our entire nation was rendered impotent when Japan declared its unequivocal renunciation of war in the postwar constitution of Japan."

The threat posed by Pakistan's national phallus disturbing the political balance of power in Asia also taps into the male neurosis that Japan has been feminized by America ever since the war, or in this journalist's words, "Japan is a nation of sluts working for money instead of men fighting for their god and country." Travel agencies are cashing in on Japanese males' captivation with the miracle drug Viagra by selling group tours to the United States. The journalist frowns at the irony of the Japanese once again relying on Americans "to get it up."

Shimamoto, puffing little rings of smoke, laughs at him. "Give me a break. It's typical. The salaryman's libido follows the logic of national economics. A decade ago he would be flying to Southeast Asia on a sex tour sponsored by the same travel agencies that are promoting Viagra tours these days. Now that the country's up the creek, they can't even get it up, so they have to go to America. Pathetic. A decade ago, buying foreign property was all the rage, now the public imagination has shriveled into this petty obsession over these little blue pills." With an I-could-careless tone which only infuriates the journalist, Shimamoto concludes, "Like the effects of this pill, this nation is just an illusion anyway."

MAP
Tokyo Hot Spots

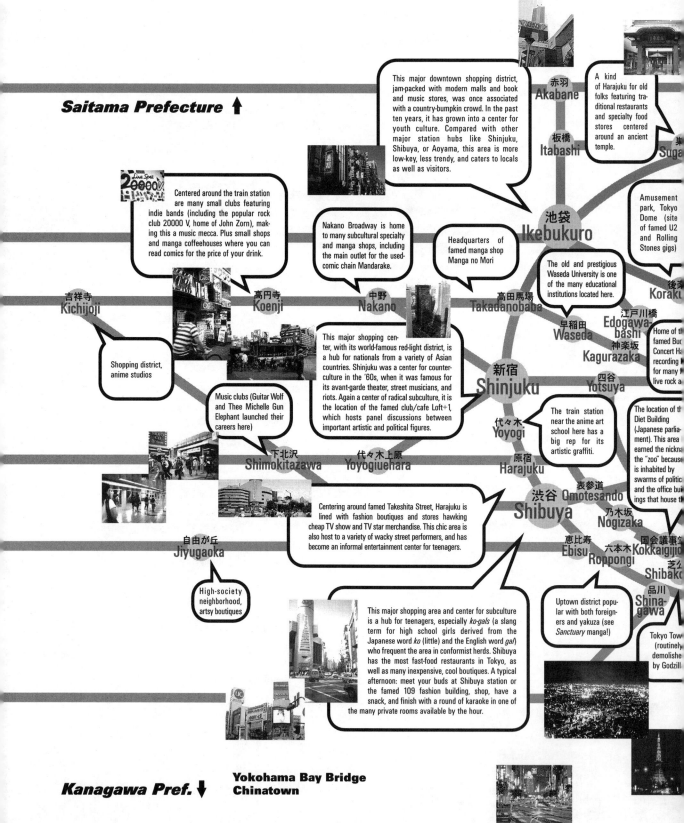

Saitama Prefecture ↑

This major downtown shopping district, jam-packed with modern malls and book and music stores, was once associated with a country-bumpkin crowd. In the past ten years, it has grown into a center for youth culture. Compared with other major station hubs like Shinjuku, Shibuya, or Aoyama, this area is more low-key, less trendy, and caters to locals as well as visitors.

A kind of Harajuku for old folks featuring traditional restaurants and specialty food stores centered around an ancient temple.

赤羽
Akabane

板橋
Itabashi

巣
Suga

池袋
Ikebukuro

Amusement park, Tokyo Dome (site of famed U2 and Rolling Stones gigs)

Centered around the train station are many small clubs featuring indie bands (including the popular rock club 20000 V, home of John Zorn), making this a music mecca. Plus small shops and manga coffeehouses where you can read comics for the price of your drink.

Nakano Broadway is home to many subcultural specialty and manga shops, including the main outlet for the used-comic chain Mandarake.

Headquarters of famed manga shop Manga no Mori

The old and prestigious Waseda University is one of the many educational institutions located here.

後楽
Koraku

吉祥寺
Kichijoji

高円寺
Koenji

中野
Nakano

高田馬場
Takadanobaba

早稲田
Waseda

江戸川橋
Edogawa-bashi

Home of the famed Bud Concert Ha recording for many live rock a

Shopping district, anime studios

神楽坂
Kagurazaka

This major shopping center, with its world-famous red-light district, is a hub for nationals from a variety of Asian countries. Shinjuku was a center for counterculture in the '60s, when it was famous for its avant-garde theater, street musicians, and riots. Again a center of radical subculture, it is the location of the famed club/cafe Loft+1, which hosts panel discussions between important artistic and political figures.

新宿
Shinjuku

四谷
Yotsuya

The location of the Diet Building (Japanese parliament). This area earned the nickna the "zoo" because is inhabited by swarms of politic and the office bui ings that house th

Music clubs (Guitar Wolf and Thee Michelle Gun Elephant launched their careers here)

代々木
Yoyogi

The train station near the anime art school here has a big rep for its artistic graffiti.

下北沢
Shimokitazawa

代々木上原
Yoyogiuehara

原宿
Harajuku

渋谷
Shibuya

表参道
Omotesando

自由が丘
Jiyugaoka

乃木坂
Nogizaka

Centering around famed Takeshita Street, Harajuku is lined with fashion boutiques and stores hawking cheap TV show and TV star merchandise. This chic area is also host to a variety of wacky street performers, and has become an informal entertainment center for teenagers.

恵比寿
Ebisu

六本木
Roppongi

国会議事堂
Kokkaigijid

芝公
Shibako

High-society neighborhood, artsy boutiques

品川
Shina-gawa

This major shopping area and center for subculture is a hub for teenagers, especially *ko-gals* (a slang term for high school girls derived from the Japanese word *ko* (little) and the English word *gal*) who frequent the area in conformist herds. Shibuya has the most fast-food restaurants in Tokyo, as well as many inexpensive, cool boutiques. A typical afternoon: meet your buds at Shibuya station or the famed 109 fashion building, shop, have a snack, and finish with a round of karaoke in one of the many private rooms available by the hour.

Uptown district popular with both foreigners and yakuza (see *Sanctuary* manga!)

Tokyo Tow (routinely demolishe by Godzill

Kanagawa Pref. ↓

Yokohama Bay Bridge
Chinatown

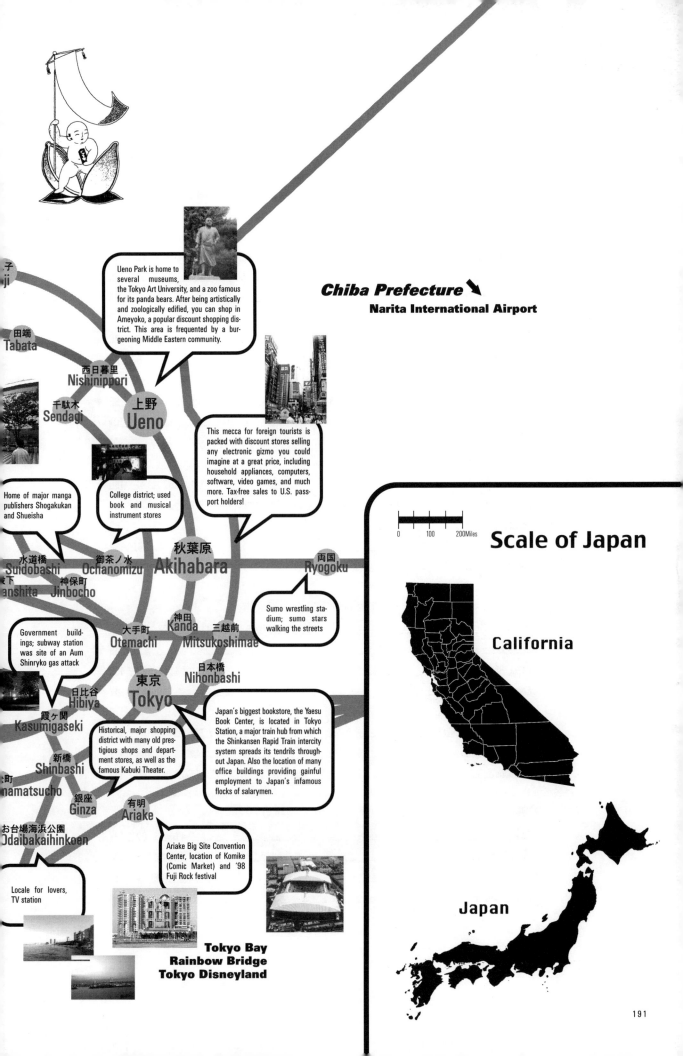

Ueno Park is home to several museums, the Tokyo Art University, and a zoo famous for its panda bears. After being artistically and zoologically edified, you can shop in Ameyoko, a popular discount shopping district. This area is frequented by a burgeoning Middle Eastern community.

Chiba Prefecture ↘

Narita International Airport

子
ji

田端
Tabata

西日暮里
Nishinippori

千駄木
Sendagi

上野
Ueno

This mecca for foreign tourists is packed with discount stores selling any electronic gizmo you could imagine at a great price, including household appliances, computers, software, video games, and much more. Tax-free sales to U.S. passport holders!

Home of major manga publishers Shogakukan and Shueisha

College district; used book and musical instrument stores

Scale of Japan

0   100   200Miles

California

水道橋
Suidobashi

御茶ノ水
Ochanomizu

秋葉原
Akihabara

両国
Ryogoku

下
anshita

神保町
Jinbocho

Sumo wrestling stadium; sumo stars walking the streets

Government buildings; subway station was site of an Aum Shinryko gas attack

大手町
Otemachi

神田
Kanda

三越前
Mitsukoshimae

日本橋
Nihonbashi

東京
Tokyo

日比谷
Hibiya

霞ヶ関
Kasumigaseki

Japan's biggest bookstore, the Yaesu Book Center, is located in Tokyo Station, a major train hub from which the Shinkansen Rapid Train intercity system spreads its tendrils throughout Japan. Also the location of many office buildings providing gainful employment to Japan's infamous flocks of salarymen.

Historical, major shopping district with many old prestigious shops and department stores, as well as the famous Kabuki Theater.

新橋
Shinbashi

町
namatsucho

銀座
Ginza

有明
Ariake

お台場海浜公園
Odaibakaihinkoen

Ariake Big Site Convention Center, location of Komike (Comic Market) and '98 Fuji Rock festival

Locale for lovers, TV station

Tokyo Bay
Rainbow Bridge
Tokyo Disneyland

Japan

ndex

A

B

C

D

S

T

U

V

W

X

Y

Z

opyrights & Credits

Front and back cover photos, "Tokyo Diary" photos:
Izumi Evers

Front cover, inside front cover, P. 1, P. 7:
Manga image from *Shinryaku Enban Kinokonga*
© Marina Shirakawa

P. 44, 74, 104, 136, 160:
Palepoli © Usamaru Huruya/SEIRINDO

P. 15:
Lupin III © Monkey Punch/NTV/YTV/TMS
Urusei Yatsura © Rumiko Takahashi/Shogakukan/Kitty Film
Riding Bean © Yumex Inc.
Speed Racer © Speed Racer Enterprises
Cream Lemon © Fairy Dust/Soeishinsha

P. 16:
The Wings of Honneamise © Bandai/Gainax

P. 24, 25:
Galaxy Express 999 © Leiji Matsumoto/Toei Animation Co./Viz

P. 30:
Key the Metal Idol © Hiroaki Sato/Pony Canyon/Fuji TV·FCC·Studio Pierrot/Viz

P. 36:
Maison Ikkoku © Rumiko Takahashi/Shogakukan·Kitty Film·Fuji TV/Viz

P. 54, 55:
Quote from *Godzilla, King of Monsters* © Toho Co., Ltd.

P. 66:
Moju © Daiei Co., Ltd.

P. 84:
Masonna: Quote from *Bananafish Magazine No. 8*, photo by Gori

P. 90:
Merzbow: Quote from *Moraigero Magazine No. 1*

P. 96:
Mayuko Hino of C.C.C.C.: Quote from *Bananafish Magazine No. 8*

P. 108:
Guitar Wolf, photo by Shigeo Kikuchi appeared in *Quick Japan No. 16*, published by Ota Shuppan

P. 114:
Demi Semi Quaver, photo by Bruce Osborn, quote © Sony Music

P. 120, 121:
Melt Banana, photo by Ken Fukuda, quote © Iguana Coax

P. 128:
Sugar Plant, photo by Takayuki Asano, quote © World Domination

Keiji Haino, photo by Hiromi Wakui, quote © Fushitsusha

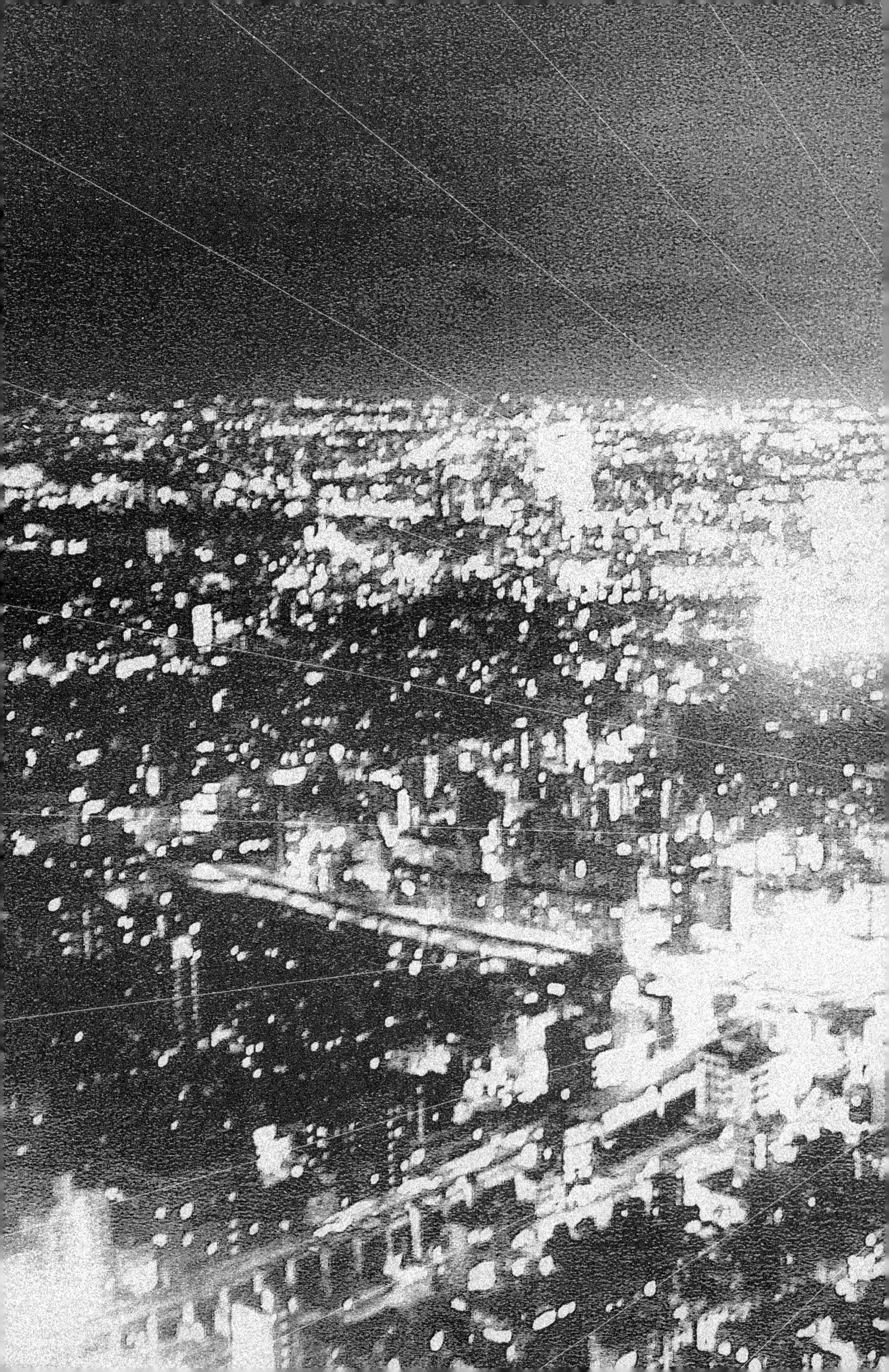